Dixie Walker

ALSO BY LYLE SPATZ
AND FROM MCFARLAND

*Yankees Coming, Yankees Going: New York Yankee
Player Transactions, 1903 Through 1999*
(2000; paperback 2009)

*Bad Bill Dahlen: The Rollicking Life and
Times of an Early Baseball Star* (2004)

*New York Yankee Openers: An Opening Day History of
Baseball's Most Famous Team, 1903–1996* (1997)

Dixie Walker
A Life in Baseball

LYLE SPATZ

McFarland & Company, Inc., Publishers
Jefferson, North Carolina, and London

LIBRARY OF CONGRESS CATALOGUING-IN-PUBLICATION DATA

Spatz, Lyle, 1937–
    Dixie Walker : a life in baseball / Lyle Spatz.
    p.   cm.
    Includes bibliographical references and index.

    ISBN 978-0-7864-4633-9
    softcover : 50# alkaline paper

    1. Walker, Dixie, 1910–1982. 2. Baseball players — United States — Biography. I. Title.
    GV865.W3348S73   2011
    796.357092 — dc22 [B]   2011010141

BRITISH LIBRARY CATALOGUING DATA ARE AVAILABLE

© 2011 Lyle Spatz. All rights reserved

No part of this book may be reproduced or transmitted in any form or by any means, electronic or mechanical, including photocopying or recording, or by any information storage and retrieval system, without permission in writing from the publisher.

Front cover: Dixie Walker in 1939, shortly after joining the Dodgers (National Baseball Hall of Fame Library, Cooperstown, N.Y.)

Manufactured in the United States of America

McFarland & Company, Inc., Publishers
   Box 611, Jefferson, North Carolina 28640
     www.mcfarlandpub.com

In memory of my parents,
Benjamin Spatz (1901–1984)
Sylvia Spatz (1904–1974)

Table of Contents

Acknowledgments ix
Preface 1

PART I — BEFORE THE DODGERS

1 • Born to Play Baseball	7
2 • A Minor League Sensation	13
3 • The Guy to Take Babe Ruth's Place	20
4 • The Lost Years	30
5 • Radical Surgery and a Career Revived	38
6 • The Most Unpopular Man in Detroit	47

PART II — THE DODGERS

7 • "All I knew about Brooklyn was that it was some strange outer world"	57
8 • The People's Choice	67
9 • An Almost Perfect Team	79
10 • A Pennant and a World Series	90
11 • The 1942 Dodgers Look to Repeat	99
12 • "Men, you are going to lose this pennant"	106
13 • The War Begins to Affect Baseball	114
14 • The 1944 National League Batting Champion	123
15 • "The most beloved baseball player of recent years"	134
16 • The War Ends and the Battle with the Cardinals Resumes	144

17 • Playoffs, Pensions, and a Promotion	156
18 • "It was the dumbest thing I did in all my life"	166
19 • Jackie Robinson Joins the Dodgers	177
20 • Dixie and Jackie Bring a Pennant to Brooklyn	186

PART III — AFTER THE DODGERS

21 • "The place doesn't look the same since you've gone, Dixie"	199
22 • Managing in the Minor Leagues	208
23 • Ending His Career in Dodger Blue	219
24 • Was Dixie Walker a Racist?	227

Chapter Notes 233
Bibliography 249
Index 255

Acknowledgments

I would like to thank the following people for their generous help and advice. Foremost among them are Maury Bouchard of Shrewsbury, Massachusetts, and Eric Sallee of Seattle, Washington. Maury and Eric read the entire original manuscript. They corrected several numerical errors and offered many suggestions to make this a better book. Tom Bourke, of St. Petersburg, Florida, the former chief of the Microforms Division at the New York Public Library, delved into the genealogical history of the Walker and Shea families, and supplied me with much of the birth and death data used in the book.

David Smith, founder and president of *Retrosheet*, and David Vincent, the keeper of the Society for American Baseball Research's home run log, were there, as always, to answer questions and supply data. Former staff members Gabriel Schechter and Russell Wolinsky of the National Baseball Library and Archive in Cooperstown provided access to Dixie Walker's player files.

Stephan Saks, Reference and Research Services, New York Public Library, helped track down some difficult-to-find 1940s New York newspaper stories. Susan Sertell, office manager at Our Lady of Sorrows Catholic Church, Homewood, Alabama, found information about Dixie and Estelle's convalidation rite in 1972 and details of his church service and burial.

Canadians Lew Cauz, Maxwell Kates, Neil Munro, and Bob Stuart helped with newspaper articles and stories from Walker's years as a player and manager in Toronto.

Patricia Kelly of the National Baseball Library and Archive, Dixie Walker's son Stephen, Dodgers team historian Mark Langill, and Ken Fenster of Stone Mountain, Georgia, furnished the photographs that appear in this book.

My two closest friends, Aaron Elkins of Sequim, Washington, and Harvey Sherman of Plainview, New York, cheered me on all through the research and writing process. Aaron and Harvey are, with me, part of that rapidly disappearing demographic that saw Dixie Walker and Jackie Robinson play together at Ebbets Field in 1947. Both took pleasure in the research tidbits I shared with them that brought back memories of our youth in 1940s-era Brooklyn.

Others who helped in one way or another are Marty Adler, Steve Gietschier, Joe Hoppel, Len Levin, Lee Lowenfish, Trent McCotter, Rod Nelson, Ted Reed, and Frank Vaccaro.

There are many ways for a baseball biographer to research a player's career, but not so many ways to learn about his private life. I owe whatever insight I brought to Dixie Walker's marriage, family, and personal memories to the wonderful cooperation I received from Dixie's son Stephen and his daughter Mary Ann Estelle.

Finally, I want to thank my wife Marilyn, who has tolerated my love of baseball, past and present, with patience and understanding for more than half a century.

Preface

Over the course of more than half a century, Fred "Dixie" Walker lived several baseball lives. He went from sure-fire prospect and successor to Babe Ruth, to a player written off for never having reached his potential, to stardom as one of the greatest heroes in Brooklyn history, to *persona non grata* because of his relationship with Jackie Robinson, and finally to redemption as a well-respected minor league manager and major league batting coach. During his playing days, he won a batting championship and played in two World Series and four All-Star games. Yet to this day, he is remembered too often only for the charge that he was the player most responsible for trying to keep Robinson from joining the Brooklyn Dodgers. He deserves better.

If you judge a player's influence by how much he changed the game, then the two most influential players of the twentieth century were Babe Ruth and Jackie Robinson. After the Red Sox converted Ruth from the game's best left-handed pitcher to an outfielder following World War I, it was the Babe's home run hitting that brought baseball out of the Deadball Era and transformed it into the slugging and high-scoring game that it is today. As every schoolchild in America knows, or should know, it was Robinson who in 1947 became the first black man to play in the major leagues. In doing so, he literally changed the face of the game, moving it away from one played exclusively by Caucasians to one that now includes not only blacks but also large numbers of Hispanics and an ever-increasing number of Asians.

Dixie Walker is the only player to have been a teammate of both these legendary figures, and not merely a cup-of-coffee kind of teammate, but one whose career and reputation were deeply affected by both: Ruth at the beginning, Robinson at the end. Dating from his major league debut as a 20-year-old in 1931, Walker's abilities were so apparent as to make many in the media and around the American League call him the eventual successor to Ruth in the Yankees outfield. Unfortunately, a series of injuries, a problem that would recur throughout Walker's eight-year American League career, would prevent that from ever happening. In May 1936, the Yanks sold Walker to the Chicago White Sox to clear a roster spot for the man who truly would be the Babe's successor—Joe DiMaggio.

Overall, Walker batted .306 and accumulated more than 2,000 hits and more than a thousand runs scored and batted in during his 18-year big league career. Tall and lean, at six feet one and 175 pounds, he was a solid hitter, a fine defensive player with an excellent throwing arm, and in his early days among the fastest players in the game. A five-time All-Star, Walker was the National League batting champion in 1944 and its runs batted in leader a year later. He also led the NL in assists in 1941 and the American League in triples in 1937.

Although a gentle man off the field, he was a fiery competitor on it, which led to his involvement in several of the more notorious brawls of the 1930s and 1940s. Among them were the 1933 battle that centered on his Yankees teammate Ben Chapman and Earl Whitehill of the Washington Senators, and a pair of 1946 melees with the Chicago Cubs, involving teammate Eddie Stanky and the Cubs' Lennie Merullo.

Nevertheless, Walker was highly respected among his peers, who elected him the National League's representative in the mid–1940s effort to secure a pension plan for major league players. During the war years, he used his popularity among Brooklyn fans, along with a pleasant singing voice, to help raise huge amounts of money for the war effort.

A son and nephew of major leaguers, Dixie, like his brother Harry, also a National League batting champion, spent his whole life in baseball. Signed as a 17-year-old by the Yankees, he followed his playing days with years of managing in the minor leagues and scouting and serving as a batting instructor for the Dodgers and several other teams. Among the Los Angeles players who praised Walker for his help with their batting were African American stars Dusty Baker, Jim Wynn, and Maury Wills.

Despite his injuries, Walker had a .295 batting average during his eight years in the American League with the Yankees, White Sox, and Tigers. But it was his years with the Dodgers, where he gained fame as "The People's Choice" and became the most popular player ever to wear a Brooklyn uniform, that make his career worth remembering. Oddly enough, before the Tigers sold him to the Dodgers in July 1939, Walker had been one of the most *unpopular* players ever to wear a Detroit uniform.

But everything changed for Walker once he landed in Brooklyn. Some early batting success against the hated Giants won him the instant love of the Brooklyn fans, a love that grew over the years, only partly extinguished by the problems of 1947. Walker's seasons in Brooklyn saw the team play in two

Harry and Dixie Walker, the only pair of brothers to each win a batting championship (private collection of Stephen Walker).

memorable World Series against the Yankees — in 1941 and 1947 — lose one pennant to the Cardinals in 1942, after squandering a ten-game lead, and another to the same team in 1946, in the first playoff series ever.

He was fortunate to have joined the team just as the mercurial Larry MacPhail was turning it from a moribund franchise into one that was exciting on the field and profitable at the gate. After MacPhail had broken the "gentlemen's agreement" banning radio broadcasts for the three New York teams, he brought Red Barber with him from Cincinnati to become the voice of the Dodgers. Barber's broadcasts would become a beloved part of life in Brooklyn and help glorify the exploits of Walker and his teammates, men like Eddie Stanky, Pee Wee Reese, Pete Reiser, Joe Medwick, Hugh Casey, Kirby Higbe, Dolph Camilli, Whit Wyatt, Harry Lavagetto, Billy Herman, Arky Vaughan, and, of course, in 1947, Jackie Robinson. Add to this wonderful mix of players such unforgettable baseball characters as Branch Rickey and Leo Durocher, and it is easy to recognize the truth in Barber's dictum that "there is never a dull day in Brooklyn."

The relationship between Dixie Walker and Jackie Robinson is one that transcends the playing field and is more a reflection of race relations in America, especially as they were in 1947. Did Walker, a lifelong Southerner, hate Robinson because he was a "Negro"? Absolutely not. Did he want Robinson, or any other black man, as a teammate? Absolutely not. Was his attitude different from millions of white Americans at the time? Absolutely not. Barber, himself a Southerner, has written of his own problem in merely *broadcasting* a game in which Robinson took part.

Yet despite his distaste for integration, Walker never went out of his way to be unpleasant to Robinson, who later described him as a man of innate fairness. At a time when players had offseason jobs and businesses to supplement their income, Walker could not easily dismiss threats by people back home in Birmingham, Alabama, to boycott his hardware store if "he played with that nigger." Undoubtedly preferring to play on an all-white team, for both personal and economic reasons, Walker proposed what he believed to be the best solution. He wrote a letter to Rickey in which he asked to be traded as the best way out for all concerned.

Rickey was unable to get what he considered fair value for Dixie and chose not to trade him. Meanwhile, Walker and Robinson became teammates, with both men making the best of a very awkward situation. Robinson went out of his way to avoid putting Walker in a position that people in Alabama might perceive as an acceptance of integration, while later acknowledging how grateful he was for a batting tip Walker gave him early in the season when he was struggling at the plate.

Walker had grown up believing blacks did not have what it takes to play at the Major League level. Robinson's athletic ability and the mental and emotional strength he exhibited in withstanding all the insults thrown at him convinced Walker otherwise. "A person learns, and you begin to change with the times," he would later say. There was too much history between them to prevent the two from ever becoming friends, but Walker would have nothing but praise for Robinson, as a player and as a man, for as long as both men lived.

Looking back, almost every big baseball story in the 1940s had a Brooklyn connection, and Walker was a major part of that history. For hundreds of thousands of young boys who came of baseball age in Brooklyn in the 1940s, Dixie Walker was their first hero. This book is for them, as well as for anyone interested in reliving what is arguably baseball's most memorable era.

PART I — BEFORE THE DODGERS

1

Born to Play Baseball

Fewer than 9,000 fans were at Pittsburgh's Forbes Field on September 22, 1949, for one of those end-of-the-season games between two teams long eliminated from pennant contention. The hometown Pirates were in sixth place and the Boston Braves, the National League's defending champions, were fourth. Johnny Sain of Boston and Murry Dickson of Pittsburgh were in a scoreless duel in the seventh inning when Pirates manager Billy Meyer sent Dixie Walker up to pinch hit for Monty Basgall. Walker singled to right and Meyer immediately replaced him, sending pitcher Vic Lombardi in as a pinch runner. The Pirates failed to score, but Danny Murtaugh, Basgall's replacement at second base, drove home Wally Westlake with a ninth-inning single to give Pittsburgh a 1–0 victory.

Both Walker's appearance and his hit, which had come two days before his 39th birthday, would be the last ones of his major league career. After sitting out Pittsburgh's final eight games, he and 42-year-old pitcher Rip Sewell were released a day after the season ended. Walker had been the oldest non-pitcher in the National League in 1949, and Sewell the oldest pitcher.[1]

The country had been deep in an economic depression when Fred "Dixie" Walker began his big-league career as a 20-year-old with the New York Yankees in 1931. He was ending it with America at the zenith of its post-war power and influence. The United States had survived the Depression, fought and won a world war, and was now in the midst of tremendous growth and social change.

An even greater transformation had taken place in the country since Fred Walker entered it on September 24, 1910, in a log cabin on his maternal grandparents' farm in Villa Rica, Georgia. Villa Rica was a small railroad and factory town located in the west central part of Georgia, approximately 35 miles west of Atlanta and 115 miles east of Birmingham, Alabama. The city traced its history back to 1826, when wagons arrived in the area from Pennsylvania, New Jersey, and Delaware, and discovered gold. It was from this boomtown beginning that the city derived its current name, which translates to "City of Riches." The city's center changed to its current location with the arrival of the railroad in 1882. Villa Rica became a railroad town, with the rails running right through its center.

Only 45 years had passed since the end of the Civil War when Walker was born. Many men in Villa Rica, and in the cities and towns around it, had fought for the Confederacy in what they called the War of Northern Aggression, and just about everyone over the age of 50 had memories of the conflict, mostly bitter ones.

Although Fred's father, Ewart Gladstone Walker, was born in the North, in Brownsville, Pennsylvania, on June 1, 1888, his parents moved to Alabama soon after his birth.[2] He was reared in the South, and except for those very earliest days, he spent his entire life there. His grandparents, Robert and Mary (née Robinson), were born in England c. 1850 and married there. Both died in Alabama in 1931. Ewart was named after William Ewart Gladstone, the four-time British prime minister in the late nineteenth century.

Ewart's two brothers also had names suggestive of England rather than America. Older brother Alfred was born in August 1886, in Pennsylvania, and younger brother Earnest in September 1890, in Alabama. Robert, who had been a policeman in England, worked in the coal mines in the United States. Both Ewart and Alfred worked in the mines from a very early age.

Ewart Walker's baseball ability allowed him to escape the difficult life of a coal miner. He was in his second season as a right-handed pitcher for the Washington Senators when his first son was born. The boy, christened Fred, would come to be called "Dixie" when he entered baseball, as his father before him had been. The name was pinned on Ewart in 1909, when he was pitching for the Zanesville (Ohio) Infants of the Central League. "I'd been there only a few days and I woke up one morning and saw a big headline that said, 'Dixie Walker Pitches Today.' It was just as simple as that. I don't know where the paper got the idea, but I was Dixie from then on."[3]

Washington brought Walker to the big leagues in September 1909. He won three of four decisions, with four complete games in four starts for a team that lost 110 games, including 26 by Bob Groom, 25 by Walter Johnson, and 19 by Dolly Gray. The Senators finished 20 games behind the seventh-place St. Louis Browns and 56 games behind the pennant-winning Detroit Tigers. Ewart's September performance impressed manager Clark Griffith and the Washington press. "With a little more coaching Walker should develop into one of the best pitchers in the league," predicted the *Washington Post*.[4] In 1910, his first full season, Walker went 11–11 for the seventh-place Senators. His most memorable performance was the 1–0 one-hitter he pitched against Ed Walsh and the Chicago White Sox on June 10.

Ewart "Dixie" Walker warms up in the spring of 1910 as Walter Johnson (second from left) and two unidentified men look on (private collection of Stephen Walker).

Walker was 8–13 in 1911, for a Washington team that again finished seventh. The highlight of this season for him was in a losing effort at home against the Yankees on September 9. After Ewart and Yankees ace Russ Ford had battled to a 1–1 tie after 12 innings, the Yanks scored four runs with two out in the 13th to win, 5–1. Despite the loss, the youngster had impressed the big city writers. The *New York Times* wrote that Dixie Walker's "smoke and curve balls were beautifully blended."[5] "When Walker is going right, he is a hard man to beat," added the *Brooklyn Daily Eagle*.[6] But by the following season, not much was going right for him. He was hit hard early in the season and fell out of favor with manager Griffith.

On May 30, when the Nationals left Boston for St. Louis to begin their first Western trip, Walker was not with them. The *Washington Post* reported that Griffith was preparing to ask waivers on him. "The pitcher has not taken care of himself and given the club his best efforts," the *Post* quoted Griffith as saying.[7] Four days later Griffith sold Walker to the Baltimore Orioles of the International League. "I said that I was done with him and have shown that I was not bluffing," said Griffith. "Every man on this club must give his best or go."[8] A few months later, on August 6, owner Jack Dunn of the Orioles sold Walker to Wilkes-Barre of the New York State League. In two full and two partial seasons with Washington, the original Dixie Walker won 25 games and lost 31.

In 1913, Dixie landed in the American Association, where he won 18 games for the St. Paul Saints and won 18 again in 1914. He won 25 games pitching in the Class B New York State League in 1916 and 11 more in 1917, but he was then 30 years old, bothered by a sore arm, and would never return to the major leagues.

Ewart stayed in baseball by playing and managing lower minor-league Class D and semipro teams, while working and raising his family. Home was now Birmingham, but he managed in various places in the South, mostly in small towns like Sipsey and Coal Valley in Alabama, but also in Pascagoula, Mississippi. It was in Pascagoula that Flossie Walker gave birth to another son, whom she and Ewart named Harry William Walker. After Ewart's arm went bad, he became an outfielder and pitched only in emergencies. His last official connection to the game was in 1930, as the manager of the Brantford Red Sox of the Ontario League.

Fred Walker's mother, Flossie (Vaughn) Walker, was born in Tennessee — as were her parents, William and Susie (née Jackson) — on January 28, 1888. Ewart and Flossie married in 1910, and moved in with Ewart's parents, Robert and Mary, in Birmingham. Ewart's 1917 World War I draft card lists the family living at 4209 10th Avenue in Wylam, Alabama, and his occupation as a machinist at a steel plant. By 1920, Ewart and Flossie were living in Sipsey, with their two boys and Flossie's 16-year-old sister Annie. Ewart was now working as a mine foreman.

With a father from Alabama and a mother from Tennessee, young Fred Walker was a true son of the South. He was also part of a baseball-playing family; when Fred was three years old, his uncle Earnest also reached the major leagues. Ernie Walker played as an outfielder for the St. Louis Browns from 1913 to 1915.

Fred and Harry would spend almost their entire adult lives associated with baseball. With Ewart pitching and managing in the minor and semi-professional leagues while they were growing up, it was natural for them to think only of baseball, he said of his sons. Harry remembered playing baseball with his older brother Fred almost from the time he was big enough to walk. Both recalled their father telling them stories about his days in the big leagues and especially about that day in 1910 when he had pitched a one-hitter to beat Ed Walsh.[9]

When Ewart was managing at Sipsey, in 1920, ten-year-old Fred was the team's batboy. Ewart would take advantage of their time together to instruct his young son in batting techniques, pitching to him, whenever possible, for a half-hour every day. He also had Fred shagging fly balls as a way to teach him the art of playing the outfield. By age 12, Fred was earning five dollars a game playing for a semipro team in Calvert, Alabama, managed by his father. The local high school had no baseball team, but they did have a football team. Fred, a speedy halfback, played for one season, during which he suffered a broken left collarbone. The injury was the first of many he would endure in his athletic career. Eventually, he dropped out of high school with the hope of starting a career in baseball that would lead him to the major leagues, as it had his father and his uncle. "The only thing I cared about was being a ballplayer," Walker later recalled. "I didn't figure I needed much of an education for that."[10]

Fred's parents were displeased with his decision to drop out of school, and Flossie objected strongly to his intention to play baseball professionally. Flossie had seen her husband's playing career end because of an injury, and she wanted her son to seek a more secure livelihood. "I wasn't a ballplayer's wife for all those years for nothing," she said. "Moving from town to town ... trying to see you get an education ... trying to live on your father's pay between seasons ... having to depend on a curve ball to pay the rent and buy groceries."[11]

Nevertheless, Fred left school at the age of 15 to take a job with the Tennessee Coal and Iron Company, a Birmingham steel mill, working at the open hearth. It was hot, backbreaking work, and Walker never forgot it. Years later, after he had achieved stardom, he recalled those teenage days in the steel mill.

"Some ballplayers complain of having to play in the heat," he said. "Why they don't know what heat is. I remember back in the mills when my shirt used to catch on fire from blazing cinders. That was when I was first starting in as a 'pull up' boy, that is pulling up the doors of the open hearths. Later when I was promoted to operating an electric crane high above the hearths, I remember how the heat would blast up and burn the soles of my feet. I couldn't stand still. I had to jump up and down to keep my feet from frying. And work! When I had a job of pushing wheelbarrows of ore for the furnaces, my arms would be so tired I could scarcely lift them at night."[12]

Still, Walker felt much good had come from those hardships. For one, they had made him appreciate the life he was living as a major-league star, and the work had actually helped him in his chosen profession. "I really believe that all that lifting work with the wheelbarrows strengthened my forearms for hitting a baseball," he added.[13]

Fred had an even greater incentive in working for Tennessee Coal and Iron; it gave him a chance to play in an organized baseball league. The company had a league with the different departments competing against one another. Dixie played for his department, named the "Open Hearths" and managed by his father. Ewart later also managed Harry on the coal company team, and, not surprisingly, was harder on his sons than he was on his other players.

"He had the right idea, though," Dixie later said. "He demanded hustle, unfailing effort, and because we were his own, and he wanted the best for us, he was more critical of us than anyone else."[14]

While playing for the Tennessee Coal and Iron Company, Fred met another teenager playing in the league, one who would be his future major-league teammate and his friend for life — Ben Chapman. Young Fred wanted to be a pitcher like his dad, but Ewart, with memories of his own shortened career in mind, advised his son to be an outfielder. Your career will last much longer as an outfielder, he said. Nevertheless, Ewart used young Fred mostly at the more demanding shortstop position for the Open Hearths.

The players on these company teams did not devote all their time to playing baseball. They had to put in a certain number of days and hours at work between games. Walker recalled time spent working as an electric crane operator, hoisting and depositing ladles of glowing, red-hot steel. One day while rushing to get this done, he snapped the cables, and after the crane was repaired, he snapped them again. The company allowed him to keep his job only because of his baseball ability.[15]

Fred continued to play baseball evenings and Sundays, all the while asking Flossie for permission to allow him to pursue his ambition of playing in the major leagues. "My mother never had any reason to like baseball as a way of earning a living," he later told sportswriter Grantland Rice. "All she had to look back on was moving from one minor league town to another, with my father getting just about enough money to keep us together and never getting a chance to put any away."[16]

Dixie still remembered what his mother had said about his job in the steel mill. "'Stay where you are,' she told me, 'and in the long run you'll be better off. You'll have a steady job and be getting somewhere and saving your money. Look at your father. After all the years he put into baseball, he wound up with nothing but a sore arm and then had to go out and look for a job.'"[17]

In due time, Fred's natural ability convinced his father he had the skills to play professional baseball. Early in 1928, Ewart told his 17-year-old son, "Fred, I think you are ready for the Southern League [sic] now. I am going to get you a trial with the Barons."[18]

Eventually Flossie Walker also gave in to Fred's wishes — but with conditions. "Go ahead, play ball if you must. But I'm not going to see you wear out your life in the minor leagues, as your father did. If you're not in the majors within three years, you'll have to quit," Flossie told her son. "I want your promise on that."[19]

2

A Minor League Sensation

The "Barons" Fred Walker got a trial with in the spring of 1928 were the hometown Birmingham Barons, a team whose history traced back to 1885. Known originally as the Coal Barons (for obvious reasons), they played in a series of Southern leagues during the early years of baseball. In 1901, they became a founding member of the Southern Association and one of the league's most successful franchises. The Southern Association was a Class A league, the second-highest minor league classification at the time.

Walker showed enough at training camp to earn his first professional contract. Birmingham scout Bill Pierre signed him for $500. Pierre had also signed Sammy Byrd, in 1926, and Ben Chapman, along with Walker, in 1928, but all were later sold to the Yankees without ever having played for the Barons.

Fred's lifelong dream of being a professional baseball player was now a reality, a reality that thrilled not only him, but also Ewart. "Dad always had his heart set on my becoming a ball player," Walker said several years later. "I was brought up with ball players."[1]

He was on the Barons' roster, listed as an infielder-outfielder, when spring training started, but it was too good a team and too tough a league for a 17-year-old. (Birmingham had finished second in 1927, and would win the Southern Association pennant in 1928.) Walker spent the season playing for three teams in three different leagues. Barons manager Johnny Dobbs sent him to the Albany (Georgia) Nuts of the Class B Southeastern League, where he played in 16 games before moving on to the Greensboro (North Carolina) Patriots of the Class C Piedmont League. Fred played in just six games for Greensboro and then spent the bulk of the season — 82 games — with the Gulfport (Mississippi) Tarpons of the Class D Cotton States League. Overall, he appeared in 104 games for the three clubs in 1928, with a combined batting average of .284.

Walker had the most success with the Tarpons, batting .293 while playing both the outfield and third base. He also learned a valuable hitting lesson from Gulfport manager Cotton Knaupp, a lesson that would help him throughout his career. Knaupp, a longtime minor league manager who had a brief stay in the big leagues with the 1910–1911 Cleveland Naps, taught him how to hit the high pitch. Before that, Walker later recalled, he had been strictly a lowball hitter and had trouble catching up with pitches above the belt.[2]

Gulfport was gone from the Cotton States League in 1929, but Walker was not. He spent the season with another Mississippi club in the league, the Vicksburg Hill Billies. Walker played in 61 games, all at third base, and batted a solid .318 for a team that finished seventh in an eight-team league.

The Birmingham club continued to own the rights to Walker by placing him on their reserve list following the 1929 season.[3] He went to spring training with them again in 1930, under new manager Clyde Milan, the former Washington Senators outfielder. While there, he attracted the attention of another Washingtonian, Senators owner Clark Griffith. "That young man is an infielder," said Griffith, the Senators' onetime manager who had released Fred's father. "He covers the ground well, and either shortstop or third base should be his position."[4] The Barons, judging Walker not yet ready for Class A competition, assigned him to the Class B Greenville (South Carolina) Spinners of the South Atlantic Association.

Walker's manager at Greenville, Joe Schepner, disagreed with Griffith's assessment of where Walker should play. Perhaps it was because in addition to managing the team, Schepner was also its third baseman, or perhaps the order had come directly from Birmingham. Whatever the reason, Walker played only in the outfield for the 1930 Spinners. Moreover, aside from playing three games at first base for the Pittsburgh Pirates in 1949, his final major league season, he would remain strictly an outfielder for the rest of his career.

The batting lessons learned the year before began to pay off in 1930, as Walker took the South Atlantic Association by storm. The tall, speedy youngster batted .481 for the first three weeks of the season. "Fred Walker, the 19-year-old son of the former Washington pitcher, is the early season sensation of the South Atlantic League," reported the *Associated Press*.[5] Johnny Nee, who scouted young players in the Southern states for the New York Yankees, recommended the Yanks purchase Walker's contract, which they did. On June 19, manager Schepner announced that the club had sold outfielder Fred Walker to the Yankees for $15,000.[6] Other sources listed the purchase price as $25,000, which if true was the highest ever paid for a Class B player at the time.[7] Walker had batted .401 in 73 games for the Spinners, with 17 doubles, ten triples, and 11 home runs.

The Yankees assigned Fred to the Jersey City Skeeters of the Class AA

International League. Before 1946, when baseball reclassified its minor leagues, Class AA was the highest level, one step below the major leagues. Two other leagues, the American Association and the Pacific Coast League, also were designated as Class AA.[8]

Playing in the International League, whose eight teams were all located in the North, would be a new experience for Walker, who had spent all his young life in the South.[9] Jersey City, his new "home," was a bustling port city, ruled by its iron-fisted mayor, Frank Hague. Located directly across the Hudson River from Lower Manhattan, it was home to many Irish, Italian, and Jewish immigrants, much like its bigger neighbor on the other side of the Hudson. Walker would be encountering a far different population mix than the mostly white Protestant milieu he had known in the South.

The 1930 Jersey City Skeeters were a bad team, one that would finish in last place, 44½ games behind the pennant-winning Rochester Red Wings. Led by future Cardinals manager Billy Southworth, the Red Wings had the league's top hitter — Rip Collins — and its top pitcher — Paul Derringer — both future major league stars.

Six weeks after Walker joined the Skeeters, they fired manager Nick Allen and replaced him with Joe Tinker, the onetime Cubs shortstop. The 49-year-old Tinker had not managed in 12 years, and after this half-season, he would never manage again.

Neither the new surroundings nor the change in managers had any adverse affect on Walker's play. More significantly, he was having no trouble with the upgraded pitching he was now facing. He continued his steady hitting, compiling a .335 batting average in 83 games with the Skeeters. Showing power and speed, he had a combined 104 runs batted in and 32 stolen bases for the 1930 season. He also exhibited a strong throwing arm, tallying 33 assists, 14 at Greenville and 19 with the Skeeters.

On July 24, Jersey City hosted the Newark Bears in its first-ever night game. Many of the New York writers were at West Side Park that night for the historic event, which was also the first professional night baseball game in the New York metropolitan area. The Bears won the rain-shortened game, but Walker, playing center field, impressed the big city writers with two sensational catches and a terrific throw.

By early 1931, sportswriter Ernie Lanigan was hailing 20-year-old Fred Walker as one of the most promising rookies of the upcoming season.[10] The Yankees had monitored Walker at Jersey City, liked what they saw, and invited him to spring training in St. Petersburg, Florida.

The 1931 Yankees were a team in transition. After a third-place finish in 1930, owner Jacob Ruppert, on the advice of business manager Ed Barrow, fired manager Bob Shawkey and replaced him with Joe McCarthy. Shawkey had been hired in 1930 to replace the late Miller Huggins; but despite having been a popular mainstay of the Yankees' pitching staff for many years, he could not survive the team's lowest finish since 1925. McCarthy had led the Chicago Cubs to the National League pennant in 1929, but he too had been let go after finishing two games behind the St. Louis Cardinals in 1930.

A number of Yankees veterans were unhappy with the hiring of McCarthy — whom they dismissed as a National Leaguer — believing the job should have gone to Babe Ruth. The Babe had begun campaigning for the position even before Huggins's death. Neither Ruppert nor Barrow thought of the free-spirited Ruth as managerial material; nevertheless, the Babe would never get over the perceived snub in the four years he played under McCarthy.

Walker caught everyone's attention the first week of training in Florida. His batting, fielding, and throwing were the sensation of the camp. Although he realized his chances of opening the season in New York were slim, he remained optimistic. "No matter where they send me," he said, "I'll work my head off to get back."[11] Also working against him joining the Yankees was the reduced roster size mandated for the 1931 season. Baseball owners, fearful of the effects of the Depression, had voted to cut their teams from 25 players to 23.

Babe Ruth and Earle Combs were fixtures in the outfield, and the third slot eventually would go to Ben Chapman, Walker's old friend from Birm-

Babe Ruth (top row, middle) with his hands on the shoulders of Dixie Walker, his rumored successor (private collection of Stephen Walker).

ingham. Chapman had played mostly third base as a Yankee rookie in 1930. McCarthy moved him to the outfield after the club signed veteran third baseman Joe Sewell, following Sewell's release by the Cleveland Indians. Other outfielders in camp included holdover Sammy Byrd and rookies Myril Hoag and Dusty Cooke. Hoag, a right-handed batter, was a natural hitter with good speed. Cooke, a left-handed batter, had difficulty with left-handed pitchers.

McCarthy had intended to keep his entire squad together as the team played its way North. But on March 26, the team's last day in St. Petersburg, he received a telegram from Barrow ordering him to option three players to the minor leagues. The *New York Times* reported the Yankees were sending Dixie Walker and 22-year-old shortstop Bill Werber to Fort Lauderdale, Florida. From there they would join the Toledo Mud Hens of the American Association.[12]

Toledo was managed by 41-year-old Casey Stengel, and included on its roster former rough-and-tumble big leaguers Carl Mays, Bruno Haas, Bevo LeBourveau, and Jack Scott, all of whom were Stengel's contemporaries. Walker played center field for the Mud Hens, and because of his great range was responsible for everything hit between him and the slow-moving corner outfielders, Haas and LeBourveau. Stengel rode his two newcomers, Walker and Werber, especially hard, and neither youngster enjoyed playing under him. "Despite the level of play that surrounded us, Stengel got on Dixie and me more often than not," Werber would later claim.[13]

Two weeks into the season, McCarthy found himself short of outfielders because of injuries and recalled Walker from Toledo. "When I told the old man that I was going away to play with a team called the Yankees, he wouldn't speak to me for a month," Walker would often jokingly recall.[14] He had not quite made it to the major leagues in three years, as his mother had asked, but when he did make it he was still only 20 years old.

Dixie Walker made his major league debut at Washington on April 28, 1931, in a game called because of darkness after 14 innings. The game lasted three hours and 46 minutes and ended tied at 7–7. Playing left field and batting sixth, Dixie had three hits in seven at-bats, including his first big-league hit, a single off Sam Jones. He also struck out three times, the only time in his career he would strike out three times in a single game.

Three days later, he played his second game as a Yankee, going hitless in three at-bats against Philadelphia's George Earnshaw. Walker later called Earnshaw the most impressive pitcher he faced early in his career. "He could always get me out. His curve ball had me folding like a pretzel; and I never even saw his fast one."[15]

Walker's first stay in the big leagues lasted just over two weeks. By May

15, sidelined outfielders Ruth, Byrd, and Hoag were healthy again; as the Yankees prepared to leave St. Louis for Detroit, they informed Dixie he was being sent back to Toledo.

Happily, for Dixie, his second stay at Toledo would also be short-lived. When the Mud Hens hit a financial crisis in mid-summer, they asked the Yankees for salary relief for both Werber and Walker. On July 8, the Yanks complied by sending Walker back to the Jersey City Skeeters. Dixie had done well in his two stints at Toledo — a .303 average in 58 games — and while he would have preferred going back to the Yankees, he was just pleased to be getting away from Stengel. George "Specs" Toporcer was the playing manager at Jersey City when Walker reported, but on July 19, the Skeeters sold Toporcer to Rochester and named Bob Shawkey to manage the club.

Walker was leading the league with a .372 average when, on August 27, Barrow sent him on option to another International League club, the Toronto Maple Leafs. It is difficult to ascertain why the Yankees would move Jersey City's best player to Toronto at that point in the season. According to Daniel R. Levitt, Ed Barrow's biographer, prior to 1932 the Yankees did not have truly exclusive working relationships with minor league teams as we know them today. Major league teams could have only 15 players out on option and they generally farmed them to "friendly" minor league teams. Meanwhile, minor league rosters could consist of players on option from more than one major league team. Most often, the relationship was a personal one between someone with the major league team and someone with the minor league team, rather than a contractual arrangement.[16]

Whatever Barrow's motive, Walker was a welcome addition to the Toronto lineup. "Dixie Walker should make the Leafs look like a ball club, something they haven't done lately," wrote Charlie Good in the *Toronto Daily Star*. "Walker can hit, run and field, and is sound in wind and limb."[17]

The *Star*, while noting that Dixie possessed one of the best throwing arms in baseball, reminded their readers it was his great speed that he had used to make one of the more memorable plays of the season. It came during the Skeeters' last visit to Toronto's Maple Leaf Stadium. Joe Rabbitt of the Leafs was on first when the next batter singled up the middle. Walker came charging in from center field, scooped up the ball and without breaking stride tagged out Rabbitt as he was rounding second base.

Ike Boone, of Newark, won the league batting title with a .356 average. Walker played in 80 games in the International League — 51 with Jersey City and 29 with Toronto — and finished third with a .352 average. Adding in the 58 games he played for Toledo, Dixie's overall average for 1931 was .331 in 138 games, at the minor leagues' highest level.

With many other clubs, the numbers Walker had put up the past few seasons would have resulted in an automatic promotion to the big leagues; but not so with the Yankees. Dixie was invited to the Yanks' spring training camp at St. Petersburg in 1932, but as a member of the Newark Bears. Ruppert had purchased the Bears the previous November and arranged for them to train with their new parent club.

Although he was still just 21 years old, Walker was disappointed at the prospect of spending another year in the International League. He recalled that after the 1931 season, he was "really tired" of the minors. "But the Yankees had no place for me," he realized. "How was I to break into an outfield whose regulars were Ben Chapman, Earle Combs, and Babe Ruth, and whose first reserves were Sammy Byrd and Myril Hoag?"[18]

Walker spent the 1932 season playing for a Newark Bears team that was among the finest minor league squads ever assembled. Managed by former major-league pitcher Al Mamaux, their roster featured a host of future major leaguers. Among those who would star for the Yankees in the 1930s were George Selkirk, Johnny Murphy, and Red Rolfe. Newark took over first place to stay in early July and breezed to their first International League pennant in 19 years.

After Newark finished 15½ games ahead of the second-place Baltimore Orioles, they defeated the American Association's Minneapolis Millers in six games to win the Junior World Series. Following the Series, losing manager Donie Bush told Mamaux, "You have the greatest minor league club I have ever seen, Al."[19]

Walker was a key contributor to the Bears' success. He batted .350, had 15 home runs, 105 runs batted in, and was voted to the International League All-Star team. He was also popular with the fans that came out to newly renamed Ruppert Stadium, as well as with one particular teenaged stadium employee.

After Walker's death, Morton Roth, a concessionaire at the stadium in 1932, wrote a piece about him in *Baseball Digest*. "The majority of players treated stadium employees as if we were part of the scenery, ignoring us for the most part," Roth wrote. But Walker was different, he remembered, always acknowledging him with a nod and willing to chat with him before games and one time inviting him onto the field for a pregame catch.[20]

On September 7, Walker was one of a group of players the Yankees recalled and directed to report to them at St. Petersburg the following spring. This time, he would be working with the major league club.

3

The Guy to Take Babe Ruth's Place

"It's the fate of some ball players to get on the wrong ball club," wrote Harold C. Burr of the *Brooklyn Daily Eagle*, referring to Sam Leslie of the Giants and Dixie Walker of the Yankees. Leslie, a first baseman, was the backup to Bill Terry, the best first baseman in the National League and the Giants manager.[1]

Walker was the Yankees' only new outfielder when he reported to spring training at St. Petersburg in 1933. The Yanks were the defending world champions and had all their key players back. The 1932 starting outfield of Babe Ruth, Earle Combs, and Ben Chapman was set to retain their positions, as was reserve Sammy Byrd, whose role was mostly as a late-inning defensive replacement for Ruth.

Despite the odds against him, Walker was not dismayed and looked forward to earning a spot on the club. "I'm down here to get and hold some kind of job with the Yanks," he said on arriving in camp. "This is my ball club. I'd like to play on it. It's the greatest ball club in the world because it doesn't ride a rookie. It tries to show him how to play the game."[2]

Walker's optimism aside, no one expected him to break into the Yankees' lineup this season. However, because he was an excellent hitter and fielder, had great running speed and a strong throwing arm, baseball experts were sure the 22-year-old outfielder was destined to be a major league star. Dixie Walker's running speed early in his career should not be overlooked. On the Yankees, he was second only to Ben Chapman, the fastest runner in the American League. In 1933, Walker may well have been the second fastest in the league.

With his overload of talented outfielders, Joe McCarthy would have trouble finding a spot for Walker. Yet the young man's skills — the strong hitting, speed, and excellent all-around play in the outfield — had made a very strong impression on the Yankees manager. Ruth, Combs, and Chapman were in place as outfield starters, with Byrd again slated for one of the two reserve outfielder slots. For the other, McCarthy had to choose between Walker, holdover Myril Hoag, and Dusty Cooke, who had missed the 1932 season with a sore arm.

Dixie did not expect to win a starting job by dislodging any member of that quartet, two of whom were longtime friends. "Dewey [Sammy] Byrd and Ben Chapman are my boyhood friends. I don't expect to beat Byrd out for Ruth's right field job. Dewey's too good."[3] Nevertheless, Walker was determined to leave his minor league days behind. "I'm not going to let anything interfere with my baseball this year. Two years ago I had the same chance, but I was a kid then."[4]

The competition was spirited, but Walker won out. The Yankees sent Cooke to Newark, before trading him to the Red Sox in May. Hoag too was sent to Newark, with Walker replacing him as the fifth outfielder. McCarthy was a taciturn man, usually very sparing in his compliments, but he telegraphed his decision when he said to reporters one day, "I think we have found the guy to take Ruth's place."[5]

McCarthy's high praise of Walker notwithstanding, the manager had what historian Bill James called a dislike for southern-born ballplayers, whom he considered "hot-headed and ignorant."[6] McCarthy, a teammate of Dixie's dad at Wilkes-Barre in 1912, often kidded the son about his Southern drawl. "Darn that Walker," he once said. "He makes the whole team sound like Amos 'n' Andy."[7]

As with many ballplayers, Walker had certain superstitions, and he carried trinkets that he felt brought him good luck. One such item was a coin given to him by an elderly fan in Newark during the 1932 season that had come to be his "lucky piece." It was made of lead alloy and had a bright penny as an inlay. Around the penny were the words, "Keep me and you'll never go broke." He had attempted to make it even luckier by adding "for base hits" to the inscription. "I've been hitting real good since it was given to me," he said. "I've never left it out of my vest pocket." Therefore, Dixie had a scare one morning in Nashville as the Yanks were barnstorming north. While paying for breakfast, he inadvertently used it thinking it was a 50-cent piece; after realizing his mistake, he was able to retrieve the coin from the cashier.[8]

Wearing number 27, Walker was primarily a spectator the first week of the season. He made just one brief appearance — as a late-inning defensive replacement for Ruth — as the Yankees opened with seven consecutive victories against the Boston Red Sox and Philadelphia Athletics. On April 23, the Yanks traveled to Washington, where the streak ended with a 5–4 loss, followed by another one-run defeat the next day. Dixie had his first major-league at-bat in almost two years in that second loss, when he flied out as a pinch-hitter for Frank Crosetti.

Washington had won 93 games in 1932, yet ended the season in third place, 14 games behind New York. The Athletics had finished second; nevertheless, the Senators were expected to pose the biggest threat to the Yankees' attempt to repeat as pennant-winners. Shortstop Joe Cronin had replaced Walter Johnson as the manager of Washington's strong, veteran club. Rounding out Cronin's infield were first baseman Joe Kuhel, second baseman Buddy Myer, and third baseman Ossie Bluege, while future Hall-of-Famers Goose Goslin and Heinie Manush led the outfield contingent. Anchoring the pitching staff were Alvin Crowder, the league's leading winner in 1932, with 26, and Earl Whitehill, acquired in an offseason trade with Detroit.

Rookie Russ Van Atta got the Yankees back on track in the final game of the series on April 25. Van Atta made his major-league debut by shutting out the Senators, 16–0. The Yankees pounded Washington starter Monte Weaver and three replacements for 21 hits, four of them by Van Atta. But Van Atta's brilliant performance was overshadowed by what one sportswriter in attendance called "the greatest fight he'd ever seen on a ball field."[9]

What would become a 15-minute near-riot, resulting in the suspension of three players and the arrest of five spectators, began innocently enough with a fourth-inning ground ball hit by Sammy Byrd to shortstop Cronin. However, the genesis of this brawl may have occurred the previous year, during the second game of a July 4 doubleheader between the two teams. Senators outfielder Carl Reynolds, while running home on a squeeze play, scored when he knocked the ball loose by barreling into Bill Dickey, the Yankees catcher. Having been stunned by Roy Johnson of the Red Sox in a similar collision at Boston the day before, Dickey reacted by throwing a punch at Reynolds's jaw.

Umpires and other players intervened and ejected both Dickey and Reynolds. Dickey's punch had fractured Reynolds's jaw in two places, causing the Senators outfielder to miss the next seven weeks. Batting above .360 at the time of the incident, Reynolds ended the season at .305. American League president Will Harridge fined Dickey $1,000 and suspended him for 30 days, the length of time he mistakenly believed would coincide with Reynolds's absence. There were no other serious incidents between the teams for the rest of the season, but the bad blood between the Yankees and the Senators remained. It was ready to explode, and Byrd's grounder to Cronin lit the spark.

Cronin tossed the ball to second baseman Myer for what should have been a routine force out on the runner, Ben Chapman, and likely the start of an inning-ending double play. But Chapman's very hard slide into Myer knocked him down. Myer, whose father was Jewish, was perceived around the league as being Jewish, while Chapman had a well-deserved reputation as a notorious racist and anti–Semite.

3. The Guy to Take Babe Ruth's Place

Furious at what he considered an intentionally dirty play — Cronin later concurred that Chapman had made a "deliberate attempt" to spike his double play partner — Myer retaliated with a kick to Chapman's thigh. Chapman then took a swing at Myer, and when Myer swung back, players from both sides joined the battle. Umpires George Moriarty and Harry Geisel eventually restored order and ejected the two combatants. Twenty years later, Frank Graham, Jr., gave this account of what happened next, as told to him by a veteran sportswriter who was there.

"Buddy left the field without an argument, but Ben, who was a redneck kid if I ever saw one, kept yelling that Buddy had hit him first and wanting to know why he should be put out. Joe McCarthy knew he had to go, of course, and he said to Dixie, who was on the bench: 'Run down to the bullpen and warm up in a hurry because you will have to take Chapman's place in left field as soon as they get the ball game going again.'

"Dixie grabbed his glove and ran down there. He was throwing a couple to the bullpen catcher to get his arm loosened up quick because Chapman was out on the play at second base and that was the third out. About this time Ben decides he has said about everything he can think of to the umpires and he starts for the clubhouse. He is still steaming and when he gets to the Senators' dugout, through which he has to pass to get to the clubhouse, there is Earl Whitehill standing at the top of the stairs leading to the tunnel.

"Whitehill was one of the best pitchers in the league in those days and a handsome, dark-haired guy, and cocky, too, and as Chapman was about to pass him, Earl said. 'Well, you swell-headed — —, you finally got what was coming to you, didn't you?' (Rookie shortstop Bill Werber, a member of the Yankees at the time, says Whitehill called Chapman "a no good southern son of a bitch.")[10]

"Chapman hit him in the mouth with a right hand that almost knocked him down the stairs and then the fight really started. All the Washington players were trying to hit Chapman and fans were climbing out of the stands trying to get to him, too, and cops were running in to put a stop to it and all of a sudden, there was Dixie. He was yanking guys off his pal Chapman and belting them, which left Ben free to do some more punching on his own, and I never saw anything like it.

"The two of them kept a small circle cleared around them and hit everybody in range — Senators' fans, everybody. It seems that a couple of guys in store clothes they hit were detectives, although, of course, they didn't know who they were. But they soon found out because the detectives and the uniformed cops closed in on them and hauled them off and down the steps to the clubhouse. The cops told them to shower and dress because they were pinched and there was a police car waiting to take them to the pokey. Just then old Griff came in and said to the cops:

"'Look, don't arrest these boys. The Yankees are going to Philadelphia right after the game. Let them leave town with their ball club. The league will take care of them, I am sure, because I am going to call Mr. Harridge in Chicago and tell him what happened and I want Chapman, anyway, suspended and fined.'"[11]

"After the contest, the Yankees required police protection. They proceeded directly to Union Station and left town."[12] Harridge ruled that Whitehill, Myer, and Chapman be suspended for five days and fined $100 each. Blaming the trouble on the fact that Chapman had to leave the field via the Washington dugout, he announced that all clubs would be asked to provide separate exits from the dugouts at their ballparks.

> "In my decision, I felt Myer had provoked Chapman by kicking the Yankee outfielder," ruled Harridge. "I did not get any report from our umpires, Messrs Moriarty and Geisel that Chapman has deliberately spiked Myer. Apparently, it was a play such as we see very often — an effort by a runner to prevent a double play.
> "I also did believe that Chapman's assault on Whitehill had been provoked, but with all that, Chapman had no right to strike either Myer or Whitehill.
> "With all facts evening themselves out, I decided that a warning, five games and one hundred dollars would be sufficient punishment."[13]

Harridge did not fine or suspend Walker. He ruled that Dixie had not participated in the brawl, but had just attempted to protect Chapman. After Walker testified at the hearing held by Harridge, the league president said, "All right, my boy. I'm satisfied you did exactly as anyone else would have done in the circumstances."[14] Nevertheless, Griffith, Cronin, and the rest of the Senators were upset that Walker and Lefty Gomez, who was also heavily involved, were let off free. In essence, Graham's source for the game agreed with the Washington position.

> "Dixie didn't start it, but, you might say, he wound it up. By the time he quit punching there were cops and detectives hanging all over him, and he would have wound up in the pokey if it hadn't been for old Griff, although all he had done was go to the aid of a pal who was in trouble.
> "Everybody was surprised to see him in there, slugging in all directions, because by nature he was a very peaceable fellow, as he is now. But he showed that day in Washington, as he was to prove in Brooklyn later on, that he was a very bad guy to monkey with and anybody who did was likely to wind up minus a few teeth."[15]

Over the years, Walker took part in several memorable on-field fights, but he claimed it was always a case of his coming to someone's aid. "I don't know why it is," he said, "but I always seem to get myself into trouble."[16]

Chapman, the man he had helped, placed the major blame on Whitehill. "When I slid into Myer at second, I was not trying to cut him down, but merely trying to prevent him from completing a double play," he said. "That's baseball and it happens every day. While I was still down, Myer kicked me, and then I got up and closed in on him. But it really wasn't much of a fight as Cronin had me by the arm and some other player was pulling Myer," he explained. "When we were ordered off the field, I was plenty sore, but I was determined to do or say nothing more and nothing further would have happened had Whitehill minded his own business. But as I went down the runway alongside the Senators' dugout he climbed over a couple of players to get close to me and called me a dirty name."[17] Moreover, Chapman claimed that McCarthy had encouraged him "to take a shot at Myer" because of what McCarthy believed was Myer's attempt to spike Lou Gehrig the day before.[18]

Chapman's suspension gave Walker the opportunity to start five of the next six games. He played right field in Philadelphia, but switched to left field at Yankee Stadium against Washington and Boston, allowing Ruth to patrol the Stadium's much less spacious right field. In his fifth start, at Detroit, Walker replaced Earle Combs as the leadoff man and center fielder.

During this run of starting appearances, Dixie was a major participant in a Yankees' baserunning blunder that is still talked about more than 75 years later. In the April 29 home game against the Senators, the Yanks were trailing Monte Weaver, 6–2, when Ruth led off the ninth with a single. Gehrig followed with a hit, and then Walker singled to score Byrd, running for Ruth. Tony Lazzeri followed with a long drive to right-center field that sailed over the head of right fielder Goose Goslin.

It appeared to be a two-run double for Lazzeri, but instead, both runners were thrown out at the plate. Gehrig had hesitated at second, thinking Goslin would catch the ball. Walker, realizing Goslin had no chance at the ball and not noticing Gehrig's hesitation, took off from first at full speed. By the time he rounded third, he was just two strides behind Gehrig. Meanwhile Cronin had gone into short center field to take Goslin's throw and then fired a strike to catcher Luke Sewell, who put the tag on both men—first Gehrig and then Walker. It was a most unusual double play, one that left the 30,000 fans stunned. Weaver then retired Dickey to end the game. "It was a swell job by Goslin and Cronin," Sewell said after the game. "I didn't have to move for the ball. I had my eye on Walker when I was tagging Gehrig."[19]

Clark Griffith's reaction to the double play was ecstatic, perhaps inspired more by the win over the Yankees than the actual play. "The greatest play baseball ever saw," said the Washington owner. "The greatest play in my 46 years in baseball and the greatest play I have ever seen in the 51 years I have been watching the game."[20]

That same week, *The Sporting News* ran a front page feature story describing how highly the Yanks thought of Walker, and how he could be next in line for a full-time spot in their outfield, maybe as the eventual replacement for Babe Ruth.[21] Chicago White Sox manager Lew Fonseca also invoked Ruth's name in praising Walker. Noting that Dixie had a batting stance similar to the Babe's, Fonseca called him one of the best youngsters to come into baseball in years.[22]

Being compared to the greatest, most popular player ever had to be heady stuff for someone with fewer than 50 games of major league experience. As with most young men of his age, Walker looked up to Ruth. "Since I've grown up my other heroes have shrunk in stature. But not Ruth. He's grown if anything."[23]

Chapman's return sent Dixie back to the bench, where he served mostly as a pinch-hitter and defensive replacement. Batting for Jumbo Brown in the first game of a June 11 doubleheader at Fenway Park, he connected against Johnny Welch for his first big league home run. A few days later, McCarthy used him to replace Ruth, when an illness kept the Babe sidelined for a week. Ruth was back on June 20, but McCarthy kept Walker in the lineup as a replacement for the slumping Earle Combs. Dixie hit a home run that afternoon in Chicago and then two more against the Browns in New York's next series.

After leaving St. Louis, the Yankees headed to Detroit for a June 25 doubleheader. The Tigers won the first game, 6–5, on a 12th-inning single by 22-year-old rookie Hank Greenberg. "A Bronx boy of giant stature supplied the winning run in the opener," wrote James P. Dawson in the *New York Times*.[24] Tigers fans cheered the victory and their rookie first baseman, little suspecting that in five years he would mount the most serious challenge yet to Babe Ruth's single season home run record.[25]

But for now the Babe was still king, and so it was big news when McCarthy benched him in the second game. "Ruth Benched for First Time," screamed the headline in the *Times*.[26] It was the first time in Ruth's career he had been benched for not hitting, although McCarthy said the reason for the benching was to rest his aging star during the current hot spell. "The heat is terrific, and Babe just asked for a little respite," McCarthy said, not mentioning that Ruth had just two hits in his last 17 at-bats.[27] After leading off and playing center field in the opener, Dixie batted third and played left field as Ruth's replacement in the nightcap. Ruth returned after one more game, and Walker went back to center field. He remained the everyday starter there through the end of June and most of July.

Washington and New York had been battling for the lead all season, and by July 4, it was clear that this was now a two-team race. The Senators held a half-game lead before the two teams met in a holiday doubleheader at Yankee Stadium. Playing before a record, standing room only crowd of 77,365, the Senators won both games, 6–5 and 3–2. Cronin's club had now moved 2½ games ahead of the Yankees, inspiring 5,000 fans to greet the team when they returned by train to Washington's Union Station.

The Yanks, meanwhile, had little to cheer about that evening. Their only satisfaction had come from driving Earl Whitehill — their chief antagonist in the April 25 brawl at Griffith Stadium — from the mound in the second inning of the opener. Walker's personal satisfaction came from a game-tying leadoff home run against Whitehill in the bottom of the first.

The Western clubs, beginning with Detroit, followed the Senators into New York. The Yanks lost two games to the Tigers, but then went on a nine-game winning streak. Win number nine, 9–4, against the White Sox on July 18, put New York back in the lead, one game ahead of Washington. Walker, "the gangling Alabama youngster with a smile that breaks his brown face into a million wrinkles," hit a two-run double and a three-run homer to drive in five of the Yankees' nine runs.[28] Dixie also hit a two-run homer the next day, his tenth of the season, but the White Sox won, ending New York's winning streak.

Despite some occasional shaky moments in the field, Walker had gradually won the center field role from Combs. He was batting just over .300 and had played a significant role in the Yanks' winning streak that allowed them to overtake the Senators.

"One of the brilliant features of the Yankees' comeback has been the hitting and outfielding of Dixie Walker," wrote Joe Vila in *The Sporting News*. "This young man has apparently obliterated the veteran Earle Combs as a regular. Dixie has knocked out nine home runs [sic] to date, and the way he is dragging down powerful wallops and making long, swift throws to the infield and plate has stamped him as a real star."[29]

The *Brooklyn Daily Eagle*'s Harold C. Burr was particularly enthusiastic about Walker's future. Burr thought young Dixie was already a better player than Combs had ever been. "This boy Dixie Walker seems capable to do everything the tired old Kentucky Colonel ever did, and has twice as good a throwing arm," he wrote.[30]

Throughout July, the Yankees and the Senators exchanged the lead several times. However, because the race between them was so close, McCarthy chose to go with experience over youth. Walker's recent slump had expedited the change. From July 19 through the first game of a doubleheader at Boston on July 26 Dixie had only four hits in 27 at bats. McCarthy put Combs back in center field for the second game saying he planned to use the veteran the rest of the way. But Combs failed to hit, and three weeks later first-year man Walker was back in center. He batted second more than first and sometimes, in Ruth's absence, batted third.

Dixie was the leadoff batter in the historic August 17 game against the Browns, played on a typical sweltering summer's day in St. Louis. By appearing in this game, Lou Gehrig extended his consecutive games-played streak to 1,308, breaking the previous record held by former Red Sox and Yankees shortstop Everett Scott. Looking beyond baseball, the day was an important one throughout the state. Asked to vote whether to uphold or repeal Prohibition, 80 percent of Missourians voted to repeal the unpopular Volstead Act. In heavily German St. Louis, the vote to repeal was an overwhelming 20–1.

Meanwhile, after Lefty Gomez retired the Browns in the first inning at Sportsman's Park, a ceremony honoring Gehrig's achievement took place at home plate. Players from both teams gathered around American League president Will Harridge as he presented Gehrig with a silver statuette donated by *The Sporting News*. Missing from the simple ceremony were Yankees manager Joe McCarthy, who was ill, and Scott, who had a business obligation in Fort Wayne, Indiana. That evening, Gehrig received a congratulatory phone call from Colonel Jacob Ruppert and was a guest at a dinner of the St. Louis Chamber of Commerce, where he received another statuette.

The Yanks had a 5–2 lead behind Gomez until Rollie Hemsley hit a three-run inside the park home run to tie the score, and the Browns eventually won, 7–6. Hemsley's sixth-inning home run was due to Walker's misplaying his fly ball. Almost 40 years later, Walker explained to St. Louis sportswriter Bob Broeg what had happened. "I'd been playing with ordinary smoked glasses, but Ben Chapman who was playing right urged me to use the flip glasses like a big leaguer. Hemsley hit the ball; I flipped the glasses, which got in my way." The ball sailed over Walker's head to the center field fence for a three-run homer. As the Yanks trotted off the field when the inning ended, Babe Ruth said to Walker, "Hell, kid, if you'd stayed put the ball woulda hit you in the glove — or on the head."[31]

Washington had taken a half-game lead back on July 24 with a doubleheader sweep at Philadelphia, while the Yanks were idle. Then the Yanks went 17–20, while Washington won 13 in a row in August. At the end of play on August 20, the Senators had an 8½-game lead. With the Yankees falling out of the race, many of their players now seemed to be going through the motions, but Walker continued to play with unbridled enthusiasm. "Young Dixie Walker," noted the *Brooklyn Daily Eagle*, "is doing great things with his centerfield opportunities."[32]

Unfortunately, the year ended on a sour note for Walker. On September 19, he injured his right shoulder sliding into the plate against the White Sox at the Stadium. He saw no action after that until the final day of the season, when he replaced Combs late in the game. Walker's totals for his rookie season, a .274 batting average, and 15 home runs in 98 games, earned him a place on *The Sporting News*'s unofficial American League rookie team for 1933.

The Yankees finished second, seven games behind Washington. Gomez's win total dropped from 24 in 1932 to 16, while Red Ruffing, an 18-game winner in 1932, slipped to 9–14, the lowest full-season win total Ruffing would have as a Yankee. Offensively, the team was showing its age at key positions.

Ruth, at 38, and Combs, at 34, were clearly nearing the end of their careers. For 34-year-old third baseman Joe Sewell, 1933 was his final season as an active player.

It had been a season of disharmony for the Yankees, including a split between those who had played under Miller Huggins and those who had not. Ruth, who thought he should have been Huggins's replacement, was the leader of "a contingent of Yankees who refused to speak to manager Joe McCarthy or any players loyal to him for nearly the entire season."[33]

When the Yankees dropped out of contention in late August, McCarthy and Barrow began turning their attention to 1934. The big question facing them was, of course, Ruth. Was the Babe finally through, as his weak batting in late 1933 seemed to indicate, or did he still "have a lot of baseball left," as he insisted? Ruth had led the American League in walks for the 11th time, but 1933 was the last year he would lead the league in any offensive category. Close observers of the club, wrote the *Daily Eagle*, believed the Babe would not be back in 1934. The paper predicted that Gehrig, Dickey, Chapman, and Walker would be the only position players returning. Walker, it wrote, had emerged as one of the best young players in the game and would replace either Combs or Ruth in 1934.[34]

4

The Lost Years

The friendship that Dixie Walker and Ben Chapman had forged as teenagers in Birmingham, when the two played for the Tennessee Coal and Iron Company, had blossomed now that they were both members of the New York Yankees. Not only were Chapman and Walker roommates, they were also neighbors in Birmingham. "They seem inseparable, both as roommates during the season and friends during the offseason," wrote *The Sporting News*.[1]

Following the 1933 season, they played in several exhibition games and did some horseback riding on visits to teammate Earle Combs's farm in Richmond, Kentucky, and teammate Herb Pennock's farm in Pennsylvania. Pennock's horses were "jumpers," a kind of riding that Ben and Dixie had no experience with, but exhibiting the bravado of the young, the two jumped several fences as they tried to outdo each other. The two young men also attempted to earn extra money by playing in exhibition basketball games after the season, but the Yankees declared basketball off limits.

Mostly, they spent the last few months of the offseason horseback riding, quail shooting (Dixie was an excellent rifle shot), and chopping down trees on a 40-acre piece of land outside of Birmingham that Chapman had recently purchased. They abandoned the outdoor life to spend a few days in New York in February, including attending the Baseball Writers dinner at the Commodore Hotel. While in the city, Dixie and Ben took in some Broadway shows, boxing matches, a few hockey games, and even some clothes shopping.[2] Both men predicted a Yankees pennant in 1934, but when training camp opened on March 1, Walker and Chapman were among the missing, along with Bill Dickey and Lyn Lary. None of the four had yet signed his 1934 contract.

Thirty-five years later, at a Shea Stadium celebration commemorating the 100th anniversary of the 1869 Cincinnati Red Stockings, Walker reminisced about that 1934 salary negotiation with business manager Ed Barrow. His 1933 salary was $5,000, and he was asking for a raise to $7,500, he told Dick Young of the *New York Daily News*. "I was in less than 100 games [98] but I hit 15 home runs and felt pretty good about it." An unimpressed Barrow told him that with a .274 batting average, he would have had to hit 25 home runs to get a raise with this club. "From that day on," Walker said, "I decided the home run was not for me and that I would go back to my natural form of hitting with the pitch and get my raises that way."[3]

His contract signed, Walker arrived in St. Petersburg on March 8. With him were his parents and what the newspapers called "a Negro cook." Babe Ruth was still the main attraction during training camp, as he always was. The Babe, claiming he was in excellent shape, had come to camp 20 pounds lighter than the year before. He said he hoped to play 100 games in 1934, but many in the press suspected baseball's most spectacular player was beginning his final season in a Yankees uniform.

Heeding Barrow's advice, Jacob Ruppert had given Joe McCarthy a three-year contract following the Yankees winning the 1932 World Series. Still, the team's subpar performance in 1933 had Ruth even more convinced that he, and not McCarthy, should be managing the team — if not this year, then in 1935 when McCarthy's contract was due to expire. Ruth would soon learn the feeling among the owners that a man who could not manage himself would be incapable of managing a baseball team.

Walker's excellent rookie year had engendered predictions of great success for him from around the league. During the offseason, White Sox manager Lew Fonseca predicted a wide-open race in 1934. In discussing the Yankees, Fonseca said, "I look for Dixie Walker, their young outfielder, to star this season, and predict he will hit 30 home runs."[4] Sportswriter Harold Parrott called Dixie "a grand young outfielder who is a great runner and a sure .300 hitter."[5]

In an article written during spring training, Washington columnist Shirley Povich pointed to the respect the opposition had for Walker's abilities. Povich wrote that the defending champion Senators feared the Yankees even if Ruth played only half the schedule. The Nats "have seen enough of Dixie Walker to note that the club will be far better off defensively with Ruth out of the lineup, with the added argument that Walker, himself, is no mean man with the bat."[6]

McCarthy's problem with Walker continued to be where to play his budding young star. Should he use him to replace Ruth at a corner outfield position or to replace Earle Combs in center field? Dixie had done an outstanding job as Combs's part-time replacement in 1933; now his play in the early March exhibition games had McCarthy ready to make him Combs's permanent replacement.

But in baseball, as in life, things do not always go as planned. Sometime during spring training Walker developed soreness in his right arm — his throwing arm — the first in a series of injuries that would greatly alter the shape of his career. When it failed to heal, he had a tooth removed, as other players had done in an attempt to cure sore arms on the theory that the soreness was caused by an infected tooth, or teeth. The "cure" had purportedly worked for some players, but it did not work for Walker. The soreness persisted, preventing him from throwing normally. "Dixie Walker has developed a mysterious lame arm," said *The Sporting News*.[7]

On April 11, less than a week before the season opener, the Yankees sent Walker ahead to New York to have the arm examined. The doctors could find neither the cause of the problem nor a way to cure it. Dixie did play with the Yanks' second-stringers in a game at Newark on April 15, where he hit a home run. He also had three hits and a home run in an exhibition game at Albany on April 23, but he did not get into a regular season game until April 26. That was as a pinch-hitter, and he did little more than pinch-hit or pinch-run for the rest of the season. From time to time, Walker's frustration at not playing would show. While on the bench in the eighth inning of a May 18 game at Detroit, Dixie, "ordinarily the most retiring of Yankee players," said something that umpire George Moriarty did not like and was ejected.[8]

McCarthy started him in an exhibition game against the Class C Wheeling Stogies at Wheeling, West Virginia, on July 27. Dixie responded with four hits and a home run. The next day, he made his only start of the season, playing left field and batting third. After going hitless in five at-bats, he would make only one more appearance in 1934, as a pinch-hitter on August 7. Two weeks later, in a game against Cleveland, a foul tip broke a finger on Bill

Yankees manager Joe McCarthy had to decide whether Walker should replace Babe Ruth at a corner outfield position or Earle Combs in center field (National Baseball Hall of Fame Library, Cooperstown, New York).

Dickey's throwing hand. Arndt Jorgens replaced Dickey as the first-string catcher, and the team purchased 36-year-old Zack Taylor from the Syracuse Chiefs of the International League to back up Jorgens. To make room for Taylor, the Yankees took Walker off the roster, believing his sore arm would not heal this season, and put him on the voluntarily retired list.

Walker's totals for 1934 were one game played in the outfield and just two hits in 17 at-bats, both singles. A year that had started with such great promise for Walker had ended with his career in jeopardy. "Dixie Walker may never recover from his injured arm and is at best a poor risk," wrote Shirley Povich, the same man who in the spring had described him as an improvement on Babe Ruth.[9]

In addition to Walker's lost year and Dickey's broken finger, which caused him to miss the final month of the season, the Yankees had other injury problems. Combs crashed into a concrete wall in St. Louis on July 24, fracturing his skull, while pitchers Johnny Allen and Russ Van Atta struggled with arm problems that reduced their effectiveness.

Lou Gehrig won the Triple Crown, as he continued to carry the Yankees' offensive load.[10] The Yanks also had the pitchers' Triple Crown winner, Lefty Gomez, who had the best season of his career.[11] However, their heroics were not enough to prevent the Detroit Tigers from winning their first pennant since 1909. For the second consecutive year, the Yankees finished in second place, seven games behind the leader.

Following the season, Walker and Chapman again visited Earle Combs at his Richmond, Kentucky, farm. Dixie's sore right arm felt well enough for him to participate with other major leaguers in a three-game postseason series in North Carolina. He and Chapman played for a team managed by Ray Hayworth, the backup catcher to Mickey Cochrane, manager of the Tigers team that lost the World Series to the St. Louis Cardinals. Max Bishop, long-time Athletics second baseman and now a member of the Red Sox, led the other team.

Although Chapman and Walker were seemingly inseparable, Chapman told the Yankees in November he would like them to trade him. He thought he would hit better away from Yankee Stadium, he said, despite having hit .335 at home in 1934, as opposed to .283 on the road. Then again, Chapman may have been unhappy playing in New York, and may have preferred a less diverse environment. Openly bigoted, he had been criticized this past season for shouting offensive and derogatory remarks at a Jewish fan in a May 10 game at the Stadium against the White Sox.

In asking for the trade, Chapman added his belief that the Yanks were a few years away from winning a pennant. The Red Sox, who had just added All-Star shortstop Joe Cronin as their manager, were his team of choice. Nevertheless, he was the most sought-after Yankee by all the teams at the winter meetings in New York. Whenever the Yanks proposed a trade, the other team always demanded Chapman in return. McCarthy's attempt to get Heinie Manush from Washington collapsed when he would not include Chapman in the deal.[12]

Sammy Byrd, another Birmingham resident, also wanted out of New York. After spending most of the 1934 season as a part-time substitute for Ruth, Byrd had told McCarthy that he wanted to go someplace where he could be a regular. Walker, the third Yankee outfielder from Birmingham, did not share the desire of Chapman and Byrd to leave New York. Anxious to rebound from the lost season of 1934, Dixie was simply looking forward to playing, and preferably in New York. "The arm feels fine," he said, "and nothing will keep me out of the lineup in 1935."[13] Walker had tested the arm during the offseason by pitching to Chapman, who was experimenting with batting left-handed. Dixie had shown good speed on his pitches and had felt no pain during these sessions.

In January, Walker visited the Yankees offices in New York to assure Barrow that after several minor operations on his throwing arm—one of which had forced him to keep it in a plaster cast for seven weeks—the arm was healed. (Walker had also had five teeth extracted and his tonsils removed to help cure his sore right arm.)

He reported to St. Petersburg early, accompanied by his parents. Before the official start of spring training, he would be out each day playing catch with his father, and when they finished, his mother would apply hot towels to his throwing arm. Yet he continued to feel twinges of pain during the Yankees' early workouts.

Undismayed, Walker remained confident that working out in the Florida sun each day would eventually cause the pain to disappear. By mid–March, he was throwing from the outfield with apparent ease, first in the workouts and then in the exhibition games. "I can throw as naturally as I ever did," he said.[14] During the winter, Barrow had sent Johnny Nee, the scout who signed Walker for the Yankees, to check on several of the Yanks' injured players.

One was Combs, who said he was ready to return in 1935. He did, but he retired at the end of the season. By then, Combs knew that Walker would not be replacing him, but that Joe DiMaggio was coming to New York to be the new center fielder. Combs accepted a coaching job with the Yankees and helped DiMaggio master the intricacies of playing the outfield in Yankee Stadium.

Dr. Robert Hyland, the renowned St. Louis surgeon, had operated on Dickey's broken hand and dislocated finger, and the Yankee catcher was ready to go. Walker, Allen, and Van Atta also checked out fine, Nee reported. The

Yankees offered all three conditional dollar-a-year contracts, which meant they had to convince McCarthy they were in shape to play before the club would offer them a specific salary. Ultimately, all did.

For the first time since joining them in 1920, Babe Ruth was no longer a Yankee. The Yanks had released him in late February, whereupon he signed with the lowly Boston Braves, based on his mistaken assumption that he would eventually be the club's manager. Ruth was gone, but McCarthy did not miss him, not on the playing field and certainly not in the clubhouse, where the Babe had long sought his job. He gave Ruth's spot in right field to George Selkirk, a minor-league standout for the past several years.

"He has shown me everything — punch, speed, defensive strength, enthusiasm.... I am going to give him every opportunity to prove he deserves to be out there every day," McCarthy said of Selkirk.[15] Meanwhile, McCarthy worked on Walker's swing, which Dixie later said made him more effective against left-handed pitchers. McCarthy had considered Walker a long-shot to come back, but Dixie's play in spring training changed his mind. "Combs and Dixie Walker are coming along very nicely," said the Yankees skipper, "and I have decided to go along with them and stop worrying about a deal for another outfielder."[16]

The outfielder the Yanks had been pursuing was Roy Johnson of the Boston Red Sox. In return, Boston general manager Eddie Collins and manager Joe Cronin asked for minor league first base prospect George McQuinn and either Walker or Selkirk. McCarthy offered Myril Hoag, but Boston said no and the deal did not get made.[17]

Walker had been timid in the early going, trying to protect his arm, but by early April, he was playing magnificently and throwing well from the outfield. He was "looking like the Walker of 1933," wrote Dan Daniel in the *New York World Telegram*.[18] Daniel thought he could possibly open the season in center field, rather than Combs, or share left field with right-hand-hitting Jesse Hill. McCarthy seemed to agree, saying, "Dixie has come along so impressively that I cannot ignore his qualifications for a regular post against right-handed pitching."[19]

Another manager Walker impressed that spring was Bill McKechnie of the Braves. McKechnie now had Babe Ruth on his roster, but after seeing Walker in an exhibition game, he said. "If I had a fielder like Dixie Walker I'd be a little happier too. This is the first time I have ever seen him in real playing shape and he could play on my club any time."[20]

After breaking camp, the Yankees traveled north, encountering cool, wet weather along the way. In Nashville, Walker came down with a fever that confined him to his room and required treatment by a physician. The illness was a minor setback, and McCarthy used Dixie as a pinch-hitter the next day in Knoxville. What mattered to the Yankees concerning Walker was that he had demonstrated his arm problem was cured, leading them to expect a big season from him in 1935.

Combs was in left field, Chapman in center, and Selkirk in right when the Yankees opened the season with a 1–0 loss to Wes Ferrell of the Red Sox. Ferrell allowed the Yanks just two hits and retired Dixie as a pinch-hitter in the ninth inning. Three days later, Walker pinch-hit successfully against Philadelphia, which earned him starts in the next two games against the Athletics. Batting leadoff and playing left field, he was a combined 1-for-8, with a double and a run batted in.

Before going to Boston for their first road game of the season, the Yanks stopped at West Point on April 22 for an exhibition game against the Army Cadets. Coach Art Fletcher was in charge of the 16 players, including Walker, who made the trip. It was a rainy day and the game, which the umpires called in the third inning, probably should never have started. But it did, and as a result, Dixie Walker's season, career, and life would be dramatically altered.

Dixie drew a walk leading off the game. Red Rolfe followed with a ground ball that the Army first baseman fielded, stepped on the bag, and threw to the shortstop in an attempt to double up Walker. On Dixie's slide into second base, he dislocated his right (throwing) shoulder. A dislocated shoulder is extremely painful, and Dixie needed the assistance of Earle "Doc" Painter, the Yankees' trainer, and an Army doctor to help him off the field and over to the Post Hospital.

The injury put Walker out indefinitely, and it would take several years before he regained his full throwing ability. He returned a month later, and made three pinch-hitting appearances in late May. One was against the St. Louis Browns, amid rumors that Ed Barrow had offered Walker, Myril Hoag, and cash to the Browns for outfielder Sam West, considered the league's best center fielder. Browns manager Rogers Hornsby was interested, but the deal fell through when Hornsby asked the Yanks to increase the amount of cash going to St. Louis.[21]

With major league rosters limited to 23 players, McCarthy now had to decide whether Walker's shoulder problem would continue to prevent him from being a full-time player this season. On June 10, the Yanks sent Dixie to Johns Hopkins Hospital in Baltimore to have the shoulder examined. The doctors at Hopkins could not say with any certainty when Dixie's throwing would return to normal. So on June 14, the Yankees, still worried about what they called Walker's "trick shoulder," sent him back to Newark.

Bears manager Bob Shawkey was glad to have him. Walker's throwing might be hampered, Shawkey reasoned, but he could still hit, run, and field at a big league level. In 89 games for Newark, Dixie batted .293 in 317 at-bats with 17 home runs and 67 runs batted in. He was the only player to hit a home run in every International League park in 1935.

Nonetheless, for Dixie Walker, it was another lost season. He had appeared in only eight major-league games, with two hits in 13 at-bats. In what should have been two prime seasons with the Yankees — 1934 and 1935 — Walker played in just 25 games for them. Perhaps even more damaging to Dixie's future was the growing talk around baseball that he was a hard-luck player, one of those multi-talented young men prevented by injuries from fulfilling their potential.

5

Radical Surgery and a Career Revived

The first indication that Dixie Walker's days in New York were numbered came in December 1935, when business manager Ed Barrow included him in a proposed trade for Cleveland's Mel Harder. Along with Walker, Barrow offered pitcher Johnny Allen, veteran second baseman Tony Lazzeri, and catcher Joe Glenn for Harder and infielder Odell Hale. Indians owner Alva Bradley turned down the offer, saying he would neither trade nor sell Harder. However, he did agree to part with two other pitchers, Monte Pearson and minor-leaguer Steve Sundra, in exchange for Allen, winner of 50 games with just 19 losses in his four seasons with the Yankees.[1]

Having survived the winter meetings untraded, Walker was one of 15 players to receive contract offers from the Yankees in January 1936, two of which were conditional. A conditional contract was a formality in baseball negotiations; it meant the player would sign for a dollar until he could prove to his team that he deserved to be offered a contract at a specific salary. Recipients of the two conditional contracts were Walker and Frank Crosetti, the team's 25-year-old shortstop. Crosetti had missed the final two months of the season as the result of a freak accident. While bending over to untie a knot in his shoelace, he tore some cartilage in his left leg.

Walker had earned his way onto the Yankees club under similar contractual conditions in 1935, but the competition for an outfield spot was even more heated this year. During the winter, the Yanks had traded for Washington outfielder Roy Johnson. Joe McCarthy had been after Johnson for a long time. In March 1935, he had failed in an attempt get him in a trade with the Boston Red Sox.

In December, Boston traded Johnson and outfielder Carl Reynolds to Washington for outfielder Heinie Manush, but Johnson never got to play for the Senators. In a trade with the Nats a month later, on January 17, 1936, the

5. Radical Surgery and a Career Revived

The 1936 New York Yankees at spring training. Walker is in the top row, second from right. To the left is pitcher Johnny Murphy with whom he would work a decade later as their respective league's player representative. Rookie Joe Di-Maggio is in the second row, third from right (private collection of Stephen Walker).

Yanks acquired Johnson and pitcher Bump Hadley for outfielder Jesse Hill and pitcher Jimmie DeShong.

The 33-year-old Johnson had spent seven years as a regular in Detroit and Boston. He had, in different seasons, led the American League in doubles (1929) and triples (1931), and had a .300 lifetime batting average, including a .315 mark for the Red Sox in 1935.[2] Also making his first appearance as a Yankee this spring was 21-year-old rookie Joe DiMaggio. The highly prized and much-discussed DiMaggio was coming off a season in which he batted .398 for the San Francisco Seals of the Pacific Coast League.

Walker again played extremely well at training camp, but the addition of Johnson and the coming of DiMaggio made his chances of making the team much less likely. Most of the training-camp buzz revolved around DiMaggio. The New York papers were unstinting in their praise of the team's prize prospect, as was McCarthy. The *New York Times* of March 6 wrote of McCarthy's "unconcealed admiration for the swiftness of his young star in pursuit of balls, and the power of his arm in returning them to the infield."[3]

A few years earlier, sportswriters had heralded Walker as the successor to Babe Ruth. That honor, or perhaps burden, now belonged to DiMaggio. However, as with Walker, DiMaggio was not immune to injury. Joe Coscarart of the Boston Bees stepped on his left instep in a game at St. Petersburg on March 22. The next day DiMaggio was still lame and the foot was swollen. Trainer Doc Painter put Joe's left foot into a diathermy machine, but left it in the machine for too long a time, and DiMaggio emerged with a burned and blistered heel. The prognosis was that he would be out of action until early May.

McCarthy used Walker to replace DiMaggio, and Dixie took advantage of the opportunity. He hit well and his throws from center field supported his claim that his arm had healed. Still, the consensus in the press box was that he was on the market. Dan Daniel, writing in *The Sporting News*, said the Yankees' outfielders in 1936 likely would be Roy Johnson, Joe DiMaggio, Ben Chapman, George Selkirk, and Myril Hoag. That left Walker out. Daniel believed the Yanks would try to sell him to the Braves or Dodgers. Either team would be wise to grab him, he wrote. "Walker would look good in Brooklyn, as he would be a threat for that right field wall," Daniel presciently predicted.[4]

But when the season opened, Dixie was still with the club, making his first appearance at Washington in the third game of the season. He replaced Chapman, who left in the fourth inning after complaining of stiffness in his chest. Walker's seventh-inning triple off Joe Bokina, making his big league debut, drove in Bill Dickey with the winning run. A week later, his second-inning, three-run homer at Yankee Stadium against Washington veteran Monte Weaver got the Yanks started on their way to a victory.

The battle for the final outfield spot had come down to Walker and Myril Hoag. McCarthy preferred Hoag, and in April offered Walker to both the Braves and the Dodgers, the latter managed by Casey Stengel. "If the Yankees let Dixie go," wrote Daniel, "Casey ought to grab him and aim him at the right field wall in Ebbets Field."[5]

Selling Walker to a National League team was the Yankees' preferred option. Sending him back to the minor leagues would be difficult, as they would have to get the other big league clubs to waive on him, which they were not likely to do. Nor did they want him joining a rival American League team and risk his becoming a star in their own league. Yet when White Sox owner J. Louis Comiskey offered a reported $20,000 for Walker on May 1, they took it. A few days earlier, the Yanks had offered to sell Walker to Chicago for $25,000. Comiskey made a counter offer of $15,000, so the $20,000 price tag is probably accurate. The Sox were looking for help wherever they could find it. After getting off to a 4–1 start, they had just lost their eighth straight, 3–2, at New York, when they made the deal.

In six games and 20 at-bats with the Yankees this season, Dixie had seven hits, including two triples, a home run, and five runs batted in. Sportswriter Fred Lieb summarized the now ex–Yankee's stay in New York this way: When he broke in, "Dixie seemed to have everything necessary for a long and brilliant big league career. Long and lean, he was a deer on the base paths and in the outfield. He hit low line drives, which sailed from his bat like machine gun bullets." Lieb praised Walker's throwing arm and said before the injuries to it and to his shoulder, Walker seemed the logical successor to Babe Ruth. The opportunity to play every day might afford him the chance to reach his potential, concluded Lieb.[6]

Joe DiMaggio would be making his major league debut in two days, still McCarthy hated to lose Walker, as did the Yankees players, among whom he was well-liked. On the day of the trade, McCarthy called him into his office and said, "Dixie, I'm sorry to say this, but we'll have to let you go. I still think you can play major-league baseball, and I've sent you to a team I think you can help, the Chicago White Sox."[7]

Six weeks later, Ben Chapman, Walker's best friend, followed him out of New York. The Yankees traded Chapman to the Washington Senators for outfielder Jake Powell. Chapman had been a Yankees regular since 1930, but had fallen out of favor with the club during spring training. First, he staged a holdout, and then he asked the Yanks to trade him, preferably to the Red Sox. He eventually signed, but missed some early-season games while working his way into playing shape. At the time of the trade, he was batting just .266 and had only one stolen base. Both marks were far below average for Chapman, a career .305 hitter and the American League's stolen base leader in 1931, 1932, and 1933.[8]

After meeting with McCarthy, Dixie made an even more significant change in his life. For the past few years he had been dating a young, native New Yorker named Estelle Shea. Estelle had been talking marriage for some time, but Dixie had wanted to wait. His fear, he said, was his injuries would end his baseball career and force him to return to working in the steel mills.

Now that his career was back on track, the two had planned to marry on May 15; but spurred by Dixie's trade to Chicago, they decided to get married immediately. They drove to Armonk, New York, in suburban Westchester County, where Judge Julius A. Raven performed the ceremony in his office at three o'clock in the morning of May 2, 1936. George Selkirk, Dixie's teammate at Newark and with the Yankees, was the best man; Agnes Rooney, Estelle's roommate, served as her maid of honor.

Judge Raven was known in and around New York as "the marrying judge," for all the weddings he performed. Raven had a reputation for being on call 24 hours a day and is said to have married more than 6,000 couples in his career. Sherman Billingsley, owner of the famous Stork Club in Manhattan, suggested "Raven in Armonk as a nice place to get married" to many of the show business people who patronized his club.[9]

Though hastily arranged, the marriage would last for 46 years, until Dixie's death in 1982. A warm and loving relationship, it produced six children and endured many personal hardships and frequent baseball-related separations. Players are often gone on road trips for up to two weeks several times each season, and it is left to the wives to keep the household going. "I remember that he wrote Mom each day and often called her several times a week," wrote daughter Mary Ann Estelle Walker, recalling those road trips.[10]

Dixie's new bride was born Estelle Mary Shea in Manhattan on October 11, 1909. Her parents were native New Yorkers Patrick and Catherine E. (Casey) Shea, both the children of Irish immigrants. They were married on October 15, 1902, at the Holy Cross Catholic Church on West 42nd Street between Eighth and Ninth Avenues. Patrick, age 40, and Catherine, 17, were the first of their families to be married in the United States.

They eventually had ten children, five boys and five girls. When Estelle, the third child and second girl, was born, the family was living on West 40th Street in the old Irish "Hell's Kitchen" section of Manhattan. Patrick drove a horse and wagon for a furniture moving company, but he branched out from there. He created a small moving company for entertainers who needed to move furniture and possessions around the city. In addition, according to his grandson Stephen, Patrick Shea started the first company to offer carriage rides in Central Park.[11]

At the time of her marriage, Estelle shared a Manhattan apartment with Agnes and worked at the Music Corporation of America (MCA) as a talent scout. Sonny Werblin, her boss at MCA, prospered there and years later owned thoroughbred horses and was a part-owner of the New York Jets football team. Estelle's job was to book bands into nightclubs and to visit the smaller clubs around the city, seeking young talent for MCA to sign.

After the trade and marriage, Estelle left her glamorous job and moved with her new husband to Chicago. When the season ended, she moved with Dixie to Birmingham. It would take several years for Flossie Walker to fully accept her chic, Irish-Catholic, native New Yorker daughter-in-law. Meanwhile, her own mother, Catherine, never spoke to her again for having married outside the faith. On June 13, 1972 Dixie and Estelle went through a rite known as convalidation at Our Lady of Sorrows Catholic Church in Homewood, Alabama in the Diocese of Birmingham. Convalidation is a process to validate a pre-existing civil marriage in the Catholic Church.

Dixie was leaving the pennant-contending Yankees for the White Sox, a team that had finished in the second division in each of the previous 15 seasons. Conversely, going to the less-talented White Sox would afford him a chance to play every day, and that pleased him. Chicago's manager was Jimmy Dykes, the longtime American League third baseman in his third season as manager and his final season as a full-time player.

Walker made his White Sox debut on May 5, at Philadelphia. Dykes put him in the third spot in the batting order and played him in center field, moving rookie Mike Kreevich from center to left. In effect, Dixie was replacing Rip Radcliff, Chicago's slumping left fielder. Walker was hitless that day, and just 1-for-18 until he broke out of the slump with a five-hit game on May 11, at St. Louis. He had three singles, two doubles, a walk, and four runs batted in as Chicago drubbed the Browns, 19–6.

Dixie's batting average was a solid .279, when on May 23 he suffered yet another career-threatening injury. The White Sox were hosting St. Louis in a Saturday afternoon doubleheader. Walker had a single and a pair of walks in the first game, won by Chicago, 8–3, behind Vern Kennedy. With two out in the first inning of the nightcap, he drew a walk, his third walk of the afternoon. Jack Knott, the Browns pitcher, saw Dixie leaning the wrong way and made a successful pickoff throw to first baseman Jim Bottomley. Walker dived headfirst to the bag with his right arm extended; he collided with the burly Bottomley and his right shoulder popped loose.

A doctor snapped the dislocated shoulder back into place after the game, but Walker was expected to miss four to six weeks of action. Some thought his absence would be longer, maybe the rest of the season, while others thought his career was over. "Estimates on the probable date of Dixie Walker's return still are vague," reported local sportswriter Edward Burns, more than a week later, "and there are several who fear he may be through as a big league ballplayer."[12]

Dykes put Walker, temporarily, on the voluntary retired list, moved Kreevich back to center field and put Radcliff back in left. Rip took advantage of Walker's injury by having one of the best seasons of his career. He batted .335, finished fifth in the league in hits, and made the American League All-Star team.

Doctors operated on Dixie's right shoulder to see why the arm continued to come loose from the socket. They did some refastening of tendons and said they had solved the problem. Walker started working out in late July, but he did not see any action until he singled as a pinch-hitter against Cleveland on August 18. Dixie pinch-hit just eight more times that season and skipped the traditional post-season City Series against the Cubs.

Although the White Sox finished in the first division for the first time since 1920, they were disappointed at losing second place to the Detroit Tigers by half a game. The injuries to Walker and pitcher Monty Stratton, they believed, had prevented them from finishing closer to the pennant-winning Yankees. In a very generous gesture by the White Sox players, they voted Walker a full share of the third-place money despite his small contribution.

He had missed three full months of the 1936 season. In all, between the Yankees and the White Sox, Walker played in 32 games, his third consecutive drastically shortened season. For most ballplayers, the ages from 24 to 26 are among their most productive. That was not the case for Dixie Walker. Of a possible 462 games at those ages, from 1934 through 1936, he appeared in only 57.

While the Yankees seemed content to let nature take its course with regard to his injuries, the White Sox took a proactive approach. Aware that Walker's career was in jeopardy unless they could get his throwing arm repaired, manager Jimmy Dykes asked eminent Chicago surgeon Dr. Philip Kreuscher to look at the shoulder.

"The shoulder kept grinding and the arm socket was chipping away," said Dr. Kreuscher after examining Dixie. "We'll have to give him a new arm socket."[13] The procedure he proposed was a radical surgery in which the arm muscle is tied with little silver wires through holes drilled in the upper arm bone. It was an extremely delicate operation, one that took great skill to perform. That it worked was a credit to the surgeon's skills, and it earned Walker's everlasting gratitude.

"Dr. Philip Kreuscher was the surgeon, and believe me I owe him a lot. He cut right through my upper arm and shoulder. He drilled a hole in the bone in my shoulder. Then he took a muscle from somewhere and put it inside the bone to hold my shoulder in place. It worked out perfectly. As a matter of fact, Dr. Kreuscher later had me come from Birmingham to Chicago at his expense so that I could be Exhibit A when he lectured to other surgeons on the operation."[14]

Following the December 1936, surgery, Walker rested his arm all winter at home in Birmingham. At the White Sox's spring training camp in Pasadena, California, he started with easy tosses, but soon was throwing as well as ever; obviously the operation had been a success. The shoulder was fine, but the injury jinx appeared to have struck again in an exhibition game against the Los Angeles Angels. The Sox were playing against the Pacific Coast League team before starting their schedule of games against other big league teams.

In the first inning, Walker pulled up lame running to first base after stroking a single. He left the game, but was back for the next two games against the Angels. In addition to his being relieved that Walker's injury was not serious, Dykes took a special pleasure in watching him uncork some excellent long throws from the outfield. Dixie homered against Pittsburgh in Chicago's first game against major league opposition; then, on April 2, against the Cubs at Phoenix, he caught two long fly balls in succession and threw to third on a line after both.

Walker was delighted at his progress. Having shaken the initial worries about his arm, he was confident about the new season. After hitting a home run against the Cubs in the weekend City Series before the opener, he said, "I've been going pretty good, and maybe I'm due for some good luck. My arm feels fine and will probably get stronger. I weigh 15 pounds less than I did last season and feel that much better."[15]

Dykes left spring training content with what he had seen of Walker. Dixie had long established he could hit, field, and run. Now with his throwing arm restored to health, the Sox felt that a full season from Dixie made them a serious pennant contender. Detroit manager Mickey Cochrane cited the return of Walker and Monty Stratton in agreeing that Chicago was a legitimate contender. The race figured to be among the defending champion Yankees, the Indians, the White Sox, and his Tigers, predicted Cochrane.

Walker's hot hitting in spring training continued into the regular season. He had three hits, including a double and a triple, on Opening Day in St. Louis. He hit safely in 12 of Chicago's first 13 games, four of which were three-hit games. One of those three-hit games came against Boston on May 8 and raised his batting average to .415.

"He's hitting the ball, he's fielding with the best of them, running like a deer, and throwing as if there never had been anything wrong with his right arm," wrote the *Chicago Daily Tribune*'s Irving Vaughan, while describing Dixie as a "tall Southerner, who drawls melodiously in a high pitched voice."[16]

Everything was going right for Walker in the spring of 1937. In addition to being injury-free and hitting steadily, he was now a father. On April 14, in New York, Estelle gave birth to the couple's first child, a son they named Fred Walker, Jr. Emerging from a barbershop after a haircut, the new father, with tongue in cheek, told a reporter, "This will have to last me for a month. On account of the new baby, I'll have to economize."[17]

On June 1, Bill Dietrich of the White Sox pitched a no-hitter at home against the Browns, the first major league no-hitter in which Walker had participated. He contributed two hits and three runs batted in to Chicago's 8–0 victory.

One week later, left-hander Thornton Lee defeated the Yankees, 5–4, at Comiskey Park for his third victory of the season. All three wins had been against New York, as the White Sox were beginning to reap the rewards of one of the best trades they ever made. The only player they had given up to get Lee in the three-way offseason deal with Washington and Cleveland was Jack Salveson. The 22-year-old Salveson had only four big-league wins to his credit. He would add only five more — with Cleveland in 1943. Lee was no youngster; he was 30 at the time of the trade, but he would pitch another 12 seasons in the major leagues and win 105 more games.

Lee's victory over the Yankees was Chicago's tenth in a row. It raised their record to 25–17, and tied them with New York for the league lead. The Sox finished the home stand on June 13 with a doubleheader sweep of Washington behind Ted Lyons and Monty Stratton. They now trailed the Yanks by just half a game, but lost four straight at Boston, scoring a combined seven runs in the four games.

The series finale, the second game of a June 17 doubleheader, was tied 2–2 after nine innings. Chicago threatened against pitcher Rube Walberg in the top of the tenth, but the rally was broken when Bill McGowan, the lone base umpire, called Mike Kreevich out on a close play at second. When Walker passed by McGowan as he headed to right field for the home tenth, he said something about the call that the umpire did not like. McGowan threw Dixie out of the game, and when Dykes came running out to protest the ejection, McGowan tossed him too.

Stratton retired the first two Boston batters, but a double by Doc Cramer and a single by Ben Chapman gave the Red Sox the win. After completing their swing through the East, with three games at New York, three at Philadelphia, and three at Washington, the White Sox had fallen three games behind the Yankees. A seven-game winning streak at the end of June strengthened Chicago's hold on second place, but got them no closer to the Yankees. The Sox never did regain the lead. They finished third, three games behind Detroit and 16 games behind the repeat champion Yankees.

Despite the success his former club, the Yankees, had enjoyed since he left, 1937 was an extremely satisfying season for Dixie Walker. He combined with Mike Kreevich (.302) and Rip Radcliff (.325) to give the White Sox an all-.300-hitting outfield. Dixie's average was .302, with 28 doubles, 16 triples, and nine home runs. He had 95 runs batted in and 105 runs scored. His 16 triples tied him with Kreevich for the most in the American League. In addition, Walker fanned only 26 times in 593 at-bats, making him the seventh-toughest man to strike out in the American League. It was the first of eight times he would finish in the top ten in his league in this category.

Walker had three four-hit games during the season, with the most productive at St. Louis on July 3. Among his four hits were his first home run of the season, and he drove home five runs in Chicago's 10–5 win.

Yet the most rewarding aspect of the 1937 season was that for the first time as a big leaguer, he played an entire season free from a major injury. Dixie was one of two White Sox players — shortstop Luke Appling was the other — to appear in all 154 games. Once again, Dixie Walker was recognized as one of baseball's emerging stars.

6

The Most Unpopular Man in Detroit

When the 1937 season ended, 27-year-old Dixie Walker had finally begun to fulfill the promise so long expected of him. He had every reason to believe he would be in Chicago for years to come — certainly, at least, for the 1938 season. Yet a bare two months after the '37 season ended, Walker was no longer a member of the White Sox. On December 2, at the minor league meetings in Milwaukee, Chicago traded him to the Detroit Tigers, along with pitcher Vern Kennedy and infielder Tony Piet. In exchange, the White Sox received outfielder Gerald "Gee" Walker, third baseman Marv Owen, and minor-league catcher Mike Tresh. Chicago manager Jimmy Dykes had asked Detroit for Birdie Tebbetts, their promising young catcher, but when the Tigers refused to trade Tebbetts, Dykes settled for Tresh instead.

To say that the deal was unpopular in Detroit would be a gross understatement. Tigers fans reacted angrily and emotionally. They were especially upset at the loss of Gee Walker, a fiery competitor and among the most well-liked players ever in Detroit. A lifelong Tiger and a .300 hitter in five of his first seven seasons, Gee Walker was coming off a year in which he batted .335 and reached career highs in hits (213), home runs (18), and runs batted in (113). This was superior in every category to what his soon-to-be replacement, Dixie Walker, had done in 1937.

The general reaction to the trade among baseball people was that Chicago manager Dykes had outsmarted Tigers manager Mickey Cochrane, his old Philadelphia Athletics teammate. Nevertheless, Cochrane defended the deal on several fronts. He noted that Dixie's .302 batting average for the White Sox was better than it looked because Comiskey Park was "the worst park on the circuit to hit in." Moreover, claimed Cochrane, the acquisition of Kennedy, a 21-game winner in 1936, made it an excellent exchange for the Tigers. "I have to bolster my pitching, and with Kennedy winning between eighteen and twenty games we will be tough next season."[1]

Although Kennedy had slipped to a 14–13 record in 1937, a significant drop-off from his 21–9 season of 1936, he ranked with the league's better right-handers. The Red Sox had been pursuing him, too, until Dykes asked for third baseman Pinky Higgins in return. "I knew I was putting myself on the spot but I had to do something to strengthen our pitching," said Cochrane. "In my opinion Kennedy will give us the needed help. He is the best pitcher that could be had."[2]

However, others, including Shirley Povich of the *Washington Post*, believed Kennedy was not that good a pitcher and, despite his inclusion, the trade greatly favored the White Sox. With tongue in cheek, Povich attributed Detroit's poor deal to the cracked skull Cochrane had suffered after being beaned by the Yankees' Bump Hadley during the 1937 season.[3] "When Detroit fans get a load of Dixie Walker in Gerald Walker's accustomed spot in the outfield and in the batting order, I, for one, would not want to be Mickey Cochrane," he wrote.[4]

Povich's words, written two days after the trade, correctly anticipated the fans' reactions. Gee Walker had endeared himself to the people of Detroit with the all-out, enthusiastic way he played the game. They so loved his style of play, they willingly forgave him when his overzealousness sometimes led to baserunning and other kinds of blunders. Whenever his antics or reckless baserunning got him into trouble with Cochrane or Bucky Harris, Cochrane's predecessor as manager, the fans always sided with Walker.

The White Sox rewarded Walker for his excellent 1937 season by trading him to Detroit (National Baseball Hall of Fame Library, Cooperstown, New York).

"Newspaper offices were besieged with telephone calls from men, women, and children, who first questioned the authenticity of the swap and then denounced it emphatically," wrote Sam Greene of *The Sporting News*. "Crowds huddled on street corners, in hotels, saloons, barber shops, and drug stores to voice indignation," he con-

6. The Most Unpopular Man in Detroit

tinued. "Taxicab drivers and newsboys, butchers and bakers, policemen and factory workers, executives and clerks joined in bitter disagreement with the Tigers management. The subject transcended all others in popular discussion." Greene called Walker "the most popular of all Tiger players, a hustling hard-hitting outfielder, chock full of the quality known as color."[5]

The fans were so outraged at Cochrane for making this trade that Tigers owner Walter Briggs was forced to issue a statement saying he had approved the deal. Briggs's support for the trade did not prevent various civic groups from threatening to boycott Tigers home games in 1938. The timing could not have been worse for Briggs; he had added an upper deck to Navin Field for the '38 season, while renaming it Briggs Stadium.

Aware of the dissatisfaction the trade had caused among Tigers fans, Dixie attempted to get them on his side. He spoke to more than a thousand attendees at the annual All-American sports banquet at the Detroit Yacht Club. Walker delivered a wonderful address, one that received even more applause than that given to Harry Kipke, the University of Michigan football coach. Kipke's recent resignation had upset the local fans as much as the trade of Gerald Walker.

Dixie did his best to put a positive spin on the trade. He promised the fans they were getting an outstanding pitcher in Vern Kennedy, who he was certain would return to his previous form in 1938. He told them he knew how popular Gee Walker was in Detroit, but how pleased he was about the trade.

"You know I could hardly believe it when I saw that I had been traded to Detroit. Why this is the best sports town in the United States," he said. "I'm still afraid I'll wake up and find it all a dream. But if I am not dreaming, I promise you I'll give everything I have for the Tigers next season."[6]

In the spring of 1938, while Walker was adjusting to his new teammates in Lakeland, Florida, the biggest baseball story of spring training was unfolding at the Yankees' training camp in St. Petersburg. Rookie sensation Joe Gordon, up from the Newark Bears, was trying to earn the second base job. Tony Lazzeri had manned that position for the previous 12 seasons, but he had slowed considerably. Anticipating the arrival of Gordon, the Yankees had released Lazzeri following the 1937 season.

Walker had his own thoughts on the problems the 23-year-old Gordon would face, having himself been a "Yankee rookie sensation" a few years earlier. Using his personal experiences as a guide, he predicted that playing in that big ballpark in New York, combined with the attitude of the veteran Yankees players, would work against Gordon.

"It happened to me, so I know," Walker said. "I was a pretty fair fielder when I reported up at the Stadium, but that place, with all those people, gave me buck fever something fierce. I was dropping fly balls all over the place. And Myril Hoag told me the same thing happened to him. The older players on the Yanks make you feel inferior," Dixie added. "They are established and they don't count you as one of them until you prove yourself. They let you know you are inferior too."[7]

This was a change of heart for Walker, who had praised the veteran Yankees for their help while he was with them. He confessed resentment toward what he considered the neglectful way the club had treated his injuries. After all, the White Sox, not the Yankees, had rescued Dixie's career by arranging for Dr. Kreuscher to perform the surgery on his shoulder.

Opening Day in Chicago was the scene of the first game between the Tigers and the White Sox, the two participants in the big offseason trade. Dixie Walker was in center field, batting second. Behind him were Charlie Gehringer and Hank Greenberg, coming off a season in which he hit 40 home runs and drove in 183 runs.

Dixie was hitless in his first game against his former team, while Gee Walker had a single for the White Sox in Chicago's 4–3 win. The game ended in an abrupt and disappointing way for the Tigers. With two out in the ninth, Dixie was on first, having reached on a force play. Gehringer, the American League's defending batting champion, was at the plate. Walker broke for second on what appeared to be a steal attempt, but may have been a missed sign by Gehringer. Sox catcher Tony Rensa threw Walker out to end the game. "Gehringer at bat, failed to move on what appeared to be a hit and run signal," wrote the *Chicago Daily Tribune*.[8]

Walker had two hits the next day, but the Tigers dropped another one-run decision. After winning the final game in Chicago, the Tigers came home and were swept in three games by the Indians. Cleveland's Mel Harder, Johnny Allen, and Bob Feller, three of the American League's best, held Walker to one hit in each game.

On April 29, Boots Poffenberger pitched the Tigers to a 5–1 win over the White Sox in a game that marked the return of Gee Walker to Detroit. Poffenberger was 10–5 as a rookie in 1937, and appeared to have a bright future. He was, however, a drinker and a carouser, and someone given to taking unauthorized "vacations" from the team. One such absence on June 7 led a frustrated Cochrane to fine Poffenberger $100, a significant sum in 1938.

Only 7,500 fans were in Briggs Stadium on the afternoon Gee Walker returned to Detroit. Gee drew a walk leading off the second but was picked off on a throw from catcher Birdie Tebbetts to first baseman Hank Greenberg. It was a reminder to the home fans of why Cochrane had not been reluctant to trade Gee. They received another reminder later in the game. Gee smacked a double to left field but was thrown out trying to stretch it into a triple.

6. The Most Unpopular Man in Detroit

Detroit's left fielder, Dixie Walker, made the throw. Dixie also had a single and a two-run homer in the game.

Although Dixie had clearly outplayed Gee, he changed no minds among Tigers fans that day; nor would he ever win them over. Dixie hit .308 in 1938, but that did not appease the fans, wrote author and longtime Tigers follower Art Hill. "Dixie Walker was hated in Detroit — not because he didn't have a good year, but simply because he wasn't Gee."[9]

Meanwhile, Vern Kennedy, the Tigers' other major acquisition in the trade, was justifying Cochrane's faith in him. Kennedy got off to a sensational start, winning his first nine decisions. By late May, the local newspapers were praising the trade, or at least that aspect of the trade. Kennedy, as Povich and others suspected, was not that special a pitcher. He soon faded and finished the year at 12–9.

By contrast, Jimmy Dykes was being criticized in Chicago for the trade, a change from the original assessments where he was thought to have swindled Cochrane, his old pal and longtime teammate. Six weeks into the season, the trade was not working out well for the White Sox. Dykes had called Kennedy vastly overrated, saying that even though he was a 20-game winner in 1936, he had a high earned run average.[10] Now, not only was Kennedy 9–0 for Detroit, but Marv Owen, the third baseman Chicago had acquired in the trade, was hitting in the .240s. Worst of all, Dixie Walker was outhitting Gee Walker, the man Dykes had wanted most. Labeled as "brittle" by Dykes, Dixie had played steadily and was hitting better than .300.

While Walker did have a history of being injury-prone, it seems odd that Dykes would label someone as brittle after he had played in all 154 games for him. Dixie would play in 127 games in 1938, mostly as a left fielder but also in center, and his fielding was superb at both positions. His .308 batting average was up slightly from the previous year's .302, but batting primarily in the number two spot, his overall production was down. Among his offensive highlights in 1938 were the four runs he scored in a May 16 game against Washington and two more four-hit games: one against Boston on May 24 and the other against Cleveland on September 9, the day before his 28th birthday.

Missed signals related to the hit-and-run play had plagued the Detroit club on several occasions this season, beginning with the Walker-Gehringer snafu on Opening Day. After three such foul-ups in a July 13–14 series at Boston, Cochrane promised to crack down, saying he would fine the next player who missed the hit-and-run sign.

The first victim turned out to be Walker, in a July 16 game at Yankee Stadium. Batting against Red Ruffing, he missed the sign for the hit-and-run and failed to swing as Chet Morgan was cut down at second. Cochrane fined

Dixie $25. "They'll learn to protect the runner even if they have to pay to learn," announced Cochrane.[11] The fine allowed Jimmy Dykes to take a verbal dig at his former outfielder. "If he [Cochrane] fines Walker every time he misses a sign, Walker will end the season owing money to the club."[12]

Oddly enough, on the day of the fine, Walker had played a sensational game in the field. Twice he took potential home runs away from Frank Crosetti, and he robbed Joe DiMaggio of an extra-base hit with a running shoestring catch.

The Tigers' 1–5 start had them struggling all season in their attempt to finish in the first division. They were even a disappointment to heavyweight champion Joe Louis. Louis was in Pompton Lakes, New Jersey, in early June training for his upcoming title defense against Max Schmeling. Detroit's slow start made it easy for Louis, normally a big baseball fan, to abandon his interest temporarily and concentrate on the fight. "The Detroit Tigers haven't been so hot and that's Joe's team," explained Jersey Jones, a public relations man for fight promoter Mike Jacobs. "If they're down," Jones told *New York Times* columnist John Kieran, "Joe loses some of his interest in baseball."[13]

In August, with his team floundering in the second division, owner Briggs fired Cochrane and replaced him with Del Baker, Cochrane's chief assistant. Under Baker, the Tigers rallied to win 37 of their last 56 games. They finished fourth, 14 games above .500, but 16 games behind the Yankees, who won their third consecutive pennant. (The White Sox finished in sixth place, 32 games behind New York.) Hank Greenberg's challenge to Babe Ruth's record of 60 home runs in a season generated the most excitement in Detroit in 1938. Greenberg fell two short, finishing with 58. Catcher Rudy York added 33 home runs, but Kennedy faded after his 9–0 start, and Tommy Bridges and Schoolboy Rowe were no longer the pitchers they had been in the pennant-winning years of 1934 and 1935. Bridges led the team in wins with just 13, and an injured Rowe pitched just 21 innings and had no wins.

Greenberg and Gehringer were back to lead the offense in 1939, along with third baseman Pinky Higgins, acquired in an offseason trade with the Red Sox. Bridges and Rowe appeared ready to regain their earlier form, and the Tigers were encouraged by the spring training work of two rookie right-handers: Fred Hutchinson and Paul "Dizzy" Trout. Yet no one considered Detroit a serious threat to prevent the Yankees from becoming the first American League team to win four consecutive pennants.

"As the Tigers shape up this season, there is nothing to disturb the belief that they are a pretty hopeless club as far as pennant prospects are concerned," wrote Shirley Povich in the *Washington Post*. Povich was particularly unimpressed with the Tigers' potential starting outfield. "At this writing, they haven't a single .300 hitter," he said, ignoring Walker's .308 batting average

6. The Most Unpopular Man in Detroit   53

in 1938. "A Detroit outfield comprised of Pete Fox, Roy Cullenbine, and Dixie Walker is by no means potent," he concluded.[14]

Del Baker, beginning his first full season as manager, also recognized that the outfield could be the team's weak spot. "My outfield is one problem," he told sportswriter Richards Vidmer. "I have seven outfielders and for the life of me I haven't an idea who the three regulars will be. Dixie Walker, Pete Fox, [Chet] Laabs, Cullenbine, [Barney] McCosky [sic]—they all look about the same. I'll just have to wait and see which one develops best."[15]

An *Associated Press* story, however, thought that Walker was clearly the best of the lot. After a visit to Lakeland, the *AP* reporter wrote, "The outfield's stick work on the whole doesn't figure on the Detroit team, although Dixie Walker was a .300 hitter last year and looks good this year."[16]

Walker had indeed looked good all spring, with some of his best games coming against the Dodgers and their new manager, Leo Durocher. With the Tigers in Lakeland and the Brooklyn club not too far away in Clearwater, the teams met often in the spring of 1939. That allowed Dixie to get his first look at 20-year-old Pete Reiser, whose spectacular hitting was the sensation of the Grapefruit League. In his first ten at-bats of the spring, Reiser had hit safely eight times and walked twice.

Baker settled on an outfield of Walker in left, McCoskey in center, and Fox in right to open the season. Dixie homered in the season's second game, one of the three hits and three runs batted in he had that day. Ten days later, on April 30 against Cleveland, he had four singles and scored five runs, and had another four-hit game on May 14 at St. Louis. A day earlier, the Tigers and Browns had engineered a huge ten-player trade.[17] Among the six players going to St. Louis were pitcher Vern Kennedy, the key man for the Tigers in the trade that brought Dixie Walker to Detroit, and outfielder Chet Laabs. The major new additions for the Tigers were pitcher Bobo Newsom and outfielder Beau Bell.

Newsom, a 20-game winner for the Browns in 1938, would win a combined 20 with the Browns and Tigers this season, and 21 to lead the Tigers to the pennant in 1940. Bell had batted .268 for the Browns in 1938, but the Tigers were hoping he could replicate the two prior seasons—.344 in 1936 and .340 in 1937.

On May 24, the Tigers made their first visit of the year to Yankee Stadium. With just under one-fifth of the season gone, the Tigers were in last place, 13 games behind the Yankees. Detroit had played the Yanks twice at home earlier in the month, losing both games. The May 2 game, a 22–2 drubbing by the New Yorkers, was the day Lou Gehrig had chosen to end his consecutive game streak at 2,130.

The Yankees came into the May 24 game riding a 12-game winning streak, while the Tigers had lost five of their last six. But in one of their most satisfying victories of the season, Detroit, behind Paul Trout, won the game, 6–1, and ended New York's win streak. It was the first major-league win for the 25-year-old rookie. Not only had Trout never seen Yankee Stadium before, he had never even been to New York. Walker helped the offense with two hits, including a home run, and two runs batted in.

Dixie's batting average was up to .309 when he tore cartilage in his left knee sliding into second base in a June 8 game against Philadelphia. The latest injury put him on the sidelines, and with the exception of pinch-hitting appearances on July 21 and 22, ended his stay in Detroit. The latest injury, which had again put Walker's career in jeopardy, turned out to be the biggest break of his baseball life. It got him out of Detroit, where he had been the team's most unpopular player with the fans, and landed him in Brooklyn, where he very soon became the most popular player the Dodgers had yet had.

Brooklyn's team president, Larry MacPhail, had been searching American League rosters, looking to add a left-handed hitting outfielder to his club. He had settled on Cleveland's Earl Averill, and all he needed was for the veteran Averill to pass through the AL's waiver process. However, when Walker injured his knee, the Tigers canceled their waivers on Averill. On June 14, the Tigers traded pitcher Harry Eisenstat and cash to Cleveland for Averill. The trade was a sure sign that Walker would soon be leaving a team whose fans had never accepted him.

"Detroit fans were wrong about Dixie Walker, obviously," wrote author Art Hill four decades later. "But they felt that the Walker playing left field for the Tigers was an impostor. And they wouldn't have it."[18]

Thwarted in his attempt to

"If they don't like me here anymore, maybe somebody else will want me. There's a place for everybody" (National Baseball Hall of Fame Library, Cooperstown, New York).

get Averill, MacPhail purchased another left-handed hitting outfielder, Mel Almada, from the Browns on June 15. When the 36-year-old Almada, playing his final big league season, failed to hit, MacPhail went into the American League for yet another left-handed hitting outfielder. On July 24, he claimed Walker from the Tigers, and Dixie headed to Brooklyn.

Twenty years later, Dixie, then the manager of the Toronto Maple Leafs of the International League, reflected on his early career moves from team to team. "I can't help what they do," he told reporter John P. Carmichael. "But if they don't like me here anymore, maybe somebody else will want me. There's a place for everybody."[19] How right he was.

PART II — THE DODGERS

7

"All I knew about Brooklyn was that it was some strange outer world"

The upcoming 1940 Census of Population would determine that nearly 2.7 million people lived in Brooklyn. It was the most populous borough of New York City, and had it still been an independent city, its population would have ranked behind only New York and Chicago. Fewer than half the states in the nation had as many people as Brooklyn, which as a city and a borough had played a significant role in the country's history and had produced many of its most honored citizens. The Brooklyn of 1939 was a wonderful place, made up of a myriad of ethnic neighborhoods, many of which had the feel of a small town. Moreover, the people of Brooklyn loved their baseball team — in good times and bad — and in 1939, there was a prevailing sense that good times were coming.

Dixie Walker had played for the Bronx-based Yankees and had married a girl from Manhattan, but he had no familiarity with Brooklyn. "All I knew about Brooklyn was that it was some strange outer world," Walker later recalled. "When they told me I'd been traded to Brooklyn, I didn't know what on God's great earth to expect."[1]

The Brooklyn team Walker was joining had finished in the second division the previous six years, and had not made a serious run at the pennant since 1924. Additionally, the club was in financial trouble. Seeking to stabilize the situation in Brooklyn, National League president Ford Frick suggested the Dodgers hire 48-year-old Larry MacPhail to run the club. The tempestuous MacPhail had entered baseball in 1930 when general manager Branch Rickey of the St. Louis Cardinal's chose him to run the Cardinal's top farm club, the Columbus (Ohio) Redbirds of the American Association.

After turning around the floundering Redbirds, MacPhail moved on to another financially strapped team, the Cincinnati Reds. In just a few years, he built a team that won consecutive National League pennants in 1939 and 1940 and the World Series in '40.

MacPhail arrived in Brooklyn in 1938 and immediately began to revitalize the franchise. He spent hundreds of thousands of dollars provided by the Brooklyn Trust Company, owner of 51 percent of the team, to refurbish Ebbets Field. The Dodgers' 25-year-old ballpark had deteriorated over the years and become an unappealing place for fans to visit. MacPhail had brought night baseball to the major leagues when he installed lights at Cincinnati's Crosley Field in 1935. Now, he used some of the money he had received from the bank to install lights at Ebbets Field. In doing so, he broke a "gentlemen's agreement" that had existed among the pre–MacPhail Dodgers, Jacob Ruppert's Yankees, and Horace Stoneham's Giants that had kept night baseball out of New York City. The Dodgers played their first night game on June 15, 1938, against Cincinnati. The fans loved it, although the game is mostly remembered as the one in which Reds pitcher Johnny Vander Meer tossed his second consecutive no-hitter.

In December 1938, MacPhail upset the Yankees and Giants again when he ended another long-standing agreement with those clubs to ban broadcasts of baseball games in the New York area. He announced that he had sold the radio rights to General Mills, maker of the breakfast cereal Wheaties, to broadcast Dodgers games over station WOR beginning in 1939. His choice to be the voice of the Dodgers was Walter Lanier "Red" Barber, who had been with him in Cincinnati. The soft-spoken Barber enthralled Brooklyn fans. His game accounts, delivered in southern drawl and peppered with "down-home" witticisms, were both entertaining and informative and an integral part of the Brooklyn landscape for the next 15 years.

Still, it was on the field where MacPhail set about to turn the Dodgers from perennial also-rans into a pennant contender. His first big move came during spring training of '38, when he acquired slugging first baseman Dolph Camilli from the Philadelphia Phillies. The Dodgers had not had a legitimate long ball hitter since trading Babe Herman back in 1932, and manager Burleigh Grimes had been asking the club to get him a slugger. In Dolph Camilli, he finally got his man.

Camilli, 31, had hit close to 100 home runs over the past four seasons with the Phillies. His 27 home runs in 1937 were only ten fewer than the entire Brooklyn team had hit. To get Camilli, the Dodgers gave up Eddie Morgan, a player with just 66 at-bats in his big league career, which was now over. The Dodgers also sent Philadelphia $45,000, a sum thought to be the most they had ever paid for a player. (Other estimates ranged as high as $75,000.)

Brooklyn finished seventh in 1938, though attendance increased by almost

200,000. Camilli was everything the Dodgers had hoped he would be. He hit 24 home runs, batted in 100 runs, and drew a league-leading 119 walks. But the addition of one power hitter clearly was not enough; the team needed an overhaul and MacPhail set about to provide it — beginning at the top. He fired Grimes as manager and in a surprise move replaced him with Leo Durocher, his 32-year-old shortstop. Durocher had just finished his first season in Brooklyn, after having played for the Yankees, the Reds, and most notably the Cardinals. MacPhail had engineered the trade of Durocher from Cincinnati to St. Louis, where Leo became the shortstop and captain on Branch Rickey's Gashouse Gang clubs.

One of the first moves Larry MacPhail made when he came to Brooklyn was to hire fiery, volatile Leo Durocher as his manager (courtesy the Los Angeles Dodgers).

Durocher was a volatile, mercurial man, just like MacPhail, and the two would clash repeatedly in the years to come. He was coarse, brash, a gambler on and off the field, and a scourge of umpires; but he knew baseball and could motivate men. Those who played with and against him mostly loved or hated him.

Dick Bartell, a big-league shortstop for 17 seasons, quoted one anonymous Dodger infielder as saying, "When Leo was shortstop and captain of the team in 1938, we hated him. We were ready to sock him for the first offside remark. Now we're ready to break our backs for him."[2]

Sportswriter Gene Karst used this eclectic string of (mostly) adjectives to describe Durocher: "supreme egotist, brash loudmouth, natural ham, narcissistic, monologist, hunch player, strategist, has-been, strutting clothes horse, manicured, pedicured, perfumed, ruthless, sarcastic, bitter, amiable, flirtatious, charming, dapper."[3]

The most significant change in the Dodgers roster on the day they claimed Dixie Walker had more to do with the loss of Van Lingle Mungo than it did with the addition of Walker. Or so it seemed at the time. Mungo had broken his ankle the previous day while sliding into second as a pinch-runner for Art Parks. His injury figured to keep him out for six weeks, and while the colorful Mungo was no longer the pitcher he had been in the first half of the decade, the team would miss him.

Meanwhile, the rest of the clubs in the National League barely acknowledged Brooklyn's purchase of Walker — with one exception. Ever since MacPhail had come to Brooklyn, the Dodgers fortunes, both on the field and at the gate, had been rising. Conversely, those of the archrival Giants had been falling in both areas. Giants general manager Eddie Brannick, who never missed an opportunity to criticize the Dodgers and their president, had this reaction to the addition of Walker. "What a ridiculous crowd they are," he said of the Brooklyn club. "MacPhail has just bought another outfielder, a tramp named Dixie Walker."[4]

The fans in Brooklyn were not sure what they were getting. They remembered Walker as a promising rookie with the Yankees in the early 1930s, but one who, because of injuries, never had lived up to that promise. James J. Murphy, of the *Brooklyn Daily Eagle,* speculated as to what might have been had Dixie stayed healthy. "If it hadn't been for an epidemic of injuries and disappointments, Fred (Dixie) Walker, newest of the Dodgers, would be one of the greatest players in major league baseball today," he wrote.[5] Murphy predicted that because of his hustle the "likeable Southerner" would become a big favorite in Brooklyn.

It was a wonderfully accurate prediction, similar to the one sportswriter Dan Daniel had made back in 1936. Aware that Walker was not likely to stick with the Yankees, Daniel had suggested manager Casey Stengel grab him for the Dodgers and aim him at Ebbets Field's right-field wall.

But Walker's great success in Brooklyn lay in the future. For the present, it was clear that despite being a steady .300 hitter after moving on to the White Sox and the Tigers, he currently was not in first-rate playing condition. "He could barely walk; he looked like a cripple," one Dodgers executive remembered thinking after Walker reported. "We needed a ballplayer who could give us a lift and we got one who looked as if he needed a blood transfusion."[6] Durocher had Dixie's leg examined and said his new outfielder would be ready for full-time duty in a day or two.

Walker reported to the Dodgers in Chicago, where they were beginning a 15-game visit to the league's Western cities. The club was in fifth place, one game below .500 and 12 games behind the league-leading Cincinnati Reds. He entered the clubhouse limping slightly, but told his new teammates, in what the *Brooklyn Daily Eagle* described as a soft Southern drawl, "Ah've never been on a second division club in my life, fellas. Don't spoil my record now."[7]

On July 25, Dixie Walker made his debut in a Brooklyn uniform; he wore number 11, the number he would wear throughout his stay in Brooklyn. He batted for pitcher Red Evans in the first game of a doubleheader and took a called third strike from Cubs veteran Charlie Root. A half-inning earlier, in the bottom of the sixth, Walker had his introduction to Leo Durocher and Brooklyn baseball.

The Cubs were trailing the Dodgers, 5–0, when Rip Russell capped a six-run Chicago rally with a home run to left field, a drive the Dodgers did not believe had cleared the fence. Durocher and several of his players argued for ten minutes in an attempt to get the umpires to reverse their decision. When they refused, Durocher announced he was playing the game under protest. The protest proved unnecessary, as the Dodgers rallied with three in the ninth to win the game, 8–6. Rookie Hugh Casey gave the Dodgers a sweep with a 3–1 win in the second game.

Casey, 25, had pitched briefly for the Cubs in 1935 before returning to the minors. MacPhail purchased him after the 1938 season from the Memphis Chicks of the Southern Association for $7,500. Durocher eventually moved him to the bullpen, where he gained his greatest fame, but in 1939 used him mostly as a starter and Casey won 15 games.

In the series finale, on July 27, Dixie got one of Brooklyn's five hits in his first start as a Dodger. He batted third and played center field in a 3–1 loss to Chicago's ace right-hander Bill Lee. Five days later, at Pittsburgh, he had a single and two triples as the Dodgers topped the Pirates and climbed back to the .500 mark. At 45–45, they remained in fifth place, 14½ games behind the Reds. The three hits gave Walker eight hits in 18 at-bats and a batting average of .444.

Walker's two triples were particularly noteworthy because it was obvious he had not regained his full speed. "The crippled Mr. Walker, whose bad left knee prevents him from getting around with his usual speed and agility, wasn't handicapped in swinging a bat," wrote Roscoe McGowen in the *New York Times*.[8]

Dixie's deftness with the bat was evident on both three-baggers. When he batted in the first inning, the Pirates outfield, being unfamiliar with the former American Leaguer, shifted over to the right, as they normally would with a left-handed hitter. But Dixie crossed them up with a drive into the gap in left-center. Then in the fifth, with the Pirates playing him as an opposite field hitter, he drove the ball into deep right-center. A healthy Walker would have had an inside-the-park home run on the fifth-inning drive. Under orders not to slide, he was thrown out at the plate on a relay from center fielder Fern Bell, to shortstop Arky Vaughan, to catcher Ray Berres. It marked the second time since joining the Dodgers that orders not to slide had gotten him thrown out at the plate.

On August 5 in Cincinnati, Durocher was ejected for the third time this season for arguing with the umpires; Bill Stewart tossed him after Leo objected to his out call on Dolph Camilli for leaving third base too soon. The Dodgers won the game, 10–4, led by third baseman Harry "Cookie" Lavagetto's four hits, and Walker's two hits and three runs batted in. Brooklyn concluded its

Western swing the next day with a split against the Reds. In addition to a nifty catch, Walker had four hits in the doubleheader and was batting .390 as a Dodger.

For two weeks, the fans in Brooklyn had been listening to Red Barber's broadcasts and reading newspaper accounts of Dixie Walker's heroics out West. They got their first chance to see him in the flesh on August 7, when he played his first home game against the Boston Bees.[9] A crowd of nearly 28,000 turned out that night, and Dixie, "the new hero of Brooklyn fandom," did not disappoint.[10] He was the hero of a ten-inning 7–6 win, with a run-scoring double in the third inning and a two-out, game-winning single in the tenth inning. Boston's manager was Casey Stengel, Dixie's old antagonist from his days with the Toledo Mud Hens, which made the victory even sweeter.

"Walker was added to the roster while the club was on its recent western trip," wrote Pat McDonough the following day. "Flatbush fans read of his hard and timely hitting in the team's successful tour of the West. But now they've seen him in his best form." Commenting on the third-inning double that had driven home two runs, McDonough wrote, "When Walker returned to center field in the fourth frame the bleacher fans stood up and cheered him lustily. They've adopted Dixie."[11]

Dixie Walker in 1939, shortly after joining the Dodgers (National Baseball Hall of Fame Library, Cooperstown, New York).

Adopted is a good word, here. Brooklyn fans fell in love with the slow-talking, affable young Southerner. By the early 1940s, his stellar play and his involvement in the civic affairs of the borough made Dixie Walker the most popular player yet to wear a Brooklyn uniform. "The fans were behind all of us," Kirby Higbe remembered, "but I guess the player they loved best in those days was Dixie Walker. When Dixie went into a slump, the whole town rallied around him."[12] And that love was returned. By the end of the 1939 season, Dixie's sense that Brooklyn was "some strange outer world" had been replaced by a sense of belonging. "When I came to the Dodgers in midseason of 1939, it was almost like coming home," he later revealed. "Maybe I didn't realize it right away, but Brooklyn is sure home to me now."[13]

Dixie's popularity in Brooklyn earned him the title of "The People's Choice." It was a well-deserved honor and one that truly reflected the esteem in which the borough's citizens held him. "He was loved by the people of Brooklyn," wrote author Rudy Marzano, "for he willingly signed autographs, kissed babies, went to his fan club meetings, and posed for pictures with the local politicians."[14]

Surprisingly, Walker had been referred to as "The People's Choice" even before coming to Brooklyn, and of all places in Detroit, a town where he had not been very popular. It was in an article in the May 1939 edition of *Esquire* magazine that discussed the difficulties Walker had while playing for Mickey Cochrane in 1938. The title of the article was, "The People's Choice: The Cheering of Fans Has Helped Problem-Child Walker More Than Any Amount of Hell from Cochrane."[15]

Durocher continued to tinker with his lineup, looking for a winning combination. By August, he had replaced his entire opening-day outfield of Fred Sington, Goody Rosen, and Gene Moore. "At last we have a workable outfield," Leo said after an August 15 win against the Giants. "Art Parks, Dixie Walker, and Ernie Koy give us the best-looking trio of outfielders we've had in the lineup at one time this season."[16]

The Dodgers won 24 of their last 37 games in 1939; still, it took victories in their final four games to allow them to slip by the Cubs into third place. Walker's plea to his teammates on joining them in late July to keep his string of never finishing in the second division was realized.[17] Along with the third-place finish, which was a big jump from seventh the previous year, there was a comparable rise in paying customers. Attendance, which had been 482,500 in 1937, had risen to 663,100 in 1938, MacPhail's first year. In 1939, it soared to 955,500.

Luke Hamlin led Brooklyn's pitchers with 20 wins, while Camilli, with 26 home runs and 104 runs batted in, and Lavagetto, who batted .300 and had 87 RBI, led the offense. Walker batted .280 but drove home 38 runs in the 61 games he played.

After his half-year in Brooklyn, Walker made this comparison between the two leagues. "One thing I've noticed is that ball players in the National League hustle more," he said. "You can notice that from the dugout. Over in the other league they just sort of lay back and wait for that big inning. Over here they try to beat out the hit or make the play that will mean a one-run difference." When asked to compare the pitching in the two leagues, he said, "The pitching is the same. By that I mean they've got good pitchers in both leagues. But the difference is that the umpires over here [the NL] give the pitchers the breaks on stuff that cuts the corners. Over in the other league those pitches are balls. It's the umpires that make the difference."[18]

During the 1939 season, Dixie took part in an event little noticed at the time, but one that would revolutionize baseball in the years to come. On August 26, the Dodgers hosted the Reds in a doubleheader in the first major-league baseball games ever televised. The games were broadcast by NBC over an experimental station W2XBS with Red Barber as the lone announcer. Between games, Barber conducted on-field interviews with Walker, Camilli, pitcher Whit Wyatt, Reds pitcher Bucky Walters, and the two managers, Durocher and Bill McKechnie.

The broadcast went to the Dodgers club offices and pressroom, the Broadway Theater, and the television building at the New York World's Fair. *The Sporting News* reported that the response was "instantaneous and amazing." Nevertheless, not everyone was convinced that televised baseball games had a future. "It's difficult to see how this sort of thing can catch the public fancy," wrote an anonymous critic in the *New York Times*.[19]

After the season, Walker went home to Birmingham, where he secured a position in the security investment business. His performance over the last half-season, along with the adoration shown him by the fans, made him confident he had at last found a place where he was wanted. In December, Dixie learned for the first time that his admirers did not include Dodgers president Larry MacPhail.

At the major leagues winter meetings in Cincinnati, MacPhail included Dixie in a package he put together to bring Boston Bees outfielder Max West to Brooklyn. In addition to Walker, MacPhail offered the Bees outfielder Gene Moore, outfielder Tuck Stainback, and catcher Babe Phelps. In return, Brooklyn would receive the 23-year-old West, a .285 batter with 19 home runs in 1939, and Al Lopez, a former Dodger and one of the better catchers in the league.[20]

To no one's surprise, Bees general manager Bob Quinn turned down the offer and Walker remained a Dodger. MacPhail remained constantly on the lookout for players to improve his club. On February 5, 1940, the Dodgers signed free agent Roy Cullenbine, a switch-hitting outfielder. The 26-year-old Cullenbine had spent the last two seasons with Detroit's Toledo club in the American Association, appearing briefly in each season with the Tigers. He was one of the 91 players baseball commissioner Kenesaw Landis had freed from the Tigers' farm system in January 1940, claiming the club was "hiding" these players.

MacPhail spent $25,000 for Cullenbine, the same amount he paid the Red Sox a week later in a waiver claim for yet another outfielder, ten-year veteran Joe Vosmik. The right-handed hitting Vosmik had slumped from a .324 average in 1938 to .276 in 1939; nevertheless, he came highly recommended. "There wasn't a better left fielder in our league last year than Vosmik," Yankees manager Joe McCarthy told MacPhail.[21] Cullenbine and Vosmik joined Walker, Mel Almada (purchased from the St. Louis Browns), and Ernie Koy (purchased from the Yankees) to give Brooklyn five outfielders that MacPhail had purchased from the American League.

Four Dodgers remained unsigned when training camp opened at Clearwater, Florida, on February 25. Foremost among the holdouts, and the most adamant, was Dolph Camilli, the team's biggest offensive weapon. Camilli had played more games than any other National Leaguer in 1939, finishing third in home runs and fourth in runs batted in, runs scored, slugging percentage, on-base percentage, total bases, and triples.

MacPhail said he had spoken to Camilli at the end of the 1939 season and had offered him a $1,000 raise to $15,000. "I told him he could go back home without signing, but that $15,000 was the top figure and he'd never get any more," MacPhail said. "Now he can stay in California (Camilli had a cattle ranch in Laytonville, California) as far as I'm concerned, until he signs the contract. Each time he returned it I fired it back via air mail without a word." MacPhail said he had done so "about eight times."[22]

The other unsigned players were Walker, second baseman Pete Coscarart, and third baseman Cookie Lavagetto. MacPhail said he was near to an agreement with Coscarart and Lavagetto, but not with Walker, which was especially upsetting to him. "He must be considered a part-time outfielder because of his knee," MacPhail said of Walker, "and how he could turn down what we offered him is beyond me."[23]

Always a hard bargainer, Dixie now had further incentive to seek a higher salary; he had a new mouth to feed. On January 27, Estelle had given birth to Mary Ann Walker, the couple's second child.

Written correspondence between MacPhail and Walker continued into the next week. On March 7, MacPhail said, "I've got a lot of letters from Walker, and he's made a different proposal in each one. But I've made him a fair offer, with a chance to make as much as last season, depending upon the number of games he plays."[24]

Camilli and Walker, the last two holdouts, arrived in Clearwater on March 10, on a day the Dodgers were in Lakeland to play the Tigers. Two days later, both men signed their 1940 contracts. MacPhail had withdrawn his original offer of $15,000 to Camilli, claiming it was based on an on-time arrival by the slugger. With ownership holding almost complete control,

Camilli had no choice. He finally signed when MacPhail agreed to the $15,000 salary that Camilli had so long resisted. Walker settled for $7,500, plus a thousand-dollar bonus if he played in 100 games and another thousand if he played in 120.

8

The People's Choice

Pee Wee Reese made his first appearance in a Brooklyn uniform in the spring of 1940. The Dodgers had acquired the 20-year-old shortstop in a deal with the Louisville Colonels the previous July. In addition to paying the American Association club $35,000 for Reese, the Dodgers also sent four players to the Colonels. Reese, a native Kentuckian, was one of several players the Boston Red Sox had kept when they purchased the Louisville franchise in 1939.

As part of the agreement, Reese was allowed to finish the season with Louisville, where he batted .279 and stole a remarkable 35 bases in 36 attempts. In addition, he was an outstanding defensive player, with excellent range, sure hands, and a strong throwing arm. Louisville manager Donie Bush called him "the best-fielding shortstop he's seen in his 31 years in the game."[1]

Reese was not pleased when he first heard he might be going to Brooklyn. "That's the last place in the world I'd want to go," he said. "All you ever read about is guys getting hit in the head with fly balls.... I don't want to go there."[2] After learning the trade was official, Reese seemed resigned to his fate. "Brooklyn's in the major leagues, isn't it?" he said.[3] As was the case with Dixie Walker, his fellow Southerner and soon-to-be lifelong friend, Reese later acknowledged that his acquisition by the Dodgers was the biggest break of his professional career.

Once thought to be the heir apparent to Red Sox shortstop Joe Cronin, Reese was now the heir apparent to Dodgers shortstop Leo Durocher. Replacing himself with Reese sometime during the season was the only infield change Durocher contemplated in the spring of 1940. First baseman Camilli, second baseman Coscarart, and third baseman Lavagetto were all back to play those positions. MacPhail's failure to get Al Lopez from Boston meant Babe Phelps would again be behind the plate.

Durocher faced a much different situation in the outfield. Gene Moore and Ernie Koy had played the most games there in 1939, but neither was assured a starting job in 1940. Nor was Walker, the Dodgers' center fielder in the second half of the season. At the opening of camp, Durocher said Joe Vosmik would be his left fielder. The other two positions, he said, would be chosen from a group that included Moore, Koy, Walker, Roy Cullenbine, Mel Almada, rookie Charlie Gilbert, and Jimmy Ripple, obtained the previous August in a trade with the Giants.

By late March, the two most likely to join Vosmik, based on what they had done in the exhibition games, were Gilbert in center and Ripple in right. After reporting late, Walker had been in just three games and was batting .200. On March 31, in a game against the Giants in Columbus, Georgia, he replaced Gilbert late in the game and in his only at-bat hit a game-winning home run. By the start of the season, Dixie had retained his position on the roster, but not as a starter.

The starting outfield against right-hander Bill Posedel in the April 16 opener at Boston was Vosmik in left, Gilbert, making his big league debut, in center, and Cullenbine in right. Whit Wyatt shut out the Bees, 5–0, in wintry weather that held the crowd to 3,517. Wyatt, another former American Leaguer picked up by MacPhail, had been a non-descript pitcher for Detroit, Chicago, and Cleveland from 1929 to 1937. Wyatt's best season was 1932, when he went 9–13 for the Tigers, but with a 5.03 earned run average. Cleveland sent him to Milwaukee of the American Association in 1938, where he won 23 games. MacPhail purchased him that summer, and he had an 8–3 record for the Dodgers in 1939.

Because of bad weather, the Dodgers did not play again until the 19th, when Hugh Casey shut out the Giants, 12–0, in Brooklyn's home opener. Four days later, the winning streak reached three when Tex Carleton beat Boston, 8–3, at Ebbets Field, with Gilbert contributing two home runs. Reese, making his big league debut, started at shortstop after Durocher benched himself with a sore arm.

Unwilling to break up what had so far been a winning combination, Durocher stayed with the outfield of Vosmik, Gilbert, and Cullenbine. Walker did not make his first appearance of the season until the team's fourth game, at home against Boston. Durocher sent him up as a pinch-hitter for pitcher Newt Kimball in the eighth inning with the game tied at 6–6. Dixie delivered a single that scored two runs, giving Brooklyn an 8–6 victory.

Walker sat the next two days, while Brooklyn won two games at Philadelphia behind Casey and Freddie Fitzsimmons, who pitched a 6–0 shutout. The Dodgers had now won their first six games, something no Brooklyn team had ever accomplished. Dixie made his first start on April 27 at the Polo Grounds, when Durocher used him in place of Gilbert, out with a bone bruise.

8. The People's Choice

Playing center field and batting leadoff, Dixie went 2-for-4 as Luke Hamlin downed New York, 4–1. The next day he again led off and played center field, going 3-for-4 as Brooklyn won its eighth consecutive game. Camilli's two-run homer off Harry Gumbert in the ninth inning gave Whit Wyatt the 5–3 victory.

The Dodgers had played only eight games, but already "pennant fever" gripped the Borough of Brooklyn. An 8–0 record can do that, but wiser heads knew the wins had come against Boston, Philadelphia, and New York, all weak teams. A truer test for the Dodgers would come out West, in Cincinnati and St. Louis. The next day the team embarked from LaGuardia Field on two 21-passenger United Airlines planes chartered by MacPhail. First stop — Cincinnati.

At Crosley Field on April 30, Carleton, another of MacPhail's rescue projects, threw a 3–0 no-hitter against the Reds, extending Brooklyn's winning streak to nine. It was the second major-league no-hitter of the season — Cleveland's Bob Feller had thrown one against the White Sox on Opening Day — after none had been thrown in 1939. Carleton was a 33-year-old right-hander MacPhail had purchased in January from Milwaukee of the American Association. He had a 94–70 record for the Cubs and Cardinals from 1932 to 1938 and was 11–9 for Milwaukee in 1939.

Cincinnati's last out was a low, twisting line drive to center by Ival Goodman that Walker caught knee-high. "I couldn't tell where the thing was going," Dixie said in the jubilant Dodgers clubhouse. "It curved one way, then seemed to curve the other way and I wasn't sure whether to come in or back up. Anyway I got it."[4]

After the catch, Carleton started toward Dixie to thank him. He made it a few steps onto the grass between the mound and second base before his teammates mobbed him. But during the postgame celebration in the clubhouse, Carleton yelled to Walker, "Come here, you lug, I want to kiss you."[5] For Walker, the right fielder for the White Sox when Bill Dietrich no-hit the St. Louis Browns on June 1, 1937, it was the second major-league no-hitter in which he had participated.

Brooklyn's nine consecutive wins to open a season tied the post–1893 major-league record set by the 1918 New York Giants.[6] At this point, they led the defending champion Reds by three games. Bucky Walters, a 27-game winner and the league's Most Valuable Player in 1939, ended the streak the next day. Walters won his third game of the young season as the Reds, led by Ernie Lombardi's grand slam off Casey, thrashed the Dodgers, 9–2.

After a pair of rainouts in Pittsburgh, the Dodgers moved on to St. Louis, where they won the first two of a three-game series. Durocher, despite saying that Reese would be the shortstop "indefinitely," reinserted himself against the Cardinals. He also put Gilbert back in center field and Walker back on the bench.

St. Louis won the final game, 18–2, lambasting Casey and Max Macon for 20 hits. The Cardinals established new major-league records for extra-base hits (13) and total bases (49), and their seven home runs in the game tied the National League record. The Dodgers were now 11–2, and Casey had both losses.

Walker and Reese came off the bench to deliver key hits in a win at Chicago, after which the Dodgers flew home — all except Babe Phelps, who refused to fly — and landed at Floyd Bennett Field in Brooklyn at 12:40 on the morning of May 10. Ten thousand fans were there to greet them; some had been waiting since 9 P.M. the night before. A large "Welcome Home Brooklyn Dodgers" sign greeted the players as they departed the two planes. Brooklyn borough president John Cashmore, there with a contingent of local dignitaries, talked about throwing out the first ball at the World Series.

Later that day both Walker and Reese were back in the starting lineup. Walker replaced the injured Vosmik in left field; he would remain in the Dodgers outfield, primarily as their center fielder, for the rest of the season. Brooklyn later sent Gilbert to Montreal of the International League, and in May 1941, traded him to the Cubs in the deal that brought Billy Herman to the Dodgers.

Dixie ran off a ten-game hitting streak from May 5 to May 17 that raised his batting average to .413. Everything seemed to be going well, but the next week, he and Estelle suffered the worst tragedy a parent can suffer — the loss of a child. On May 23, four-month-old Mary Ann Walker died of pneumonia at South Nassau Communities Hospital in Rockville Center, Long Island. Walker missed the next three games as he and Estelle accompanied the body of their baby daughter home for burial in Birmingham.

Walker told of receiving a letter from a woman in Brooklyn. She was not a baseball fan, but she had a young daughter who was crazy about the Dodgers and was very sick. "She was writing me," Dixie said, "because she knew I'd lost a youngster recently. She said her girl was in a coma. Her best times were in the afternoon, when they turned the radio to the broadcast of the Brooklyn game; she would almost come out of it. In some obscure way the doctors could not understand, she seemed vaguely conscious of what was going on. If the Dodgers won, her condition improved toward night. If they lost, she was worse."[7]

By late May, MacPhail, still dissatisfied with his outfield, made three moves in the space of four days. He purchased Jimmy Wasdell from Washington, sold Gene Moore to the Boston Bees, and traded Roy Cullenbine to the Browns for Joe Gallagher. During that period of late May and early June,

8. The People's Choice

Durocher was using a different lineup almost every day, with Walker remaining one of the few constants.

When the Dodgers began their second swing through the West, in Chicago on June 1, they were two games behind Cincinnati. They lost that day to the Cubs, but suffered a more serious loss when a pitch by Chicago's Jake Mooty hit Pee Wee Reese in the head. Reese spent the next 18 days in a Chicago hospital. After taking the next three from the Cubs, the Dodgers won two at St. Louis. On June 4, in the first night game played at Sportsman's Park, they scored five first-inning runs and beat the disappointing Cardinals, 10–1. Veteran Vito Tamulis raised his record to 3–0, while Mort Cooper dropped to 0–3. After an offday, the Dodgers won again for their fifth straight. Walker had a triple, a home run and three runs scored to back Luke Hamlin.

In the process of winning two of four games in Cincinnati, the Dodgers handed Bucky Walters his first defeat of the season, after nine straight wins. The next day Durocher's club suffered its most embarrassing loss of the season, a 23–2 shellacking by the Reds. The teams then split a June 9 doubleheader in which Walker had five hits, including three doubles. Two wins in Pittsburgh gave the Dodgers a 9–3 record for the trip, and they returned home in a virtual first-place tie with the Reds.

On June 12, MacPhail set the hearts of Brooklyn fans racing with the announcement that he had acquired 28-year-old outfielder Joe Medwick from the Cardinals. Medwick was among the most productive hitters in the game. He had led the National League three times each in runs batted in, total bases, and doubles, and had never hit below .300. He was the league's MVP in 1937, the year he won the Triple Crown with a .374 batting average, 31 home runs, and 154 runs batted in. No National Leaguer has won the Triple Crown since.

MacPhail sent the Cardinals Ernie Koy, Montreal infielder-outfielder Bert Haas, little-used pitchers Carl Doyle and Sam Nahem, and cash, for Medwick and pitcher Curt Davis. At age 36, Davis was a sore-armed right-hander with an 0–4 record, but he had won 22 games in 1939, his best season ever. While the personnel in the deal made it clearly one-sided in favor of Brooklyn, the $125,000 going from MacPhail's Dodgers to Branch Rickey's Cardinals helped serve as an equalizer.

The trade for Medwick further convinced Dodgers fans that this year's pennant would be theirs. Crowds at the Dodgers ticket office in downtown Brooklyn grew so large and unruly, police had to be called out, and streets blocked off to control them. Tickets for two upcoming series, against Cincinnati and St. Louis, were particularly in demand.

Medwick and Davis were with the Cardinals in Buffalo when they heard news of the trade. The Dodgers had assumed their two new additions would be coming by train, but instead they took a plane to New York, arriving several hours before they were expected. "I'm the happiest guy in the world," said Medwick. "Nothing ever happened to me that tickled me so much."[8]

"We've got a chance to win now," said Durocher, Medwick's former roommate and probably his closest friend. "I know Medwick," said Leo. "I ought to. I roomed with him for six years. For us he'll hustle three times as much and be twice as good a hitter as he was in St. Louis."[9]

Less than a week later, Medwick faced his old teammates in a three-game series at Ebbets Field. St. Louis won the first game, their fifth straight under new manager Billy Southworth.[10] Facing Bob Bowman the next day, June 18, Walker led off with a single, followed by a Lavagetto double and a Vosmik single. Medwick was the next batter, and Bowman's first pitch hit Joe flush on the left side of his head. Durocher and several players went after Bowman, accusing him of deliberately trying to injure Medwick. There was bad blood between Bowman and Durocher and between Bowman and Hugh Casey dating back to a game in 1939 when each pitcher accused the other of throwing beanballs. Casey would do anything to win, remembered his teammate and friend, Whit Wyatt. "He didn't care if he hit you right between the eyes; it wouldn't faze him a bit."[11]

Southworth immediately removed his pitcher from the game, and several policemen escorted him off the field. MacPhail called for Bowman to be banned from baseball and indicted for murder. Both calls went unheeded, and Medwick was back in the lineup within a week; he would still be a productive player, but never the aggressive hitter he had been before the beaning.

Pitcher Max Lanier, Bowman's roommate, had a different take on the Medwick incident. He said Bowman had no reason to throw at Medwick and was very upset over what happened. Lanier believed it was the result of a wrong sign flashed to Medwick by third base coach Charlie Dressen, a notorious sign stealer. "Bowman was wrapping his curve ball, and then he wrapped a fastball the same way, and it faked Dressen," thought Lanier. "Medwick stepped right into it, thinking it was going to be the curve. I think that's what happened. And Joe got hit hard."[12] Intentional or not, Bowman's beaning of Medwick set off an animosity between the Dodgers and the Cardinals that would endure for the rest of the decade.

Meanwhile, Walker, in just his first full season with the Dodgers, kept delivering on the field and participating in the civic functions that earned him the title of "The People's Choice." Both sides of the Walker appeal to Brooklynites were on display over a three-day period in late June. On the night of the 27th he attended a dinner at the St. George Hotel in Brooklyn in honor of 61-year-old Brooklyn native Jack Norworth, the famed songwriter

8. The People's Choice

who wrote "Shine on Harvest Moon" and "Take Me Out to the Ball Game." Two days later, Walker's grand slam off Boston's Bill Posedel helped Curt Davis to his first win as a Dodger and kept Brooklyn just a half-game behind Cincinnati.

Since Reese's return from his hospital stay, on June 21, Durocher had installed him in the leadoff position and moved Walker into the third spot. Reese had shown in his first game back that he was unaffected by the beaning. He had three hits, including a double and a triple.

The Dodgers had climbed back into the lead, and after a doubleheader sweep of the Giants on July 4, they were a game ahead of the Reds. The next day, Brooklyn's 6–2 win at Boston in 20 innings set a major-league record for elapsed time, going five hours and 19 minutes. Walkers single to start the 20th inning began the four-run rally that gave the Dodgers their tenth win in their last 11 games. Tot Pressnell's 2–0, three-hitter the next day raised the current winning streak to seven, which ended a day later with two tough defeats by Boston, 1–0 and 2–1. The double loss and Cincinnati's win moved the Reds ahead of Brooklyn into first place.

Dixie's popularity in Brooklyn earned him the title "The People's Choice" (National Baseball Hall of Fame Library, Cooperstown, New York).

Although Walker had hit over .400 early in the season and stayed among the league's top five hitters — he was second after play on July 4 — he was left off the National League All-Star team. Six Dodgers were chosen for the team (Coscarart, Durocher, Lavagetto, Medwick, Phelps, and Wyatt), but the omission of Walker greatly angered the Brooklyn fans. He was, they reasoned, widely outhitting Terry Moore, one of the center fielders chosen, while the other, Hank Leiber, had not played in a while because of illness. Moreover, the Dodgers faithful were quick to point out, Walker was outhitting every National League outfielder chosen. "Dixie Walker's hitting has been almost astounding," wrote the *New York Times*'s John Kieran in reference to the snub.[13]

Sportsman's Park in St. Louis hosted the All-Star Game on July 9, with the National League winning, 4–0. Red Sox outfielder Lou Finney, the American League's leading hitter at .359, did not appear until the sixth inning, nor did Detroit's Hank Greenberg, the major leagues RBI leader with 71. Of the ten leading hitters going into this game, five from each league, only White Sox shortstop Luke Appling was in the starting lineup. Five did not even make the team: the Browns' Rip Radcliff, the White Sox's Taft Wright, and the Tigers' Barney McCoskey, the numbers two, four, and five hitters in the AL; and Walker and the Cubs' Jimmy Gleeson, the numbers two and four hitters in the NL.[14]

Walker's omission from the All-Star roster prompted his ever-growing legion of fans to honor him in their own way. The "Friends of Dixie Walker" committees from Brooklyn and Long Island chose Sunday, July 28, to stage a Dixie Walker Day and a Dixie Walker Night. They presented him with a set of golf clubs between games of that afternoon's doubleheader against St. Louis. Adding to the pleasure of the crowd was a sweep of the Cardinals: a 3–0 shutout by 32-year-old Wyatt and a 7–4 win by Fitzsimmons, two days past his 39th birthday. Dixie celebrated his afternoon with four hits, including a triple, three runs batted in, a perfectly executed squeeze bunt, and a terrific catch in deep left-center to rob Don Gutteridge of an extra-base hit.

The evening celebration, staged at Brooklyn's Hotel Bossort, afforded Walker the opportunity to show off his singing voice. When Dixie walked up to the microphone in the Grand Ballroom, he got an ovation equal to the ones he had received at Ebbets Field that afternoon. Performing with The Eddie Lane Band, he led off with a pleasant tenor rendition of "I'll Never Smile Again," as Leo Durocher and his teammates looked on proudly. He followed with "You Thrill Me," with lyrics he had written with Eddie Lane and Tom Connelly. Walker concluded with "Melancholy Baby," after which Reese and Tamulis sang.[15]

Leo Durocher's Dodgers were a rambunctious, combative team that played the game with a no-holds-barred approach. No longer the lovable losers of Wilbert Robinson and Casey Stengel, they had begun to earn the enmity of players and fans around the league once reserved for John McGraw and his New York Giants. "Both at home and away the Dodgers were embattled," wrote the late baseball historian Jack Kavanagh. "At Ebbets Field they were viewed as playing aggressive baseball. On the road they were vilified as dirty players with head-hunting pitchers and a manager without a conscience."[16]

The Brooklyn club would have three significant rivalries during the 1940s, rivalries that went beyond the everyday struggles teams normally waged against one another. One, the rivalry with the Giants, was based on proximity. It had been a constant since Brooklyn joined the league in 1890, and flourished regardless of either team's position in the standings. The 1898 incorporation of the then independent city of Brooklyn into Greater New York likely inflamed the sense of inferiority many Brooklynites harbored when comparing their city-turned-borough, large parts of which were still farmland, to Manhattan, the "sophisticated" colossus across the East River. Similarly, those living in Manhattan had little or no interest in what went on in Brooklyn.[17] The passions were much greater on the Brooklyn side, as evidenced by the many Dodgers fans that would show up when their heroes played at the Polo Grounds. By contrast, far fewer Giants fans would be visible when the teams played at Ebbets Field.

The other two rivalries the Dodgers of the 1940s had were with Chicago and St. Louis. Both began in earnest in 1940 and went through 1946 with the Cubs and 1947 with the Cardinals, and both featured a series of beanballs, spikings, and on-field brawls. Bob Bowman's beaning of Joe Medwick may have been the opening blow in the "war" with the Cardinals—shortstop Durocher and Cardinals baserunner Mickey Owen got into a confrontation at second base the next day.

With the Cubs, it may have begun with Jake Mooty's beaning of Reese—though that likely was unintentional—and started in full on July 19, at Wrigley Field. After Casey plunked Cubs pitcher Claude Passeau, Passeau responded by throwing his bat at the Brooklyn pitcher, which led to players from both dugouts rushing onto the field. Brooklyn's Joe Gallagher grabbed Passeau, and while Cubs manager Gabby Hartnett attempted to free his pitcher, third baseman Stan Hack took a punch at Gallagher. It took the umpires, ushers, and members of the Chicago police force to end the brawl.

Hugh Casey. "He didn't care if he hit you right between the eyes; it wouldn't faze him a bit" (courtesy the Los Angeles Dodgers).

Faced with declining attendance, and seeing the success of night baseball elsewhere, Giants owner Horace Stoneham accepted the inevitable and installed lights at the stately old Polo Grounds. The Giants played their first home night game on May 24, 1940, and their first night game at home against Brooklyn on August 7. The latter date was the night the Giants chose to honor their longtime star, Mel Ott, which helped draw a crowd of just under 54,000, the largest crowd ever for a National League night game.

However, once the ceremonies were over and Ott had received his gifts, the Dodgers spoiled things for the home fans with an 8–4 victory over Carl Hubbell. Walker delighted the usual large contingent of Brooklyn fans at the Polo Grounds with four runs batted in and four hits, including a triple and a home run. Two days earlier, the teams had met at Ebbets Field for their first-ever night game, and Walker had four hits in that one—a 6–0 shutout by Wyatt. Walker was rapidly cementing his reputation as a "Giants killer," the surest way for a player to win the hearts of fans in Brooklyn.

Dixie further solidified that reputation by going 5-for-5 in the nightcap of a September 1 Brooklyn sweep, their ninth consecutive win over Bill Terry's club. The five hits raised Walker's average to .3295, putting him in a virtual tie for the league lead with Boston's Bama Rowell, whose average was .3298.

"He has been one of the most consistent hitters imaginable, with many good days and a few great ones," wrote Tommy Holmes, who covered the Dodgers for *The Sporting News*. "Settling down at Ebbets Field for almost all his remaining games, Dixie is in a perfect spot to drive his way to the title."[18]

On the morning of September 7, Walker was leading the league at .326. Two days later, he had five singles against Hal Schumacher in 7–4 loss to the Giants, but slumped after that and fell out of contention for the batting title.

Pittsburgh's Debs Garms was far ahead in the race, but there was some doubt he would have enough at-bats to qualify for the title. Later in the month, National League president Ford Frick proclaimed there was no written rule that Garms would have to bat 400 times, as long as he played in 100 games.[19] At the conclusion of the season, Garms was officially proclaimed the National League's batting champion for 1940. He had a .355 average and 358 at-bats in 103 games.

Brooklyn had stayed neck-and-neck with the defending champion Reds for the first half of the season. But in the two weeks after the All-Star break, the Dodgers played at a .500 level, while the Reds won 12 of 14. By the time Cincinnati concluded a sweep of a three-game series at Ebbets Field on July 24, they were eight games ahead of the second-place Dodgers.

In late July, the Dodgers recalled Pete Reiser and pitcher Ed Head from the Elmira Pioneers of the Eastern League. Reiser gave Dodgers fans a glimpse of what was to come, batting .293 in 58 games, mostly as a replacement for Lavagetto at third base. Lavagetto had been stricken with appendicitis in late August, two weeks after Reese broke a bone in his foot while sliding into second base in Philadelphia. Both Lavagetto and Reese were lost for the rest of the season. The Dodgers never mounted a serious challenge in the second half and finished 12 games behind Cincinnati. A 14–7 home loss to St. Louis on September 18, a game in which Cardinals first baseman Johnny Mize drove in six runs, eliminated them.

Over the final week of the season, even more honors and gifts were bestowed on Brooklyn's favorite son. On September 24, Walker celebrated his 30th birthday on the stage of the Flatbush Theater, at Flatbush and Church Avenues. Three thousand fans were there to see Dixie cut the cake and sing "I'll Never Smile Again" and "Sierra Sue," as Estelle watched from the wings. Then it was Walker's turn to listen, as the crowd sang "Happy Birthday" to him. After Dixie received his birthday gifts, which included a watch and a camera, he spoke to the audience of his baseball travels and assorted injuries. "I appreciate all the nice things the Brooklyn rooters have said about me," he told them. "Some way, next year, if I'm with Brooklyn again, I'll repay this kindness."[20]

Walker was presented with another award — a gold cup — two days later, for being voted the "spark plug" of the Dodgers in a contest conducted by the Electric Autolite Company in conjunction with the *Brooklyn Daily Eagle*. State Tax Commissioner David F. Soden made the presentation between games of a doubleheader with Boston.

"In all the years I've been in baseball this is the first thing of its kind I have ever received," Dixie said. "One of the minor disappointments of my career is the fact that I wasn't picked for the All-Star team this summer and that was simply because I wanted the souvenir that goes to an All-Star player. And next year here in Brooklyn I hope to rate one of those World Series rings."[21]

Dixie again had every reason to expect he would be back in Brooklyn in 1941. He had led the club in batting (.308), and been especially effective against the Giants, compiling a sensational .435 average against the New Yorkers. One of the toughest men in the league to strike out, he fanned only 21 times in 605 plate appearances. Walker finished sixth in the voting for the National League's Most Valuable Player award, won by Cincinnati's Frank McCormick. Fred Fitzsimmons, the only Dodger ahead of Dixie, finished fifth, after a season in which he won 16 of his 18 decisions with a 2.81 ERA.

Prior to the voting, Jimmy Powers, the sports editor of the *New York Daily News,* wrote that his colleagues in the Baseball Writers' Association of America should make Walker their choice as MVP. "Dixie should be a shoo-in," said Powers. "Walker hits to all fields. Can bunt, run, and is a reliable man in the clutch," he said in calling Dixie "the key player of the Brooklyns."[22]

Walker credited much of his success to a line he had read some years back in Bruce Barton's *The Man Nobody Knows*. The line is "attributed to Christ," Walker said, "and reads, 'No man ever added a day to his life by worrying.' I took that in. I used to be the most worrying player in the game. If I went hitless one day I worried myself into a slump. I just quit doing that. I play for today and let tomorrow take care of itself."[23]

Walker's spring holdout had ended when he agreed to a salary of $7,500, plus two bonus clauses: a thousand dollars if he played in 100 games and another thousand if he played in 120. By playing in 143 games, he collected both.

Barnstorming and postseason exhibitions were standard fare for many players during this time. So before returning to Birmingham, Walker took advantage of the opportunity to pick up some extra money. In October, he played several games with Giants shortstop Billy Jurges's All-Stars in exhibition games against the Brooklyn Bushwicks.

9

An Almost Perfect Team

Brooklyn fans were hoping the natural progression from a third-place finish in 1939 to a second-place finish in 1940 would lead to a first-place finish in 1941. Larry MacPhail believed he could make that happen; but he knew that to compete with the two-time defending champion Cincinnati Reds and the young and talented St. Louis Cardinals, he had to make some improvements to his club.

MacPhail's first priority was another quality starting pitcher. He filled that need on November 11, 1940, by completing one of the most favorably one-sided deals in Brooklyn history. He traded pitcher Vito Tamulis (8–5 in 1940), pitcher Bill Crouch and catcher Mickey Livingston, both of whom had been in the minor leagues in 1940, and $100,000 to the cash-strapped Philadelphia Phillies for pitcher Kirby Higbe. MacPhail predicted that leaving the last-place Phillies would do wonders for Higbe, a brash, hard-throwing, 25-year-old right-hander. He said he fully expected his new pitcher would be a 20-game winner in 1941.

Priority number two was obtaining a catcher to replace the aging, non-flying Babe Phelps. MacPhail seemed to have targeted Mickey Owen of the Cardinals, though some skeptics thought that was a ruse, and his first choice was the Giants' Harry Danning, generally recognized as the league's top catcher. A deal that would send Danning to Brooklyn had first been reported in the October 17, 1940, edition of *The Sporting News*. According to that report, Giants manager Bill Terry had offered Danning and Mel Ott to Brooklyn for Phelps, Dixie Walker, and pitcher Luke Hamlin. The thought that Ott, the longtime Giants hero, might go to Brooklyn shocked New Yorkers in much the same way that Leo Durocher's going from the Dodgers to the Giants would in 1948.[1]

Yet the skeptics were wrong; MacPhail had been more interested in getting Owen than Danning. On December 4, he got his man in a trade for catcher Gus Mancuso, minor-league pitcher John Pintar, and $65,000. Owen had been the Cardinals first-string catcher the past three seasons and was not yet 25 years old—five years younger than Danning.

The additions of Higbe and Owen made the Dodgers a legitimate contender for the pennant, and to some, the favorite. "The Dodgers are generally rated as having an excellent chance to win the National League pennant," wrote *Time* magazine in a preseason issue. "Rival fans, accustomed to Brooklyn's bragging, usually laugh it off. But this year there is no laughing off the Dodgers. Even Bill Terry, manager of the Brooklyn-hating New York Giants, admitted last week that the Dodgers are the team to beat in the National League. Bolstered by nearly $200,000 worth of new material this year's team is rated 50% better than the team that finished second to the pennant-winning Cincinnati Reds last year."[2]

Cincinnati first baseman Frank McCormick was unconvinced, seemingly unimpressed by MacPhail's acquisitions. The National League's Most Valuable Player told reporter John Lardner he expected the Reds to repeat in 1941. When told that MacPhail had predicted a Brooklyn pennant in '41, McCormick was dubious. "How does he figure that? I can't see it," he said. He agreed that Kirby Higbe would help, but did not consider Mickey Owen much of an upgrade. As for Brooklyn's best pitcher and hitter in 1940, McCormick was dismissive. "Fred Fitzsimmons, he won't win any sixteen games next year like he did this year. Dixie Walker, their best hitter, is no kind of hitter at all for my dough. No power. Lots of his hits are leg hits and bloopers and swinging bunts. For me, a hitter should bat in those runs."[3]

Walker signed his contract on January 29, making 1941 one of the few seasons he did not hold out. While MacPhail continued to underestimate Dixie's value, tossing his name into almost every trade discussion, he could not avoid what Walker had accomplished in 1940. Because Dixie signed so quickly, it is likely that MacPhail had given his team's leading hitter a nice raise.

Nevertheless, Walker seemed to be the forgotten man at Brooklyn's spring training camp in Havana, Cuba. Pete Reiser had played shortstop, third base, and right field in the second half of 1940, but Durocher was now trying him in center field, the position Dixie had played in '40. Also in camp was outfielder Paul Waner, signed by MacPhail in January, following Waner's release by Pittsburgh, where he had spent 15 glorious seasons. Waner hit extremely well all spring while playing right field, and with Joe Medwick back to play left field, it appeared that Walker would be out of a job.

Dixie had reached the majors with the Yankees ten years earlier, which led some to think of him as an "old man." However, the *Brooklyn Daily Eagle* wrote that at age 30, Walker was at the peak of his career and was currently "the most valuable athlete discarded by one major league to another."[4]

9. An Almost Perfect Team

Because the people of Brooklyn fully agreed with that assessment, they were infuriated when Durocher announced that Waner, not Walker, would be his opening-day right fielder. "You can't win a pennant with a man in the outfield who can't catch a fly ball below his belt buckle, and that is why I am not using Walker," Durocher was quoted as saying.[5]

Dixie vigorously protested his demotion to both Durocher and MacPhail, while back home, 5,000 outraged Brooklyn fans signed a petition supporting him. The fans threatened a boycott if Durocher did not play Walker, which put Leo right in the middle of the firestorm. MacPhail had threatened to fire Durocher if he yielded to the fans and did play Walker.

When Reiser wrenched a muscle in his side four days before the opener, it solved Durocher's dilemma. Walker began the season in center, with Waner in right. But Waner got off to an atrocious start (.171 in 11 games), and on May 11 the Dodgers released him. Reiser had returned to play center, with Walker moving back to right, where, with occasional exceptions, he would remain a fixture for the next seven years.

Pennant expectations were high when the Dodgers opened the 1941 season at home against the Giants. "In Brooklyn, Dodger fans, believing reports from spring training, are all set for their first pennant in 21 years," wrote *Time* magazine. "So, when Boss Larry MacPhail's fabulous collection of stars was beaten by the New York Giants, 6-to-4, in the opening game, impatient Brooklynites hastily dubbed them Larry MacPhailures."[6] Two more defeats by the Giants followed, so unlike the previous season, when they started with nine straight wins, the Dodgers had started 1941 with three straight losses.

Reiser was injured ten games into the season, on April 23, when a pitch from Philadelphia's Ike Pearson struck him on the side of the head. The ball hit Reiser partially in the face and partially on the new helmet liners all the Dodgers were wearing.[7] (Reacting to the beanball wars of 1940, MacPhail had ordered all his players to wear liners in their caps.) Reiser crumpled to the ground and was removed on a stretcher. He never lost consciousness, and X-rays taken at Brooklyn's Caledonian Hospital showed no fractures. Expected to be out for two weeks, Pete returned to the lineup on April 30, a game in which the Dodgers won their ninth in a row, matching the winning streak they had to open the 1940 season. Trailing Johnny Vander Meer, 3–0, going into the home eighth, they tied the game on home runs by Walker and Medwick, and won it in the ninth on Reese's double off Joe Beggs.

Since losing their first three games of the season, the Dodgers had won 13 of 14, to finish April with a 13–4 record. Pitching had been mainly responsible, and Walker was quick to praise the Dodgers staff. "I can hear the Reds whisperin' to each other," he said in the clubhouse, "and they're sayin', Wyatt yesterday, Hamlin today, Higbe tomorrow, and either Davis or Casey the next day.... Dawgone if I've ever been on a club that had four or five starters working that way in the spring."⁸ St. Louis had also started quickly, finishing April with a 10–3 record. The scene had been set. The Dodgers and Cardinals would spend the whole spring, summer, and fall trading places at the top of the standings before Brooklyn finally clinched the pennant three days before the season ended.

Billy Southworth's St. Louis squad had an infield that included slugging first baseman Johnny Mize and second-year shortstop Marty Marion, and a strong, speedy outfield of Johnny Hopp, Terry Moore, and Enos Slaughter. Mort Cooper, Max Lanier, Ernie White, and veteran Lon Warneke anchored the pitching staff.

Brooklyn had Dolph Camilli at first, Billy Herman at second, Pee Wee Reese at short, Cookie Lavagetto at third, and an outfield of Joe Medwick, Pete Reiser, and Dixie Walker. Mickey Owen caught a staff led by Wyatt, Higbe, Casey, and Curt Davis.

The difference-maker in Brooklyn's winning the pennant may have come in the early morning hours of May 6. Chicago Cubs owner Philip K. Wrigley had made some changes in his club's leadership. He brought in former Phillies manager Jimmie Wilson to replace Gabby Hartnett and hired Jim Gallagher, a former sportswriter, as his new general manager. The Cubs were in town playing the Giants, and Gallagher was having drinks and talking trades with MacPhail in Gallagher's room at Manhattan's Commodore Hotel. At 3:28 A.M., the meeting concluded with Brooklyn sending second baseman Johnny Hudson and outfielder Charlie Gilbert, both of whom were at Montreal, and $65,000 to Chicago for second baseman Billy Herman.⁹ With the aid of money provided by the Brooklyn Trust Company, MacPhail had engineered another extremely one-sided trade. The 31-year-old Herman had been an All-Star for the past seven seasons and had a .309 lifetime batting average.

Herman was batting just .194

Kirby Higbe teamed with Wyatt as each won 22 games in 1941 to lead Brooklyn to its first pennant in 21 years (courtesy the Los Angeles Dodgers).

this season, but the move from last-place Chicago to the pennant-contending Dodgers revitalized him immediately. After being notified of the trade, Herman said goodbye to his Cubs teammates at the Commodore and crossed the East River to Brooklyn. He arrived at Ebbets Field at 12:30 in the afternoon and made his Dodgers debut by going 4-for-4 in a 7–3 win over the Pirates. The victory was Wyatt's fifth in a row since losing to the Giants on Opening Day. Herman's and Wyatt's performances notwithstanding, Walker was the day's star; Dixie hit two home runs off Rip Sewell, including a grand slam in the seventh inning that broke a 3–3 tie.

On May 8, Pete Reiser had his first serious encounter with an outfield wall. He injured his left hip crashing into a metal gate at Ebbets Field while catching a drive hit by Enos Slaughter of the Cardinals. Reiser missed the next five games; Walker moved back to center field and Jimmy Wasdell took Dixie's place in right.

On May 10, Wyatt, Herman, and Walker again combined in beating the Phillies, 4–1. Herman went 5-for-5, including two triples, as he raised his average as a Dodger to .667. Wyatt won his sixth straight, all complete games, and Walker equaled his 1940 home run total with his sixth of the season. Dixie had a financial incentive to hit home runs, one that came not from MacPhail but from a diaper company. Back on April 21, Estelle gave birth to a daughter the couple named Mary Ann Estelle Walker.

"Dixie gets a free week's diaper service for his month-old daughter, Mary Ann Estelle, for every homer he hits. This is the gift of an Elmhurst diaper service," wrote *New York Daily News* columnist Jimmy Powers.[10]

The Dodgers were at 20–6 and the Cardinals at 16–6, when Brooklyn opened its first Western swing in Cincinnati. Hugh Casey raised his record to 5–0 and Wyatt's seventh consecutive win dropped the two-time defending champions 10½ games behind the Dodgers. But after a rainout, a loss at Pittsburgh was followed by three losses in Chicago and two more in St. Louis, dropping Brooklyn a game and a half behind the Cardinals. The streaky Dodgers followed this six-game losing streak with a nine-game winning streak. The highlight of the streak was a Memorial Day sweep of the Giants before a huge crowd of 59,487 at the Polo Grounds. Wyatt pitched a five-hit shutout in the opener, and a five-run ninth-inning rally took the nightcap. June was just beginning, and the Dodgers had already compiled winning streaks of seven, eight, and nine games.

Reiser's first-inning, two-run homer off Mort Cooper on June 3 helped Wyatt defeat St. Louis, 6–0, Wyatt's ninth win of the season and fourth shutout. The Dodgers and the Cardinals were now both 32–13 and tied for first place. By June 13, the start of a four-game series in St. Louis, the Dodgers had fallen two games behind the Cardinals. They could take the lead with a sweep, or gain a tie by winning three of the four games, but the best they could do was a split. The two Brooklyn losses were shutouts, the first blankings they had suffered this season: 1–0 to Max Lanier (beating Wyatt) and 3–0 to Ernie White.

As major league baseball approached the June 15 trading deadline, Bill Terry heard the Dodgers were interested in one of his players, a right-handed hitting veteran outfielder named Frank Demaree. Terry said he was willing to trade Demaree to Brooklyn for Pete Coscarart or Walker, preferably Walker. "If I could land Walker," Terry said, "I would find a spot in the outfield for him right away. He's always been tough for us to get out, and this park is certainly Walker's spot. I'd like to have a victory for every time he was instrumental, indirectly or otherwise, in beating us."[11] The Dodgers declined, and on July 21, the Giants sold Demaree to the Braves on waivers.

Terry, the last man to hit .400 in the National League (.401 in 1930), obviously appreciated Dixie Walker's talents, even if Walker's boss, Larry MacPhail, did not. Later in the season, Durocher began platooning Walker, suggesting he could not hit lefthanders. Dodgers fans knew that was not true and began to wonder why their hero was not in the lineup every day. After a pinch-hit double against Cliff Melton and a ninth-inning triple against Carl Hubbell (both left-handers) led to two wins over the Giants, it had become apparent even to Durocher that Walker certainly could hit lefties. "The guy ruins us. We just can't seem to get him out no how," Terry said.[12] What more could Dodgers fans want to hear?

"Every time I looked up it seems to me Walker is around and getting in my hair," complained Terry in late August. "How MacPhail has shunned that fellow is beyond me. To me Dixie is as good as any outfielder in the league and without him the Dodgers would not be in first place."[13]

Following their grueling series in St. Louis, the Dodgers won two of three in Chicago and three of four in Cincinnati, including a dramatic doubleheader sweep on June 22. Playing on a blistering hot afternoon before a record-breaking Crosley Field crowd of 35,792, the Dodgers won, 2–1, in 16 innings, and 3–2.

The first game was a classic matchup between Wyatt and Paul Derringer. Neither man allowed a run until Wyatt homered on the first pitch of the 11th inning—his first of the season. After his home run, Wyatt, exhausted by the heat, became sick on the bench. Durocher called on Hugh Casey to seal the victory, but the Reds got doubles from Lonny Frey and Frank McCormick to even the score. The Dodgers finally pushed across the game-winner in the 16th inning when Walker's squeeze bunt scored Reiser. The Dodgers fell behind Johnny Vander Meer, 2–0, in game two, but rallied to win behind Higbe's route-going performance.

Following his normal three-day rest, Wyatt raised his record to 11–4, as Walker's four hits helped Brooklyn thump the Braves, 11–2. The win raised the Dodgers' record to 45–21 and brought them back into a tie with the idle Cardinals. On July 1, the Phillies scored their first win of the season against the Dodgers, a ten-inning triumph that dropped Brooklyn a game behind the Cardinals. A five-game winning streak coupled with the Cardinals five-game losing streak put the Dodgers 3½ games ahead after play on July 11.

Then it was St. Louis's turn to get hot; they won eight of nine, including four in extra innings. Matching the red-hot, back-and-forth-race for the pennant between these two excellent, evenly matched teams was the race for the batting championship between Reiser and Cardinals first baseman Johnny Mize. At the All-Star break, Reiser was at .360 and Mize at .348. Both men were in the National League's starting lineup at the All-Star game in Detroit. So too were the Cardinals' Terry Moore in left field and the Brooklyn battery of Whit Wyatt and Mickey Owen.[14] Wyatt pitched two scoreless innings in the game, eventually won by the American League on Ted Williams's dramatic ninth-inning home run off Chicago's Claude Passeau with two on and two out. Williams was on his way to batting .406 and Joe DiMaggio was in the midst of compiling his 56-game hitting streak, lending even more excitement to a season author Robert Creamer has called baseball's best ever.

The second half of the season continued to see the Dodgers and the Cardinals taking, retaking, or sharing first place. In all, Brooklyn was in first place 99 days of the season and St. Louis 82 days.

On August 17, the Dodgers swept a doubleheader at Boston, while the Cardinals were splitting a pair at Pittsburgh. As a result, the 72–40 Dodgers moved a half-game ahead of the 72–41 Cardinals. After Higbe won the opener, his 17th win of the season, Wyatt took a perfect game into the ninth inning of the nightcap. With the Braves' biggest crowd in recent years looking on, Wyatt struck out pinch-hitter Paul Waner to open the ninth. He got two strikes on Phil Masi, but the Boston catcher spoiled the perfect game, and the no-hitter, lining a clean single to center. Wyatt struck out pinch-hitter Bama Rowell and retired pinch-hitter Frank Demaree — waived by the Giants to the Braves in July — to preserve the 3–0 victory. It was Wyatt's fifth shutout of the season and the Dodgers' 13th.

With the Dodgers having taken over first place a week earlier, pennant fever gripped Brooklyn when the Cardinals came to Ebbets Field for an August 24 doubleheader. "We could have sold 200,000 tickets for this doubleheader," MacPhail claimed. "Only the facilities to accommodate such a crowd are lacking."[15] Lines began forming early in the morning and countless thousands had to be turned away. National League president Ford Frick recognized the importance of the games by assigning four umpires rather than the customary three.

Time, the weekly newsmagazine, captured the excitement of the series in its September 8 edition.

> Ethel Barrymore came early, carrying a box lunch. Alfred Gwynne Vanderbilt flew down from Saratoga. By 10 P.M., three and a half hours before game time, 50,000 fans had been turned away. Extra policemen were called to form a cordon around the park. Mobs, stampeding out of nearby subways, were urged to go back home unless they had reserved seats.
>
> What was going on at Ebbets Field last week was of interest to not only Ethel Barrymore, young Vanderbilt and the 31,000 other Ethels and Als who were lucky enough to get in. Brooklyn's fabulous Dodgers were playing a four-game series with the daredevil young Cardinals of St. Louis — a head-on clash in one of the most exciting pennant races in major-league baseball.[16]

The Cardinals came into the series minus their two best outfielders: Terry Moore and Enos Slaughter. Max Lanier, who in 1952 was a teammate of the young Willie Mays, called Terry Moore "the greatest outfielder I ever played with."[17] Slaughter, the team leader in home runs and runs batted in, had broken his collarbone in an outfield crash with Moore on August 10. Ten days later, a pitch by Art Johnson of Boston hit Moore in the head, putting him out of action. Both men would play very little for the rest of the year.

Injuries had crippled the Cardinals all season. In addition to Slaughter and Moore, catcher Walker Cooper missed several weeks with a broken collarbone; brother Mort was out from mid–June to mid–August with bone spurs on his right elbow, and Mize's broken finger and sore shoulder contributed to his home run total dropping from 43 in 1940 to 16 in 1941.

After Moore and Slaughter went down, Branch Rickey chose not to make any moves to strengthen his outfield. It was not until mid–September that he brought up Stan Musial from the International League's Rochester Red Wings, the Cardinals' top farm club. "Why didn't he bring Musial up earlier? That's what all the players wanted to know," remembered Johnny Mize. "We might have gone ahead and won the pennant."[18]

St. Louis had no trouble with Higbe in the opener, winning 7–3 behind Ernie White. Veteran Larry French, picked up on waivers from the Cubs four days earlier, made his Dodgers debut in relief of Higbe. Game Two was a battle between the veteran Wyatt and Cardinals rookie left-hander Howie Pollet, recently recalled from the Houston Buffs of the Texas League. The 20-year-old Pollet had a record of 20–3 at Houston, after going 20–7 for the Buffs in 1940. "Pollet isn't yet 21," Cardinals owner Sam Breadon told sportswriter Grantland Rice, "but he's the smartest young pitcher I ever saw."[19]

Pollet had defeated Boston, 3–2, in his first start, and though he was pitching in a pennant race in front of a hostile crowd, he showed no sign of nervousness. The score was 2–2 going into the home ninth; St. Louis had scored single runs in the first and eighth innings, and Brooklyn had scored two in the fourth. Walker drove in both Dodgers runs with a double to left. Dixie had two hits in each game against left-handers White and Pollet, further proving to Durocher that he could indeed hit left-handed pitching.

Darkness was setting in when Reese led off the ninth by beating out a perfectly placed bunt down the third base line. Owen sacrificed him to second. Wyatt was the next batter and Durocher allowed him to bat for himself. He came through by slashing Pollet's first pitch back through the box and into center field. Reese came home with the winning run, and Wyatt had his 17th win of the season. The Dodgers had begun the day with a game and a half lead, and their second-game win allowed them to retain it. Had they lost, they would have dropped a half-game behind St. Louis.

A rainout the next day forced another doubleheader, witnessed by a crowd of more than 39,000 and with the same result — a split. This time Brooklyn won the opener behind Curt Davis, and St. Louis the nightcap behind Mort Cooper in a game that rain halted after eight innings. Augie Galan, acquired from the Cubs that morning, substituted in center field for Reiser, who was ill. During the 1941 season, the Dodgers got Billy Herman, Larry French, and Augie Galan from the Cubs in three separate deals. All would help the Dodgers, while the Cubs got next to nothing in return. After these four crucial games, Brooklyn (79–44) remained a game and a half ahead of St. Louis (77–45).

Following their September 7 doubleheader sweep of the Giants, the Dodgers had only two home games left. They embarked on a 17-game road trip that would take them to six different cities, before finishing the season with two games at Ebbets Field against Philadelphia. The Cardinals would play most of their games at home, but finish with six on the road.

On September 11, the two contenders met in St. Louis in the first of the season's final three games between them. The local press was calling it the "Little World Series," reclaiming the title they had used for the crucial series between the Browns and Yankees in 1922. Baby Doll Jacobson, the star center fielder of that Browns team, visited the Cardinals dressing room before the game to wish them luck.[20]

A day earlier, the Dodgers had seen their three-game lead reduced to one game, losing both ends of a doubleheader in Chicago while the Cardinals were sweeping Philadelphia at home. The crowds were as rabid at Sportsman's Park as they had been at Ebbets Field two weeks earlier. Tension on the field was as great as it was in the stands. The two best teams in the league each committed four errors in the opening game. Brooklyn took that one, 6–4, on Walker's two-run, game-winning single in the 11th inning. Fitzsimmons, with relief help from Casey, picked up the win, while Ernie White, who took the loss, went the distance.

Walker said he'd had trouble early in the game with White, a pitcher with four consecutive wins against the Dodgers this season. Dixie also admitted White's first pitch in the 11th had fooled him. "But I had the second one right," he said. "I was expecting a fast one and that's what he gave me."[21] Bob Considine of the *Washington Post* wrote, "The curious part of Walker's hit is that it probably didn't decrease by one whit the disdain in which Larry MacPhail holds him."[22]

Considine was right. MacPhail had never liked Walker nor had he ever understood his popularity with the fans. His most outrageous and slanderous attack on Dixie came during the summer when reporters asked him to rate the team's most valuable players. MacPhail named Camilli, Wyatt, Owen, Reiser, Herman, and Reese. "What about Walker?" asked one writer. "If the St. Louis club will promise to play Walker every day, I will give Walker to the Cardinals for nothing," answered MacPhail. "I will pay his transportation to St. Louis and I will pay his salary for the remainder of the season, and the Dodgers will win the pennant."[23]

In that first game in St. Louis, the teams exchanged barbs with one another and both lodged complaints with umpire Al Barlick. The aggressively belligerent Durocher was at the forefront of all the complaints and arguments, as he always was. Before the next day's game, Ford Frick met with Leo, Billy Southworth and the umpires and ordered them to tone down the badgering and arguing.

Extra-base hits by Gus Mancuso, Estel Crabtree, and Frank Crespi helped the Cardinals defeat Curt Davis in the middle game of the series. Brooklyn's lead was again down to one game, and if the Cardinals could win the final game, they would take over the lead on percentage points. The game attracted the biggest weekday crowd in St. Louis since 1927.

Because of the stakes involved and the quality of play, the September 13, 1941, battle between the Dodgers and Cardinals was among the most dramatic ever in the history of these longtime rivals. Whit Wyatt and Mort Cooper were the opposing pitchers, and through seven innings, neither team could score. Wyatt, pitching at a much more deliberate pace than usual, was in trouble in several innings. Meanwhile, Brooklyn managed five walks against Cooper, but the Cardinals right-hander allowed no hits.

Walker ended Cooper's potential no-hitter with an eighth-inning double to right-center. Next up was Herman, who also ripped a double to right-center, driving in the game's only run. "Walker, running as if a horde of red demons were on his heels, galloped across with the all-important run," wrote

Roscoe McGowen in the *New York Times*.²⁴ Walker said after the game that he stole catcher Mancuso's sign and signaled Herman that the next pitch would be a curve ball. "Billy's eyes bugged out so far that I was sure the Cardinals would catch on and switch," he said.²⁵

Wyatt set down the last six St. Louis batters to notch his 20th victory, including a strikeout of Slaughter to end the game. Slaughter, along with Moore, had taken batting practice, but his shoulder was still too sore to play the field. The pinch-hitting appearance was Slaughter's first game action since his injury a month earlier.

Speaking of the game years later, Wyatt said, "I think that was the best game I ever pitched in my life." When Slaughter came up to pinch-hit

Apparently, Larry MacPhail did not like Dixie's "pokey, easy-going manner" (National Baseball Hall of Fame Library, Cooperstown, New York).

in the ninth, Durocher came out and said, "You know this fellow can hurt you, don't you?" Wyatt did know, but he struck out the rusty Slaughter on three fastballs.²⁶

That winter, Walker discussed the three games in St. Louis with *Sporting News* editor J.G. Taylor Spink. "I have been in baseball for some years, but that series of three games with the Cardinals was the most thrilling of my life," Dixie told Spink. "We won that series because we rode the younger St. Louis players into the jitters," he said. Walker called Wyatt's win over Cooper "one of the greatest games in the history of the major leagues."²⁷

10

A Pennant and a World Series

On September 14, a day after Brooklyn's stirring 1–0 win at Sportsman's Park, Dixie Walker, one of the heroes of the series, suffered his only ejection of the season. In the fifth inning of a game at Cincinnati, plate umpire Jocko Conlan ruled that Walker had gone around on a third strike. Dixie argued the call, and when he threw his bat in the air on the way back to the dugout Conlan threw him out of the game. Throwing the bat cost Walker $50, a fine imposed on him the next day by National League president Ford Frick.

Billy Herman's home run and Joe Medwick's RBI single in the ninth inning gave the Dodgers a 7–5 win that day, but they lost a half-game in the standings when St. Louis swept a dramatic doubleheader from the Giants. Lon Warneke won the opener, 1–0, although the Cardinals had just three hits against Carl Hubbell. Trailing 5–3 in the second game, the Cardinals scored two runs in the ninth inning and won it in the tenth when Giants shortstop Dick Bartell threw wildly on Terry Moore's bases-loaded grounder. Rookie Howie Krist, the winner in relief, raised his season's record to 10–0.

The following day, the Dodgers played their longest game of the season. Having already won 15-inning and 16-inning games this season, they downed the Reds, 5–1, in 17 innings. The game was scoreless through the first 16 innings. Paul Derringer had gone all the way for Cincinnati, while Johnny Allen had pitched the first 15 innings for Brooklyn before giving way to Hugh Casey. Allen, yet another American League veteran added to the Brooklyn roster by Larry MacPhail, had been picked up on waivers from the St. Louis Browns at the end of July.

Pete Reiser finally broke the scoring drought when he led off the 17th inning with a 400-foot home run, his 13th of the season. Brooklyn added four more runs against Derringer and two relievers, more than enough to offset the run Casey allowed in the home half of the inning. While the Dodgers were batting, Reds manager Bill McKechnie protested to the umpires that it had grown too dark to see adequately. He demanded for safety's sake that they should call the game, which, of course, would nullify the Dodgers' runs. McKechnie's two pitching changes in the inning, both made at an agonizingly slow pace, were designed to get the game called, but the umpires denied his request. The Dodgers' lead was now two games and back in Brooklyn the club announced they were accepting mail-order applications for World Series tickets.

Reiser's big hit was just one of so many he contributed that season. It raises the question of how good a player Pete Reiser was, and how good might he have been had he not played so recklessly. We will never know, but many of those who saw him in 1941 said he had the potential to be among the greatest ever. "Maybe Pete Reiser was

Pete Reiser. Leo Durocher said he "might have been the best ballplayer I ever saw" (courtesy the Los Angeles Dodgers).

the purest ballplayer of all time," wrote sportswriter W. C. Heinz. "There is no exact way of measuring such a thing, but when a man of incomparable skills, with full knowledge of what he is doing, destroys those skills and puts his life on the line in the pursuit of his endeavor as no other man in his game ever has, perhaps he is the truest of them all."[1] Heinz quoted something Bob Cooke, sports editor of the *New York Herald Tribune,* wrote in 1958, at a time when Willie Mays and Mickey Mantle were at their peaks: "I didn't see the old-timers, but Pete Reiser was the best ballplayer I ever saw."[2]

Leo Durocher, who managed Reiser and Mays, ten years apart, thought Reiser was as good as Mays. "There will never be a ballplayer as good as Willie Mays," wrote Durocher years later. "But Reiser was every bit as good as Mays. He might have been better. Pete Reiser might have been the best ball player I ever saw. He had more power than Willie. He could throw as good as Willie. You think Willie Mays could run in his hey-day? You think Mickey Mantle could run? Name whoever you want to, and Pete Reiser was faster. And knew how to run the bases. Willie Mays had everything. Pete Reiser had everything but luck."[3]

Heinz cited that lack of luck, detailing the long list of injuries and recurring mishaps that shortened Reiser's career and prevented him from attaining the numbers of a Mantle or a Mays.

"In two and a half years in the minors, three seasons of Army ball and ten years in the majors, Pete Reiser was carried off the field 11 times. Nine times he regained consciousness either in the clubhouse or in hospitals. He broke a bone in his right elbow, throwing. He broke both ankles, tore a cartilage in his left knee, and ripped the muscles in his left leg, sliding. Seven times he crashed into outfield walls, dislocating his left shoulder, breaking his right collarbone and, five times, ending up in an unconscious heap on the ground. Twice he was beaned."[4]

As the Dodgers headed toward the pennant, an interesting item appeared in the September 20 edition of the *Chicago Defender*, that city's Negro newspaper. It was in an article covering heavyweight champion Joe Louis's training routine for his September 29 title defense against challenger Lou Nova. The *Defender* wrote that Louis would be rooting for the Dodgers to win the World Series should they get there "because of the presence of his old pal Dixie Walker on the club."[5]

His old pal Dixie Walker? We know Louis was a big fan of his hometown team, the Detroit Tigers; we also know that Walker played for the Tigers in 1938 and half of 1939. Therefore, this "friendship" may have dated back to when Walker played for the Tigers. A similar article had appeared around Opening Day of 1938. Louis was in training for his rematch with Max Schmeling, the German heavyweight who had stunned the boxing world two years earlier by knocking out the previously unbeaten Louis. Joe wasn't worried about Schmeling, the paper said, but was "much concerned how his friends the Detroit Tigers of the American League are going to come out in this season's baseball race."[6] Could Louis and Walker have met, chatted about their Alabama roots, had dinner together? In light of what was to happen later in Dixie's career, the idea of a friendship between the two men is intriguing.

On the morning of September 24, Dixie Walker's 31st birthday, Brooklyn's lead was one and a half games over St. Louis, with each team having four games left. The Cardinals were in Pittsburgh for the final two games of a four-game series, and the Dodgers were in Boston for two. The Dodgers trailed Jim Tobin, 2–0, in that first game when Walker hit a bases-clearing triple with two out in the seventh inning. Brooklyn added another run in the eighth to win, 4–2. Kirby Higbe, with relief from Casey, earned his 22nd victory of the season. (Recall, MacPhail had predicted that Higbe would be a 20-game winner for the Dodgers.) At Pittsburgh, Harry Gumbert shut out the Pirates, 4–0, keeping the Cardinals a game and a half behind.

Leo Durocher recalled what happened in the Brooklyn clubhouse prior to the next day's pennant-clincher. Whit Wyatt, his choice to pitch that day, had already beaten the Braves five times in 1941. He put a hand on Durocher's shoulder and said, "Get me one run today. They won't score."[7] Walker opened the game with a single and later scored, giving Wyatt his one run.

The Dodgers eventually scored five more as Wyatt shut out the Braves, 6–0, for his 22nd win. Walker, a key figure in both wins, had three hits. With the Braves batting in the bottom of the ninth, the final score from Pittsburgh came in; the Pirates had defeated the Cardinals. At 5:08 P.M., Boston's Max West grounded out, third baseman Cookie Lavagetto to first baseman Dolph Camilli, clinching the pennant for Brooklyn, their first in 21 years. Rud Rennie of the *New York Herald-Tribune* called it "the longest and closest pennant struggle in the history of baseball."[8]

"WE WIN," read the headline in the *Brooklyn Daily Eagle*. Another local newspaper, the *Brooklyn Citizen*, had erected a board near Brooklyn's Borough Hall for fans to follow the game. Thousands gathered to watch, but their presence served to disrupt traffic for blocks around. People throughout the borough, both indoors and out, followed Red Barber's transcription of the game on radio.

"Last Thursday, at 5:08 P.M., bedlam broke loose in Brooklyn," wrote *Time* magazine. "Staid citizens dashed out of their homes and shops, yelling 'We're in, we're in!' Housewives stood on their stoops, beating dishpans; kids tooted tin horns; barkeeps opened their taps, 'set 'em up on the house.' For 21 long years, Brooklynites had waited for this moment. Their beloved Dodgers ("Our Bums") had just clinched the National League pennant in Boston. Many another baseball town has gone wild over a pennant victory. But Brooklyn's faithful fans — victims of an inferiority complex provoked by the pompous, pennant-heavy New York Giants and Yankees across the river — burst into a demonstration last week that looked like New Orleans' Mardi Gras, New Year's Eve in Times Square and the 1918 Armistice."[9]

Before leaving Boston, the victorious Dodgers celebrated in the traditional fashion of winning teams. They drank and sprayed champagne all over their Braves Field clubhouse and then continued celebrating on the train ride back to New York. MacPhail had gotten word to the conductor to tell Durocher to have the train make a stop at the 125th Street Station in upper Manhattan before arriving at Grand Central Station. MacPhail's plan was to board the train there and share in the glory by accompanying his champions to Grand Central. But the train never even slowed as it approached 125th Street; it sped right by the station, leaving MacPhail red-faced, furious, and ready to fire Durocher for not stopping. Later that night he did fire his pennant-winning manager, but rehired him the next day. "He fired me 60 times if he fired me once," Leo would later say.[10] "There is a thin line between genius and insanity," Durocher once said of MacPhail. "In Larry's case it's sometimes so thin you can see him drifting back and forth."[11]

Durocher claimed he never got the message from the conductor. While that may be true, he had what he considered a good reason not to stop. Durocher had overheard some of his players saying they would get off the train at the uptown stop to avoid the anticipated mob scene at Grand Central. Leo did not want the long-suffering Brooklyn fans snubbed in that manner. "I don't care if they tear your clothes off," he recalled saying. "We belong to those fans. They've been waiting twenty-one years for this chance to celebrate, and we've gotta go through with it. There'll be no stop."[12]

Durocher's decision was an appropriate one, a recognition that Dodgers fans had supported the team in record numbers. Attendance at Ebbets Field reached a new high in 1941— more than 1.2 million people. Four days later, after the last game of the regular season, more than a million people marched down Flatbush Avenue behind their heroes in a gigantic Victory Parade.[13]

In calling the 1941 Dodgers "that close to being a perfect team," baseball historian Bill James noted they had future Hall of Famers Leo Durocher as their manager, Joe Medwick in left field, Pee Wee Reese at shortstop and Billy Herman at second base. They had a near-Hall of Famer, Dixie Walker, in right field, the league's MVP, Dolph Camilli, at first base, the MVP runner-up, Pete Reiser, in center, and quality players Cookie Lavagetto at third base and Mickey Owen behind the plate. Whit Wyatt and Kirby Higbe were 20-game winners, and Hugh Casey was one of the early outstanding relief pitchers.[14]

Camilli led the league with 34 home runs and 120 runs batted in. Reiser, in his first full season, led in batting (.343), triples (17), runs scored (117), total bases (299), and slugging percentage (.558) and tied Johnny Mize for the lead in doubles (39).

Finishing third in the MVP race was Whit Wyatt, the first time one team had swept the top three spots. Wyatt tied Higbe for most wins in the league (22) led in shutouts (7), and was second in complete games (23), strikeouts (176), and ERA (2.34). Higbe finished seventh in the MVP voting, Walker tenth and Billy Herman 11th. "No one man carried our club," said Camilli. "We all had great years."[15]

Walker batted a solid .311, and along with Reiser and Joe Medwick (.318) gave Brooklyn an all-.300-hitting outfield. Walker delivered numerous clutch hits throughout the season, and was among the National League's top ten in hits, singles, doubles, triples, walks, and on-base percentage. The Dodgers Victory Committee of fans voted Walker the team's most popular player, quite an honor for a relative newcomer. Walker, with more than 32,000 votes, had more than three times as many as Camilli and Reiser. Dixie was also a close second to Camilli in the voting for most colorful player, while the exciting young Reiser was a surprising third. The awards were presented the night of September 26 at the Brooklyn Paramount Theater.[16]

What prevents the 1941 Dodgers, this almost perfect team, from consideration as the greatest team ever is that they lost the World Series.[17] The New York Yankees, the team that defeated them in five games, had won the American League pennant in much different fashion from the Dodgers in taking the NL flag. Joe McCarthy's Yankees had clinched on September 4, the earliest ever for a 154-game season. Even without a contested pennant race, the season had been an eventful one for the New Yorkers. The highlight was Joe DiMaggio's record 56-game hitting streak, and the lowlight the untimely passing of Lou Gehrig.

New York had three of the league's top four home run leaders: Charlie Keller (33), Tommy Henrich (31), and DiMaggio (30). Rookie shortstop Phil Rizzuto, who batted .307, and second baseman Joe Gordon, with 24 home runs, were not only good offensive players, they were instrumental in helping the Yankees lead both leagues in double plays, with 196. Brooklyn had the lowest number of double plays in the majors, just 125. The Yankees had no 20-game winners, but Red Ruffing, Lefty Gomez, Marius Russo, and Spud Chandler all had double-figures win totals, and bullpen ace Johnny Murphy was the New Yorkers equivalent of Hugh Casey.

When Dixie Walker was asked if he thought the Dodgers could beat the Yankees, he replied, "I do, definitely. I'd hate to have us come this far and not think we're going to win. We all do."[18] Walker also had a new good luck token for the Series, one that came all the way from Ireland. A Brooklyn fan had sent him a piece of the Blarney Stone set in a gold horseshoe. "Wear it, Dixie, my boy," he wrote, "and the Dodgers can't lose."[19]

But those who made the odds on sporting events saw it differently. They made the Yankees 2-to-1 favorites to win the World Series for the fifth time in six years. *Time* magazine gave the reasons why the Yanks were such heavy favorites. "The smooth-running Yankee machine may hit on all cylinders after four weeks of coasting; while the high-strung Dodgers, after a neck and neck race with the St. Louis Cardinals since the first week of the season — a race during which the Dodgers were in and out of the lead ten times — may be on the verge of collapse."[20]

Walker's parents came up from Birmingham to watch their son play in the Series.[21] Ewart, the former Washington Senators pitcher, was working as a night watchman in a department store and had a small peach farm. "This visit of ours is the kick of a lifetime," he said.[22]

"You know I always said I hoped to see Fred in a World Series," said Flossie, who had warned her teenage son against his pursuing a career in baseball, "and I wondered if I ever would. But this has taught me a lesson — I'll never give up again."[23] (One year earlier, Walker's former team, the Detroit Tigers, had lost a seven-game World Series to Cincinnati.)

The Series opened at Yankee Stadium on October 1 before a World Series record crowd of 68,540. The Yanks' Red Ruffing went the distance in defeating Brooklyn's surprise starter Curt Davis, 3–2. Wyatt got the Dodgers even the next day, by the same score, 3–2. Starter Spud Chandler took the loss for New York. Game Three, following a day of rain, was the first World Series game at Ebbets Field since 1920. As in the first two games, pitching dominated this arduous duel between Brooklyn's 40-year-old Fred Fitzsimmons and the Yankees' Marius Russo.

Fitzsimmons, another surprise pick by Durocher after he appeared in only 13 games during the season, matched Russo through seven scoreless innings. The last out of the seventh was a Russo line drive that hit off Fitzsimmons's left knee and caromed on the fly to shortstop Reese. However, the injury to the knee prevented Fitzsimmons from coming out for the eighth

Prior to the 1941 World Series, Dodgers coach Charlie Dressen points out the dimensions of Yankee Stadium to pitchers Whit Wyatt, Curt Davis, Fred Fitzsimmons, Hugh Casey, and Kirby Higbe (private collection of Stephen Walker).

10. A Pennant and a World Series

inning. The Yankees jumped on his replacement, Hugh Casey, with consecutive singles by Red Rolfe, Henrich, DiMaggio, and Keller that scored two runs. Walker doubled to lead off the Brooklyn eighth and later scored on Reese's single to cut the lead to one. Russo preserved the 2–1 victory, retiring Reiser, Medwick, and Lavagetto in the ninth. "I don't think the Yankees would have touched him the rest of the way if he'd been able to stay in there," Camilli said of Fitzsimmons.[24]

Until Bobby Thomson's pennant-winning home run ten years later, Game Four of the 1941 World Series was the bitterest defeat in Brooklyn baseball history. The Yanks got off to a quick 3–0 lead against Higbe, with a run in the first and two more in the fourth. Brooklyn came back with two in the fourth against Atley Donald and took the lead in the fifth when Walker led off with a double and Reiser followed with a home run over the scoreboard in right.

Needing a win to tie the Series at two games each, the Dodgers held a 4–3 lead with two outs in the Yankees ninth. The pitcher was Hugh Casey; the batter was Tommy Henrich; and the count was full. When Henrich swung and missed on the next pitch, plate umpire Larry Goetz raised his right hand indicating strike three as the crowd erupted in joy. But the third strike had gotten away from catcher Mickey Owen and rolled back to the screen behind home plate. Before Owen could retrieve it, Henrich had reached first base. Given a new life, the Yankees took full advantage. As the crowd looked on in disbelief, DiMaggio singled, and he and Henrich scored on Keller's double off the right field screen. New York now led, 5–4.

Durocher never left the bench, even as Casey allowed two more Yankees runs to score. He had Curt Davis warming up but did not bring him in, even though Casey was clearly floundering. Even the pitch sequence to Keller indicated the veteran Casey was no longer in control. He had gotten ahead of the Yankees slugger, 0–2, and then threw him a pitch that Keller could smash off the screen.

Johnny Murphy retired the Dodgers in order in the ninth, as he had in the eighth, to get the win. On the Brooklyn side, Casey became the first pitcher to lose two World Series games on consecutive days.[25] "I had Henrich 3–2 on the count so I figured I'd rear back and throw him the curve," Casey told reporters after the game. "It broke too much."[26] Instead of the Series being even, the Yankees now held a commanding 3–1 lead. When Ernie Bonham topped Wyatt, 3–1, the next day, the Series was over.

"The Lord must be on their side," Walker had said of the Yankees after Game Four.[27] When the Series was over, he uncharacteristically called the Yanks the luckiest team ever. "Every break in the book went to them," he lamented. "Why, even in that big ninth-inning rally that ball that Keller hit fiddled around on top of that concrete wall and let DiMaggio go home with the second, or winning run. Not that it would have meant anything as things turned out, you understand but it just shows you. That ball stayed up there on the fence like somebody was holding it."[28]

Owen was understandably disconsolate after his error in the fourth game.[29] "I don't mind being the goat, Harold," he told *Brooklyn Daily Eagle* reporter Harold Parrott in the Dodgers dressing room, "but the tough part is that it costs these other fellows money. I'm square with myself. I knew I gave it everything I had, although I can't tell you for the life of me how that ball got away in the ninth."[30] Owen took complete blame for the incident. "I was late getting my glove down there and it went right by me. My fault."[31]

Yet over the years, revisionist historians have attempted to shift the blame from Owen to Casey, claiming the pitch by Casey was not a curveball, but a spitball. Casey's manager, teammates, and others at the scene have always disputed this.

"Hugh Casey didn't even know how to throw a spitball," said Leo Durocher. "Why should he? Casey had a natural sinker — that's why he was a relief pitcher. A good spitball acts exactly the same way. It breaks down and away. Common sense tells you that a man wouldn't bother to develop a pitch that acts the same as a pitch he's already throwing." According to Durocher, Casey made a great pitch, but Owen reached for the ball instead of shifting his feet, and the ball rolled off his glove.[32]

Billy Herman agreed that the fault was Owen's, not Casey's. "I think Owen might have 'nonchalanted' the ball, putting his glove out instead of shifting his whole body to make the catch," Herman said. "Owen had a habit of doing that, and maybe that's what happened there."[33] Whit Wyatt discounted the notion that Casey had thrown a spitball in a 1986 interview with *Sports Collectors Digest*. "I really don't think it was a spitter," he told author Paul Green. "I think it was Casey's curve ball."[34]

11

The 1942 Dodgers Look to Repeat

In July of 1941, Harold Parrott of the *Brooklyn Daily Eagle* had asked Dixie Walker if he now considered New York his town and the people who lived there his real friends. Walker's response about his adopted home was positive and enthusiastic. "I found that out during the last month or so. I never knew I had so many friends. They helped me set up my store in Rockville Center. Why I owe them everything. A town that goes to bat for me like that is my town. I'm not going South again in the offseason. I'm staying here, going to become part of the community. I want to send my children to school up here. I'm a storeowner now, but baseball, for as long as I can play it, will be my first love, will have my main attention. After I've wound up my major league career, I have hopes that I may return some of the favors, perhaps by coaching a high school or a college team hereabouts. That's my dream."[1]

So for the first time in his career, Dixie Walker did not return to Birmingham for the winter. He, Estelle, Fred Jr. and Mary Ann Estelle remained in their house in Rockville Center on Long Island. Dixie looked after the store he owned, The Dixie Walker Liquor Store, at 312 Sunrise Highway, while also continuing his in-season practice of making civic appearances. Hardly a week went by when the *Brooklyn Daily Eagle* did not report Walker's attending some local civic or community function. Moreover, he was completely ecumenical in his appearances, attending Church Bazaars, meetings of the Knights of Pythias, and a series of Holy Name Society gatherings, as well as meetings for the American Legion and other patriotic groups, and just about any event that involved children or orphans.

He was at 120 Empire Boulevard in Brooklyn on January 8, 1942, when a crowd of 3,500 people attended the opening of Freddie Fitzsimmons's bowling alley. "It was the toughest day's work I ever had," said an exhausted Fitzsimmons after it was over. "Boy, I certainly did plenty of handshaking."[2]

Also attending the opening were Giants catcher Harry Danning, Brooklyn borough president John Cashmore, district attorney William O'Dwyer, county court judge Samuel Leibowitz, and Sid Luckman, the former Columbia University quarterback. Luckman, a Brooklyn native, recently had led the Chicago Bears to victory over the New York Giants for the National Football League championship.

Walker's involvement with the community would continue throughout his tenure in Brooklyn. In June 1942, he spoke to 1,500 workers for the Atlantic Basin Iron Works and the Ocean Shipscaling Company, urging them to contribute to the Greater New York Fund. The Fund helped support 400 welfare agencies throughout the city. After his talk, Dixie stayed around to sign hundreds of autographs. He also talked baseball with the workers, predicting that the Dodgers would repeat as National League champions this year.

Walker not only enjoyed giving these talks and making these appearances, he felt an obligation to do so. "I've found most fans think big league players are stuck up and big headed. I've spent a lot of time trying to break that feeling down. I've tried to get next to Brooklyn fans socially, because I don't think a fellow's duties to a team ends when he peels off his uniform. And I think I've succeeded," he told Harold Parrott.[3]

Larry MacPhail continued to wheel and deal during the winter, attempting to improve on his pennant-winning team of 1941. At the major league meetings in Chicago he made it known that he was interested in Cardinals first baseman Johnny Mize, who had fallen out of favor with manager Billy Southworth. Of course, MacPhail already had a first baseman in Dolph Camilli; he also hinted he would be willing to trade Camilli, a fan favorite and the league's reigning MVP.

A trade for Camilli never materialized. He remained in Brooklyn, and while Mize landed in New York, it was not with the Dodgers, but with the Giants. However, MacPhail did make two significant additions that winter. On December 12, he sent pitcher Luke Hamlin, catcher Babe Phelps, second baseman Pete Coscarart, and outfielder-first baseman Jimmy Wasdell, none of whom figured in the Dodgers' plans for 1942, to the Pittsburgh Pirates for shortstop Arky Vaughan. Although Vaughan had been the National League's premier shortstop for the past decade, there were no plans to have him replace Pee Wee Reese.

However, war had broken out five days earlier, and all personnel decisions were now subject to the vagaries of the military draft. Walker and his family had been at the Polo Grounds on December 7 to see the football Dodgers upset the Giants. It was there they learned of the Japanese attack on Pearl Harbor.

MacPhail also added another outfielder to the club, purchasing Don Padgett from St. Louis, the team the Dodgers were likely to battle again for the pennant. Trades between contenders are unusual; although Padgett had played in 107 games for the Cardinals in 1941, Branch Rickey had no need for him. Manager Southworth had Terry Moore and Enos Slaughter healthy again, plus rookie Stan Musial, who had made a spectacular debut the previous September. Johnny Hopp had split his time between the outfield and first base in 1941, but with Mize gone, Hopp figured to play mostly at first this year.

Soon after acquiring Padgett, a rumor surfaced that the Dodgers had offered Walker and Cookie Lavagetto to Cincinnati for ace right-hander Paul Derringer.[4] That trade too fell through, and MacPhail announced that Walker, who had finished eighth in the batting race and 10th in the MVP voting, ranked a lowly eighth among Brooklyn's outfielders. Why MacPhail, a clever judge of talent, continued to disrespect and undervalue Dixie Walker is difficult to fathom, yet in spite of his denials, clearly he did. Before Thanksgiving, he complained that the press continued to write that he did not like Walker. "When are you fellows going to kill the story that I am mad at Dixie Walker," he asked in a booming voice. "If you don't kill it soon it will kill me! I'm nice to the guy; I smile at him whenever we meet. I'm going to send him a Christmas card."[5]

When asked why he and Durocher had tried to replace Dixie with Paul Waner in the spring, MacPhail shouted, "That's a fiction. Walker was never our right fielder the season before, in 1940. He couldn't throw well enough to play right field for the Bloomer Girls that year. He was our center fielder — and Pete Reiser took his job in camp last spring." MacPhail pointed out that Walker had made more money in Brooklyn than anywhere he had played and that Durocher had gotten more out of him than any previous manager.[6]

Durocher paid no attention to MacPhail's calling Walker Brooklyn's eighth best outfielder; he had watched Dixie come through time after time during the 1941 stretch drive. In assessing the club's prospects for 1942, Leo said, "The right field job is Dixie Walker's until somebody can take it away from him." He also said that if he lost Reiser to the draft, he would use Walker to replace him in center field.[7]

If Dixie was upset at the way MacPhail treated him, he was not ready to show it, at least not openly. Speaking to the Brooklyn Rotary Club at the Hotel Bossert, he said. "The only time I disagree with MacPhail is when it comes contract time. I hope to spend my remaining days in baseball in Brooklyn. I'd never want to play with any other club."[8]

Shortly after America's entry into the war, Commissioner Landis wrote to President Roosevelt asking if baseball should operate in 1942, and if so, how. Roosevelt answered on January 15, 1942, with his famous "green light" letter. "I honestly feel," said the president, "that it would be best for the country to keep baseball going."[9]

The 1942 season would see a limited loss of players to military service, primarily Cleveland's Bob Feller and Detroit's Hank Greenberg. Yet even in the first weeks after Pearl Harbor, teams began to feel the war's impact. On January 31, the day Durocher signed his contract to manage the Dodgers in 1942; he learned he had lost his third baseman. Harry Lavagetto, who had an amateur pilot's license, informed the club from his home in California that he had joined the Navy Air Corps.[10] Recently acquired Arky Vaughan would be the Dodgers third baseman in 1942.

During the first week of February, the owners held a special meeting to discuss the implementation of wartime regulations. They decided to allow 14 night games for each club that had lights, with Washington allowed 21. Two All-Star Games would be played, the traditional one, plus one with a military All-Star team. Curfews were set for night games, with no inning to start after 12:50 A.M.

Teams with key players past age 30 were less likely to be hurt by their players being drafted than were the younger teams. The Dodgers worried about losing Pee Wee Reese and Pete Reiser, but with a core of older veterans, like Walker, Dolph Camilli, Fred Fitzsimmons, Billy Herman, Arky Vaughan, and Whit Wyatt, they figured to fare better than the younger Cardinals.

Nonetheless, most prognosticators were predicting the Cardinals would replace the Dodgers as National League champions. The return of Slaughter, having Musial from the beginning of the season, and an outstanding young pitching staff were the major factors in making St. Louis the preseason choice. Billy Southworth's team lacked power, but they had speed, defense, and solid pitching.

On February 18, the Dodgers, with some notable absences, left Miami to fly to their training camp in Havana, Cuba. Walker was still holding out, as was Wyatt, who was demanding a $7,500 raise over his $12,500 salary of 1941. Kirby Higbe had signed his contract, but said he did not want to go to Havana. "I just don't like the place," he said. "Besides the food being terrible, the water is bad."[11]

With Walker continuing to hold out, Roscoe McGowen wrote in the *New York Times*, "There is increasing evidence in the Dodger camp that Dixie Walker (whom McGowen called 'Brooklyn's most popular Dodger') is threatened with serious competition."[12] The three men mentioned were newcomer Padgett, and veterans Johnny Rizzo and Augie Galan.

Walker and MacPhail finally agreed to terms in a telephone conversation on February 23. Dixie said the salary he accepted was the best he ever had, although he believed he deserved more. He flew from Birmingham to Havana, arriving the same day as Higbe, who promised to win 30 games this season. "It would have been 40 if I'd stayed in Miami," he added.[13]

Spring training for Walker in Havana, and later when the team moved to Daytona Beach, Florida, was in one disturbing way much like it was the previous year. In 1941, the Dodgers had brought in Paul Waner to replace him. Irate fans back in Brooklyn had written letters and telegrams demanding Dixie be given back his old job. MacPhail's response was to tell the fans that he and Durocher, and not they, were running the ball club, and Waner was his right fielder. Waner started poorly, and Walker did get his job back, just in time in the opinion of some. "That MacPhail almost lost the pennant for the Dodgers because of his stubbornness in keeping Walker out of the lineup," said one sportswriter who covered the team.[14]

Estelle Walker and several other Dodger wives were in Daytona this spring, and so too was 19-year-old Dottie Walton. Dottie, Pee Wee Reese's girlfriend, had come at the invitation of Mrs. Billy Herman. The couple planned to marry in the fall, but that changed one night after going to dinner with the Walkers. Estelle wondered why they were waiting until the fall. "Why don't you two get married now?" she asked. The couple agreed to get married the next Sunday with Dixie as the best man.[15] The Reeses and the Walkers would remain friends for life.

Unlike 1941, the Dodgers had designated no specific player as Walker's replacement this year. Yet as the team played exhibition games across Florida, Walker, much to the dismay of the fans back in Brooklyn, remained in Daytona with the second-stringers. Those fans were bombarding Durocher with telegrams asking him to start playing their beloved Dixie. Durocher remained adamant, saying he was the manager, and he would decide who plays.

MacPhail backed up his manager, while also issuing him a veiled threat. "Durocher is running the Brooklyn ball club on the field. But he won't be running it long if I find he's being influenced by telegrams or protests from fans or other groups of fans who think they know more about the job than he does."[16]

When asked about Walker's seeming demotion, Durocher said. "I like him like a brother, but I wouldn't give my own brother a place on the team unless he earned it." Durocher went on to say Walker had reported late to Havana and had to work himself into shape. "As a matter of fact, he likes to bat whenever he feels like it, sit down when he feels like it, and go out and snag flies when he feels like it," Leo said disapprovingly.[17]

Brooklyn fans found Durocher's response unconvincing. They just could not understand why Walker, the "long-legged drawling Georgian," as sportswriter Tommy Holmes called him, a man who batted .311 and was so valuable in 1941, was playing with the B Team in spring training.

Shirley Povich thought MacPhail's dislike of Walker was attributable to Dixie's style of play. "MacPhail wants his players full of dash and fire, in his own image," Povich wrote. "Apparently he doesn't like the pokey, easy-going manner of Dixie, who doesn't like to be hustled."[18]

Meanwhile, MacPhail charged that the Brooklyn fans were trying to usurp his and Durocher's roles and trying to run the team. Walker told *New York Daily News* sportswriter Jimmy Powers he hoped MacPhail realized he was not responsible for the thousands of letters and proposed boycotts from the fans. "I certainly appreciate their praise, but I certainly never agitate those fan clubs into deluging the club with mail every time I'm left out of a ball game."[19]

Walker had worked his way back into the starting lineup by Easter Sunday, when the Dodgers stopped off in Atlanta to play the Crackers at Ponce de Leon Park. The *Atlanta Daily World*, a newspaper whose readership was mostly African American, carried another intriguing reference to the relationship between Walker and Joe Louis. Lucius (Melancholy) Jones, a columnist for the paper, described the Brooklyn outfield as consisting of Joe Medwick in left, Pete Reiser in center, and "Dixie Walker, the idol of World Heavyweight Champion Joe Louis, in right."[20]

Stephen Walker recalled his father telling him that Joe Louis was the best fighter he had ever seen. It was during a 1966 conversation — when he was 12 years old — at the family's farm in Odenville, Alabama, just outside of Pell City. They were sitting on Dixie's Ford tractor and eating Estelle's "famous cheese and grape jelly sandwiches" while discussing whether Louis was better than Muhammad Ali. Dixie said it was a "close call," as they were different types of fighters, from different eras, but he would give the edge to Louis. Stephen suspects it was because Joe was from Alabama. "Dad loved everything about Alabama and was very loyal to people that came from there."[21]

Having won his job back, Dixie was in right field when the Dodgers battered Carl Hubbell to defeat the Giants, 7–5, in the 1942 opener. Johnny Mize, playing his first games as a Giant, had a three-run homer as the Giants rallied back from a 7–0 deficit. As at all parks on the East Coast, the Polo Grounds had a supply of sand and fire extinguishers available, and instructions on what to do in case of an air raid. More than 32,000 fans showed up to celebrate the return of baseball, though the grim news from Asia and Europe clouded their joy. The Japanese government reported Japanese forces had taken 40,000 captives on Bataan, including 6,700 Americans, and were continuing their relentless assault on Corregidor. In addition, President Roosevelt had to deal with the previous day's shakeup in the French cabinet, in which pro-Nazi Pierre Laval returned to take control of the Vichy government.

11. The 1942 Dodgers Look to Repeat

Walker had his first home run of the new season the next day, but rookie Willard Marshall had a grand slam as the Giants defeated Kirby Higbe, giving new manager Mel Ott his first win. Later in the week, Dixie threw out the first ball as Brooklyn Technical High School opened their baseball season against James Madison High. The student body at Brooklyn Tech had voted Walker the most popular Dodger.

Somehow, Walker's popularity continued to mystify many of the writers, particularly those who did not see the Dodgers on a regular basis or were not familiar with his civic endeavors. This was especially true of writers more attuned to the Yankees and Giants. Because their idea of a hero was the majestic and reclusive Joe DiMaggio, they chose to denigrate the less sophisticated fans on the other side of the East River.

"Mr. Dixie Walker occupies an important position in the eyes of the Brooklyn fan," wrote Joe Williams in the *New York World Telegram*. "He is the big hero — and for reasons only the B[rooklyn] F[an] can convincingly explain. At one time, it looked as if he might develop into a real star but it never happened. Now, in his 30s, it is reasonable to assume a large part of his future is behind him. Nevertheless, he is the idol of Flatbush. You can have the brilliant Reiser, who led the league in hitting, and the masterful Wyatt, whose pitching genius sewed up the pennant; Flatbush will take Mr. Walker."[22]

Off to another flying start, the Dodgers put together two five-game winning streaks in April and ended the month with a record of 14–3. Their lead over the second-place Pirates was four games, while the Cardinals were five and a half games back. Walker, playing right field almost exclusively, had an excellent April, batting .349 with 13 runs batted in. On April 19, he had a single, a double, and a home run, and drove home four runs in Curt Davis's 6–2 win over the Phillies. Six days later, his three-run double in the first inning was more than Johnny Allen needed in beating Philadelphia, 4–1.

On May 3, the Dodgers made their first visit of the year to St. Louis. This first meeting between the bitter rivals hinted at what a wild battle the two teams would stage this season. Both managers were ejected, along with four Brooklyn players — Camilli, Fitzsimmons, Wyatt, and rookie pitcher Chet Kehn. Durocher's ejection came in the first inning of the first game. The Cardinals won both contests, 14–10 and 4–2 in a game called in the sixth inning because of darkness.

The double loss cut Brooklyn's lead to one game, but the Dodgers won 11 of their next 12. Aided by Walker's three hits against the Cubs on May 19, the club had its eighth straight win and their lead over second-place Boston was up to seven games.

12

"Men, you are going to lose this pennant"

The Cardinals made their first 1942 visit to Ebbets Field on May 20. In third place with a disappointing 17–15 record, the team had played sloppily and "lacked the proper mental attitude," according to manager Billy Southworth. "I'm cracking down on everybody, myself included," he said. "We're not going all-out, but we will from now on, I assure you. You'll see a change in this ballclub."[1] That afternoon, Mort Cooper's two-hitter defeated Wyatt, 1–0, to end Brooklyn's winning streak at eight games. It was yet another stirring pitching duel between the two right-handers, with the only run coming on a fifth-inning triple by Walker Cooper and a fly ball.

The Dodgers concluded the month of May with a home doubleheader sweep of Boston, the team's 14th consecutive victory over the Braves. Curt Davis raised his record to 7–1 in the opener, while Wyatt's win in the nightcap was his fourth of the season and tenth straight over Boston. Brooklyn's 10–2 win in the first game featured a rarity, an inside-the-park grand slam. It came in the fourth inning when Dixie Walker's line drive into the right-field corner ended up under the Dodgers bullpen bench, situated against the wall in foul territory. Braves right fielder Paul Waner searched frantically on his hands and knees for the ball, but by the time he retrieved it, Reese, Reiser, and Vaughan had scored, and Walker was sliding across the plate. The two losses by Boston allowed St. Louis to move ahead of them into second place, six games off the pace.

St. Louis was riding a seven-game winning streak, and Brooklyn's lead was four and a half games, when the teams began a five-game series at Ebbets Field on June 18. Before the game, Dolph Camilli received a medal denoting him as "the outstanding father in sports" for 1941. Camilli called the award, presented by actress Jean Cagney, the sister of James Cagney, "the proudest moment of my life."[2]

12. "Men, you are going to lose this pennant"

However, the spirit of love and family that prevailed on the field was short-lived. Another brawl broke out during the game, won by Brooklyn, 5–2, which led to ejections and fines for Joe Medwick and Cardinals second baseman Frank "Creepy" Crespi.

The confrontation took place in the sixth inning after Medwick tried to advance to second on a passed ball. Catcher Walker Cooper's throw to shortstop Marty Marion retired Medwick, but Joe's hard, spikes-high slide upended Marion. After the play was over, both men came up ready to fight. Crespi quickly came between them, but soon he and Medwick were wrestling on the ground. Camilli, the batter, raced out and jumped on Crespi, and Dixie soon followed.

Max Lanier, the Cardinals pitcher that afternoon, remembered Walker running past him and diving at third baseman Whitey Kurowski. Lanier and Cardinals second baseman Jimmy Brown then went after Walker.[3] Soon other players from both teams joined in, creating a full-scale melee around second base. Walker strained his left leg during the tussle and had to leave the game. To add insult to injury, Dixie also took a punch to the jaw from an unidentified Cardinals player. The leg injury would reduce his status to primarily that of a pinch-hitter until after the All-Star break, with Johnny Rizzo and Augie Galan filling in. Brooklyn won four of the five games with St. Louis to increase their lead to seven and a half games.

Walker did not realize until a year later that he had broken his right ankle. "The bone was sticking out kind of funny in my ankle," he told Harold C. Burr. "At first I thought it was just a spur. But when I started to limp a year later at the Polo Grounds during a War Bond game, I had the ankle X-rayed, and I declare if the pictures didn't show a fracture." ("I declare" is one of his favorite phrases, added Burr.)[4]

Long after he retired, Marty Marion recalled the 1940s rivalry between the Cardinals and the Dodgers and his personal rivalry with Reese, who also had come to the majors in 1940. "In those days it seems we were always battling the Dodgers for the pennant, and people were always comparing me with Reese. The Dodgers were our enemies. We hated them and they hated us, but it was nothing personal. It was just that we were fighting for the same prize."[5]

Yet in many cases, it was personal. The Cardinals, like every other team in the National League, considered the Durocher-led Dodgers to be bullies. The Dodgers had become the league's most hated team, primarily because Durocher always had his pitchers throwing at the opposing team's hitters. In 1942, six of the seven teams complained about beanballs from Brooklyn pitchers. The poorer clubs in particular resented Brooklyn pitchers throwing at their batters.

Another incident in the Dodgers' ongoing feud with the Cubs broke out at Wrigley field on July 15. Before it was over, Kirby Higbe had thrown a pitch behind Bill Nicholson's back, seemingly on orders from Durocher; Chicago's Paul Erickson had knocked down Medwick and dusted off Billy Herman three times in retaliation, seemingly on the orders of his manager, Jimmy Wilson. Erickson had replaced Hi Bithorn, whom Durocher had ridden so hard that as he was walking off the mound he threw the ball at Leo sitting in the dugout. Mickey Owen reached in front of his manager to catch Bithorn's well-aimed throw.

Brooklyn's lead was eight games when they traveled to St. Louis for back-to-back doubleheaders on July 18 and 19. With the Cardinals starting two left-handers, Ernie White and Max Lanier, Durocher replaced Walker in the starting lineup with right-handed hitters: Johnny Rizzo in the first game and Frenchy Bordagaray in the second. The teams split the pair, with Larry French taking the loss in the opener, his first defeat after ten straight wins.

St. Louis won both games the following day to cut Brooklyn's lead to six games. Mort Cooper beat Wyatt for the third time this season, 8–5, and the Cardinals won the second game, 7–6, in 11 innings. The winning run came on an Enos Slaughter inside-the-park home run. The ball sailed over the head of center fielder Reiser, who crashed into the wall in a vain attempt to catch it. "It might have been the greatest catch I've ever seen," said left fielder Medwick. "I'll swear that Slaughter hit that ball beyond Reiser and that Pete overtook it. He was traveling like a bullet when he hit the fence."[6]

Reiser was taken to the hospital, where he was diagnosed with a concussion and advised by Dr. Robert F. Hyland, his personal physician, not to play any more that season. Defying his doctor's orders, Reiser continued to play, though continually bothered by dizzy spells, and ended the season with a .310 average. The most gifted young player in the National League would never again be the same. "They [MacPhail and Durocher] never asked me if I could," Reiser said years later. "They always asked me if I would."[7]

Writing about Reiser in his book, *The Future of Being Human*, Paul Olson said, "If there was a hero soon to become the anti-hero, a man who epitomized the frustration and impotence of all of us, it was Pete Reiser, the wunderkind outfielder of the Brooklyn Dodgers. In 1942, he was destined to become perhaps the greatest baseball player in the history of the game.... He could do it all—run, field throw, but especially hit—with an authority that caught your breath short."[8]

Reiser never regretted Durocher playing him after the injury in St. Louis. "I have never, ever blamed Leo for keeping me in there. I blame myself. He wanted to win so badly it hurt, and I wanted to win so bad it hurt. I've heard a lot of guys knock Leo for all sorts of things, but I've always said this about him: If you don't know him, you hate his guts, but if you do know him, you love him. He was the best. He was aggressive, and he always fought for you. Always."[9]

Organized Baseball, along with the individual clubs, staged many special events to raise money for the war effort in 1942. As early as May 8, the Dodgers played the first twilight game at Ebbets Field in 24 years. More than 42,000 fans saw them top the Giants, 7–6, with Dolph Camilli's seventh-inning home run onto Bedford Avenue the big blow. The game raised close to $60,000, with all the proceeds donated to the Navy Relief Fund. Everyone, including the ball players and the umpires, paid their way into the park.

On August 1, the Dodgers defeated the Cubs while the Cardinals were splitting a doubleheader with the Giants. The Dodgers (71–29) now had a nine-game lead over the Cardinals (61–37). Two days later, the Giants and Dodgers played another twilight game, this one hosted by the Giants. A crowd of 57,305 raised $80,000 for the Army Emergency Relief Fund. The Dodgers won again, 7–4, and Camilli again led the offense, this time with a fifth-inning bases-loaded home run.

The game, as so many between these intra-city rivals did, ended in controversy. The Giants had two on with no one out in the last of ninth, but because it was now 9:10 P.M., wartime regulations required plate umpire George Magerkurth to halt the action. (Military regulations required that games be ended one hour after sunset). The game, which started at 6:45, went into the books as an eight-inning affair. Fans booed lustily, temporarily drowning out the popular Fred Waring Band's attempt to play the national anthem.

Giants owner Horace Stoneham announced there would be no more night or twilight games at the Polo Grounds until after the war. "We will play the twilight game tomorrow against Brooklyn," he said, "and after that twilight baseball and night baseball will be discontinued at the Polo Grounds for the duration."[10]

As if to emphasize Stoneham's point, the next night the game again ended with a portion of the crowd booing. Only this time it was the Brooklyn fans who were unhappy. They had just watched Pee Wee Reese's bases-loaded, inside-the-park home run in the top of the tenth inning negated by another "dim out" with the game reverting to a nine-inning, 1–1 tie.

On August 5, the teams played a third successive twilight game, this one at Ebbets Field. It was Rockville Center night at the park, and Walker and his fellow Rockville Center resident, Billy Jurges of the Giants, were honored before the game. Dixie received a fishing outfit and a watch, while Jurges got a watch and a ping-pong set. No controversy in this game — a two-hit, 4–0 shutout by Brooklyn's Max Macon that raised the Dodgers lead over St. Louis to ten full games.

The Cardinals had also won that day, and they continued to win. On August 18, Max Lanier shut out the Cubs while the Dodgers were losing, 3–1, to Philadelphia's Rube Melton, cutting Brooklyn's lead to 6½ games. Melton, a 25-year-old right-hander, would lead the last-place Phillies in losses this season with 20, but he had been tough on the Dodgers; in two earlier encounters, he had beaten them, 2–1, and lost, 1–0. Melton had been especially tough on Walker, who praised him after this loss.

"He really gives me the miseries," Walker said. "He can throw that ball at so many different speeds, I cannot get set up there." Dixie, along with some of his teammates, also praised other pitchers toiling for weaker teams, like Al Javery and rookie Johnny Sain of the Braves. "He starts it up over his shoulder," Walker said of Sain's curveball, "and by the time he sweeps it down at you, you don't know whether it's coming — or gone."[11]

A doubleheader sweep of the Giants, combined with a St. Louis-Pittsburgh split, upped the lead to 7½ games on August 23. Next up for the Dodgers was a four-game series at Sportsman's Park with a chance to all but end the Cardinals' pennant hopes. But St. Louis bounced back to take three of four, as Max Lanier, Mort Cooper, and Johnny Beazley allowed the Dodgers one run each in the first three games. Cooper's win was in 14 innings and Beazley's in ten. Curt Davis won the final game for Brooklyn, whose lead was now 5½ games.

By the end of the month, with the lead down to three games, MacPhail sought to bolster his faltering club by purchasing much-traveled pitcher Bobo Newsom from the Washington Senators. Newsom had won 11 games this year, but just two years earlier had won 21 for Detroit and two more in the World Series.

"Congratulations on buying the pennant," Newsom telegraphed Durocher. "Will report tomorrow in fine shape, rarin' to go."[12] Three days later, Newsom shut out Cincinnati, but the best he could do in September was split four decisions.

MacPhail was now telling everyone how he had warned about the Cardinals catching and then passing the Dodgers, but no one had listened. "I didn't like the attitude of the team when I held that meeting a couple of weeks ago. They were blowing games they should have won because they were overconfident and they should have known they were due for trouble later on. Guess that meeting I called didn't do any good," he continued. "Dixie Walker offered to bet that they'd win by the eight games that was their lead then. I'm not singling out Walker, but just emphasizing that this was the spirit of the whole club."[13] Walker gave his version of that memorable incident a dozen years later in a newspaper interview. "It was in August," he recalled, "and MacPhail came into a club meeting at Ebbets Field. We were nine games in front. Larry said, "Men, you are going to lose this pennant just as sure as I stand before you." Dixie offered to bet MacPhail $100 that not only would the Dodgers win, they would keep their present lead. His purpose, Walker said, was to get the players fired up, but MacPhail thought he was just being cocky and overconfident.[14]

Walker was correct; that is exactly what MacPhail thought. In response to Dixie's offer to bet $100 that the Dodgers would retain their lead, MacPhail said. "I'll bet $100 you ought to win it by 20 games. Here's a club that has been in a slump and nobody worries about it except me. An eight-game lead in the middle of August isn't anything to sleep on. Leads like that have been lost."[15]

MacPhail was not alone in predicting the race was not over. After the Dodgers played an August series with Boston, in which both teams had thrown beanballs, Braves manager Casey Stengel expressed surprise to the reporters that Durocher would engage in such tactics. "If I had a ballclub as good as Durocher's," he said, "I wouldn't throw at a ballclub as bad as mine. We're going to battle these guys all the harder from now on. I've talked to [Pirates manager Frankie] Frisch, [Cubs manager Jimmy] Wilson, and other managers who feel the same." Then, despite the laughter of the reporters gathered in the clubhouse, Stengel predicted that despite Brooklyn's ten-game lead, the Cardinals were not out of the race. "Sure, they've got a big lead," he said of the Dodgers, "but they're not in yet. In case you guys didn't notice it, St. Louis is winning steadily."[16]

On September 10, the Dodgers lead slipped to just two games after they lost to Chicago's Lon Warneke, recently acquired from St. Louis, while the Cardinals were beating the Giants. The next stop for the red-hot Cardinals was Ebbets Field, where a sweep of the two games would put them in a first-place tie.

Before the series, a now optimistic Southworth gave the press a history lesson on late-season blown leads and comebacks. "Did you ever hear of the 1921 Giants winning after being 7½ games behind in late August? The Yankees blowing a 13-game lead in 1928 and just barely limping home? The 1936 Giants coming from ten games behind in August? The 1935 Cubs staging a 21-game late-season winning streak? The Pirates building a World Series press box in 1938 that was never used? And the Giants blowing a 7½-game Labor Day lead in 1934?"[17]

The pitchers for the first game were Whit Wyatt and Mort Cooper, as they had been in so many big games between Brooklyn and St. Louis these last two seasons. In a similar showdown between the two almost a year to the day earlier, doubles by Walker and Herman had given Brooklyn a 1–0 victory. But today Cooper, on his way to winning the Most Valuable Player award, outpitched Wyatt. Wearing number 20 rather than his usual number 13, he tossed a 3–0 shutout and allowed only three hits.[18] The win was his 20th of the season, his fifth in a row, his fifth over the Dodgers, and the third time he had blanked Brooklyn this year.

The next day, September 12, St. Louis won again, as Max Lanier defeated the Dodgers for the fifth time this season. His 2–1 victory brought the Cardinals even with the Dodgers, after having trailed them by ten games as late as August 5. Both teams now had a record of 94–46. "I think we're in," gloated Cardinals president Sam Breadon, while confidently ordering the printing of World Series tickets.[19]

Meanwhile, neither Durocher nor MacPhail seemed outwardly discouraged. "All right, they caught up," Durocher said. "It took them five months to do it. Let's snap out of it and get after them now." MacPhail told his players that he felt better now than he had in a couple of days. "They're even with us and I know you can win," he said. "Something's going to happen soon — a break that will start our rally...."[20]

But the Dodgers promptly lost two more to the Reds, and the Cardinals took over possession of first place. Brooklyn rallied to win their last eight, but despite winning 104 games, they finished two games behind St. Louis. Brooklyn's 104 wins tied the 1909 Chicago Cubs as the most ever by a second-place club, while the Cardinals' 106 wins were the most by a National League team since the Pittsburgh Pirates won 110 in '09.

Win number 100 for the Dodgers was Larry French's brilliant one-hit, 6–0 shutout of the Phillies at Ebbets Field on September 23. Nick Etten got the lone hit in the second inning, a soft liner that just eluded Reese. Etten, the only man to reach base, was erased on a double play, so French faced just 27 batters that afternoon. French called it the best game he ever pitched; it was also the last start of his career. After a season in which he had gone 15–4 with a 1.83 earned run average, he accepted a commission in the Navy. French served to the war's end. He was called back during the Korean War and eventually retired with the rank of Captain.[21]

Beginning with an August 9 doubleheader sweep at Pittsburgh, St. Louis won 43 of their final 51 games. The Dodgers were in first place for 148 days, and the Cardinals only 16 days. However, the Cardinals were there the only time that counted, the last day of the season.

"You've got to give the Cardinals credit for a drive like that," Walker said. "There isn't anything you can take away from a bunch that can come far from behind when they should have known they were beaten. Remember — they won it. We didn't lose it."[22]

An ankle injury in late April and the leg injury he sustained in the June brawl with the Cardinals limited Walker to 118 games in 1942. He batted

12. "Men, you are going to lose this pennant"

.290—his only sub-.300 full season as a Dodger and the only one in which he failed to get any MVP votes. Younger brother Harry, after seven-game stays with the Cardinals in 1940 and 1941, contributed a .314 average in 74 games for St. Louis this season.

During all the years Dixie and Harry were in the National League, they would often have dinner together on days their teams played each other, with Dixie usually playing the big brother role. "Fred is more like a father than a brother to me. And if I were his own son, he couldn't worry more about me," Harry said.[23]

The "St. Louis Swifties," a nickname given to them by a New York newspaper cartoonist, concluded their miracle season with a five-game World Series upset of the New York Yankees. The "Swifties" name can be misleading; the 1942 Cardinals were not a great base stealing team, but they were excellent at other aspects of baserunning, like going from first to third on singles. Several of the league's other managers, who had problems with Durocher's clubs' aggressiveness, had only admiration for Southworth's club's all-out style of play. "Too much energy, entirely too much," complained Cubs manager Jimmy Wilson. "No team can keep charging around a park the way they do and stay in one piece. The Cardinals knock you out of the way just for fun."[24] Boston's Stengel called them "a track team that ran like uncaged rabbits."[25]

Yet these Cardinals had a lot more than speed; they led the National League in batting, runs scored, doubles, triples, and slugging percentage. They allowed the fewest runs in the league and posted the best ERA (2.55). Mort Cooper (22) and Johnny Beazley (21) were the league's top winners, and Cooper (1.78) and Beazley (2.13) finished one-two with the lowest earned run averages. "When baseball fans talk about great teams of baseball's past, the 1942 St. Louis Cardinals are hardly mentioned," wrote baseball historian Rick Van Blair. "They should be. They deserve a better place in the history of the game."[26]

13

The War Begins to Affect Baseball

Harry Walker had only one at-bat in the 1942 World Series, but unlike brother Dixie the year before, he was on the winning team. After losing the first game, the Cardinals swept the next four from the Yankees in what many viewed as a stunning upset. John Drebinger of the *New York Times* called the Cardinals' victory the most amazing World Series upset since 1914, when the miracle Braves defeated Connie Mack's Philadelphia Athletics.[1]

The same day as the Cardinals' triumph, October 5, Dixie Walker was in Flatbush Court, along with teammate Mickey Owen, two Ebbets Field ushers, and four fans. All were there to dispute assault charges and counter-charges related to a pregame incident on September 16. Before the game against Pittsburgh that afternoon, the ushers became involved in a brawl with four young men behind the Brooklyn dugout. Walker, Owen, and several other players jumped into the stands to help the ushers. Once peace was restored, the Dodgers pounded the Pirates, 10–3, led by Dolph Camilli's two home runs and Walker's four hits in four at-bats. By the time of the court hearing, all was forgiven on both sides and all charges were dropped.

In late September, with the pennant race still undecided, Larry MacPhail announced that he had resigned as the Dodgers president and was preparing to join the Army. To replace him, the Dodgers chose Cardinals mastermind Branch Rickey, who had grown unhappy in his relationship with owner Sam Breadon in St. Louis. Rickey, recognized as baseball's shrewdest trader and judge of talent, had built the great Cardinals teams that battled Brooklyn throughout the 1940s. Now his job would be to do the same with the Dodgers, a team with many aging stars and about to lose many of their younger ones to military service.

The change in the presidency from MacPhail to Rickey may have been responsible for keeping Walker in Brooklyn. The tempestuous MacPhail had not forgiven Dixie's ridiculing of his August prediction that despite their big lead the Dodgers would lose the pennant. "I'll tell you one thing," MacPhail

13. The War Begins to Affect Baseball

said after he proved to be right. "If it's the last thing I do, Walker will be found in new pastures next year."[2] With MacPhail now in the Army, Walker would remain a Dodger.

MacPhail's purchase of Walker in 1939 had been almost a desperation move, and while Walker produced far beyond expectations, MacPhail never truly appreciated him. "Dixie has been such a ballplayer's ballplayer that he is just about the most popular player in the National League," wrote *United Press* correspondent Jack Cuddy, "and now that MacPhail has left for the army, Walker's star may really shine under Rickey."[3]

Walker and Rickey met for the first time at a January 13, 1943, Rotary Club luncheon at Brooklyn's Hotel Bossert. Injuries to his knee and shoulder had exempted Dixie from military service, but he was determined to contribute in any way he could. Since the end of the 1942 season, he had been working for the Sperry Gyroscope Company, which had five locations in the New York area. Walker was the company's personnel director in charge of recreational activities and had seriously considered giving up baseball and staying with Sperry for the duration of the war. He had mentioned this in talks he delivered to the Montauk Club and to the Holy Name Society of St. Francis Xavier Church.[4]

"I hate to think of it, for the fans of Brooklyn have been the most loyal since I took up professional baseball 14 years ago, but I am beginning to think of retiring," he told the Holy Name Society. He said if he did retire from baseball, he would take up a full-time position with the Sperry Company. "If I feel I am unable to give the kind of service the fans expect of me I will quit and stick to my current efforts rather than have somebody else acquaint me with the fact that I am through."[5] Walker insisted he was sincere and not using this as a bargaining chip in a potential salary negotiation. Still, at the relatively young age of 32, it's hard to believe he was completely serious.

At the Rotary Club luncheon, Dixie sat at the end of the dais as Rickey, a mesmerizing orator, held forth as only he could. Rickey said that Walker seemed to find himself "amid a confusion of honest ideas," wrote the *New York Times*. By this, the *Times* explained, Dixie was anxious to do the right thing, but was unable to decide whether that meant a return to baseball or staying with Sperry.[6] And while never looking directly at Walker, Rickey likely had him in mind when he spoke of the debt that baseball idols owed to their public, and how they must never break faith with them.[7]

Working for Sperry was quite a change from Walker's earlier offseasons. Early in his career, he had spent his winters dabbling in real estate, using his baseball earnings to build houses and then selling them at a profit. After becoming a Brooklyn idol, Dixie, a non-drinker, had opened a liquor store in Rockville Center.

"I've enjoyed my winters," Walker said. "I've made some money during the cold months and I've met a lot of different people. But most of all I've learned things that will help in later life." Walker's constant striving to improve his lot in life came as no surprise to sportswriter Tommy Holmes. "His intelligence and his personality would make him stand out no less in a business far removed from sports," wrote Holmes.[8]

At Sperry, Walker generally got to the plant at 10 in the morning and often did not get home until 11 at night. Sperry had three plants in Nassau County and two in Brooklyn, one at the Bush Terminal on the waterfront, and one near the Flatbush Avenue extension. As the director of athletics and recreation, Dixie arranged for employees to bowl once a week at the Nevins Bowling Center on Flatbush Avenue and Fulton Street in downtown Brooklyn. "I haven't bowled much, but there is no doubt about it being a great conditioner," he said. "Frankly, I was introduced to bowling in recent years and I'm not in the same class with Freddie Fitzsimmons, for example. But I'll get there."[9] Dixie also had to get involved with bridge and ice skating, two other leisure interests he was completely unfamiliar with.

One recreational activity Walker was accustomed to was square dancing. On February 6, 1943, he spoke at Brooklyn's Bedford branch of the YMCA, where he taught a once-a-week class in country dancing to the city folks. Three hundred employees were there as Dixie tried to encourage the women, who were enduring dateless nights because their husbands and boyfriends were in the military. He said the best thing after working hard all day was to relax their muscles and brains at least once a week. "I enjoy doing the square dance with the young people," Walker said. "It is the best way for relaxing nerves and makes them fit for their hard tasks." He said square dancing was not the only form of exercise for the ladies. "Life becomes humdrum for the women who go home to iron, sew, or perhaps cook every night. Spending one night a week bowling, swimming, dancing, or playing tennis does the trick. I suggest that everyone doing overtime work go in for something like this."[10]

In addition to his work at Sperry, Dixie used his popularity among Brooklynites to aid the war effort in any way he could. In November 1942, he kicked off an American Red Cross blood drive with a speech at Brooklyn's Boys High School. He also spoke at other schools, appealing to the students to get their parents and relatives to sign up for the blood bank.

Three weeks before the start of spring training, Walker said he was still unsure whether he would report to the Dodgers or continue with Sperry. "I'm not worrying about that now. I've got a job to do here and I intend to do it. I have security at Sperry's that I don't have in baseball. I know that the Sperry plants will be active for the war, and I'm not sure about baseball. After the war is another story, but I like my chances better here."[11]

13. The War Begins to Affect Baseball

The lack of financial security in Walker's youth obviously had affected his outlook as an adult. Dixie Walker was always looking to make money, and that no doubt played a part in his early opposition to Jackie Robinson. Above any other objection he may have had, Walker knew that playing with a black man would adversely affect business at his liquor and hardware stores in Alabama.

On February 16, 1943, Estelle Walker gave birth to the couple's fourth child. Susan Ellen Walker, eight pounds, two ounces, arrived in Rockville Center the same day as Dixie's 1943 contract did. The new father assured the press that he would keep his daughter but he was not sure about the contract.

Dixie eventually signed and reported to spring training the last week of March. But it was not to Cuba or sunny Florida. Spring training in 1943 was limited to locations north of the Potomac or Ohio Rivers and east of the Mississippi River. The Dodgers' training camp was at Bear Mountain, New York, not far from the United States Military Academy at West Point. To the delight of Dodgers fans everywhere, Rickey announced that Walker "is not going to do any part-time work for the Sperry Company but will be a full-time player."[12] Rickey's statement was not entirely accurate. Dixie would be a full-time player in 1943, but he would retain his ties with Sperry.

By Opening Day, several of the biggest names in the game were in the military, including Joe DiMaggio, Ted Williams, Johnny Mize, and Enos Slaughter. Among the Dodgers now serving were Pete Reiser, Pee Wee Reese, Larry French, and Hugh Casey. Kirby Higbe would be with the Dodgers in 1943, but he would miss 1944 and 1945. Higbe believed the Dodgers rather than the Cardinals might have won pennants in 1943 and 1944, after the two teams had battled so closely in 1941 and 1942. "They didn't lose the men to the service the Dodgers did. They sure didn't. We had pretty nearly an All-Star team. The best infield in baseball. Until the war."[13]

Higbe may have been correct. There is every likelihood that these two teams would have battled for the pennant in the three years from 1943 to 1945, just as they had in the two years prior to the war and the two years after. Of course there are many "might have beens" regarding World War II and baseball, and we can deal only with what actually happened.

The Cardinals, with a lineup composed of players all under 30 years old, breezed to the 1943 pennant by 18 games over Cincinnati. Stan Musial, Harry Walker, Marty Marion, and Walker Cooper were all back to lead the offense, while Mort Cooper (21–8) and Max Lanier (15–7) led the pitchers. Musial won his first batting title, with a .357 average, and his first Most Valuable Player award; Cooper's 21 wins tied him for the league lead with Cincinnati's Elmer Riddle and Pittsburgh's Rip Sewell.

Brooklyn's only regular under 30, at least for the first half of the season, was catcher Mickey Owen. Luis Olmo, a 23-year-old rookie from Puerto Rico, filled an outfield spot in the second half. The Dodgers had six players with at least 200 at-bats who batted above .300, including Walker, who batted .302 with 71 runs batted in. The others were Billy Herman, Arky Vaughan, Frenchy Bordagaray, Paul Waner, and Olmo. Billy Herman was the team's offensive leader, batting .330, second best to Musial. Herman was second in doubles and was third in the league in runs batted in and hits. Despite getting little production from Dolph Camilli, the Dodgers topped the National League in runs scored and finished second to St. Louis in batting average.

Whit Wyatt led the pitchers with a 14–5 record and a .737 winning percentage, which tied Cincinnati's Clyde Shoun for tops in the league. But the loss of French and Casey and the falloff of Kirby Higbe made for an overall mediocre pitching staff. Higbe, a 22-game winner in 1941 and a 16-game winner in '42, won only 13 in 1943 (13–10). Curt Davis, 10–13, was the only other Brooklyn pitcher with a double-digit win total. The Dodgers' team earned run average was 3.88, the second worst in the league. For an August 18, 1943, home doubleheader, Durocher, desperate for pitching, brought two youngsters—Hal Gregg (22) and Rex Barney (18)—up from Montreal to start against the Cubs.

The Dodgers got off to another good start, winning eight of their first ten, and were in first place, a half-game ahead of the Cardinals, on July 1. But a St. Louis sweep of three games at Ebbets Field a few days later dropped the Dodgers 3½ games behind. They never recovered and finished third, 23½ games behind the Cardinals. Attendance in Brooklyn dropped to 661,739 in 1943, the lowest total in six years, but still the highest in the major leagues.

While most other teams had avoided signing young players because of the uncertainty of the draft, Rickey had taken the opposite tack. He had his scouts scouring the country for young talent, and while some went to war and others never worked out, many of the players he signed would contribute greatly to Brooklyn's postwar success. In 1943 alone, the Dodgers signed teenagers Gil Hodges, Duke Snider, Ralph Branca, and Rex Barney.

By the middle of July, the Dodgers were falling out of serious contention, giving Rickey an excuse to start unloading some of his veterans. The team released Fred Fitzsimmons days short of his 42nd birthday, and traded 35-year-old Bobo Newsom to the St. Louis Browns. Rickey's most significant move, one for which many Brooklyn fans never forgave him, was the July 31 trade of Camilli to the Giants. Along with Camilli, the Dodgers sent pitcher Johnny Allen to New York, receiving pitchers Bill Lohrman and Bill Sayles, and infielder Joe Orengo in return. Rickey called up Howie Schultz from the St. Paul Saints of the American Association to take over at first base. The 21-year-old Schultz was six-feet-six and a part-time professional basketball player.

The fans were upset at the loss of Camilli, a popular player and the team's premier slugger since 1938. "I don't think you could ever get a first baseman better than Camilli," said Whit Wyatt. "He was a great hitter and the best fielding first baseman I ever saw."[14] But at age 36, Camilli was no longer the player he had been just two years earlier; he was batting just .246 with six home runs. Rather than report to the Giants, Camilli chose to return to California to be a player-manager with the Pacific Coast League's Oakland Oaks. Years later, Rickey gave the reason for the trade. "Failure to pull the ball to his own field with customary power is the first sign a player is slipping. It shows his reflexes are beginning to get dull. Camilli wasn't pulling the ball."[15]

In 1984, Dodgers fans elected the popular first baseman to the Brooklyn Dodgers Hall of Fame. "I only wish I could receive the Dodgers' Fans Hall of Fame plaque in front of those great fans who supported me during my stay in Brooklyn," he said when he received the plaque. "All they cared about was their family, their job, and the Dodgers. And I don't know which was the most important."[16]

The Dodgers lost 15 of their 22 games with St. Louis in 1943, including one that featured the annual melee between the two rivals. Only they were not really rivals when the battle took place at Sportsman's Park on August 1. The Cardinals were in the midst of a four-game sweep over the Dodgers, a sweep that stretched their lead over Brooklyn to 13½ games.

In the sixth inning of the first game of a doubleheader, Walker Cooper of the Cardinals was out by five steps after hitting a routine ground ball. But as he crossed the bag, he stepped on first baseman Augie Galan's right foot. Mickey Owen, backing up the play, jumped on Cooper, who easily tossed him aside. Almost immediately, players from both teams gathered around. So did the umpires and some policemen, who restored order. The huge crowd let loose on the visitors, not just with boos but also with pop bottles.

The trigger for Cooper's seemingly unsolicited attack may have been Stan Musial, the previous batter, having to dodge four balls thrown at his head by Brooklyn pitcher Les Webber. Musial did not react physically, but his longtime teammate Max Lanier said it was the angriest he ever saw Stan get on the ball field.[17]

Leading the league at .352, Musial was by far the best player in the game now. Walker was as impressed as everyone else was with the young slugger. Before an August 16 home game against the Cardinals, Dixie, with tongue in cheek, said Musial should not be allowed to take batting practice. "A guy like Musial should never be allowed to hit before the game," Dixie said.[18]

Walker's best game of the season came at Ebbets Field on June 19, a time when the Dodgers were still in the race. He went 4-for-4 with two home runs, a double, and a single, while driving in three runs and scoring four in a 7–5 win against Philadelphia. Dixie also appeared in his first All-Star Game, hitting a run-scoring fly ball in a pinch-hitting role in the National League's 5–3 loss at Philadelphia. The NL's starting lineup included five Cardinals, highlighting St. Louis's domination this season: starting pitcher Mort Cooper, catcher Walker Cooper, shortstop Marty Marion, left fielder Stan Musial, and center fielder Harry Walker. The 1943 All-Star Game was the first time Dixie and Harry played on the same team as professionals.

Paul Scheffels of the *Brooklyn Daily Eagle* praised Walker's selection to the All-Star team. Scheffels called Dixie "something of a legend in baseball for his unbelievable popularity in Brooklyn." He noted that MacPhail had helped solidify Brooklynites' love for Walker by the way he treated him. "MacPhail blasted his outfielder at every turn," Scheffels wrote, "refused to even negotiate salary terms with him one spring [1941], and ordered him benched as long as possible that year."[19]

That summer, the newspaper *PM* did a feature story on Walker in which he described a typical day during the season when the team was at home. He woke up between nine and ten in the morning, Dixie said, ate a big breakfast, played with the kids for a while, and then headed to the ballpark. He would either drive or take the train, depending on the state of his gas-ration book. At the park, he would talk with the other players, have a glass of milk for lunch, and then go to work. On the way home, he would sometimes stop and

Brothers Mort and Walker Cooper and brothers Dixie and Harry Walker at the 1943 All-Star Game (National Baseball Hall of Fame Library, Cooperstown, New York).

check on things at his liquor store. He would eat a big dinner and stay home with Estelle, or several times a week they would go to the movies. He would usually be in bed by midnight.[20]

The low point of the Dodgers' 1943 season came on July 10 before a scheduled game with Pittsburgh at Ebbets Field. The previous day, Durocher had suspended pitcher Bobo Newsom for insubordination, a move that upset Arky Vaughan. In Vaughan's mind, Durocher had lied to the press in describing his reasons for the suspension. During pregame practice, Vaughan handed his uniform to Durocher. "Take this uniform and shove it right up your ass," he said, and threw the uniform in Leo's face. "If you would lie about Bobo," Vaughan said, "you would lie about me and everybody else. I'm not playing for you."[21]

Arky Vaughan was so upset at Durocher's suspension of pitcher Bobo Newsom, he told the manager, "Take this uniform and shove it right up your ass" (courtesy the Los Angeles Dodgers).

By now, the players were on the field going through their pregame preparations. Durocher ordered them all into the clubhouse for a meeting. After he spoke, Walker, the acknowledged leader of the team, responded first, siding with his teammate Vaughan against his manager. "I don't see why this boy should suffer, and if he's out, I guess I'm out too," said Dixie.[22] Others followed Walker's lead. Facing a full-blown strike, Durocher was reduced to calling for volunteers to play, but as game time neared only pitcher Curt Davis and catcher Bobby Bragan had agreed to take the field.

What made a terrible situation even worse, it was Kitchen Fat Day at Ebbets Field. In addition to the 8,748 paying customers, more than 4,000 women had been granted free admission for bringing a pound or more of household fats to the park. Also in the crowd were 930 servicemen and 441 blood donors. Ballplayers striking in the middle of a war would have been a public relations nightmare for the Brooklyn club.

Finally, Branch Rickey intervened and calmed everyone down. Durocher, worried about a possible forfeit, said he would take no disciplinary action against Vaughan and convinced his players to call off their strike. The still seething Dodgers took out their anger against the Pirates with ten runs in the first inning and ten more in the fourth to win, 23–6.

The following day, Durocher and Vaughan explained their positions. "I had a talk with Vaughan and he explained his reasons for turning in his uniform to me," Durocher said. "Now that I see those reasons, I can understand them. But I cannot tell you what Vaughan's reasons were for getting so mad and wanting to quit." Vaughan said, "I boiled over because I thought Newsom was wrongly treated, and I thought to myself the same thing could just as well happen to me. I could be the next victim."[23]

Rickey traded Newsom to the St. Louis Browns five days later, and even Durocher's job appeared to be in jeopardy. Meanwhile, angered by Walker's siding with Vaughan against him, Leo was threatening to trade Dixie. Durocher and Walker had had an up-and-down relationship in the past, one that would continue as long as the two men were with the Dodgers.

However, that was true of many of the men who played with and against Durocher. "I didn't agree with all the things he did and said, especially his treatment of us on the ball field, and I don't suppose anyone else did either," said Howie Schultz. "But I don't think anyone ran a ballgame, once that first pitch was thrown, any better than Leo did."[24]

The gentlemanly Larry French called him the best manager he ever played for. "He handled each man individually," said French. "I wouldn't care to have him in my living room, but if I owned a ball club I would want him running it."[25]

14

The 1944 National League Batting Champion

Dixie Walker had learned that in Brooklyn, as in no other city, the ball club was a civic institution. "I figure that a ballplayer owes the fans who pay to see him play more than just a chance to see him in the ball park," he said. "In Brooklyn, especially, there are a lot of important people who like to know the players a little more intimately than that. When the folks in this town are getting up any kind of an affair, the first people they think of inviting are the ballplayers."[1]

Aware of his position, Walker continued to use his celebrity and popularity to raise money for good causes throughout the 1943 season. Three days before the opener, he spoke at Jamaica High School in Queens in support of the school's restoring its baseball team, which had not played in five years. The school's principal had answered a threatened student strike by saying he would resume the sport if the students could raise $400 for the equipment needed to field a team. That was all the encouragement the students needed; they staged a big rally and invited Walker to attend. Dixie spoke to the group and donated the first ten dollars. By the time it was over, the rally had raised more than $700 and baseball was once again a varsity sport at Jamaica High School.[2]

Early in May, he was on stage at the Brooklyn Paramount Theater, where three blind men and a blind woman were being honored at the opening of Brooklyn Week for the Blind. Walker presented a $25 bond to the woman who demonstrated that blind people could operate complicated machinery.[3] Later that month, with the Cardinals in town, several team members were guests of Sperry at the Central Queens Branch of the YMCA. The workers had the opportunity to mingle with the players, who in turn watched as Dixie directed a gymnastics program followed by dancing and refreshments.

Above all, it was the war-related events that could always depend on

Walker's presence and participation. On July 2, he christened a pair of new submarine chasers at the Brooklyn Navy Yard, saying he "got more kick out of sending this ship down the ways than from any home run I ever made."[4]

This came shortly after the first of two days Commissioner Landis had designated as "War Charities Days." On those days, a portion of the proceeds for all major league games would go to the armed forces. The first was June 30, and Brooklyn drew the biggest crowd (26,893) and raised the most money ($32,134). The Dodgers rewarded the Ebbets Field faithful with a doubleheader sweep of the Cincinnati Reds that allowed them to temporarily slip by St. Louis into first place. Players from both teams participated in field events before the game, and Walker entertained the crown by singing "My Buddy" and "Mexicali Rose." Dixie then hit his team-leading fifth home run in the nightcap.[5]

By far the most lucrative money-raising effort for the war came on June 8. That afternoon the New York and Brooklyn chapters of the Baseball Writers' Association of America held a luncheon at the Waldorf-Astoria Hotel to raise money for the Baseball War Bond League. The league's bond campaign, directed by the United States Treasury and the baseball writers, hoped to raise a staggering one billion dollars. With Jimmy Walker, the former mayor of New York City, and announcers Red Barber and Mel Allen acting as the auctioneers, this one event raised $123,850,000 by "selling" players from the three New York teams in exchange for pledges of War Bond purchases.

Walker attracted the most spirited competition and drew the largest bid, $11,250,000 from the Brooklyn Club, a social organization. Arky Vaughan drew the second highest bid, $11,000,000, from Esso (the Standard Oil Company). Joe Gordon of the Yankees and Carl Hubbell of the Giants were the most sought-after players from their teams, drawing bids of $3,500,00 and $3,000,000 respectively. In all, the money bid for the Dodgers players far exceeded those for the Giants and the Yankees.

Mayor Walker provided the most amusing moment of the auction when he announced a bid of $350 million for one player. While correcting himself to say the bid was actually for $3.5 million, Walker, one of New York's legendary corrupt politicians, quipped, "I've made a mistake with people's money before."[6]

Later in the summer, on August 26, the three New York teams, playing as the War Bond All-Stars, defeated a team of Army players that included Enos Slaughter and Hank Greenberg, 5–2. The game attracted 38,000 fans to the Polo Grounds and earned $800,000,000 in War Bond pledges. Overall, the Dodgers, Yankees, and Giants sold enough War Bonds to account for almost 25 percent of New York City's War Bond goal.[7]

14. The 1944 National League Batting Champion

Those unfamiliar with Branch Rickey's admiration for Leo Durocher's managerial skills had not expected Leo to survive the dissension of the 1943 season. Expectations that Rickey would fire Durocher continued into the offseason. Among those rumored to replace him were two of his players: Walker and Billy Herman. Two others prominently mentioned as replacements were Burt Shotton and Ray Blades, both of whom had managed for Rickey in the Cardinals organization.

After Durocher was rehired, reporters questioned him about discord on the team. Leo responded that he got along with all of his players except one. Although Arky Vaughan had been the instigator of the team's revolt in July, the press assumed the "one" was Walker, whom Durocher had never forgiven for siding with Vaughan that afternoon. (The possibility that Walker could be his possible successor likely did nothing to strengthen their relationship.)

Walker was noncommittal as to whether he was the player Durocher had in mind. "Only he (Leo) knows who it is, and he isn't going to say," Dixie said. "It wouldn't be smart. He wouldn't go around saying 'I don't like Walker, or, I don't like Herman, or, I don't like Vaughan.'" Walker said he had always gotten along with Durocher and commended him for retaining his job. He also said he did not believe Leo disliked Vaughan. "I believe Leo admires Arky for his courage in getting right up and backing a teammate," he said. "Besides, Vaughan showed more courage than anybody I know last summer. Hustling like he did when he wasn't well."[8]

The mystery player that Durocher could not get along with made for an ongoing story in the New York newspapers during the offseason. After Walker signed his 1944 contract, a reporter asked Rickey if Dixie was the man Durocher was referring to when he said that he got along with all of his players except one. "I think I'll let Leo wriggle off the limb on his own," was his response. Rickey said that when he spoke to Walker at the end of the season, "Dixie spoke in high praise of Leo ... but seemed to feel that this year there were some changes in Durocher's method of handling the team that were not desirable." Walker was not speaking necessarily in criticism, just the facts as he saw them. Rickey also refused to say if Dixie's contract had a bonus clause as all his previous ones had.[9]

Durocher cleared up any mystery as to the player was referring to — not that there was much mystery — in his 1948 book, *The Dodgers and Me*. This is from UPI sportswriter Oscar Fraley's review of the book.

> Durocher said he feared Walker's popularity and called him a player "picked up out of the waiver ash can in 1939." Durocher said, "Dixie had charm, he could kiss babies, sign autographs, and talk at smokers and meetings of the Ladies Aid Society. He developed a tremendous personal following." Recalling the rebellion of 1943, Leo said that Walker had threatened to follow the walkout

of Vaughan but agreed to play only after Durocher convinced him that he hadn't suspended Vaughan. "As usual," Durocher said, "the players all went along with Walker." When Rickey fired and rehired Leo following the '43 season, Leo said he asked that Walker be traded. He admitted that as was speculated at the time, Walker was the man he referred to as the one player he couldn't get along with.

When a writer asked Walker how he came to be the "people's choice," Leo said he answered with a three-point program. "First, he answered every question the fans shouted at him when he was playing the outfield. Second, when they rode him he dropped his head and made no reply; when they applauded he tipped his hat. Third, he was generous with autographs."[10]

In October 1943, Walker resigned his position with Sperry and returned home to Birmingham. Then, in December, he embarked on a two-month USO tour that entertained American troops stationed in Alaska and the Aleutian Islands. Walker was part of a group led by Pirates manager Frankie Frisch that included three players who two months earlier had taken part in the World Series: Cardinals outfielders Stan Musial and Danny Litwhiler, and Yankees pitcher Hank Borowy.

Borowy won praise from the others for his work in washing dishes, making beds, and preparing breakfast for the troops, but the trip took its toll on him. While in the Aleutians, he lost his footing during a windstorm and fell on some rocks, injuring his knee. Overall, the tour was physically debilitating for Borowy, who reported to spring training weighing 160 pounds, 15 pounds below his normal playing weight.

Walker talked about the trip in a letter from Alaska that appeared in the *Brooklyn Daily Eagle* on New Year's Eve Day 1943.

> "Since arriving we have been quartered in a bungalow and everything has been perfect. We even have our own icebox and stove. I find that Litwhiler and Borowy are pretty fair bacon and egg cooks. Musial has turned out to be a fine dish washer. I have been given the job of mailman and, as is fitting, Frisch is foreman of the whole shebang. I might add he is still raising cane with the umpires, we four being umps at this time. He gets the crying towel out quite often, says he feels sure one of us is going to get lost before we get back home."[11]

The knee injury Walker suffered when he was with Detroit had kept him out of the Army originally. That injury had not gotten the newspaper play that some of his other injuries did, but the Tigers' team physician warned him at the time to be careful running the bases or he could end up permanently disabled. In early March 1944, Walker, 33 years old and the father of three, was temporarily reclassified 1-A. His draft board ordered him to report from his home in Birmingham to Ft. McClellan, Alabama, where he spent several days undergoing a thorough physical examination. The doctors took awhile in their evaluation before ruling his draft status should remain 4-F. Only this time, they decided it was Dixie's shoulder problem that should keep him from active service.[12]

Rickey, in his role as the general manager, was glad to have his best player stay with the team, but Rickey the American patriot wondered at the decision. Speaking to 300 department store employees of Frederick Loeser & Company on behalf of the Brooklyn 1944 Red Cross War Fund, he said, "I don't know why the army can't use him, for a man who can throw a baseball like that can surely carry a gun, even if he has got wires on his shoulders."[13]

Walker and catcher Mickey Owen were the only regulars left from the 1941 pennant winners when the Dodgers assembled at Bear Mountain in the spring of 1944. Billy Herman was in the Navy and Arky Vaughan had chosen to retire to his California cattle ranch. Gone too was pitcher Kirby Higbe, now in the Army. "All I can say is that we will have a large number of human beings at the training camp," said Rickey.[14] Brooklyn's roster, like those of all the other 15 big-league teams, consisted mostly of retreads and untried youngsters.

Walker, the senior member of the Dodgers, was generous in giving hitting tips to all the young players in camp. Durocher even tried him at third base in an attempt to fill the hole left by Vaughan's departure. Dixie had not played third since he was at Vicksburg 15 years earlier, and it showed. He played there in some exhibition games, but he looked uncomfortable and had trouble making accurate throws to first base.

The St. Louis Cardinals, with only one regular lost to the military—outfielder Harry Walker—went into the season as prohibitive favorites to win their third straight pennant. Billy Southworth's club did not disappoint. Led on offense by Musial, Walker Cooper, and Johnny Hopp, St. Louis won 105 games and finished 14½ games ahead of second-place Pittsburgh. Mort Cooper led the pitchers with 22 wins, Max Lanier and rookie Ted Wilks each won 17, and Harry Brecheen won 16. The Cardinals then defeated the American League's surprise winner, the St. Louis Browns, in an all–St. Louis World Series.

The Dodgers were never in the race; they finished in seventh place, 42 games behind St. Louis, and just a game-and-a-half ahead of the last-place Phillies. Their 16 wins in 22 games with Philadelphia was the major factor in keeping them out of the cellar.

Brooklyn lost 18 of their 22 games against both the pennant-winning Cardinals and the second-place Pirates. The Dodgers' only win of the season at Sportsman's Park was Curt Davis's dramatic 2–1 victory on May 11, which went down to the final play of the game. With two out in the bottom of ninth and Pepper Martin on first base, Ray Sanders hit a ball against the right-field screen. A relay from right fielder Paul Waner to shortstop Bill Hart to catcher Mickey Owen retired Martin to seal the victory.

The 40-year-old Davis led the team in wins, with ten, followed by Rube Melton — acquired from the Phillies in December 1942 — and Hal Gregg, each of whom won nine. All three lost more than they won. One Dodgers pitcher with a winning record was Ben Chapman, Walker's longtime pal who had last appeared in the major leagues with the White Sox in 1941. Chapman had been a player/manager for Richmond in the Piedmont League in 1942,

Walker and Augie Galan at Bear Mountain, New York, for spring training in 1944 (National Baseball Hall of Fame Library, Cooperstown, New York).

but after punching an umpire, he was banned from organized baseball for the entire 1943 season. On August 2, the Dodgers signed the volatile career outfielder as a pitcher, and he won five games with just three losses. Chapman vowed he was a "changed man when it comes to respecting the other fellow on the field."[15] His unconscionable treatment of Jackie Robinson three years later would prove how empty a vow that was.

If the signing of Chapman was indicative of the wartime recycling of former stars — Paul and Lloyd Waner were also with Brooklyn this season — the call-up of Tommy Brown from the minor leagues was indicative of the untried youth that teams used during the war. The Dodgers had invited the 16-year-old Brown to spring training after having seen him in a special tryout session in 1943. He started the season with Newport News in the Class B Piedmont League, before the Dodgers recalled him in August. Aware he was not ready for the big leagues, Brown asked Rickey to send him back to the minors. "I needed schooling and experience," he later said. "I wanted desperately to go back to the minors." Nevertheless, the Dodgers kept him until after the war. "Some players the war helped. They got to play. It hurt me 'cause I wasn't ready," Brown said.[16]

A sign of the kind of year Brooklyn would have in 1944 came early — in the season's tenth game. Before a crowd of more than 58,000 at the Polo Grounds, the Giants annihilated the Dodgers, 26–8, in the first game of a doubleheader. Twenty-six runs was the most scored against a Brooklyn club since a 28–5 loss at Chicago on August 25, 1891. First baseman Phil Weintraub led the way for New York with two doubles, a triple, a home run, and 11 runs batted in. Five Brooklyn pitchers combined to issue 17 walks, tying the National League's single-game record. "I had nothing but humpty-dumpties on my staff that year," Durocher later wrote.[17]

In late May, with the Dodgers in seventh place, Durocher tore into his club, accusing them of not hustling, while excepting Walker and French Bordagaray. The team, which had been six games under .500, began to improve. After a June 25 doubleheader sweep of the Phillies, which extended their winning streak to five games, the Dodgers record stood at 33–30. They were in a third-place tie with the Giants, albeit a distant 11 games behind St. Louis. But following two days off, they began a road trip that turned out to be the worst one in franchise history. Playing in Chicago, St. Louis, Cincinnati, Pittsburgh, and Boston, the Dodgers lost 16 straight — 14 before the All-Star break and two after — and went on to lose 61 of their last 91 games.

Overall, 1944 was a terrible year for Brooklyn fans. In addition to a seventh-place team, they had to endure a particularly hot summer. At a time when very few people had air conditioning in their homes or apartments, temperatures in New York City reached 90 degrees or higher on 37 different days. Then, on August 12, the borough lost one of its landmarks when Luna Park, a Coney Island attraction since 1903, burned to the ground.

Jokes and stereotypes about Brooklyn and Brooklynites, long the staple of comedians, intensified during the war years. Merely mentioning the word Brooklyn was sure to get a laugh, while the soldier, sailor, or marine from Brooklyn who just wanted to end the war so he could go home to see the Dodgers play was a stock character in almost every war film. Justly so, perhaps; Brooklyn had more men and women in the service than 39 of the then-48 States in the Union.[18]

The one highlight for Brooklyn baseball in 1944 was Dixie Walker. Dixie started strong with hits in 12 of the Dodgers' first 13 games and had a .442 batting average for April. Stan Musial, the defending batting champion, was at .447, and the two staged a terrific race all season. Walker had a fantastic May, going 46-for-106, to open up a big lead on Musial, .436 to .364. Then Musial caught fire in June, and by the end of the month had edged ahead of Dixie, .379 to .378.

It was during his early-season hot streak that Walker took a jab at Joe McCarthy, his former manager with the Yankees. McCarthy had a well-known dislike for Southern players, also for players who smoked a pipe, which he felt made them "too contented." McCarthy always claimed that he said this in jest, and that a player's performance was more important to him than his pipe smoking. He offered Lou Gehrig as his prime example, but other players confirmed that McCarthy did not like his players to smoke a pipe. "I don't know whether I'm a ballplayer or not, but I'm contented," said Walker, who had started smoking a pipe on the Aleutians tour the previous winter.[19]

About that same time, Cincinnati manager Bill McKechnie paid tribute to Dixie and his many skills as a player. "If I had Walker here with the Reds," he said, "I think I'd have a shot at the pennant." McKechnie did not even mention Walker's league-leading batting average, but instead stressed his overall qualities as a player. "Walker is a sound ball player," he said, "a good hitter, steady going, reliable, the kind that can help you win."[20]

Dixie had his only extended slump, an 0-for-21 drought, during the Dodgers' 16-game losing streak. He ended it on July 15, during loss number 15, with a ninth-inning home run off Boston's Nate Andrews. A keen student of hitting, Walker had once explained the cause of slumps to *New York Daily News* sportswriter Jimmy Powers. "If a man is hitting poorly, it's one of several things. Either he's striding too soon or too far, or is lunging at the ball and hitting with a stiff elbow instead of snapping and rolling his wrists with the proper timing. Or else he's bobbing his head and therefore taking his eye off the ball."[21]

More than a decade later, Bill Roeder recalled Walker as "a craftsman

14. The 1944 National League Batting Champion

with the bat," and "the best left-handed hit-and-run artist" he had ever seen. Opposing players paid Dixie a daily tribute that marked him as an extraordinary hitter. "When he took his turn in batting practice, all players in the vicinity of the cage stopped whatever they were doing and gazed admiringly at the enviable swing." In his days of covering baseball, Roeder wrote, he had seen that done only with DiMaggio, Williams, Musial, and Mantle.[22]

Musial led Dixie .363 to .353 on August 4, but Walker took over the batting lead for good on August 29 with three hits against Philadelphia. He eventually captured the batting title with a .357 mark, while Musial finished second at .347. The 23-year-old Musial, a zinc worker in his hometown of Donora, Pennsylvania, during the offseason, was gracious in surrendering his batting title to the 34-year-old Walker. "You can't take anything away from Dixie," he said. "He really hit from town to town with hardly a break in production. I'm just a rookie yet and have a lot of years left to shake it up. If it had to be anybody, I'm glad it was old Dixie. Time's running out on him."[23]

On October 1, the final day of the season, the fans in Section 8 (behind first base) held a Dixie Walker Day. To honor his winning the batting title, they presented Walker with war bonds and other gifts. Dixie made two nice running catches during the game, but after two hitless at-bats, he called it a season. Walker was the sixth different Dodger to win a batting title, joining Dan Brouthers (1892), Jake Daubert (1913 —14), Zack Wheat (1918), Lefty O'Doul (1932), and Pete Reiser (1941).

In addition to winning the batting title, Walker finished second in on-base percentage (.434), and fourth

"If it had to be anybody, I'm glad it was old Dixie," said runner-up Stan Musial after Dixie won the 1944 batting championship. "Time's running out on him" (National Baseball Hall of Fame Library, Cooperstown, New York).

in hits (191), total bases (283), doubles (37), and slugging percentage (.529). He went 2-for-4 as the National League's starting right fielder in the All-Star Game, finished third behind Marty Marion and Bill Nicholson in voting for the league's Most Valuable Player, and was named by *The Sporting News* to their All-Star Major League team.

In yet another honor, the National Fathers Day Committee named Walker "Father of the Year" in Sports. He was presented with the General Eisenhower Medal, which two young girls pinned on him before a June 13 game at the Polo Grounds.

One does not win a batting championship without having numerous multi-hit games during the season. Walker had 40 two-hit games, 16 three-hit games, and three four-hit games. In the third four-hit game, at home on September 2, Dixie hit for the cycle in an 8–4 win against the Giants that allowed the Dodgers to escape last place. He had a run-scoring single off Bill Voiselle in the first, a leadoff home run against Voiselle in the third, a triple off the right-center field screen against Ace Adams in the fourth, and a double off Adams in the sixth. Walker was the only National Leaguer to hit for the cycle in 1944.

Dodgers first base coach Red Corriden said, "Walker right now is the most deadly hitter I've seen, and I go back as far as Honus Wagner."[24] Corriden, who had also seen Ty Cobb, said, "Walker is one of the great hitters of all time and without a doubt the best left-handed hitter against southpaws I've ever seen."[25] Dixie had come a long way from his early days in Brooklyn when Durocher would often use a pinch-hitter for him against left-handers.

"I changed my stance slightly, and I used a little heavier bat," Walker said about his 1944 success. "I feel as though a lot of things may have helped, but I don't want to elaborate. I'd rather just take the batting average and leave well enough alone."[26] Later he said, "I honestly believe I wasn't a better hitter—I was just a luckier hitter. I stepped into the ball as I always did, but more drives were dropping safe. I used to think that I had to place my hits. No more, though. Now, I believe a batter should just meet the ball as hard as he can and let fly where it will. That system worked for me."[27]

At the 1946 All-Star Game in Boston, Walker talked about that heavier bat, the one he discovered at spring training at Bear Mountain in 1944. "It was 36 inches long and weighed 38 ounces, far bigger than any bat I had ever swung before. I had been considering experimenting with a longer bat against left-handed pitching, which I had been falling away from in 1943. So I decided to adopt that 36–38 for tests against southpaws. I have been using it exclusively ever since. It turned out to be just what I had needed. That bat I found at Bear Mountain was labeled 'Chick Hafey Model.'"[28]

Some baseball historians have discounted Dixie Walker's .357 batting average in 1944 by attributing it to the watered-down pitching that year. Yet it is important to remember that the second-place finisher was Stan Musial, who did not hit .500, or even .400 against the presumably weaker pitching of 1944. He hit .347, ten points below Walker.

Moreover, there were many other legitimate major leaguers in the National League in 1944. In addition to the two top MVP finishers, Marion and Nicholson, were Joe Medwick, Mel Ott, Tommy Holmes, Johnny Hopp, and Phil Cavarretta. And the top two batting leaders in the American League were future Hall of Famers Lou Boudreau and Bobby Doerr, who batted .327 and .325 respectively, well below Walker's mark. Author David Jordan, who has studied wartime baseball extensively, concluded, "it was a serious game played by serious professional ballplayers."[29] Additionally, Walker's wartime batting average of .313 (1942–45) was not that far above the .303 average he maintained for all other years.

15

"The most beloved baseball player of recent years"

As the 1944 season wound down, the Special Services Division of the Army announced that in November, five groups totaling 23 players, managers, umpires, and writers would visit war theaters as part of a USO-sponsored program. Walker had been part of a group that visited servicemen in Alaska and the Aleutian Islands the year before; nevertheless, he volunteered to leave home again and take part in this year's tour. His traveling companions this time were Paul Waner and Luke Sewell. The Yankees had signed Waner in September following his release by the Dodgers. Sewell, the man who had made that famous double tag at the plate on Walker and Lou Gehrig back in 1933, was the manager of the American League champion St. Louis Browns.

Dixie's announcement that he would again be going overseas to entertain the troops triggered an editorial tribute to him in the *Brooklyn Daily Eagle*. Entitled "The People's Cherce," the *Eagle* wrote: "On this occasion as last year, the most popular player figures to be 'The People's Cherce,' Brooklyn's Dixie Walker." With Walker on the verge of winning the batting championship, the *Eagle* concluded that "Dixie bids fair to become the most beloved baseball player of recent years."[1]

Walker, Waner, and Sewell traveled 35,000 miles around Asia, visiting army camps in India, Burma, and China. The trip lasted eight weeks before the men landed in Miami on January 15. Three weeks later, Walker and Bill McKechnie were the guests of honor at the 15th annual dinner of the New York chapter of the Baseball Writers' Association of America. McKechnie had won the Bill Slocum Memorial award for long and meritorious service to the game, while Walker had won the Player of the Year award for 1944, the first Dodger to win that award. Larry MacPhail and war correspondent Quentin Reynolds were the main speakers at the dinner, held at the Hotel Astor in Manhattan. MacPhail and Reynolds both used the occasion to argue against

15. "The most beloved baseball player of recent years"   135

the recent edict issued by the War Mobilization Board's Director James F. Byrnes that baseball players should find work to aid the war effort.

Walker spoke mostly of his recent journey to the Pacific war zone. He recalled a poignant moment when he was leaving an airfield the troops had built in the jungles of Burma.

> I stood there talking to Buddy Lewis. Finally, Buddy said that he'd have to get back to quarters. And so he picked up his lunchbox, or maybe it was a tool kit, and started back on the road through the jungle. I watched him until he was out of sight, and he never looked back.
>
> A lot of things happened on our USO trip that I'll remember for the rest of my life, but somehow that moment seems to have made the biggest impression on me. I had known Lewis only casually, just from playing against him in the American League. But all of a sudden I felt very close to him and unaccountably lonely as he walked away. It was like having a brother on the other side of the world.[2]

Lewis, a fine infielder for Washington, had not played since the 1941 season. He was an Air Force lieutenant who had recently received the Distinguished Flying Cross.

Late in the 1945 season, Walker would get to meet Major General Claire Chennault, the head of the famous Flying Tigers that helped China in their war against Japan. Chennault sat behind the Dodgers dugout at Ebbets Field for the September 19 game with the Giants. He recalled that Walker, Sewell, and Waner had played a game with his team in China.[3]

Walker, who made $14,000 in 1944, was asking for $23,000 in 1945. With Rickey supposedly offering $17,000, Dixie was hoping that they could split the difference and agree on $20,000. He had even tried asking for $21,000 in war bonds, which was fine with Rickey. That would have cost the club only $15,000 and it would be ten years before those bonds would be worth $21,000. However, Rickey balked when he discovered that Walker wanted Rickey to *purchase the bonds for $21,000.*

After some more back-and-forth negotiating between the two men, Walker ended his holdout and signed on March 30 for $18,000. Dixie then told the Dodgers he would be late in reporting to spring training because his house needed a new coat of paint, the same excuse he had used in 1944. Rickey did not seem particularly bothered by his salary dealings with Walker or with Dixie's late arrival to training camp. Earlier in the negotiations, he had said. "Walker and I are not at loggerheads. We've had some discussions. He could play ball tomorrow. He's in excellent shape. Let him paint his house for another ten days. He's a star, and I've never had any real trouble signing a star since I've been in baseball. Dixie's really the easiest fellow in the world to handle."[4]

Walker's later memory of his 1945 contract negotiations with Rickey was less convivial. After signing to manage the Atlanta Crackers in 1950, he said, "One year after I led the league in hitting, with .357, Rickey wrote me a long letter explaining that I really wasn't a good player and actually should be happy just to be in the big leagues."[5]

Late in spring training, the Dodgers sold Walker's pal Whit Wyatt to the Phillies. Wyatt had been the ace of the pitching staff in 1941; he continued to have good years in 1942 and 1943, but appeared in only nine games in 1944, with a 2–6 record. Wyatt's departure left only Walker, Augie Galan, Mickey Owen, and Curt Davis from the 1941 pennant winners, and Owen would enter the Navy early in the '45 season.

But another of Dixie's old friends, Ben Chapman, was back. Though Chapman was now a pitcher, he was helping his young roommate Tommy Brown and some of the other young players with their hitting. Chapman was not only a future big-league manager, but at this point in his career had more major-league hits (1,939) than anyone on the Brooklyn club, including Walker.

On August 20, the 17-year-old Brown blasted a pitch from Pittsburgh's Preacher Roe into the upper deck at Ebbets Field to become the youngest player to hit a major league home run. However, his mentor Chapman was long gone, having been traded to Philadelphia for catcher Johnny Peacock on June 15. Two weeks after the trade, Chapman replaced Fred Fitzsimmons as manager of the Phillies.

Walker reported to camp the first week in April, after completing his painting chores in Birmingham. He appeared to be in excellent shape, noting that when he got on the scale it read 182½ pounds, the same weight he was on his first day of camp the year before. Still, Dixie refused to predict he would win another batting title, something no one had done in the National League since Rogers Hornsby won six straight in the 1920s. With Stan Musial gone, he thought his biggest rival would be teammate Augie Galan, but said that the relatively unknown Frank Colman of the Pirates was a dark horse contender.[6]

With even more players lost to the military, including Musial, talent for the 1945 season was at an all-time low. "With most rosters as full of unknown names as YMCA hotel registers, everybody agreed that the caliber of big-league 1945 baseball would be somewhere between AA and A — but it would still be baseball,' wrote *Time* magazine. The Cardinals, they thought, were the favorites to win again, even without Musial, with the major opposition coming from the Cubs and the Pirates. "The Brooklyn Dodgers," wrote *Time*, "will try to get along on fanatical fan-enthusiasm and the league-leading (.357) bat of Dixie ('Pride of Flatbush') Walker."[7]

All big league teams during World War II, and especially in 1945, were a mixture of legitimate major leaguers, players past their prime, and youngsters not ready for the big league stage. Walker, veteran Goody Rosen, and 25-year-old Luis Olmo gave the Dodgers an outfield that was among the most productive in baseball that year. Second baseman Eddie Stanky, acquired in a June 1944, trade with the Cubs, batted just .258, but his 148 walks set a new National League record.

Augie Galan played first base, third base, and the outfield and had one of his finest seasons: a .307 batting average and 92 runs batted in. Galan had been a switch-hitter since making his big league debut with the Cubs in 1934, but beginning in 1943, he batted only left-handed. Charlie Grimm, his manager in Chicago, said, "Augie was almost — just almost — a complete ballplayer. He could run, he could hit, a good outfielder, and he could throw good. But he just wasn't quite the guy that you could say has got it all."[8]

Galan shared the first base position with right-handed hitting Howie Schultz, who spent most of the season in the minors, and Ed Stevens, a 20-year-old left-handed hitting rookie. Stevens was at Montreal and leading the

Babe Herman. At age 42, and after being out of the big leagues since 1937, Brooklyn's legendary Babe Herman made 39 plate appearances for the war-depleted Dodgers in 1945. Herman is flanked by coach Charlie Dressen and Walker (National Baseball Hall of Fame Library, Cooperstown, New York).

International League in home runs and runs batted in when the Dodgers called him up in August. But Stevens refused to go. "I didn't want to play for Leo Durocher," he said in a 1981 interview. "I didn't like the treatment I had gotten from him in spring training."[9] The Dodgers dispatched Branch Rickey, Jr., to get Stevens, but he still refused to come to Brooklyn. Eventually he did report and batted .274 with 29 RBIs in 55 games.

Second-year man Hal Gregg led the pitchers with an 18–13 record, assisted by veteran Curt Davis, retread Tom Seats, and rookie Vic Lombardi, each of whom had ten wins. Rookie Cy Buker and 21-year-old Clyde King each appeared in 42 games, almost all in relief. After Owen left for the Navy, Mike Sandlock, Fats Dantonio, and Johnny Peacock shared the catching duties. Even 43-year-old Clyde Sukeforth, who had not played in a major-league game since 1934, caught some games. On April 24, Sukeforth got two singles and a double off Boston's Jim Tobin.

Thirty-five-year-old third baseman Frenchy Bordagaray and 22-year-old shortstop Eddie Basinski made up the left side of the Brooklyn infield. Dodgers fans could be forgiven for dreaming of the day when Cookie Lavagetto and Pee Wee Reese would again be manning those positions. Bordagaray, and more so Basinski, are now mostly forgotten, but for many Brooklynites they symbolized the replacement players of the war years. "No one remembers Eddie Basinski," said Howie Schultz, his former teammate. "Eddie could really play the violin. As a kid he had played in the Buffalo Symphony, and after he left the Dodgers, he ended up playing for the Seattle Symphony."[10]

Brooklyn surprised by winning 87 games and finishing third, 11 games behind the pennant-winning Cubs. Walker hit an even .300, joining left fielder Olmo (.313), and center fielder Rosen (.325) to give the Dodgers an all-.300 hitting outfield, as he had done with the 1937 White Sox and the 1941 Dodgers.

Dixie had gotten off to the worst start of his career at the plate, getting just seven hits in his first 39 at-bats. He broke out of his slump with three singles, three doubles, three walks, and three RBI in a May 5 doubleheader at Philadelphia. Brooklyn's sweep that day launched them on an 11-game winning streak in which Walker batted .452, with six doubles, two triples, and ten runs batted in.

Walker was again selected to the All-Star team, but the 1945 All-Star Game never was played. Looking for ways to keep their full season schedules intact, the owners decided to cancel the game, which had been set for July 10 at Boston's Fenway Park. According to calculations made by National League president Ford Frick, travel by players, press, and various league and club officials to Boston would have totaled approximately 500,000 passenger miles.

15. "The most beloved baseball player of recent years"

Canceling the game would allow the teams to apply those miles to regular-season travel.

Dixie finished ninth in the MVP voting, and while he did not repeat as batting champion — Phil Cavarretta of Chicago led with a .355 mark — he did win the National League's RBI title with 124. (Walker is the last man to lead both leagues in RBIs while hitting fewer than ten home runs.) Tommy Holmes of Boston batted .352 to finish second to Cavarretta; Holmes was also second in runs batted in with 117. During the '45 season, the Brooklyn native made the first serious challenge to Joe DiMaggio's four-year-old record consecutive-games hitting streak. Holmes's streak ended at 37 games, 19 short of DiMaggio's mark; it was, however, the longest in the NL since another Brooklyn native, Willie Keeler, had a 44-game streak for the 1897 Baltimore Orioles.

Olmo and Chicago's Andy Pafko tied for third in RBIs with 110. Seven of Olmo's runs batted in came on May 18 in a 15–12 victory over the Cubs when he hit a triple and a home run, each with the bases loaded. Walker's single-game high was six in the second game of a doubleheader at home against the Giants on August 25. Dixie also had two five-RBI games, and they came two days apart.

Several National Leaguers, including Walker, had claimed Chicago's Wrigley Field was the league's most difficult park for batters. But Dixie had no difficulty in the second game of a doubleheader at Wrigley on July 18, smashing a two-run single off Lon Warneke and a three-run double off Bob Chipman. Two days later, he had five more runs batted in against the Cubs in their home park.

In that July 20 game, Chipman hit Walker in the knee with a pitch. Dixie limped to first but then later barged into shortstop Lennie Merullo at second. There were no repercussions, but Walker and Merullo would renew their feud a year later. Bad blood had existed between the Dodgers and the Cubs all season, mostly about pitchers hitting batters. Cavarretta was hit twice, once in the face, and Olmo and Rosen were also hit. The animosity between the clubs would renew itself in 1946.

Dixie's home run total dropped from 13 in 1944 to eight this season. Yet several helped win games, and none more so than home run number seven, against Cincinnati on August 8. It was the game's only run, and came in the bottom of the fourth inning off Vern Kennedy, who, with Walker, had been traded from the White Sox to the Tigers back in December 1937. The 1–0 win was Hal Gregg's first big league shutout; at 15–6, Gregg had developed into one of the top pitchers in the league.

Moreover, this was no ordinary home run. Walker's drive stuck in the right field screen at Ebbets Field, allowing him to circle the bases while Reds right fielder Al Libke waited for the ball to come down. But it remained enmeshed in the screen until Dixie went out to right field in the top of the fifth and dislodged it with a thrown ball. He caught his home run ball as it came down, eliciting cheers from the fans. Dixie Walker thus became the answer to the trivia question "Who is the only player to catch his own home run?" (Robert Ripley's "Believe it or Not" erroneously listed this as having taken place in 1946, rather than 1945.)

With the Dodgers still in the race as they prepared to open an important late-July series in St. Louis, sportswriter Bill Roeder recalled how often they had depended on Walker in big games. "Walker began exploding tough ball games for the Dodgers the day he was waived into Ebbets Field from Detroit in 1939. He's still at it, and he goes along so effortlessly it doesn't seem logical he will ever stop. It's got so you automatically expect big things from Dixie any time the big game or the inning materializes."[11]

One of those big hits Walker always seemed to get, particularly against the Giants, would have repercussions for the Dodgers for the next decade. In the first game of a September 2 doubleheader against New York, Dixie's 11th-inning single drove in the winning run. The hit came against a rookie pitcher named Sal Maglie, working in relief. "For some reason that made me resent the Dodgers," Maglie later said.[12] That resentment would manifest itself in the many bitter clashes Maglie and the Dodgers would engage in over the years.

In early September, the Dodgers played one of the more raucous series in their long and tumultuous history. *Time* magazine called the four-game set at Forbes Field a battle between "the rowdy Pittsburgh Pirates and the noisy Brooklyn Dodgers."[13] During the series, umpires Tom Dunn and George Barr ejected both managers, Leo Durocher and Frankie Frisch, along with Bob Elliott of the Pirates and Walker, Olmo, Galan, and Stanky of the Dodgers. All except Walker received fines of between $50 and $100 from NL president Frick. Dunn had tossed Dixie in the third game for flinging his glove in the air in disgust, the most innocuous transgression of the four games.

Walker and Dunn had clashed once before during the season. At Ebbets Field on August 17, Dixie grounded out for the final out of a 4–3 loss to the Cubs. Insisting he was safe, he and Durocher argued with Dunn, the first base umpire, as fans came out of the stands to join in. With the game over, there were no ejections.

Although Walker escaped the fine in Pittsburgh in September, he had not gotten off so easy earlier in the season. In a game against the Braves at Ebbets Field on the night of June 23, the Dodgers pushed across four runs in the eighth inning to take a 14–10 lead. The first three runs scored on Galan's bases-loaded triple. As the second runner, Eddie Stanky, was coming home,

Braves pitcher Ewald Pyle, backing up the plate, reached out his foot and tried to trip Stanky. Walker, the on-deck hitter, rushed at Pyle, threw him to the ground and started pummeling him.

The umpires threw both men out of the game, and the next day Walker received a telegram from Frick informing him he had been fined $75. Walker had no regrets for what he had done. "In all my years in baseball I never saw anything like it," he said referring to what had set him off. "I saw Pyle stick out his foot to send Stanky sprawling. I could have killed him."[14]

Leo Durocher's club dealt a serious blow to their old rivals, the Cardinals, winning a twi-night doubleheader on September 14. The two losses combined with a split by the Cubs upped Chicago's lead to 3½ games. The first-place Cubs were next for the Dodgers, who left St. Louis by train the following morning heading for Chicago. In Manhattan, Illinois, about 40 miles southwest of Chicago, their train was hit by an oil truck, causing a fiery explosion, killing the engineer, and severely burning the truck driver. The fire spread to a lumberyard and a nearby hotel before it was finally extinguished. All of the Dodger players were shaken up, but none was seriously hurt. Olmo, with a bruised right arm, and coach Charlie Dressen, with a bruised knee, suffered the only visible injuries. Eight players, including Walker, Galan, Rosen and Stanky, escaped the accident entirely, having left St. Louis the night before.[15]

Shortly after the season ended, Walker formed a team of major league players, including Ben Chapman, Marty Marion, and Red Sox rookie pitching sensation Dave Ferriss, and took it barnstorming in the South. The war was over and everyone in baseball was looking to a return to normalcy in 1946. But an event in Montreal on October 23, 1945, made it a certainty that in one very significant way baseball would never return to what once had been considered normal. Branch Rickey's signing of Negro Leaguer Jackie Robinson, a former UCLA football and basketball star, to play for Brooklyn's top farm team, the International League Montreal Royals, signaled the end of racial segregation in Organized Baseball was coming.

While no laws existed specifically barring black players, that none had appeared in Organized Baseball since Fleetwood Walker in 1884 was hardly a coincidence.[16] Commissioner Landis had been no fan of baseball integration, but Landis had died in November 1944. His replacement was Albert "Happy" Chandler, a former governor and United States senator from Kentucky. Chandler was in full support of Robinson's signing. "I'm for the Four Freedoms," he said. "If a black boy can make it in Okinawa and Guadalcanal, hell, he can make it in baseball ... I don't believe in barring Negroes from baseball just because they are Negroes."[17]

Not everyone directly connected to baseball felt the same as Chandler.

Reactions to Robinson were decidedly mixed. Fay Young of the *Chicago Defender* wrote a column detailing some of those reactions.

Among those in favor was Hector Racine, president of the Montreal club, whose sentiments echoed those of Chandler. "Negroes fought alongside of whites, and shared foxhole dangers," argued Racine. "They should get a fair trial in baseball."[18] Giants president Horace Stoneham approved Rickey's action and said his own club would now begin scouting Negro players. Alabama-born Rudy York, first baseman for the World Series champion Detroit Tigers, also applauded the move. "I wish Robinson all the luck in the world and hope he makes good," said York, who was part Cherokee Indian.[19]

Pittsburgh Pirates president Bill Benswanger was noncommittal. "It is an affair of the Brooklyn and Montreal clubs whom they sign, whether white or colored," Benswanger said.[20] Three other executives had no comment on the signing of Robinson: manager Connie Mack of the Philadelphia Athletics, owner Powell Crosley of the Cincinnati Reds, and Jack Zeller, general manager of the Tigers.

Opposition to Robinson came from players and front office personnel alike. Young quoted Dixie Walker as saying, "As long as he isn't with the Brooklyn club I'm not worried."[21] Pirates coach Spud Davis and Reds pitcher Elmer Riddle had similar reactions. Signing Negroes is fine with them, they said, as long as they were not with their teams. Others were much more vocal in their opposition. Rogers Hornsby, inducted into baseball's Hall of Fame three years earlier, said that Negro players ought to stay in their own league where they belonged.

Larry MacPhail, now a co-owner of the Yankees, received income when Negro League teams played at Yankee Stadium, income he thought he would lose if the major leagues signed players from the black leagues. MacPhail was no different from the majority of club owners, including Mack, who feared bringing black players into Organized Baseball would hurt them financially. "When Rickey brought in that colored boy, he depressed the value of every franchise in the majors," said MacPhail. "Our fans

Branch Rickey. The other owners opposed Rickey's signing of Jackie Robinson. The signing changed baseball forever (courtesy the Los Angeles Dodgers).

don't want to watch colored baseball. We ought to sue Rickey's self-righteous ass."[22]

Red Sox scout George Digby expressed the opinion of many in the game. "Personally I think it is the worst thing that can happen in organized baseball. I think a lot of southern boys will refuse to compete with Negroes in baseball."[23] Branch Rickey, Jr., agreed there would be some opposition, but he was convinced that the players would eventually come around. "The signing of Robinson might cost the Brooklyn club some prejudiced players," he said, "but even if they quit, they'll be back after a year or two in the cotton mills."

Years later, Shirley Povich of the *Washington Post* called the statement by Rickey Jr. the most unfortunate one of the times. It was a slanderous and provincial remark that set off a wave of condemnation. The most pointed response came in a letter to Branch Rickey, Sr., from Bill Werber, a Duke University graduate, an 11-year big leaguer, and a successful businessman. Werber wrote: "A large segment of the ball players who have in the past and who are presently contributing to the continued success of major league baseball are of Southern ancestry or actually lived in the South. Your effort to force them to accept socially and to play with a Negro, or Negroes, is highly distasteful.

"You are, in fact, for some unaccountable reasons, discriminating against the majority. The attitude that your son has assumed is certainly not conducive to the morale of your own organization or baseball in general. His reference to ball players from the South is a definite insult to every Southern boy."[24]

16

The War Ends and the Battle with the Cardinals Resumes

The war's end lifted the travel restrictions imposed on major league baseball, allowing the teams to return to Florida or California for spring training in 1946. At each of the training sites, the camps were overflowing with players, making the competition for roster spots extremely intense. A reporter from *Time* magazine described the competition as a battle between three groups: a crop of rookies just blooming when draft boards nipped them; big-name stars, back after a year or two in service and looking for their old spots; and the wartime stand-ins who refused to believe all the bad things said about them.[1]

Walker had staged his usual holdout before signing the first week in March. Rather than "painting his house this spring," Dixie had been busy with a new hardware and general merchandise store he was opening near Birmingham in Hueytown, Alabama. As usual, negotiating money matters with Branch Rickey had been difficult. Rickey had gone so far as to say he was not necessarily impressed that Walker had led the league in RBIs in 1945. "There are too many dependent factors in runs batted in which are out of the control of you hitters," Rickey had said. "You probably never considered the on-base average of the men ahead of you or their speed."[2] Rickey was probably right, but then not many people in baseball, on the field or off, were thinking about on-base average in 1946.

When Walker arrived at the Dodgers' training camp in Daytona Beach, Florida, he found yet another group of players vying for spots on the roster. Rickey had signed lots of young talent during the war years, and now he was ready to have them step in and contribute. With the Dodgers committed to a youth movement, there did not seem to be much room for the 35-year-old Walker. "Brooklyn's Dixie Walker, the pride of Flatbush, was no cinch to be a regular," wrote *Time*."[3]

16. The War Ends and the Battle with the Cardinals Resumes

So, despite Walker's batting title in 1944 and his runs batted in title in 1945, Leo Durocher had all but ceded his old spot in right field to Gene Hermanski, a left-handed hitter with power. The 25-year-old Hermanski was one of the young men Rickey had signed during the war; he had appeared briefly for the Dodgers in 1943. "Walker can't play right field on my ball club," Leo told the press during spring training. "He can't beat Hermanski out now."[4]

With Durocher committed to Hermanski as his right fielder, Walker announced that he would play anywhere the team wanted him. "If they want me to play left field, that's where I'll play," he said. "I was originally a center fielder, but I don't think they'll consider me there even if Reiser is moved to third base, because I'm not as fast as I used to be." Walker said he thought he could serve the club best in right field. "I say this," he explained, "because I've played it most and because I've been able to study the wall in Ebbets Field, toughest right field in the league."[5]

Walker played in his first exhibition game on Sunday, March 17, at Daytona Beach. The Dodgers were playing the Montreal farm club, a team that included Jackie Robinson at second base. This was Robinson's first game against the parent team, and if anyone feared there might be racial problems, they were pleasantly surprised. There were none on the field and there were none in the stands, which were segregated by local law.

"The precedent-setting appearance of a Negro in a baseball game with whites here this afternoon seemingly was taken in stride by a majority of the 4,000 spectators," wrote Roscoe McGowen in the *New York Times*.[6] Walker's first-inning bases-loaded triple was the big blow in Brooklyn's 7–2 victory. Robinson went 0-for-3 but stole a base and scored a run. More than a thousand fans sitting in the Jim Crow section in right field cheered Jackie's every move.

Dixie Walker was not the only veteran Brooklyn star his manager was disparaging this spring. Durocher had also warned Pete Reiser that if he continued to hold out he might lose his job to a youngster named Marv Rackley. Rackley "looks like another Paul Waner — stands at the plate just like Paul — and he's as fast as George Stirnweiss," claimed Leo.[7] Stirnweiss was widely considered among the fastest men in the game. The Yankees' second baseman had led the American League in stolen bases in 1944, with 55, and in 1945, with 33.

Throughout spring training, Durocher continued to search for youth and speed in the outfield, using veterans Walker, Augie Galan, and the soon-to-be-gone Goody Rosen mostly as pinch hitters.[8] When the Dodgers opened the season in Boston, the starting outfield consisted of three rookies: Dick Whitman in left, Carl Furillo in center, and Hermanski in right. It was the first time Walker had not been in the opening-day lineup since 1940. He did pinch-hit in the ninth for Pee Wee Reese, Pee Wee's first game in a Dodgers uniform in nearly four years.

Four days later, on April 20, Kirby Higbe made his first start in Brooklyn since 1943. The Dodgers beat the Giants, 9–8, with another prewar stalwart, Hugh Casey, getting the win in relief. In a pregame ceremony, the fans rose and cheered as Brigadier General Dominick Sabin, on behalf of the War Department, presented Walker and several others an Asiatic-Pacific campaign ribbon for their USO work entertaining the troops in the China-India-Burma Theater. Walker then capped his day with an eighth-inning pinch-hit home run onto Bedford Avenue that tied the score at 8–8.

After three years of "making do," the fans were thrilled to have prewar stars like Casey, Higbe, Reiser, Reese, and Cookie Lavagetto back in the lineup. The early postwar years were a wonderful time to live in Brooklyn, to be a Dodgers fan, and to be able to spend time at Ebbets Field.

Author Wilfrid Sheed wrote of the joy Brooklynites found in living there and going to that wonderful old park. "Just walking from the subway to the ballpark past the Botanical Gardens reminded one of what an elegant, mellow old city Brooklyn was in those days. The jokes which made it sound like a saloon attached to a bowling alley in no way prepared you for the range and variety of the architecture or the populace."[9]

Hermanski played poorly in the first four games; he had only two hits and committed two errors in right field. His shaky start, combined with Walker's pinch-hit home run, led the hunch-playing Durocher to start Dixie against the Giants the next day. Walker responded by making a sensational one-handed catch against the right-field wall of an eighth-inning drive by Mickey Witek. The fans, pleased to have their old favorite back in the place they considered rightfully his, loudly applauded the catch. Dixie's grab preserved rookie left-hander Joe Hatten's 2–1 win, Hatten's first big-league victory.

Cookie Lavagetto. Dodgers fans were happy to have Lavagetto and other prewar stars back in the lineup in 1946 (courtesy the Los Angeles Dodgers).

16. The War Ends and the Battle with the Cardinals Resumes 147

"When that ball left the bat," said Durocher, "I was thankful we had Walker out there. He made a great catch." Nevertheless, Durocher said he planned to return Hermanski to right field and Walker to the bench as soon as Hermanski built up his confidence.[10] Evidently Hermanski never did build up his confidence, as Walker played right field in all but one game the rest of the season.

Pitcher Ed Head, who had missed the 1945 season because of military service, returned to action in a spectacular way on April 23. Head threw a no-hitter, beating Boston, 5–0, before 26,787 at Ebbets Field. Head's outstanding performance was no surprise to Walker. Dixie had been impressed with Head's ability ever since the Dodgers faced him in a July 1940, exhibition game, when Head was with Elmira. "He has more stuff than any pitcher I've seen this year," Walker said. "His curve dropped like something rolling off a table and his fast ball sailed. So far as I was concerned, the ball might just as well have disappeared."[11]

Dixie continued to encourage Head after he joined the Dodgers. The young pitcher was trying to develop a slider, similar to the one Whit Wyatt threw. He asked the Dodgers batters for their reaction, and Walker had given him the most positive advice. "Pretty good, but stay with it and you'll make it better," he told Head. "And that's all you need — a pitch with some quality of deception to go with your other stuff. You've got everything else."[12]

After losing the opener to the Braves, the Dodgers won eight in a row. The streak led Durocher to predict his team would be in the thick of the race not only this season, but would dominate the National League for a decade. "After this year," he boasted, "Brooklyn will win five of the next ten pennants."[13] (They would actually win six and come agonizingly close in two other years. The Dodgers won in 1947, '49, '52, '53, '55, and '56.)

Brooklyn's 8–1 record had them in first place, but their old antagonists, the Cardinals, were right behind at 8–2. Management had traded away the Cooper bothers — pitcher Mort and catcher Walker — but for the most part, St. Louis had all their best players back, making them solid favorites to win another pennant. The Cardinals' major change had been at the top, where Billy Southworth had left to take over the Braves. Eddie Dyer, long a manager in the St. Louis farm system, was now leading the big club.

Walker had gone hitless in his first start, but then went on a tear, compiling a seven-game hitting streak in which he batted .519 (14-for-27). Now installed as the everyday right fielder and cleanup hitter, Dixie had an even longer streak, batting safely in 16 consecutive games from May 11 through June 2. Pirates left-hander Fritz Ostermueller stopped the streak in the Dodgers' first-game loss at Pittsburgh on June 4, but Dixie came back with four hits in the second game.

In only five of the 16 games was Walker limited to one hit, including May 22 when his 13th-inning double off Johnny Schmitz gave Brooklyn a 2–1 win over the Cubs. Dixie's hit sent the Ebbets Field crowd home happy, but the real fireworks had occurred three innings earlier. The longstanding animosity between the Brooklyn and Chicago clubs had erupted in the top half of the tenth inning. In an effort to break up a possible double play, Cubs shortstop Lennie Merullo slid into Brooklyn second baseman Eddie Stanky with his spikes high.

Merullo and Stanky had feuded when they were Cubs teammate in 1943–44. Now they began swinging at each other, precipitating a brawl between the two teams. Reese and umpire Dusty Boggess broke up the fight; however, Reese allegedly punched Merullo, and Cubs pitcher Claude Passeau ripped off Leo Durocher's jersey before peace was restored.

The peace lasted until batting practice the next day. According to Cubs historian Art Ahrens, Merullo walked into the batting cage to show Reese his black eye. He reportedly told Pee Wee that if he wanted to hit him again to do it while he was looking so that he could break Reese's neck. Ahrens says Walker sneaked up from behind Merullo, hit him on the back of the head, and then headed for the Dodgers dugout. Merullo charged after Walker, tripped him to the ground, and knocked out one tooth while breaking another in half.[14]

Cubs outfielder Peanuts Lowrey remembered that after Walker hit Merullo, Phil Cavarretta went after Dixie, but Cubs pitcher Paul Erickson got there first. Erickson, who was six feet two and weighed 200 pounds, dragged Walker over to a clear patch of ground, and Merullo followed. "Players from both clubs made a big circle around Merullo and Walker," Lowrey remembered. "We all spread out our arms and touched them to the next guy's shoulders, and pretty quickly we had ourselves a nice ring and a nice little fight to watch. I couldn't say who won the fight," Lowrey continued, "but they were both going at it real good. They'd both be on the ground and then up and down again, and all the time swinging and cuffing or wrestling. A little park cop broke through the ring but Clyde McCullough grabbed him and tossed him right out again. Finally a whole bunch of cops broke through and that was it."[15]

While admitting he struck the first blow, Walker denied hitting Merullo from behind and then running away. "After I hit him, Merullo attacked me," he said. "It was a regular football tackle and it knocked me down and took all the breath out of me. Then he started pummeling me, using his knee and his fists."[16]

The game that followed the fight resulted in another 2–1 Brooklyn win, this time in 11 innings. No more on-field tussles occurred, but there was much arguing and sniping; Durocher and four of his players — Augie Galan, Joe Hat-

16. The War Ends and the Battle with the Cardinals Resumes

ten, Hal Gregg, and Stan Rojek — were ejected. Walker and Reese had their shirts torn so badly in the pregame fighting they had to get new ones for the actual game. Reese had a spare jersey with his number one on the back, but Walker had to wear number nine instead of his familiar number 11. The league fined Walker $150 and suspended him for five days. Reese, Merullo, and Cavarretta also drew fines, and Merullo and Cubs coach Red Smith also drew suspensions.

One other game during Walker's 16-game hitting streak is worth mentioning: the second game of a May 30 doubleheader against Boston at Ebbets Field. The game was one of two in which Dixie Walker played a tangential part in what became iconic scenes of Americana. In the second inning, Braves outfielder Carvel "Bama" Rowell hit a drive off Brooklyn's Hank Behrman that shattered the famous Bulova clock that stood

Eddie Stanky. When Chicago's Lennie Merullo slid into Stanky with spikes high, it set off a two-day battle between the Cubs and Dodgers in May 1946 (courtesy the Los Angeles Dodgers).

atop the right-field scoreboard. Despite glass raining down on him, Dixie was able to field the ball and hold Rowell to a double. (The ball hit the clock at 4:25 P.M., and exactly one hour later the clock stopped.) This event was likely the inspiration for a scene in Brooklyn native Bernard Malamud's 1952 novel, *The Natural*. In the book, Roy Hobbs, the title character, hits a home run that strikes a light tower, bringing glass down onto the field.

The Bulova Clock Company had promised a free watch to anyone who hit the clock, but Rowell, for some reason, did not receive his gift during his playing days. More than 40 years later, in 1987, on "Bama Rowell Day" in Citronelle, Alabama, Bulova presented Rowell with his wristwatch.[17]

At the end of play on June 7, Walker was leading the league in batting average (.368). He was also tied with Enos Slaughter for the lead in RBI (35) and with Stan Musial for the lead in hits (57). Dixie's four hits in the second game with the Pirates on June 4 had launched him on another hitting streak, this one of 12 games, which was also stopped by a Pittsburgh left-hander, Ken Heintzelman.

On the night of June 20, Walker, still leading the NL in batting, appeared on the Columbia Broadcasting System's television quiz show "See What You Know?" on WCBW. The other guests on the show were actress Lucille Ball and writer Ben Hecht, but it is not likely many people saw it.[18] Television was very much in its infancy in 1946. New York City, the communications capital of the nation, had only three channels, each of which had a few hours of evening programming.

The previous night, Joe Louis's eighth-round knockout of Billy Conn at Yankee Stadium had been the first heavyweight title fight ever televised. People with access to television sets in New York, Washington, Philadelphia, and Schenectady, New York, watched Louis successfully defend his title.[19]

On June 26, Walker had two triples and knocked in three runs as the Dodgers defeated the Reds, 4–2, to maintain their three-game lead over St. Louis. It was the second time in four days that the 35-year-old Walker had two triples in a game, also the fifth and final time in his career with two three-baggers in a single game. He hit another triple the next day, giving him five in five games, while going 11-for-19 and raising his average to .376.

Meanwhile, as the Dodgers continued to battle for first place, their intra-city rivals, the Giants under manager Mel Ott, were stuck in last place. Giants' fans were not blaming Ott, whom they had treasured since he first joined the club as a 17-year-old in 1926. One of the all-time greats, Ott had set National League career records during the 1945 season for most runs scored, total bases, extra base hits, home runs, years with one club, and most times with two or more home runs in a game.[20] Yet like an earlier Giants idol, Christy Mathewson, the fans loved Ott not only for what he accomplished, but for what he represented.

"Ott is liked for his modesty and character, and admired and appreciated for the many times during these many seasons that he came through in the clutch with the play that meant the ball game," wrote George Coleman of the *Brooklyn Daily Eagle*. "The Giant manager is to the Polo Grounds fans what Dixie Walker is to the Brooklyn Dodger customers."[21]

While Walker would never come close to matching Ott's batting feats, the Ott-Walker comparison was an apt one. The two men were similar for the admiration in which their team's fans held them.

"Probably never in the annals of baseball history has a player so captured the hearts of the fans as this soft-spoken, drawling southerner from Villarica [sic], Georgia," wrote *Associated Press* sportswriter Joe Reichler. "To Brooklyn fans Walker can do no wrong. In their humble opinion, Dixie is the greatest baseball player who ever lived."[22]

Reichler's comments were pure hyperbole. Even the most rabid Brooklyn fans would not suggest "Dixie is the greatest baseball player who ever lived";

16. The War Ends and the Battle with the Cardinals Resumes

however, many would argue he was the most popular. Harold C. Burr of the *Eagle* wrote a feature story on Dixie a few days later, after Walker had been declared Brooklyn's "Man of the Week." Burr said he was the man of the months and the years ever since he came to Brooklyn in 1939. He had always been in battles with the front office "but if any attempts were made to take him out of right field now, his millions of friends in the stands would burn down Ebbets Field." Burr wrote that Dixie often was asked to speak at events; but he had to limit them because Estelle complained the couple hardly ever got an evening home alone.[23]

August 13 was an off day for the Dodgers, but rather than rest, Dixie joined Babe Ruth as a guest at a United Orphans outing on Long Island's Long Beach. Transported by bus, with motorcycle policemen leading the way, more than 3,000 children from 30 different orphanages got to spend a day at the beach.

Dan Parker of the *New York Daily Mirror* tried to explain that Brooklyn's love for Walker went beyond his being one of the best players in the National League. "Where other ball players are bored or annoyed by requests for autographs," wrote Parker, "Dixie will turn on the charm and sign score cards, veal cutlets, baby's diapers, celluloid collars or short snorters with that 'pleasure-is-all-mine' spirit. He has never turned down a request to make an appearance at a Holy Name Society rally, an Epworth League meeting or a Bar Mitzvah. Chamber of Commerce meetings give him a thrill, or at least he lets the committee on invitations think so."[24]

Supposedly, it was in 1888 that Mike "King" Kelly of the Boston Beaneaters first suggested that the team that was in first place on July 4 would win the pennant. Brooklyn fans believed that the old adage would hold true this season. After splitting a doubleheader with the Giants on July 4, the Dodgers had a comfortable seven-game lead on the Cardinals. Dan Daniel also believed the Dodgers were World Series bound and credited much of their success to Walker. Even Durocher, no lover of Walker, had to admit it, wrote Daniel. Branch Rickey, whose proposed youth movement would have kept Dixie on the bench this season, went even further. "We have an outstanding star on the Brooklyn club of whose qualities I had not been fully aware. I am talking about Walker."[25]

Dixie, still leading in batting (.368) and RBI (63) at the All-Star break, was the National League's starting right fielder in the game at Fenway Park. He was the lone starting position player who was not a member or former member of the Cardinals. Around the infield were Johnny Mize at first, Red Schoendienst at second, Whitey Kurowski at third, and Marty Marion at shortstop. Joining Walker in the outfield were Stan Musial and Johnny Hopp.

Walker Cooper was the catcher. (Mize and Cooper were now with the New York Giants. Hopp was in his first year with the Braves.) However, the NL's best were no match for the American League this day. Two home runs and five runs batted in by Boston's Ted Williams powered the AL to a 12–0 victory.

The race for the pennant between the favored Cardinals and the scrappy Dodgers was reminiscent of the bitter battles of 1941 and 1942. Brooklyn had no pitching to speak of, wrote *Time* magazine. Instead, they pointed with pride to scrappy little Ed Stanky, who had a talent for getting on base, and Dixie ("The Pride of Flatbush") Walker, who had a talent for driving him in. "If there is a way to beat a team, you may depend on Stanky finding it," said Branch Rickey.[26]

"About all second-place St. Louis, the hottest team in preseason dope, had to offer were moans about sore pitching arms. They knew they had better start going places before the close-up and dangerous Chicago Cubs did."[27]

Brooklyn's lead over St. Louis was 4½ games when they opened a four-game series at Sportsman's Park with a July 14 Sunday doubleheader. The Cardinals won both games, cutting the lead to 2½ games. They broke a 3–3 tie with two eighth-inning runs in the opener, and scored a 2–1 win in the nightcap. Game Two was a well-pitched, tightly-played marathon that Musial ended with a leadoff home run in the bottom of the 12th inning. Winner Murry Dickson and loser Vic Lombardi both pitched the entire game.

Harry Brecheen handled the Dodgers easily the next day, and St. Louis completed the sweep with a dramatic 5–4 victory in the final game. Joe Hatten took a 4–2 lead into the ninth, but he hit the leadoff batter, Marion, with a pitch and then gave up a single to Clyde Kluttz. Dyer sent Erv Dusak up to bat for pitcher Howie Pollet. Down in the count, 0–2, Dusak drove the next pitch into the left field seats to give St. Louis the 5–4 win. Dusak was mobbed by his teammates as the large crowd roared its approval. Brooklyn's lead as they headed to Cincinnati was down to a half-game.

Walker had hits in all four games at St. Louis and in the three at Cincinnati as part of an 11-game batting streak. After the final game against the Reds, on July 19, his average was at .373, but Johnny Hopp, at .380, was now leading the league. On that date, Brooklyn and St. Louis were in a tie for first with identical 50–34 records.

At the All-Star Game in Boston, Walker had spoken to Dan Daniel about Brooklyn's chances of winning the pennant. "They are wrapped up in Reiser," Dixie said. "Every day, sitting around in the clubhouse, we ask each other, 'Can Pete play through the season?' If you have the answer to that question, you need ask no more." Walker went on to say he thought Brooklyn had the best balanced team in the league, but would make no predictions. No doubt

16. The War Ends and the Battle with the Cardinals Resumes 153

remembering his assurance of a pennant to Larry MacPhail in 1942, he said, "I have seen the Dodgers on top in July and beaten in October too often to get cocky."[28]

Less than a month after Walker wondered whether Reiser could play through the season, the hard-luck Pistol Pete again had to be carried off the field after running into an outfield wall. The crash into the left field wall at Ebbets Field came on August 1 as Reiser attempted to a catch a drive hit by Whitey Kurowski. An ambulance took Reiser to Peck Memorial Hospital, but he returned to action a week later.

During the All-Star break, the Dodgers had signed 22-year-old Joe Tepsic, a former Marine who had been wounded on Guadalcanal. Rickey signed him out of Pennsylvania State University for a $17,000 bonus, the highest bonus ever given by the Dodgers. However, as part of the agreement, they had guaranteed Tepsic he would stay with the team for the entire season.

Tepsic clearly was not ready to play at the major league level, and the Dodgers were in a tight pennant race. Durocher wanted to send him to the minors and replace him with someone who could contribute. The likely choice would have been outfielder Chet Ross, who was at Montreal.[29] Rickey offered Tepsic $1,500 if he would agree to go, but Tepsic believed he was a better player than some other Dodgers reserves and refused. Walker and Durocher both tried in vain to get Tepsic to accept Rickey's offer, but he refused them too.[30] Forced to keep Tepsic on the roster, Durocher used him sparingly; for the season, Tepsic would appear in only 15 games, ten of them as a pinch runner.

One of Chet Ross's teammates at Montreal was Jackie Robinson, the International League's leading hitter and unquestionably its best player. Rickey later said he never considered bringing Robinson to Brooklyn in 1946. "But even if Robinson got no chance at a Brooklyn uniform until 1947," wrote *Time* magazine, he had already accomplished his mission. Other big-league moguls were already hunting around for Negro rookies of promise.[31]

St. Louis was up by 2½ games in early September, but no one was ready to concede the pennant to Eddie Dyer's club. The big surprise of the season continued to be the way the Dodgers had stayed in the race. It was a tribute to Durocher's managerial skills, wrote *Time*. "For 15 weeks, with only about four first-rate men (Ed Stanky, Pee Wee Reese, Dixie Walker and Pete Reiser), Durocher had held the Dodgers at the top of the league. It was a great performance, worthy of making Durocher 'manager of the year,' but it was not enough to keep the talented, slow-starting Cards out of first place last week."[32]

Dodgers announcer Red Barber always claimed, "There's never a dull day at Ebbets Field," and September 11, 1946, was no different. That afternoon the Dodgers and Reds played 19 innings with neither team scoring, which is still the longest scoreless tie game in major league history. The game took 4 hours 40 minutes before the late-summer evening darkness settled over Ebbets Field, forcing the umpires to end play.

Johnny Vander Meer pitched the first 15 innings for Cincinnati, striking out 14 and allowing seven hits. Harry Gumbert pitched the last four, allowing just one hit. Durocher used four pitchers: Hal Gregg went ten innings, Hugh Casey five, Art Herring three, and Hank Behrman one.

While the Dodgers never came close to scoring, Cincinnati had two men thrown out at home plate. In the fifth, Eddie Lukon was out as he tried to stretch a triple into an inside-the-park home run on a relay from left fielder Pete Reiser to shortstop Pee Wee Reese to catcher Bruce Edwards. Walker saved the Dodgers in the last inning by throwing out Dain Clay at the plate, trying to score from second on Bert Haas's single. (The game was made up September 20, with the Dodgers winning, 5–3.)

Rookie Bruce Edwards, who made the two tag plays at the plate, had been Brooklyn's first-string catcher since being called up from the Mobile Bears of the Southern Association in June. After Mickey Owen left for the Mexican League, the Dodgers tried Mike Sandlock, Don Padgett, and Ferrell Anderson behind the plate before recalling Edwards. The 23-year-old combat veteran played an important role in Brooklyn's success, particularly on defense. In an August 15 game against the Giants, he had three assists in an inning, only the fourth major league catcher to accomplish that feat. After the season, New York sportswriter Jimmy Cannon asked Durocher what single player had helped the Dodgers most. "Bruce Edwards. He's the reason we're up there," responded Durocher.[33]

Red Barber enthralled Brooklyn fans with game accounts delivered in a Southern drawl and peppered with "down-home" witticisms (courtesy the Los Angeles Dodgers).

On the night of September 24, as part of an

Eddie Stanky-Pee Wee Reese Day celebration at Sanford's Restaurant in the Sheepshead Bay section of Brooklyn, there was a surprise 36th birthday party for Walker. The Dodgers Sym-phony band, with its two most prominent members, Shorty Laurice and Eddie Battan, was there to sing "Happy Birthday" to Dixie.

With five days left in the season, the Cardinals had a one-game lead. "Home and office radios blared play-by-play descriptions; earnest discussions went on at every street corner and water cooler. "The Dodgers and the Cards were going down to the wire in the closest of all National League pennant races," wrote *Time* magazine. The Rev. Benney S. C. Benson of the Brooklyn Dutch Reformed Church knelt on the steps of Borough Hall and prayed for the Dodgers: "Oh Lord, their chances don't look so good right now, but everyone is praying for the Bums to win. We ask you not to give ... St. Louis any better break than you give us...."[34]

That same day Durocher used eight pitchers — a league record at the time — in an unsuccessful attempt to beat the Phillies. The next day, Reiser broke a leg sliding back into first base, ending his season. After three years in the military, Reiser was no longer the player he had been, but he was still an important part of the team. He had lost his center field job to rookie Carl Furillo and was splitting time with Augie Galan in left field. Still, he batted .277 in 122 games and led the league with 34 stolen bases, including a then-record seven steals of home.

Going into the final weekend the teams were tied at 95–57. On Saturday afternoon the Dodgers defeated Boston, 7–4, behind Joe Hatten. That evening, the Cardinals kept pace with Harry Brecheen's 4–1 win against the Cubs. Another long and bitter race between Brooklyn and St. Louis had come down to the last day of the season.

17

Playoffs, Pensions, and a Promotion

Mort and Walker Cooper had always caused the Dodgers problems when they were with St. Louis. Now both were gone. The Cardinals had traded Mort to the Braves for Red Barrett in May 1945, and sold Walker to the Giants in January 1946, to make room for rookie catcher Joe Garagiola. Mort was only 12–11 this season, but he had always been a tough big-game pitcher against Brooklyn, and his old manager, Billy Southworth gave him the final-day start. Cooper responded in magnificent fashion, as he did his old teammates a favor by shutting out the Dodgers, 4–0, on four hits.

Vic Lombardi was the starter for Brooklyn; he allowed just one unearned run through eight innings, but the Braves jumped on Kirby Higbe for three in the ninth. The home fans sat there in silence until midway through the game when they had their first opportunity to cheer. The scoreboard showed the Cubs had scored five runs in the sixth inning at Sportsman's Park to take a 6–2 lead. After the game in Brooklyn ended, many fans remained, gathering on the Ebbets Field grass in right field to await the final score from St. Louis. The Cubs held on to win, 8–3; after 154 games, the Cardinals and Dodgers stood even, each with 96 games won and 58 lost.

The 1946 National League pennant winner would be decided in the first two-out-of-three playoff in big league history. A coin toss was held to decide where the games would be played. Brooklyn won the toss and chose to play two games at home. Under that scenario, the first game would be at Sportsman's Park and the second and third (if necessary) games would be at Ebbets Field.

Time magazine expressed surprise that either team had even been a pennant contender. They pointed out the Dodgers did not have a single 20-game winner (Kirby Higbe was tops with 17), while the Cardinals had one, Howie Pollet. The Dodgers had two regulars who batted .300 (Walker and Augie Galan); the Cards had three, including league-leader Stan Musial. "But," claimed *Time*, "when it came to managers, the Dodgers had a big edge: at

156

getting the most out of his mediocre material, the Cards' polite little Eddie Dyer was no match for flamboyant, volatile Leo the Lip Durocher."[1]

Playing at home, the Cardinals opened the playoffs with their ace, Pollet, 20–10 with a league-leading 2.10 earned run average. When asked whom he would start in Game One, Durocher said, "I'll pitch either Kirby Higbe or Ralph Branca, probably Branca."[2] Leo's decision might have been influenced by Higbe's disastrous relief appearance against the Braves on the last day of the season. Branca was just 20 years old and had won only three games during the season, but he had pitched two important shutouts down the stretch, including one on September 14 against St. Louis.

Branca claimed that coach Charlie Dressen had told him before that September 14 game, "We're going to start you. But Vic Lombardi is going to warm up and you're going to pitch to one batter, and then we're going to bring him in." A very angry Branca took the mound and retired the Cardinals on five pitches. When he returned to the dugout, Durocher told him, "Keep throwing like that, kid. We're going to keep you in."[3]

However, Branca failed to survive the third inning, while Pollet went the distance to win, 4–2. Captain Terry Moore and rookie catcher Joe Garagiola each had three hits for the winners. Moore had played only 91 games during the season, but he remained the team leader, playing much the same role for the Cardinals that Walker did with the Dodgers.

"You could say that he was the father of the ballclub," said Whitey Kurowski about Moore. "If we had any troubles or anything, we would go to Terry. He's the one that kept us in good spirits." Harry Walker agreed. "Terry was our captain and was respected by everyone on the club. He would do more talking to players than the manager did; everyone respected him for that."[4]

After a travel day, Game Two of the playoffs was on October 3, at Ebbets Field. The Cardinals won easily, 8–4, to finish two games ahead of Brooklyn in the pennant race. Murry Dickson allowed just two hits until the ninth inning, before the Dodgers scored three runs against him. Harry Brecheen relieved Dickson with one out and the bases loaded and struck out Eddie Stanky and Howie Schultz to end the Dodgers' season. Joe Hatten, the first of six Dodger pitchers, was the loser. Brooklyn had been in first or tied for first on 124 days of the season, but not at the end. As author Tom Oliphant wrote, "A powerful team being slowly assembled under Branch Rickey had been beaten by a St. Louis Cardinals team that Rickey had already helped build."[5]

The Cardinals went on to defeat the Red Sox in seven games to capture their third World Series in five years. Harry Walker's eighth-inning double drove home Enos Slaughter with the winning run in the final game.

Ebbets Field. It "gave your heart a lift on sight" (courtesy the Los Angeles Dodgers).

The playoff had generated criticism on two fronts in Brooklyn. One involved the decision to open on the road rather than at Ebbets Field. A National League record 1,796,824 fans had watched the Dodgers play at home in 1946 and they were well rewarded, esthetically and in the won-lost column. As author Wilfrid Sheed wrote of Ebbets Field, "The spanking blue seats gave your heart a lift on sight, and they seemed to have been gathered close to the field, the way people pull up their chairs to get a better look at something."[6]

Speaking from a player's perspective, Pirates first baseman Elbie Fletcher said, "Ebbets Field was the most fantastic place to play in. I think everybody in the league always enjoyed going to Brooklyn. Never a dull moment."[7] On the field, the '46 Dodgers compiled a phenomenal .727 winning percentage at home, winning 56 of 77 games. On the road, they were barely above .500, winning 40 and losing 37.

Five years later, when the Dodgers were again involved in a playoff, they again won the toss and this time chose to open at home. They lost to the

17. Playoffs, Pensions, and a Promotion

Giants in the 1951 playoff opener at Ebbets Field, won the second game at the Polo Grounds, and lost the third game at the Polo Grounds.

The other point of criticism was directed against Durocher and his selection of the inexperienced Branca to start Game One. In Branca's mind, there never should have been a playoff in 1946. "The three of them, Rickey, Dressen, and Durocher, blew the pennant, 'cause I had pitched very effectively in '45, but I had held out, and they didn't pitch me in '46. If they had pitched me, you know we would have won at least one more game than we did."[8]

After the season, Walker told Jimmy Cannon he believed Durocher was the best manager in baseball and had pulled off a small miracle in getting the Dodgers into the playoff. He also believed that Durocher had changed over the years. "In the old days, Leo said he could not manage young ball players," Walker said. "But this season his patience with young ball players improved a hundred percent. That's the most important change in him as a manager. In other years, there was tenseness about the ball club all the time. We had older ball players then. Now we have young ball players who figure to blow sky high. But Leo really builds the young fellow up. Gets them ready, makes the whole team feel as though it would fight through fifty hells."[9]

Walker had just completed a wonderful year, cementing his status as one of the game's finest players. He batted .319, third-best in the league, while finishing second in runs batted in with 116 and hits with 184. He also finished in the top five in triples and, at age 36, stolen bases. Walker's second-place hit total of 184 was 44 behind Stan Musial's 228. That set a record for the largest hit differential ever in one league by a first- and second-place finisher. The record lasted until 2004 when Ichiro Suzuki of the Seattle Mariners had 262 hits, 46 more than American League runner-up Michael Young of the Texas Rangers.

Musial, who won the batting title with a .365 mark, had an interesting head-to-head battle with Dixie this season. Musial led all Cardinal batters against Brooklyn with a .418 average. Among his 41 hits were eight doubles, six triples, and three home runs. Similarly, Walker led all Dodger batters against St. Louis with a .363 average. Among his 33 hits were seven doubles and three triples, but no home runs. Both men had 18 runs batted in against the other team. Musial won the Most Valuable Player award and Walker finished second. St. Louis and Brooklyn dominated the MVP voting just as they had dominated the pennant race. Enos Slaughter finished third, Howie Pollet fourth, Pee Wee Reese sixth, Eddie Stanky seventh, and Pete Reiser ninth.

Baseball had enjoyed an enormously successful season in 1946. Record attendance in many parks and the closest pennant race ever contributed to make the first postwar season a memorable one. The game also took the first steps toward financially bettering the lives of the players, both while they were active and after they had retired.

In May, Robert Murphy, a Boston lawyer and former National Labor Relations Board examiner, attempted to form a union of the players he called the American Baseball Guild. On June 7, Murphy came very close to convincing members of the Pittsburgh Pirates to stage a one-day strike. The strike was aborted when the players in favor could not get agreement from the required two-thirds of their teammates.

Murphy's plan had failed, and so too had the offers of big money by Mexico's Pasqual brothers to play in their league; nevertheless, "it convinced some owners that it would be prudent to head off potential difficulties in the future by making some changes."[10]

Led by Larry MacPhail of the Yankees, a Joint Major League committee was set up to deal with the issues raised by Murphy. In addition to MacPhail, the other members were American League president Will Harridge, National League president Ford Frick, and three club owners: Phil Wrigley of the Cubs, Sam Breadon of the Cardinals, and Tom Yawkey of the Red Sox. On July 18, the committee called for a meeting with the players to discuss reforms and decide on a uniform contract. Each team was asked to select representatives to meet with the owners, and each league was to select three players to take part in the Joint Committee meetings.[11]

Each National League team sent two representatives, while most AL teams sent one. All the teams selected veteran players, including eight who were future managers. The Dodgers selected Walker and Augie Galan. On the agenda was money for spring training, new rules regarding exhibition and barnstorming games, a minimum salary, and a pension plan. The pension plan became the special province of Cardinals representative Marty Marion. Terry Moore may have been the Cardinals' team leader, said Stan Musial, but Marion was the team spokesman. "He was always talking about trying to improve the conditions for ballplayers," said Musial.[12]

Dixie Walker was not only one of the game's top stars, he was also one of its most respected men. At a July 8 meeting of NL and AL player representatives prior to the All-Star game, he had proposed giving a portion of the game's receipts to the families of the eight Spokane ball players killed and the many others who were burned in a June 24 bus accident. The proposal passed unanimously.[13] On September 16, his fellow National Leaguers chose Walker to represent them on a seven-man committee that would include two players, two owners, Commissioner Chandler, and league presidents Frick and Harridge. Later, the American League chose Yankees pitcher Johnny Murphy as their representative.

The negotiations resulted in the establishment of a minimum salary of

$5,000, as well as a maximum of 25 percent that owners could cut a player's salary from the previous year, and a provision to provide $25 a week in spring training money for the players. The major gain was the creation of a pension plan, funded by the players with matching contributions of revenue from World Series radio (and later television) broadcasts.[14] Bob Feller, an eventual player representative himself, called Walker and Murphy visionaries. "They insisted that money from the television rights, not just radio, be included in the contribution to the plan."[15]

Responding to criticism that the players had not gone far enough in their demands, Walker said, "As some of those inconsequential points were brought up I warned our delegates not to make their stipulations too numerous, and to concentrate on a few important things. I said don't ask for a dozen concessions because you will get six or seven of the minor ones and miss out on the big ones. Ask only for what matters vitally."[16]

Dixie Walker was one of baseball's most respected men. In 1946, his fellow National Leaguers chose him as their representative in talks with the owners that would eventually lead to pensions for former players and their wives (National Baseball Hall of Fame Library, Cooperstown, New York).

Led by Walker, the National League representatives called for midseason interleague play to benefit the pension fund. Under their proposal, there would be games between the teams in the same position in the standings as of July 4 — first in the NL would meet first in the AL, second would meet second, and so on down the line. "I believe that if the sort of interleague schedule we propose had been played this year, we would have averaged about 30,000 fans per contest and taken in more than $200,000 net for the pension fund," Walker said.[17]

Overall, the NL players believed the AL players were less determined and not as strong about negotiating as they were. Walker said he was opposed to going into any negotiation with a mind-set of not hurting anyone's feelings or of being afraid to oppose anything. "I don't believe that was in the minds of the players when they chose us to represent them in negotiations with the club owners," he said.[18]

Baseball's 1947 winter meetings were held in late January at New York's Waldorf-Astoria Hotel. At their conclusion, Commissioner Chandler announced the creation of a pension plan for major leaguers. The hard work and vision of Walker, Marion, Johnny Murphy and the other player representatives was beginning to reap benefits. Players with five years' experience would now receive $50 a month at age 50, and an additional $10 a month for each of the next five years. The plan extended to coaches, players, and trainers active on Opening Day. It would require $675,000 annually to fund the pension plan, claimed the underwriter, with the money coming from owners, players, the receipts from the All-Star game, and at least $150,000 from the World Series.[19]

The players' pension plan went into effect on April 1, 1947. The first recipient was Ruth Bonham, the wife of Pirates pitcher Ernie Bonham, who died in 1949 at age 36 while still active. Bonham died from appendicitis complications on September 15, just 18 days after pitching his final game. Ruth Bonham, his widow, with two young children, reportedly received $90 a month for ten years.

Dixie's life also included a lighter side in 1946, as he took part in an amusing baseball short titled *Brooklyn, I Love You*. The Paramount one-reel film opened with actors playing stereotypical Bostonians, Southerners, and Brooklynites. A question is posed, "What's Brooklyn got that no other city's got?" The answer, of course, is "Dem Bums." The Dodgers cited in the script include Walker, Leo Durocher, Pee Wee Reese, Eddie Stanky, Pete Reiser, and Howie Schultz. There is wonderful footage of Ebbets Field, Hilda Chester in the stands, groups of raucous fans, the Dodgers Sym-Phony, Durocher entering the ball park and comical shots of him arguing with umpires. There also is footage of Red Barber calling a Dodgers-Giants game, with radio sidekick Connie Desmond by his side. Brooklyn is described as a "fightin' town," and the Dodgers are a "fightin' team."[20]

At the end of the 1946 season, just before the playoffs, *Time* predicted a bright future for the Dodgers. "Whether Brooklyn wins or loses this week's playoffs, Dodger fans have a really rosy future to contemplate during the long winter months. The twelve-club farm chain collected by President Branch Rickey is busting with young talent. Most likely to succeed: Negro Jackie Robinson."[21]

Another comment concerning Jackie Robinson did not get much coverage, but its significance would soon affect all of baseball, and Dixie Walker more than most. Speaking about Robinson, who had completed a spectacular year with the Montreal Royals, Montreal manager Clay Hopper said, "The boy is a very fine ballplayer and although he would be the first Negro player to go up, I wouldn't be surprised to see him stick with the Brooklyn Dodgers next season. He's every inch a big leaguer."[22]

17. Playoffs, Pensions, and a Promotion

Hopper's comments were in sharp contrast to those of a year earlier when he learned that he would be managing Robinson. "Please don't do this to me," he asked Rickey. "I'm white, and I've lived in Mississippi all my life. If you do this, you're going to force me to move my family and my home out of Mississippi."[23] When the season was over, Hopper said to Robinson, "You're a great ballplayer and a fine gentleman. It's been wonderful having you on the team." He also told Rickey that Robinson was a "gentleman" and also "the greatest competitor" he had ever seen.[24]

Robinson won the International League batting championship (.349) and it appeared almost inevitable that Rickey would bring him to Brooklyn in 1947. Robinson's success at Montreal had alerted the owners to that possibility; during the '46 season an ownership group headed by MacPhail issued a secret report on the ramifications of Robinson's coming to Brooklyn. The report warned of dangers to the "physical properties of franchises." In other words, too many black fans in the park might cause more prosperous white fans to stay away.[25]

Happy Chandler recalled that at the winter meetings in January 1947, none of the other 15 owners was in favor of Robinson joining the Dodgers. "Horace Stoneham was a good baseball man and one of my best supporters," Chandler said, but the Giants owner predicted that if Robinson played for the Dodgers the Negroes in Harlem, site of the Polo Grounds, would burn down the park. MacPhail, Lou Perini of the Braves, and Clark Griffith of the Senators all spoke against Robinson's coming to Brooklyn. "They voted 15–1 not to let him play," said Chandler. The reason for their opposition was not so much racism — though there was no doubt that was part of it — as it was a "business decision."[26] Their opposition was the same as Walker's: racism for sure, but based primarily on the effect it would have on their business interests.

Red Barber, who was born and raised in the segregated South, recalled a lunch he had with Rickey in March 1945, when Rickey first revealed his plan to integrate baseball. "I don't know who he is, or where he is, but I'm going to put a Negro on the Brooklyn Dodgers," Rickey told him. Barber said Rickey's announcement had shaken him to his foundations.[27] Remember, Barber was a radio announcer, not a player. If Rickey's plan was successful, Barber's job would not be to play on the same field as a black man, but simply to broadcast the games. That alone was enough to make him consider quitting a job he loved. A conversation with his wife Lylah led him to reconsider.

Rickey had announced even before the winter meetings that Robinson would appear for the Royals in two spring training exhibition games against the Dodgers at Ebbets Field. In that same announcement, Rickey made it known that Dixie Walker would be with the team in 1947. The *New York*

Amsterdam News wrote that Rickey's statements "throws down the gauntlet to Dixie," whom the widely-read Negro newspaper called (incorrectly, we would learn that spring) "the one anti–Robinson man in the Dodgers fold."[28] Walker remained evasive when asked about Robinson. "Everybody asks me about Robinson. I don't know why," he said. "After all, Durocher picks the ball club. I'm just one of the guys taking orders from him."[29]

Because of the existing "Jim Crow" laws in Florida, the Dodgers returned to Havana, the Cuban city where they had trained in 1941 and 1942, for spring training in 1947. This time they brought with them the Montreal club, including Robinson. Rickey had scheduled the Dodgers and Royals to play seven exhibition games against one another. His hope was that after seeing Robinson in action, the Dodgers players would demand his promotion to the big-league roster.

During batting practice on the first day of camp, a line drive hit minor league first baseman Lou Ruchser on the jaw. The accident inspired Walker to build a makeshift safety device that is still in use today. "First basemen tend to be vulnerable when they are throwing grounders to the other infielders at the same time batters are taking batting practice. They are particularly vulnerable to a line drive off the bat of left-handed hitters," wrote Roscoe McGowen in the *New York Times*.

"Walker, seeing a need, put together a rudimentary screen in a frame nine feet wide and six feet high and set it up in front of the first baseman. It was an immediate hit, as the first day it was used it stopped several line drives that might have caused damage."

"I thought of it the moment I saw Ruchser go down the other day," Walker said. Leo Durocher called it a great idea and couldn't understand why nobody had thought of it previously. "But I'll bet everybody in the league will be using it during batting practice this season," he said. Plans were already underway to widen the screen and make it sturdier.[30]

As he prepared for his ninth season in Brooklyn, a reflective Walker spoke of his mutual love affair with the fans. "There's no doubt fans have made old legs go further than maybe the law of averages intended," he told sportswriter Lester Bromberg, "but don't think it isn't appreciated. Thanks to the Brooklyn public, I've got myself set for life, down home in Birmingham."[31]

He had been the MVP runner-up in 1946, yet as so often had happened during his career in Brooklyn, there was no guarantee Walker would be in the opening-day lineup. In the past, the disrespect had come from MacPhail and Durocher; but MacPhail was gone and Durocher was pleading innocence. In his by-lined column in the *Eagle*, called *Durocher Says*, Leo devoted the March 2, 1947, column to Walker. Durocher said in the past he had often been accused of benching Walker, but this year it was the members of the press who were writing him off. They were figuring him for a part-time player who would probably get into only 75 or so games in 1947.

Nevertheless, Walker told Durocher he was preparing himself to play all 154 games. "I am going slower than I usually do," he told Leo, "because this heat will tire me if I work too hard. You will remember that I had my best year when I had the benefit of less than three weeks' work in freezing Bear Mountain."[32] Leo said he expected Walker to play about 125 games, and that he would rest him as needed.

During the offseason, the Pirates, at the instigation of Billy Herman, their new manager and Dixie's former teammate, had expressed an interest in trading for Walker, but nothing had come of it. Now there were rumors out of Havana saying the Dodgers would trade Walker. They would do so, the theory went, as a way to work their younger players into the lineup, enabling them to mount a challenge to the Cardinals in 1948. "Watch us in '48," Rickey had said, though not admitting that he did not consider the Dodgers a legitimate contender in 1947.

Durocher had been impressed with the youngsters in camp and was particularly high on 20-year-old Duke Snider. Charlie Dressen, Leo's former top lieutenant who was now with the Yankees, agreed. "That Snider kid can't miss," Dressen said. "I saw him play out in California. He hits a long ball and can run." Durocher had gone so far as to say he could be another Ted Williams. Several teams were mentioned as Walker's destination, including Chicago, where he would be traded even up for Bill Nicholson.[33]

Despite his protests, Durocher may have had a reason beyond the youth movement for getting rid of Walker, a player with whom he had never fully gotten along. Speculation that Dixie would succeed him as manager had been around for years.

18

"It was the dumbest thing I did in all my life"

Dixie Walker often acknowledged his involvement in the 1947 petition to keep Jackie Robinson from joining the Dodgers as the most regrettable decision of his life. The petition and his initial opposition to Robinson were actions he soon regretted and would spend the rest of his life explaining. In his later years he often told his son Stephen he wished he could go back and change a few things, no doubt with the petition in mind.[1]

"I organized that petition in 1947, not because I had anything against Robinson personally or against Negroes generally," Walker told author Roger Kahn in 1976.

"I had a wholesale hardware business in Birmingham and people told me I'd lose my business if I played ball with a black man. That's why I started the petition," said Walker, who was then a Los Angeles Dodgers batting coach. "It was the dumbest thing I did in all my life. If you ever get a chance, sometime, please write that I am deeply sorry."[2] This was the same Roger Kahn who four years earlier had called Walker "the most extreme of Dodger racists" in his book *The Boys of Summer*.[3]

However, Walker put a different spin on the petition story in a 1981 telephone interview with *New York Times* columnist Ira Berkow. "I've been called the 'ringleader' to try to stop Jackie from playing with the Dodgers," Walker told Berkow. "I was no ringleader," he said. "I was supposed to have organized a meeting of some of the players to boycott Robinson. When it was announced that Robinson was to join the Dodgers, the team was playing an exhibition game in Panama. I was in Miami, meeting my family. We then took a boat to Havana, where the Dodger training camp was. I met the team plane there when it flew in from Panama. I heard a good deal of talk about Robinson. But I didn't know a thing about any insurrections, as it was later called. But I get a message that Mr. Rickey wants to see me. I went to the Hotel

18. "It was the dumbest thing I did in all my life" 167

Nacional — or whatever it's called — and I sat down with Mr. Rickey in his room. He really reamed me out. I was so mad at him accusing me of being a ringleader that a few days later I wrote him this letter requesting to be traded."[4]

"Recently the thought has occurred to me that a change of ball clubs would benefit both the Brooklyn baseball club and myself. Therefore I would like to be traded as soon as a deal can be arranged. My association with you, the people of Brooklyn, the press and radio has been very pleasant and one I can truthfully say I am sorry has to end. For reasons I don't care to go into, I feel my decision is the best for all concerned. Very truly yours, Dixie Walker."[5]

"Well I had been with the club nine years," Dixie said, "and I resented being the scapegoat." He did admit there was pressure put on him back in Alabama about playing with Robinson. "I didn't know if they would spit on me or not, and it was no secret that I was worried about my business. I had a hardware and sporting goods store back home."[6] In Reggie Jackson's autobiography, the future Hall-of Famer described the virulent racism he encountered playing for Oakland's Birmingham team in the Southern Association in 1967. That was 20 years after Robinson integrated the major leagues, so one can only imagine the mind-set of Birmingham's white population in 1947.

That summer, Walker asked Rickey to return the letter, as the trouble he expected had never materialized and the existence of the letter bothered him. "I don't mind being traded, but I don't want to be traded for the reason I gave," he said.[7]

"Dixie Walker has a good mind," said Rickey, who chose to retain the letter. "In my book he is a high-class gentleman, a quiet assimilator. He was bold enough, strong enough to write me that longhand letter asking me to trade him, that he couldn't play on a team with a colored fellow, and then to come back to me and ask me to give him the letter back. He didn't want to be traded because he didn't want to hurt the club."[8] Author David Falkner believes the probable reason Walker has been accused of organizing the petition is that he was the only one to put his feelings in writing.[9]

Arthur Mann, a special assistant to Rickey, recalled the Walker letter in a 1950 article in the *Saturday Evening Post*. Rickey, said Mann, "viewed it as a note from a man in grave emotional difficulty."[10] Rickey immediately set out to accommodate Walker's wishes, and within three days he had received a written offer. The potential deal, scribbled on stationery from the Floridian Hotel in Miami, read as follows.

Mr. Branch Rickey:
  Pittsburgh agrees to accept player Walker for $40,000 cash [Al] Gionfriddo and [Frank] Kalin.
Pittsburgh Baseball Club
H. Roy Hamey
Gen. Mgr.

While Rickey was willing to accommodate Walker's trade request, Mann wrote, he had no intention of doing so for two minor league outfielders.[11] Walker had been his best offensive player in 1946, the only Dodger to bat above .300 and drive in more than 100 runs. Rickey countered with two alternatives to Gionfriddo and Kalin. One was rookie outfielder Wally Westlake, coming off a season in which he'd batted .315 for Oakland of the Pacific Coast League. The other was second-year man Ralph Kiner, the National League's home run leader in 1946. Not surprisingly, Hamey refused both counter-offers and the deal fell through. In May, according to the Mann article, the Giants rebuffed Rickey's offer of Walker, outfielder Carl Furillo, and pitcher Vic Lombardi for slugging first baseman Johnny Mize. Later in the summer, Rickey again tried to trade Walker to Pittsburgh, this time for pitcher Nick Strincevich and $40,000, but canceled the offer after outfielder Pete Reiser fractured his skull.[12]

Duke Snider was a rookie at the Dodgers training camp in 1947. Snider was a Southern Californian, seven years younger than Robinson, who had idolized Jackie when he starred in football, basketball, and track at UCLA. He was thrilled that he was now playing with Robinson, but understood not everyone felt the same way. Snider called Walker's opposition to Robinson a "cultural thing," something ingrained in him from childhood. He also recognized that Walker began to change his opinion during the season, and even more so over the years. Yet, Snider acknowledged that to many people Walker never was able to erase the stigma of his original stance.

"It's an old, familiar story," Duke wrote. "An attack on someone often makes page one of the newspaper, while the retraction ends up in the back of the paper and never catches up with, or gets the same attention as, the original story."[13]

The following players are generally acknowledged to have been involved in the petition to one degree or another: Walker, second baseman Eddie Stanky, outfielder Carl Furillo, backup catcher Bobby Bragan, and pitchers Kirby Higbe, Hugh Casey, and Ed Head. Furillo, a Pennsylvanian, always claimed he had been wrongly implicated and that his only opposition to Robinson was the same as it was to any rookie who might take his job. Over the years, Bragan, who like Walker was a resident of Birmingham, has spoken most often about the petition.

"I was born and raised in Birmingham, Alabama," he said in a 1997 interview. "You'd go to church and Sunday school on Sunday, and the bus station was across the street. And if you go over there, they have a 'white' drinking fountain and a 'colored' fountain. A white restroom and a colored restroom. Even at the lunch counter, you have a white place to eat a sandwich and a black one. So when you're born and raised in that kind of atmosphere,

18. "It was the dumbest thing I did in all my life"

you don't feel the same toward the blacks as you do the white."[14]

Bragan acknowledged that while some of the other Dodgers did not seem to mind the idea of having a black teammate, he did. "I never mixed much with blacks. The only ones I ever talked to were the maid who helped my mother around the house and the men who'd come over every once in awhile to ask my father, who ran a road-grading crew, for an advance."[15]

Walker, of course, had also had limited contact with blacks. "I grew up in the South, and in those days you grew up in a different manner than you do today," he said in 1981. "We thought that blacks didn't have ice water in their veins and so couldn't take the pressure of playing big league baseball. Well, we know now that's as big a farce as ever was. A person learns and begins to change with the times."[16]

Pitcher Kirby Higbe was also opposed to playing with blacks. Higbe had spent many hours throwing rocks at blacks while growing up in South Carolina, and he believed in segregation, telling Rickey he

Bobby Bragan. In 1981, Bragan said, "Some of the other Dodgers didn't seem to mind having a black teammate, but I sure did" (courtesy the Los Angeles Dodgers).

preferred not to have to play with a "negruh." Yet Hank Greenberg, Higbe's teammate on the 1947 Pirates, remembered him as "a blithe spirit" whose problems about playing with Robinson were strictly a function of the times.[17] "I think if Higbe were playing today," said Greenberg after Higbe's death in 1985, "he wouldn't have any problem playing with blacks. People like Higbe didn't know any different back then. They thought they were supposed to object, otherwise they'd be turning their backs on Southern tradition."[18]

Although Bragan admitted being opposed to Robinson's joining the team, he denied that the group had circulated an anti–Robinson petition. However, Pee Wee Reese, the team's veteran shortstop, said that such a petition did exist.[19] Reese opposed it, although he would later say when he was introduced to Robinson, "It was the first time I'd ever shaken the hand of a black man." Playing with a black man "was a difficult adjustment for a lot of people," Reese said. "It wasn't easy for me either. I'd grown up in Kentucky, and I'd never had any contact with black people."[20]

Kentucky was quite a bit different from Alabama or South Carolina, but Reese's feelings were very similar to Walker's and Higbe's. Pee Wee admitted that like most Southerners he believed blacks were inferior to whites. "You hear this all your life, you believe it."[21] Pete Reiser, Reese's friend and fellow star, had no problems playing with blacks and he too wanted nothing to do with the petition.

Ed Stevens, a young first baseman and a Texan, would seem to have been someone the petitioners would have targeted. But Stevens, who would soon lose his job to Robinson, knew nothing about it. "There has been much made of that petition, but I never saw it. Never heard talk of it, and I don't know who in the world started the rumor, but then I was just a young player and nobody let me know anything."[22]

The Dodgers were in Panama for a series of exhibition games when word of the petition leaked. Harold Parrott, the team's traveling secretary, found out about it from Higbe when he ran into the inebriated pitcher in a Panama bar. Higbe, as he so often did, had been doing some heavy drinking. "Ol' Hig just won't do it," he said to Parrott. "The ol' man [Rickey] has been fair to Ol' Hig. So Ol' Hig ain't going to join any petition to keep anyone off the club."[23] Parrott immediately informed Rickey and Durocher of what he had heard.

Rumors of the petition had already reached Durocher, and when Parrott confirmed them, Durocher swung into action immediately, calling a meeting in the middle of the night. He gathered all the players into the kitchen of the army barracks at Fort Gulick, where the team was staying. When Leo entered the room, wearing his pajamas and bathrobe, "he looked like a fighter about to enter the ring," Parrott remembered.[24]

"Listen, I don't care if this guy is white, black, green, or has stripes like a fucking zebra. If I say he plays, he plays. He can put an awful lot of fucking money in our pockets. Take your petition and shove it up your ass. This guy can take us to the World Series, and so far we haven't won dick."[25] In his memoir, *Nice Guys Finish Last*, Durocher elaborated on what he had said to the players that night.

> I hear some of you fellows don't want to play with Robinson and that you have a petition drawn up that you are going to sign. Well boys you know what you can do with that petition. You can wipe your ass with it. Mr. Rickey is on his way down here and all you have to do is tell him about it. I'm sure he'll be happy to make other arrangements for you.
>
> I hear Dixie Walker is going to send Mr. Rickey a letter asking to be traded. Just hand him the letter, Dixie, and you're gone. *Gone!* If this fellow is good enough to play on this ball club — and from what I've seen and heard, he is — he is going to play on this ball club and he is going to play for *me*.

Leo then warned his players that Robinson was only the first and soon there would be other black players in the league. "So," he said, "I don't want to see your petition and I don't want to hear anything more about it. The meeting is over; go back to bed."[26]

The next day Rickey spoke to the dissidents, including Walker and Bragan. "Mr. Rickey called us all in one by one," Bragan remembered. "He told us in no uncertain words that the guy's skin color has nothing to do with his ability. If he can play better than the guy we got, he's going to play. Do you understand that?" Bragan said he did and when Rickey asked if he preferred staying with the Dodgers or being traded, Bragan said, "I'd rather be traded." Rickey then asked if he remained with Brooklyn would he play any different if Robinson were on the team. Bragan said he wouldn't, and the meeting was over.[27]

Robinson was still a member of the Royals as the Brooklyn and Montreal clubs prepared to play a pair of exhibition game at Ebbets Field. Along with the mainstream press, columnists for two Negro weeklies made their own assessments of Robinson's chances of joining the Dodgers. Sam Lacy of the *Baltimore Afro-American* wrote, "The Dodgers to a man, feel that Jackie will be one of them before the club completes its exhibition series here. And they're prepared to take it — or else."[28]

Wendell Smith of the *Pittsburgh Courier*, Robinson's companion throughout spring training, wrote that Robinson had proved himself as a player, but still had to reach the point where his teammates accepted him.

"No player in history has tried harder to become a big leaguer. And no owner in history has tried harder to make a player a big leaguer," Smith wrote of Robinson and Rickey. He summed up the importance of Robinson succeeding. "If Robinson fails to make the grade, it will be many years before a Negro makes the grade. This is IT." Smith then gave his opinion on how the Dodgers regulars felt about Robinson joining the club.

> ED STEVENS: Definitely against Jackie because he exists as a threat.
>
> ED STANKY: He appears to be prejudiced, but will play with him.
>
> PEE WEE REESE: He will play. His attitude is not known nor has it been revealed in any way.
>
> ARKY VAUGHAN: He will go along with the mob. If they want Robinson, he will be for him. If they are against him Vaughan will be also.
>
> BRUCE EDWARDS: He is all right. Whatever Rickey says, he will do.
>
> PETE REISER: A great ballplayer. He will play with anyone.
>
> GENE HERMANSKI: He will definitely play with a Negro.
>
> DIXIE WALKER: He is against Robinson. Would rather have him elsewhere. But will tolerate him because he [Walker] is one of the highest-paid players in the majors.[29]

Although Smith had written the column a few days earlier, by the time it appeared on April 12, Robinson was a Dodger. During the sixth inning of Brooklyn's April 10 game against the Royals, the club announced they had purchased Robinson's contract from Montreal and "he will report immediately." Rickey said after the game that he decided to make the move just five minutes before he made the announcement.

"Dodgers Purchase Robby," blared the back page of the next day's *New York Daily News*. The *Times* led its sports section with an eight-column headline about the purchase, while the story in the *Brooklyn Daily Eagle* called Robinson "the first Negro boy ever to reach the big leagues."

The front-page headline in *The Daily Worker*, the Communist newspaper, exclaimed, "Robinson on Dodgers!" *Worker* sportswriter Lester Rodney, to his credit, had been agitating for integration for years. Rodney had no use for Walker, whom he called "a southern racist to the core" and explicitly anti–Communist. He quoted Walker as saying, "It's the Commies who want to break down the [color] lines."[30] Oddly, Rodney found a problem with someone being anti–Communist at a time when his newspaper's hero, Josef Stalin, was enslaving half of Europe.

Robinson's promotion to Brooklyn surprised no one, especially the players. "We all knew it was coming," pitcher Joe Hatten told the *Des Moines Register* decades later. "As a matter of fact, we thought we should have had him the year before. When he first came up, I read all this stuff about dissension in the clubhouse—about Eddie Stanky and Dixie Walker, guys from the south—but I never saw any conflict in the clubhouse or anyplace else."[31]

Robinson made his Dodgers debut the next day in an exhibition game against the Yankees. The game drew more than 24,000 people to Ebbets Field, both white and black, to witness the historic event. "White Brooklynites were not any more liberal than most white Alabamians when it came to

Jackie Robinson officially joins the Dodgers (courtesy the Los Angeles Dodgers).

welcoming blacks next door," wrote author Scott Simon. But Rickey was convinced he could get them to accept a black ballplayer if he could help the Dodgers.[32]

Rickey had gauged the Brooklyn fans' devotion to their team correctly. The mostly white crowd cheered Robinson throughout the game. "Hundreds of kids surrounded him and he literally had to fight his way through the press of admirers," wrote the *Eagle*. "Joe Louis never received such a reception."[33] Yet while the white fans cheered Robinson almost to a man, many of the black fans took every opportunity to boo Walker. That prompted the *Eagle* to editorialize against this first-ever booing of Dixie Walker at Ebbets Field, calling it a disgraceful performance.

"It was hard to understand the open exhibition of hostility toward Dixie Walker on the part of many in the stands, including some who were drawn there especially to witness Robinson's debut," wrote the *Eagle*. "We are delighted to see this opportunity given to a young Negro athlete but if, concurrently, we are to find a man like Dixie Walker — one of the most popular stars in the game and a Brooklyn sports idol — being subjected to such mistreatment, there is a danger that it will react seriously against the expansion of the Dodgers' experiment in bringing a Negro into the national game."[34]

Columnist Dan Burley took a similar position in his "Confidentially Yours" column in New York's Harlem-based *Amsterdam News*. "I can't emphasize too strongly the dumbness of fans, white and colored, who boo or otherwise annoy the 'People's Cherce' on a mistaken notion that he took a public anti–Jackie Robinson attitude in 1945 when Rickey announced he was going to use a Negro player in the Dodger system."[35]

Walter White, the longtime executive secretary of the National Association for the Advancement of Colored People and a leading voice for civil rights for blacks, also chimed in. White wrote a weekly column in the *Chicago Defender* titled "People, Politics, and Places." His April 26 column, subtitled "Jackie Robinson 'On Trial,'" was a caution to black fans not to conduct themselves in ways that would offend white patrons and thereby harm Robinson's chance of making good. He cautioned against drinking and fighting in the stands and other excessive action, and asked black fans to not see racism in every incident on the field that went against Robinson.

White cited the April 11 exhibition game against the Yankees as an example of the type of "bad manners" to avoid. "Whenever Dixie Walker came to bat he was lustily and even profanely booed for allegedly having said he would not play on the same team with a Negro." The ardently pro-Robinson New York newspaper *PM*, wrote White, quotes Walker and asserts its belief he is telling the truth in denying he made any such statement. "Whatever the circumstances," White concluded, "Walker and Robinson ARE playing on the same team. Let's wait and see what happens."[36]

The *PM* quote to which White referred had also appeared in the April 19, 1947, edition of the *Richmond Afro American*. It contained Walker's denial that he had opposed Robinson's promotion from Montreal and was an early sign that Walker had come to accept Robinson as a teammate.

"I was misquoted," Dixie said. "I didn't say anything about not being concerned about Robinson as long as he wasn't with the Dodgers. What I said was that it was Montreal's business when they signed him, not mine. The only thing that matters now is whether he can help the team. It's up to him to prove that he is the best man for the position. That's all there is to it."[37]

Robinson's signing on April 10 had been momentous news, but it had not stirred the baseball world as had the previous day's announcement of a one-year suspension for Leo Durocher — especially in Brooklyn. "The banning for a year of the Brooklyn manager, Leo Durocher, by Baseball Commissioner Chandler has attracted much more attention than has the signing of Robinson," wrote the *New York Times*. "The latter seems to us to be more important."[38]

The *Times*, of course, was correct. In retrospect, the Durocher incident merits little more than a footnote, while the Dodgers' bringing of Robinson to the major leagues is justly recognized for its extraordinary impact on baseball and on America itself. But that was not the case on that tumultuous April weekend. The Durocher suspension was the bigger national story and it made headlines all over the country.

Several factors contributed to Durocher's suspension, including a history of his friendships with known gamblers and his recent marriage to actress Laraine Day after Day's quickie Mexican divorce. Beginning in Havana, Durocher and his old boss Larry MacPhail had been trading accusations about associations with gamblers Memphis Engelberg and Connie Immerman. Columnist Jimmy Powers of the *New York Daily News* predicted Durocher would soon be gone. Powers even predicted who he thought would replace Leo. "With each outburst, the Lip is rapidly washing himself up," wrote Powers. "We still believe the day is not too far when it will be manager Dixie Walker."[39]

On the day of the suspension, Durocher spoke to a players-only meeting in the clubhouse. When it was over, Red Barber asked Walker what had taken place. Walker said Durocher was not angry with Chandler and did not make any alibis. He told the players to have faith in Rickey to get them a good manager for the coming season. "I want you to believe in Mr. Rickey, and I want you to believe in yourselves. You're good enough to win the pennant no matter who Mr. Rickey gets as your manager."

18. "It was the dumbest thing I did in all my life"   175

Pete Reiser says goodbye to suspended manager Leo Durocher prior to the 1947 season. Gene Hermanski and Dixie Walker are to the right, while Hugh Casey and Pee Wee Reese stand behind their longtime skipper (National Baseball Hall of Fame Library, Cooperstown, New York).

Walker then said to Barber, "Red, you know, I never liked Leo. I never liked him at all, and everybody knows I never liked him. But he showed me something in there. I'll tell you, the way he talked in that meeting, the way he went out of here today—he'll be back."[40]

The next day, New York sportswriter Tom Meany asked Walker if he would take over as Dodgers manager until Durocher returned in 1948. Many who followed the Dodgers thought Walker would not take the job on a pro-tem basis, but Dixie said he would. "Sure, I'd take it as a fill-in," he told Meany, "if I thought it would insure the return of Durocher."

Meanwhile, *The New York World-Telegram* reported that while Walker and Stanky were being mentioned as possible successors to Durocher (they were the number one and two choices among the fans), Rickey had said he "did not now have in consideration any of the players."[41] Rickey claimed he had a specific replacement in mind. That replacement was Joe McCarthy, but the former longtime Yankees manager turned down Rickey's offer of a one-year contract.

Charlie Dressen, Durocher's longtime assistant, would have been the logical choice, but MacPhail had hired Dressen and another Brooklyn coach, Red Corriden, to work under new Yankees manager Bucky Harris. Ray Blades, a former Cardinals manager had replaced Dressen. Blades's long history with Rickey put him prominently on the list of candidates to be Durocher's replacement. The 1947 season was about to open and the Brooklyn Dodgers did not have a manager.

19

Jackie Robinson Joins the Dodgers

Coach Clyde Sukeforth, another "Rickey man," served as the Dodgers interim manager during their final preseason series with the Yankees. Sukeforth had played a major role in bringing Robinson to Brooklyn and had managed Jackie in his first big-league action; nevertheless, he was content to be a coach and had agreed to fill the manager's role only until Rickey found a permanent replacement for Durocher. Because Rickey had not yet announced his new manager by Opening Day, Sukeforth found himself leading the Brooklyn club on that groundbreaking afternoon.

Jackie Robinson's major league debut on April 15 was a significant day for America and we now treat it as such. But that was not the case in 1947, not even on the sports pages. Robinson's debut had to compete in the mainstream New York press with other opening-day stories on the three New York teams and with speculation about who would replace Durocher.

The *New York Herald Tribune* led its sports section with Joe McCarthy's rejection of Rickey's offer to manage the Brooklyn club. The Robinson story was buried in a preview of the Dodgers' upcoming season, just below the news that "Gladys Gooding will accompany herself at the organ as she sings the national anthem."[1]

The *Daily News* beat writer, Dick Young, did not mention Robinson until the 17th paragraph of his story, and then only in reference to where he should hit in the Brooklyn lineup. Louis Effrat's article in the *New York Times* previewing the opening day's games mentioned that "the first of his race to make the grade since 1884, Robinson will cover first base for the Brooks." But that was well down the page, as the *Times* evidently deemed the history-making event in Brooklyn less important than the expectation of 50,000 fans at Yankee Stadium; Durocher's suspension; the Dodgers-Braves pitching matchup; and John Cashmore, the Brooklyn Borough President, throwing out the first ball.[2]

There was no mention in any newspaper in the nation of a story that first surfaced fifty years later on the ESPN television show *Outside the Lines*. The show alleged that opposition to Robinson playing in 1947 was far wider than previously thought. Interviews with 93 former National Leaguers suggested a conspiracy to boycott Robinson if he stepped on the field in Brooklyn on Opening Day. "I think every team in the league voted," said Al Gionfriddo, then with Pittsburgh but soon to be a teammate of Robinson.

According to Cubs pitcher Hank Wyse, team captain Phil Cavarretta held a meeting in which he said he had a telegram saying all the other clubs would strike if Robinson played in the opener. The Cubs vote was either 25–0 or 24–1 in favor of the strike, said Wyse. Dewey Williams, a little-used catcher, recalled all the Cubs players just waiting for a phone call from Dixie Walker when Robinson took the field. That would be the signal for the strike to take place. "Everybody was sitting around waiting for Dixie to call, which we thought for sure he was going to do," said Williams. The call never came, and the Cubs took the field against the visiting Pirates.[3] As mentioned, this story was aired in 1997, 15 years after Walker's death. Dixie never had the opportunity to confirm or deny it.

Seating capacity at Ebbets Field was generally listed in the 34,000 to 35,000 range, but there had been numerous occasions in which the number of customers far exceeded that total. Yet only 26,623 showed up for Brooklyn's opener against the Boston Braves. Sukeforth batted Robinson second, behind Eddie Stanky and in front of Pete Reiser and Walker. Facing Braves ace Johnny Sain, Robinson went hitless in three at-bats, but he successfully handled 11 chances at first base, a new position for him, in Brooklyn's 5–3 win.

When the Dodgers took the field in the ninth inning, Robinson remained on the bench as veteran Howie Schultz took over at first base. Sukeforth had put Schultz in as a defensive measure, but the Dodgers soon realized Robinson needed no help. Schultz played in only one more game before Brooklyn sold him to the Phillies. The next day Rickey announced he had given up his attempts to trade for Giants first baseman Johnny Mize; and Ed Stevens, the Dodgers' other first baseman, played in just five games before Rickey sent him back to the minors.

Jackie Robinson's big-league debut produced no front-page banner headlines or the type of breathless coverage the news media would bring to a similar story today. For that kind of coverage, one had to turn to the black weeklies or *The Daily Worker*. Lester Rodney of the *Worker* wrote, "But it's hard this Opening Day to write straight baseball and not stop to mention the wonderful fact of Jackie Robinson. You tell yourself it shouldn't be especially wonderful in America, no more wonderful for instance than Negro soldiers being with us on the way overseas through submarine infested waters in 1943."[4]

19. Jackie Robinson Joins the Dodgers

Reiser, a very popular player coming back from yet another injury, had struck the big blow for Brooklyn — a game-winning double — and it was he, not Robinson, who was the focus of the story in the next day's *New York Times*. Roscoe McGowen's game account mentioned Robinson only in relation to his play, leaving columnist Arthur Daley to take note of his debut, which he called "uneventful."[5]

Herb Goren, in the *New York Sun*, also wrote about Reiser with an accompanying story about Robinson. Like most New York reporters, Goren treated Robinson as another Dodger, writing that Robinson's "debut yesterday was not altogether disappointing: in fact, he set up the winning rally for Pete Reiser by the deftness of his bunting ability."[6] Without mentioning Robinson's race, the game story of *New York Daily Mirror* writer Gus Steiger noted that Robinson "was on first for the Brooks but showed a decided strangeness with big league pitching."[7]

The press seemed unsure of how to describe Robinson. In the *Eagle*, columnist Tommy Holmes wrote, "For the first time ever, an acknowledged Negro played in a major league championship game."[8] Daley's comments in the *Times* about Robinson were couched in the condescending and patronizing manner common at the time: "The muscular Negro minds his own business and shrewdly makes no effort to push himself. He speaks intelligently when spoken to and already has made a strong impression."[9]

Arch Murray, of the left-leaning *New York Post*, wrote, "Jackie Robinson, the first colored boy ever to don major league flannels, started at first base and batted second for the Dodgers."[10] At various times, Robinson was referred to as "The Black Meteor" and "the fleet-footed Negro" (*Eagle*), "the Negro star" (*Sun*) and the often-repeated phrase, "first Negro in modern major league history."

In retrospect, it would be easy, and fashionable, to attribute the writers' casual treatment of this history-making game to racism. More likely, however, they handled Robinson's debut in this way because it took place at a time when baseball reporters believed that's what they were: baseball reporters, men who felt their sole duty was to report what took place on the field. Red Barber and Connie Desmond, the Dodgers' radio broadcasters, did the same. The mind boggles to think how the media would cover such an event today.

Rickey announced his new manager on April 18, naming 62-year-old Burt Shotton, an old friend who had last been a full-time big-league manager with the Phillies in 1933. Shotton, now retired, was living in Florida and serving as a part-time scout. Sukeforth went back to being a coach, but would often represent the team in on field-arguments. Because Shotton managed in civilian clothes, he could not come out of the dugout. We can only wonder how different Robinson's first year might have been if he'd had Leo Durocher out on the field fighting for him.

A week after Shotton's appointment, Walker and Stanky addressed two assemblies totaling 2,000 students at Brooklyn's Lafayette High School's baseball rally. Both men praised their new manager and predicted the Dodgers would win the pennant.[11] But Shotton had been out of the game for many years, and it would take him a long time to reacquaint himself with the National League's current players and style of play. Some members of his own team believed he never did. "We'd sit on the bench, and we'd laugh at some of the moves Shotton made," said Ralph Branca. "After having Durocher, who was three or four steps ahead of everybody — to have this man who was a step behind or two steps behind as far as strategy went, it was a big comedown to me."[12]

Of course, this was the same Branca who had criticized Durocher for the way he had used him in 1946. Moreover, it was under Shotton in 1947 that Branca had his best major-league season. Nonetheless, Pee Wee Reese, in his usual kindly way, agreed with Branca that Durocher was the better strategist. "If I ever manage, I'll try to run a ballgame like Durocher did and handle the players Shotton's way," he would later say.[13]

The majority of preseason forecasters had predicted another pennant for the defending world champion St. Louis Cardinals. Some thought the Braves were ready to win their first pennant since 1914, while others held out for the Dodgers. Despite taking the Cardinals to a playoff before bowing out in 1946, the loss of Durocher made it difficult to assess the Brooklyn team. The Dodgers showed up anywhere from first place to sixth in these preseason polls.

"Whether Durocher's Dodgers can beat the Cardinals (or even finish in the first division) is a question strewn with ifs," wrote *Time*. "They have the pitching. If Pete

Burt Shotton. Branch Rickey's longtime friend came out of retirement at age 62 to replace the suspended Leo Durocher as Brooklyn's manager (courtesy the Los Angeles Dodgers).

19. Jackie Robinson Joins the Dodgers

Reiser's lame shoulder mends, and if Carl Furillo and Bruce Edwards are as good as they were last year, and if veteran Dixie Walker comes through, they will have hitting. First-base problem will not be settled until Rickey decides whether to let Jackie Robinson become the first Negro in the big-leagues."[14]

As the schedule had it, Robinson played 13 of his first 15 games at Ebbets Field — the other two were at the Polo Grounds. The Dodgers won ten of those games, but the homestand was not without incident. In a three-game series against Philadelphia, the Phillies, led by manager Ben Chapman, assaulted Robinson with a steady barrage of the vilest kinds of racial insults. "Hey coon, do you always smell so bad?" "Hey nigger, why don't you go back to the cotton fields where you belong?" "They're waiting for you in the jungles, black boy." "Hey, snowflake, which one of those white boys' wives are you shacking up with tonight?" And "We don't want you here, nigger," among others.[15]

It became so offensive that Walker, a lifelong friend of Chapman, told him to lay off. Stanky, another Dodger who had not welcomed Robinson originally, called Chapman a coward and dared him to "pick on somebody who can fight back."[16] Robinson had gotten his own revenge in the series opener. He singled in the eighth inning and later scored the game's only run in Hal Gregg's one-hit shutout of the Phillies.

Robinson later wrote that the ordeal with Chapman "brought me nearer to cracking up than I have ever been." Years later, he revealed how close he had come to letting loose. "I thought of what a glorious cleansing thing it would be to let go.... I could throw down my bat, stride over to that Phillies dugout, grab one of those white sons of bitches and smash his teeth in with my despised black fist. Then I could walk away from it all."[17]

For Rickey, the whole Chapman incident proved to be a positive, for Robinson and for the Brooklyn team. "Chapman did more than anybody to unite the Dodgers. When he poured out that string of unconscionable abuse, he solidified and united thirty men, not one of whom was willing to sit by and see someone kick around a man who had his hands tied behind his back — Chapman made Jackie a real member of the Dodgers."[18] Rickey was very impressed that all the Southern players had stood up for Robinson, especially Walker, Chapman's close friend.

Robinson also had a hit in the second game against Philadelphia, but then went hitless in his next 20 at-bats. It may have been at this time, or perhaps in July, that Walker gave Robinson a batting tip that Jackie later called an important part of his first season success.

"Soon after the '47 season began, Dixie's innate fairness and love of baseball made him cross the color line," Robinson wrote years later. "I was lying on the trainer's table in Boston while [team trainer] Doc Wendler was giving me a rubdown. Dixie poked his head through the door. Now Dixie was one of the most scientific hitters of all time. His level swing and wrist action enabled him to place a ball almost anywhere he wanted to. That morning he started to talk to me. In his soft Southern voice he gave me a lecture on how to hit behind runners, how to avoid hitting into double plays, how to shift my feet with a runner on third so that a fly ball would enable him to score standing up. And much more as he talked on, adding percentage points to my future batting average and RBI figures."[19]

Walker also remembered the advice he had given to Robinson. "It was early in the first season. Jackie was having a problem at the plate. I saw something. And I went to him one morning when he was on the rubbing table and told him. It was just a suggestion. I think it worked."[20] In a 1949 interview with 200 high school and college sportswriters at the CBS studios in New York, Robinson said that Walker and Branca were the two Dodgers who had helped him the most when he was a rookie.[21] Walker would later say about those batting tips, "When you're on a team, you got to pull together to win."[22]

The Chapman-led tirade against Robinson had been beyond shameful, but a more serious assault on his right to play in the National League surfaced two weeks later.

The St. Louis Cardinals had one of the largest contingents of Southern-born players in the National League. Stanley Woodward wrote in the *New York Herald Tribune* that several Cardinals players were organizing a protest against playing against the Dodgers in the scheduled May 6 game at Ebbets Field if Robinson participated. Woodward wrote that owner Sam Breadon talked the players out of striking. National League president Ford Frick jumped in, telling the players that if they did strike, he would suspend anyone involved.

> "If you do this you will be suspended from the league. You will find that the friends that you think you have in the press box will not support you, that you will be outcasts. I do not care if half the league strikes. Those who do it will encounter quick retribution. They will be suspended and I don't care if it wrecks the National League for five years. This is the United States of America, and one citizen has as much right to play as another. The National League will go down the line with Robinson, whatever the consequence."[23]

Much like the Dodgers players' petition in Havana, there are many differing recollections of what actually happened with the Cardinals' purported strike. Breadon denied that his team had planned a strike. He said the only reason he had gone to New York was to try to put a spark into his struggling club. However, Breadon did admit he had heard from a St. Louis reporter that there were some complaints among National League players about playing against Robinson. Breadon thought that would be a "terrible thing" and added that he discussed it with two of his leading players. "I was happy to find there was no dissatisfaction," he said. "They never intimated that such a thing was thought of." Manager Dyer and center fielder Terry Moore also denied there had been talk of a strike by the Cardinals players.[24]

But Freddy Schmidt, a pitcher on that team during spring training and for the first few weeks of the season, said otherwise. In a 2008 interview, the then 92-year-old Schmidt said he clearly remembered a letter being passed around the Cardinals clubhouse before he was traded. The letter, he said, called for players to refuse to take the field against Robinson.[25]

Stan Musial, in the hospital with appendicitis at the time, said that "there was some feeling there," but denied there was any plot directed at Robinson. Musial called the talk "rough and racial," but denied the existence of any strike vote.

Marty Marion said he could not vouch for any private conversations, but that nothing ever happened in the clubhouse. The Dodgers and Cardinals were bitter enemies and nobody on either team liked anyone on the other team, he explained. "I don't think we had any personal love for anybody on the whole club, and I'm sure they didn't for us."[26]

By May 17, Walker, leading the league with a .357 average, and Robinson, with his batting and fearless base running, had the Dodgers in the thick of the race. Yet neither Walker nor many of the other Dodgers had fully accepted Robinson. Walker, who was being called a "nigger lover" back in Alabama, had refused a request from Judge Sam Leibowitz, a friend of both men, that he pose for a photo with Robinson.

That Walker and Leibowitz were "friends" says much for both men. Their backgrounds could not have been more different. Leibowitz was a Romanian-born Jewish immigrant who had arrived in New York City in 1897 at the age of four. Before becoming a judge, he had been a defense lawyer, one who helped defend the "Scottsboro Boys," nine black youths charged with raping two white women in Alabama in 1931. A New York Jewish lawyer defending black men accused of raping white women in Alabama at that time made Leibowitz the most hated man in the state and led to threats against his life.

Dixie said he gradually began to respect Robinson for the way he handled the abuse he received. "God knows how many times he was thrown at, how many times he was hit."[27] One of those times was on May 17, when Pirates left-hander Fritz Ostermueller threw a pitch aimed at Robinson's head. Jackie instinctively threw his arm up and the ball hit him there. The Dodgers started shouting profanities at Ostermueller in defense of their teammate. "It was then that they displayed, probably for the first time, that they regard him as a teammate," wrote Wendell Smith.[28]

Seeing what Robinson could do on the field eventually led Walker and others to accept Robinson as a valuable teammate, if not a friend. Don Newcombe, a black pitcher who joined the Dodgers in 1949, called Walker a cracker from the South who hated everything black. In Newcombe's opinion, Dixie changed because Robinson helped get him into the World Series and make some extra money.

Yet Robinson was aware that Walker was in a difficult position. He was nearing the end of his career and would have to depend on the businesses he owned in Birmingham for his future income. Robinson understood that if Walker acted too friendly toward him it would hurt those businesses. Robinson claimed he would even avoid the customary handshake at home plate if he scored after a Walker home run. "I wasn't sure if he'd take my hand, and I didn't want to provoke anything," he later said. The handshake aside, Robinson admitted that Walker always acted politely toward him.

The *Daily Worker*'s Lester Rodney, who never missed an opportunity to castigate Walker, took Dixie to task for those supposed handshake avoidances. Rodney wrote "that he [Walker] never waited at home plate to congratulate

Gene Hermanski (22) and batboy Stan Strull greet Walker after his home run off Allie Reynolds in Game Two of the 1947 World Series. Yogi Berra is the Yankees catcher and Babe Pinelli is the home plate umpire (National Baseball Hall of Fame Library, Cooperstown, New York).

Jackie after he hit a home run with Dixie on base."[29] Also from Rodney: "During the season, Walker avoided the traditional handshake at home plate any time Jackie hit a homer."[30]

That is just not true. Robinson always batted *ahead* of Walker. In Jackie's 151 games, he batted second 140 times, third 10 times, and fourth one time. Walker usually batted fourth against right-handers and fifth against left-handers, and on the day Robinson batted fourth—September 10, against Cubs left-hander Bob Chipman—Dixie batted sixth. Walker was never on base when Robinson hit any of his 12 home runs, half of which came with the bases empty. Furthermore, Robinson was on base only twice when Walker homered. And just to complete the possibilities, Walker was never the on-deck batter when Robinson hit a home run; nor, of course, was Robinson ever the on-deck batter when Walker homered.[31]

Another charge often made against Walker concerns a team picture of the 1947 Dodgers where Walker is turning his head away from the camera, supposedly in protest of Robinson's presence on the team and in the picture. Yet there is another photo of the '47 team where Dixie is staring straight ahead. This picture was taken later in the season and also includes Dan Bankhead, the major leagues' first black pitcher.[32] There is also a photograph of the 1943 Dodgers where all the players are standing with their arms at their sides except for Walker. Dixie is standing arms akimbo, looking away from the camera. So what was Dixie Walker protesting in that 1943 photo?

In his 2007 book, *Opening Day*, Jonathan Eig argues that while Walker and other Dodgers may not have truly befriended Robinson in 1947, their "cruelty" to him has likely been exaggerated, especially as they came to see him as a teammate and fellow player. "From the start of the season to its finish, he [Walker] never criticized Robinson publicly for mistakes on the field," wrote Eig. "He never publicly questioned the right of black ballplayers to compete in the major leagues. And as far as anyone could tell, he never again spoke of organized protest. Faced with a dilemma, he decided to set aside his anger and play ball, which is all Robinson had asked in the first place."[33]

20

Dixie and Jackie Bring a Pennant to Brooklyn

Dixie Walker did not lead the National League in any offensive category in 1947, and only in bases on balls (97) did he reach a career high. Yet overall, this may have been his finest season. His consistent play and veteran leadership, combined with a sensational rookie season by Jackie Robinson, were the major factors in leading Brooklyn to their first pennant in six years. Since winning the flag after a hard-fought, season-long battle with the Cardinals in 1941, the Dodgers had suffered heart-breaking pennant losses to St. Louis in 1942 and 1946.

After bouncing in and out of first place during the first half of the '47 season, the Dodgers took the lead for good in the final game before the All-Star break. Ralph Branca's three-hit shutout of the first-place Braves — his 12th win of the season — allowed the Dodgers to leapfrog Boston into first place. Aided by a 13-game winning streak, the Dodgers opened a ten-game lead by July 31. That lead would never fall below three games, and the final margin of victory over St. Louis was five games.

Kirby Higbe had been the team's leader in wins for both the pennant-winners of 1941 and the runner-ups of 1946; however, three weeks into the season Branch Rickey traded Higbe to Pittsburgh. Twenty-one-year-old Branca emerged as the team's ace with 21 wins and a 2.67 earned run average. Left-handers Joe Hatten and Vic Lombardi won 17 and 12 games respectively, and rookie Harry Taylor won ten. Hugh Casey appeared in 46 games, all in relief. In addition to his ten wins, he "saved" 18 games more than any other pitcher in the National League.[1]

The veteran Casey also served as an advisor to manager Burt Shotton, who relied on him almost as much as he did on his coaches. Casey told sportswriter Tom Meany he would sit next to Shotton in the shade of the dugout until the seventh inning, when he would trudge down to the bullpen. Casey also credited Shotton for much of his individual success in 1947. "He asked me how much work I thought I could do, and I told him I could work three innings almost every day if necessary. So Shotton told me he would never call on me before the seventh."[2]

Second-year catcher Bruce Edwards had a "career" season, with a .295 average and 80 runs batted in, while catching in 128 games. Walker considered Edwards the most valuable player on the team. "That Edwards boy is my all-time durability champion. I have been in baseball for a good many years but have seen no one even approaching our catcher in the physical ability to take it."[3] The nation's sportswriters evidently agreed; Edwards finished fourth in the MVP voting in 1947, the highest of all the Dodgers.

Pee Wee Reese and Eddie Stanky were solid up the middle all season, and when they were both injured in an August 23 game in Cincinnati, backups Eddie Miksis and Stan Rojek filled in admirably during their absences. Rookie Johnny "Spider" Jorgensen won the job at third base out of spring training and batted a respectable .274.

Second-year outfielder Carl Furillo batted .295 with 88 runs batted in. Furillo's batting average stayed above .300 for most of the season, including a stretch where he ranked among the league leaders. In a midseason interview with Gordon Williams of his hometown newspaper, the *Reading Times*, Furillo said that Shotton wanted to convert him into a long-ball hitter and constantly urged him to swing hard. But Furillo "is satisfied with his doubles and singles and refuses to change his timing," wrote Williams. "In this, he is supported by Dixie Walker, veteran outfielder, who advised Carl not to cut from the heels, but to hit the way he has been doing. Walker has taken an interest in Furillo and coaches him with his batting."[4]

In a 1970 interview with his biographer Ted Reed, Furillo elaborated on his relationship with Walker. "I always liked Dixie Walker and I respected him, and he used to say that I wasn't a smart kid like some other kids that come up and are a little fresh and stuff like that. In other words, I knew my place and I respected the older ballplayers. After I moved to right, I used to always be compared to Dixie Walker because they would say, 'Well, who was the best who ever played right field for the Dodgers? Was it Furillo or was it Dixie Walker?' Because it was a thing you had to learn, playing right field at Ebbets Field, and I guess that the two of us were there longer than anybody else. They always used to say that Dixie Walker had helped me a lot when I came up, but that wasn't the truth because he didn't really help me all that much. Because after all, let's face it: I was trying to take the man's job away from him."[5]

The arguments over who was better at the position began after Furillo succeeded Walker as Brooklyn's right fielder in 1948. Those arguments, fruitless as they may be, continue to this day among elderly men who in their youth rooted for the Brooklyn Dodgers. None dispute Furillo had the superior arm, only about which man was better at handling Ebbets Field's tricky right field wall.

Charlie Dressen coached the Dodgers under Leo Durocher during Walker's years in Brooklyn and managed Furillo from 1951 through 1953. Dressen declared, in 1951, that Furillo was the best right fielder in Dodgers history. "Dixie Walker was a good hitter," said Dressen, "but Furillo is also a .300 batsman and miles ahead of Dixie in the outfield."[6]

Bobby Bragan, a teammate of both men in 1947, hinted in his autobiography that he would choose Walker. "My roomie Dixie Walker played right field at Ebbets Field as well as anyone. The brick wall behind him was slanted and went up 18 feet, and there was a wire fence for 10 feet above that. Caroms were tricky, and Dixie became known as 'the People's Cherce' as much for his fielding as for his hitting, which was always excellent."[7]

Furillo had begun the '47 season as the left fielder, but he took over in center after Pete Reiser crashed into yet another outfield wall. Reiser's collision with the center-field fence came in a June 4 game against Pittsburgh. In the sixth inning, with Brooklyn comfortably ahead, 7–2, Pete chased a long drive hit by Culley Rikard. The Dodgers had added additional box seats in the outfield after the 1946 season, thereby cutting the distance from home plate to the center-field wall from 420 feet to 390 feet.

"Walker is guarding Reiser like a mother hen this year," noted one New York writer. "Every time Pete comes within crashing distance of a wall ... Dixie's warning voice prevents him from making a hole in the concrete with his head."[8] But neither Walker nor left fielder Gene Hermanski was able to prevent the June 4 collision.

Reiser, who later claimed he had forgotten about the short distance, was going at full speed when his head hit the wall. He fell to the ground and yet

Carl Furillo. After Furillo succeeded Dixie in 1948, the arguments began as to who was the better right fielder (courtesy the Los Angeles Dodgers).

again had to be carried off the field on a stretcher. His condition appeared so dire that the man who might have been the greatest player ever was given the last rites by a Catholic priest. Reiser would miss the next five weeks recovering from a brain injury that was even more serious than originally thought. Pete was batting .274 when he went down, but came back strong and finished the season with a .309 average.

Yet despite the solid play of Reese, Edwards, Furillo, and Reiser, it was Robinson and Walker who, in starkly different ways, led Brooklyn to the pennant. Robinson batted .297, led the league with 29 stolen bases, finished second with 125 runs scored, and won *The Sporting News* Major League Rookie of the Year Award. Those numbers only begin to tell the story of Robinson's contribution. He was the most exciting base runner baseball had seen since Ty Cobb, and his aggressiveness on the base paths continually disrupted the opposition, causing balks, wild pitches, and defensive errors.

Dan Daniel wrote that while Walker had not been "too hot about Robinson as a teammate in the spring," that had changed drastically during the season. He had now become one of Robinson's staunchest supporters.[9] After Robinson won the Rookie of the Year Award, Walker offered this tribute to his teammate. "No other ballplayer on this club, with the possible exception of Bruce Edwards, has done more to put the Dodgers up in the race than Robinson has. He is everything that Branch Rickey said he was when he came up from Montreal."[10]

Jackie had accomplished all this while under orders from Branch Rickey not to respond to the insults, the pitches aimed at his head, or any other on-field actions against him. As the season wore on, opposing teams began to realize that trying to intimidate Robinson made him an even better player. The most serious incident in the second half of the season came on September 11 at Sportsman's Park, the opening game of the final series between the Dodgers and the Cardinals. Brooklyn's lead was four and a half games, making it an almost must-win for St. Louis. It was a tension-packed game that the Dodgers eventually won, 4–3. Branca was the winning pitcher, raising his record to 20–11 and making him Brooklyn's first 20-game winner since Higbe and Whit Wyatt in 1941.

When Robinson came to bat in the third inning, he confronted Cardinals catcher Joe Garagiola. Jackie was convinced that Garagiola had deliberately stepped on his foot in a play at first base the previous inning. Garagiola responded with harsh words of his own before home-plate umpire Beans Reardon stepped between the two men. Robinson, as he so often did, later had his revenge on the field. His fifth-inning, two-run home run off Harry Brecheen tied the game at 2–2; but it was pinch-hitter Cookie Lavagetto's single in the eighth that won the game for Brooklyn, 4–3.

Garagiola, only 21 at the time, went on to have a decent major-league career and then was a successful baseball broadcaster and a host on the *Today* show. However, much like Walker, his 1947 encounter with Robinson haunted him all his life. In an interview with Jonathan Eig, who recounted the incident in *Opening Day*, his book about Robinson's rookie season, Garagiola "begged for his encounter with Robinson to be forgotten." Even children's books had portrayed the incident, causing Garagiola's grandchildren to ask him why he had hated Robinson. "I've lived with this thing unfairly. It was a little bit of jockeying to break his concentration, that's all ... it wasn't even an argument.... You just don't know the grief and aggravation this has caused."[11]

Dixie Walker's daughter Susan also had difficulty dealing with people's misperceptions and lack of all the facts about her dad. "It became difficult for me every time it came up," she said of being Dixie's daughter. "So after a while, I would seldom tell people who I was."[12] In a 2010 book written with

Estelle with sons Fred, at her right, Sean and Stephen, on her lap. Daughter Susan is to the far left and daughter Mary Ann Estelle to the right (private collection of Stephen Walker).

sportswriter Maury Allen, Susan tried to explain her difficulty in reconciling this supposedly racist villain with the kind and decent man she knew as her father.[13] Walker's other surviving children, Stephen and Mary Ann Estelle, felt much the opposite about their identity. "Mary Ann and I have always been very proud to let people know Dixie Walker was our dad," said Stephen.[14]

Ironically, in light of his later being spiked by Garagiola and his St. Louis teammate Enos Slaughter, Robinson had said back in July, "Of all the clubs in the league, I'd say the Cardinals have been the nicest to me." He particularly praised manager Eddie Dyer, Marty Marion, and Joe Medwick for going out of their way to treat him well. He said that the Brooklyn players had accepted him without incident and that it had gone more smoothly with them than it had even the year before in Montreal. "If I don't seem to mix easily," he said, "that's my own fault. I sort of keep to myself by habit. Even in the colored leagues, I was that way. But I feel the Brooklyn players are with me." Robinson had praise for Stanky and Walker, the two star players who had not been anxious for him to join the club in April. "Eddie Stanky is always showing me how to play the hitters, and up in Boston I got some good advice from Dixie Walker. He took the trouble to explain to me when to bunt and when to swing away. No matter what you might have heard, Dixie has been fine to me."[15]

In addition to being an invaluable asset on the field, Jackie also put money in the Dodgers' coffers, as his appearances set attendance records in almost every National League city. Blacks came in droves to see him wherever he appeared. Typical was Brooklyn's first game in Chicago, on May 18, which drew 46,572, the largest paid attendance for any single game in Wrigley Field history. "There was no doubt that the new paid record was set because Robinson, the much discussed Negro athlete, was making his first baseball appearance in Chicago, as a big leaguer," wrote the *Chicago Daily Tribune*.[16] The *Chicago Defender* quoted a Cubs official as saying the fans were "The most orderly large crowd in the history of Wrigley Field.... We were pleased to note that the Negro fans behaved better than our average Sunday fans." The *Defender* noted that "other than Robinson [the fans] paid attention to one Dixie Walker who was the recipient of plenty of boos."[17]

Dixie would hear boos from black fans repeatedly on the Dodgers initial road visits to every city, but the abuse subsided on subsequent visits. At home, he was still the fan's favorite. "Because he was a castoff, retread, human," the people of Brooklyn took Walker to their hearts in a way they could never quite take Pete Reiser, Red Barber had said in the early 1940s. They appreciated Reiser for the great player he was, but he was just too perfect for the Ebbets Field crowd.[18]

Walker was also the team leader off the field, a position he had held for

Walker and Al Gionfriddo after Game Six of the 1947 World Series. Gionfriddo remembered that all the Dodgers looked up to Walker as their leader (courtesy the Los Angeles Dodgers).

years. At a 1985 gathering celebrating Dixie's induction into the Dodgers Hall of Fame, several of his former teammates discussed Walker's leadership. Ralph Branca, Vic Lombardi, and Al Gionfriddo agreed that in his years with the Dodgers, Dixie was at the center of the goings on in the clubhouse. In addition to assisting the rookies, he was the one who would administer the fines and make the humorous comments that went along with them. He often sat in an easy chair near the entrance to the clubhouse, puffing on his pipe, making comments to the players as they passed by, again in a humorous way. All the players enjoyed Dixie's banter and looked up to the veteran as their leader.[19]

Walker got off to a good start and a month into the season was batting over .400. He struggled in June and was down to .279 at the All-Star break; nevertheless, the fans voted him to the All-Star team. He batted second and went 0-for-2 in the National League's 2–1 loss. Batting ahead of him and playing in center field was his brother Harry, who was also 0-for-2. Harry, whom the Cardinals had traded to the Phillies on May 3, would win the 1947 National League batting title with a .363 average.

Harry thought his hitting this season was due partly to being an everyday player and partly to some advice about his batting stance from Dixie. Though when they met around the circuit, Harry said, they usually discussed their Alabama hardware business.[20]

Harry Walker is the only National Leaguer ever to win a batting title playing for two teams in the same season, and he and Dixie, the winner in 1944, are the only two brothers to have won batting titles. Dixie was one of five members of the 1947 Dodgers who were past or future National League batting champions. The others were Arky Vaughan in 1935 (with Pittsburgh), Pete Reiser in 1941, Jackie Robinson in 1949, and Carl Furillo in 1953.

Walker got hot again after the All-Star break. In the next 20 games, he hit close to .400, had three home runs, and drove in 19 runs. On August 4, Dixie hit the 100th home run of his career, a two-run blast in the tenth inning that beat the Braves, 4–2, and ended a three-game Brooklyn losing streak. Walker had now played in 101 of the Dodgers' 104 games. In the spring Durocher had predicted he would play in 75 games. "Seventy-five games," Branch Rickey had said disapprovingly at the time, "I want him to play 154 games."[21]

Durocher, of course, was gone and despite Shotton's many critics in the press, he did have his club on the way to a pennant. In mid-summer, Walker was asked to assess his new manager. Although Dixie had not always seen eye to eye with Durocher, he refused to criticize him when being asked for a comparison with Shotton.

"Listen, I liked Leo and I thought he was a darned good manager. Anything I say is in no way a criticism of Durocher. But darned if I can see a thing wrong with the way Shotton has managed, and is managing this club. It seems to me he has done everything as well as it possibly could be done and I think the whole club feels just as I do about him. Shotton is a good manager."[22]

Overall, Walker seemed quite content with Shotton having replaced Durocher. "We seem to be doing well enough and drawing the fans in as great numbers as we did in 1946. And don't forget this," he said in what could be construed as a shot at Durocher as well as praise for Robinson. "The 1947 Dodgers are as aggressive as any club you have ever seen in Brooklyn."[23]

Red Barber later said that although most of the writers covering the Dodgers cared little for Shotton, particularly Dick Young of the *Daily News* and Harold Rosenthal of the *Herald Tribune,* the manager was "the unsung hero of 1947." He brought calm to a very unsettled situation, won the pennant, and carried the Yankees to seven games in the World Series."[24]

During the season, Walker had two four-hit games and eight three-hit games. His first four hit game — all singles — was on April 26 at home against the Giants. The second was August 22 against Cincinnati, also at Ebbets Field. Dixie's hits included a double and a triple, and he scored the winning run in the 12th inning. He even came in from right field to make a putout in the infield during a rundown. "There's life in the old boy yet," wrote Harold C. Burr. "Dixie Walker, whose obituary has been written more often than any of the other aged gaffers of the game, had quite a game for himself at Ebbets Field yesterday."[25]

Days short of his 37th birthday, Walker said he had never felt better at this late stage of a pennant race. He claimed it was due to his conserving his energy by limiting the amount of batting practice he took and the amount of pregame running he did. "I guess I have done my share of running," he said.[26] However, a week later, with the Dodgers on the verge of clinching the pennant, Walker, still insisting he wasn't tired, said he would like to get away for a few days. "As you know," he told Dan Daniel, "our spring plans contemplated a week's vacation for me around midseason. But I never did get it. In fact, I would have refused had it been offered. Now things are different."[27]

Brooklyn clinched the pennant on September 22, an off-day, when St. Louis lost the night portion of a day-night doubleheader against Chicago. More than 100,000 people, black and white, lined Flatbush Avenue to watch the Dodgers victory parade. When the motorcade reached its destination, Borough Hall, the team's two most popular players — Walker and Robinson — addressed the crowd. Both men assured their adoring fans they would beat the Yankees. "We've won two pennants for you now, but never a World Series. However, I think we're going to do that this time," Walker said.[28]

The other pennant, of course, was in 1941 when the Dodgers lost the World Series to the Yankees in five games. Dixie, Reese, Reiser, and Lavagetto were the only members of the 1947 Dodgers who had played against the Bronx Bombers in that last prewar Series. The only remaining Yankee participants were Joe DiMaggio, Tommy Henrich, and pitcher Spud Chandler. (Charlie Keller was injured and not on the Series roster.)

The Boston Red Sox had been heavy favorites to repeat as American League champions, while for the New Yorkers it was supposed to have been a rebuilding year. The Yanks were not the dominating team they had been before the war, but new manager Bucky Harris led them to 97 wins. Led by MVP DiMaggio, the Yanks breezed to the pennant, finishing 12 games ahead of the second-place Detroit Tigers.

Allie Reynolds, acquired in a trade with Cleveland for Joe Gordon, led in wins with 19, and Frank "Spec" Shea, a rookie, had 14. During the season, Harris turned left-hander Joe Page, a high-living, failed starter into a reliever. Page responded with 14 wins and "saved" 17 games, the most in the American

20. Dixie and Jackie Bring a Pennant to Brooklyn

Hugh Casey, Pee Wee Reese, Joe Hatten, and Eddie Stanky (left to right) exchange congratulations with Dixie Walker following Brooklyn's 9–8 victory in Game Three of the 1947 World Series (National Baseball Hall of Fame Library, Cooperstown, New York).

League. He was in every way the Yankees' counterpart to Hugh Casey, much in the same way Johnny Murphy had been in 1941.

A dramatic hit by Cookie Lavagetto and a dramatic catch by Al Gionfriddo are the most vivid remembrances from the 1947 World Series. Lavagetto's two-out, pinch-hit double in Game Four broke up Bill Bevens's almost-no-hitter and won the game for Brooklyn. Gionfriddo's twisting catch of a DiMaggio drive against the Yankees bullpen in Game Six preserved the Dodgers victory and tied the Series at three games each. The next day the Yankees won the clinching game behind Page's five innings of one-hit relief.

Shea won two games for New York and Casey won two for Brooklyn. Casey had not pitched well late in the season, but with Brooklyn having lost the first two games, he won Game Three in relief. "Hell, I might beat these guys four straight," he said after the game. Casey was also the winner the next day in Game Four (the Lavagetto game), even though he threw only one

Pete Reiser, Hugh Casey, Pee Wee Reese, and Dixie Walker (left to right) surround Cookie Lavagetto after his game-winning hit in Game Four of the 1947 World Series (National Baseball Hall of Fame Library, Cooperstown, New York).

pitch. He became the first pitcher ever to win World Series games on successive days.[29] Over the course of the Series, Casey set records by appearing in six games and pitching five games in a row, the last five.[30]

Walker had a disappointing Series, with six hits in 27 at-bats (.222) and four runs batted in. Robinson hit only .259, with Furillo (.353) and Reese (.304) topping the .300 mark. Dixie's single off Shea in the first inning of Game One at Yankee Stadium drove in the first run of the Series, and he had a home run off Reynolds in Game Two at the Stadium. The home run was only the third for the Dodgers in a World Series game; Hy Myers hit one off Boston's Ruth in 1916, and Reiser hit one off the Yankees' Atley Donald in 1941.

Thanks primarily to the addition of Jackie Robinson the Dodgers drew 325,000 more people on the road in 1947 than they had in 1946. However, at Ebbets Field, paid attendance increased by only 10,000. Considering the Dodgers won the pennant and played fewer doubleheaders at home this season, their home attendance total was very disappointing to the team's owners.

"Decades later," wrote Michael D'Antonio in his biography of Walter O'Malley, "one academic study would blame the Dodgers poor performance at the gate on a decline in white attendance, which might suggest that the borough was not as open-minded as the team."[31]

On June 26, Dixie was honored when he was selected as one of the nine men voted into the first class of the International League's Hall of Fame. His plaque cited his .335 lifetime average in 396 games played with Jersey City, Newark, and Toronto. However, his achievements of the 1947 season went unrecognized by the voting members of the Baseball Writers' Association of America.

Seven members of the pennant-winning Dodgers received votes in the balloting for the National League's Most Valuable Player Award, including six of the top 13. The winner was Boston Braves third baseman Bob Elliott, followed by Cincinnati Reds pitcher Ewell Blackwell and New York Giants first baseman Johnny Mize. Bruce Edwards finished fourth, followed by Jackie Robinson. Other Dodgers receiving votes were Pee Wee Reese (eighth place), Ralph Branca (11th), Hugh Casey (12th), Eddie Stanky (tied for 13th), and Walker (19th).

The Walker vote is one of the more intriguing in the history of postseason awards. Dixie received one first-place vote, but all 23 other writers omitted him from their ballots. Walker had played a key role in the preseason resistance to Robinson, but he had evolved into a good and a helpful teammate to Jackie. In addition to his leadership qualities, he batted .306 and led the team with 94 runs batted in.

Walker's one first-place vote seems undeserved, but even more undeserved was his being completely overlooked by the other writers. That 23 voters left the RBI leader of the pennant-winning team off their ballots seems very curious. In hindsight, this appears to be a case where dogma, not performance, dictated the votes of at least some of the writers.

PART III — AFTER THE DODGERS

21

"The place doesn't look the same since you've gone, Dixie"

In April 1975, CBS canceled its long-running television show, *Gunsmoke*. The show was still doing well in the ratings, but the audience was showing signs of aging and were no longer the group that advertisers wanted for their show. However, the ratings were not what killed the show, said Alan Wagner, CBS vice president for program development. Although it was still a viable show, "it was a question like this," he said. "The Dodgers traded Dixie Walker when he was batting over .300. Did they trade him too soon? It's better to get rid of a program one year too soon than one year too late."[1]

Rumors that Branch Rickey was preparing to trade Dixie Walker resumed shortly after the World Series. "Rickey might peddle Dixie Walker, but the People's Choice holds a peculiar spot in the hearts of the Flatbush fans," wrote Harold C. Burr. "He's become a Brooklyn institution and resentment might run high if he was disposed of summarily in cold blood. Rickey would have to feel out public sentiment first."[2]

Yet Burr knew as well as anyone that Rickey did not pay any attention to public sentiment, that he had a long history of trading or selling veteran players while they still had market value. Tommy Holmes, Burr's associate at the *Brooklyn Daily Eagle*, offered a more accurate reading of Rickey. "The fact that the customers would like to see Walker patrol right field until a wheel chair becomes an essential part of his equipment cuts no ice with Mr. Rickey, who likes to talk as though baseball were a sport but always acts as though it were a business."[3]

By Thanksgiving, it had become clear that Walker would not be back in Brooklyn in 1948. The only question remaining was whether Rickey would trade him or offer him a managing job in the Dodgers organization. Holmes wrote that Walker was anxious to start his managerial career and would likely manage the Dodgers' American Association farm team in St. Paul.[4]

In early December, Branch Rickey, Jr., confirmed that the club had offered Walker the St. Paul job, at a salary of $15,000. Dixie turned it down. He was not ready to give up playing or to take the steep cut in salary.[5] "The fact that we offered Walker a place in our organization," said Rickey Jr., "indicates, doesn't it, that we no longer consider him a topflight ball player."[6] Speaking after he retired as an active player, Walker agreed with that assessment. "Rickey [Sr.] knew I was slowing up. I wasn't getting around into the ball in time. I had trouble pulling the ball like I used to."[7]

The Dodgers announced the trade of Dixie Walker from Brooklyn to Pittsburgh on December 8, 1947. Along with Walker, the Pirates received pitchers Vic Lombardi and Hal Gregg. Coming to Brooklyn from Pittsburgh were left-handed pitcher Preacher Roe, shortstop Billy Cox, and utility infielder Gene Mauch. Al Abrams, sports editor of the *Pittsburgh Post-Gazette*, believed Pittsburgh had gotten the better of the trade; however, the deal would turn out to be one of the best in Dodgers history. Over the next seven years, Roe and Cox would be key contributors to three pennant-winning seasons in Brooklyn. Roe compiled a 93–37 record, including a 22–3 mark in 1951, and made four National League All-Star teams. The Dodgers moved Cox to third base, where he teamed with first baseman Gil Hodges, second baseman Jackie Robinson, and shortstop Pee Wee Reese to form one of baseball's all-time great infields.

Given all that had transpired at spring training in Havana, many people jumped to the conclusion that Rickey was trading Walker because of his early opposition to Jackie Robinson. That false perception exists to this day. True, Dixie had asked for a trade during spring training, but he later changed his mind, as Rickey well knew.

It is important to emphasize that the trade of Dixie Walker to Pittsburgh had nothing to do with Jackie Robinson. Tommy Holmes wrote that after playing a full season with Robinson, Dixie would have had no problem staying in Brooklyn. "No one could ever detect wherein Walker's natural graciousness toward Robinson differed in any way from his attitude toward any other player on the club."[8]

Rickey had a well-deserved reputation for parsimony, and Walker, the 1947 team leader in batting average and runs batted in, was seeking a substantial raise for 1948. Dixie's excellent '47 season, at age 36, allowed Rickey to exercise one of his guiding principles in trading players, one that evidently had been adopted by CBS. It was better to get rid of them a year too early rather than a year too late. Moreover, the Dodgers were loaded with young outfielders, including Duke Snider, Carl Furillo, Gene Hermanski, and George Shuba.

According to Mike Gaven, who covered the Dodgers for the *New York*

Journal-American, Rickey had told Walker to play the season in Brooklyn, and then he would send him to the club of his choice and give him the purchase price. Walker chose Pittsburgh.[9]

Jackie Robinson wrote in 1955 that Walker made $30,000 in 1947, and did not want his salary cut in half to manage at St. Paul. Rickey engineered the deal with Pittsburgh so that Dixie would receive the same $30,000 salary. Knowing the Pirates were willing to pay Walker $20,000, Rickey put him on waivers, allowing the Pirates, last in 1947, to claim him for one dollar. The Pirates then added the $10,000 waiver price to bring Walker's 1948 salary up to $30,000. Both clubs covered up the details of the transaction to make it seem that Walker was part of the trade for Roe and Cox.[10]

Walker was home in Birmingham when Pirates general manager Roy Hamey called to tell him of the transaction. Dixie said he had known the trade to Pittsburgh was coming since November, after he told Rickey he preferred to stay in the major leagues rather than manage at St. Paul. Dixie was his typically gracious self in his remarks about leaving the Dodgers. "Naturally, I regret leaving Brooklyn but I cannot say I am unhappy over going to Pittsburgh," he said. "In nine years with the Dodgers I've made many close friends. I love those Brooklyn people." Walker said that for the past nine years he had played before "the finest and most sincere group of people a man could ever hope to play before." He added that "the newspaper and radio men have been most kind and generous in their treatment of me."[11]

In a 1974 interview, Dixie recalled those days in Brooklyn and at Ebbets Field. "There was a feeling in that ballpark that probably will never be recaptured again. I'll always be fond of my years in Brooklyn, even though I didn't know what I was getting into when I went there. The people loved the Dodgers as if they were a part of them."[12]

Walker's youngest son, Stephen, attested to his love of playing in Brooklyn. Dixie often told Stephen he felt he had a few more years left in him and wanted to end it in Brooklyn. It broke his heart when he had to leave the Dodgers.[13] "He loved those days in Brooklyn," remembered Harry Walker. "He doesn't care much about those other teams, just the Brooklyn Dodgers."[14]

Rickey claimed he had received only a dozen or so letters critical of the trade. "They were without exception from people who liked Dixie," he said. "I understood all of the letters. I might have written them myself if I'd been in the public's place. I like Dixie too. But all of them were tempered and friendly. Nothing like the violent communications I received when I traded Dolph Camilli."[15] Of course, the Camilli trade had been unexpected, while the fans had been reading about Dixie's likely departure for several months.

Walker arrived in Pittsburgh on January 17, 1948, and signed his contract in Hamey's office. Entering his 21st season as a professional, Dixie was realistic about his future. "I know I'm not a fellow they can bank on for too long, but I think I have some baseball left and will give them my best." He admitted that he would miss the Brooklyn fans, who had treated him so well. "But starting from scratch with a club like this is a great opportunity." Walker predicted the other ex-Dodgers involved in the trade — Lombardi and Gregg — plus shortstop Stan Rojek and first baseman Ed Stevens, whom Pittsburgh had purchased from Brooklyn the previous November, all would help the Pirates in 1948.[16]

The Pittsburgh club had changed ownership recently. A group of four men — John Galbreath, Frank McKinney, Thomas P. Johnson, and singer Bing Crosby — had purchased the team in August 1946. With the addition of Hank Greenberg and the blossoming of Ralph Kiner, the 1947 Pirates had their largest attendance ever, 1,283,531, an increase of more than 530,000 over 1946. It was the first time the club had ever drawn a million fans. But the team that finished seventh in 1946, finished seventh again in 1947. When they went to spring training in 1948, they had a new manager. Billy Meyer had replaced Walker's old teammate, Billy Herman. Greenberg had since retired, but in addition to Walker, Lombardi, and Gregg the Pirates had added proven veteran Johnny Hopp and a group of promising rookies, led by pitcher Bob Chesnes and catcher Ed Fitz Gerald.

When Walker arrived in Hollywood, California, for spring training, he found himself in a familiar situation, one he had dealt with almost all his baseball life, trying to nail down a regular position. Meyer had said his outfield was set in left field with Ralph Kiner and in center field with Hopp. Walker would have to compete for the right field job with Wally Westlake, coming off a productive rookie season.

Dixie's first league game as a Pirate was against the Reds on Opening Day in Cincinnati. Facing Ewell Blackwell, he tripled in his first at-bat and later singled, but Pittsburgh lost, 4–1. Blackwell had been the league's best pitcher in 1947, leading in wins and strikeouts and finishing second to Boston's Bob Elliott in the MVP voting. "He looked like a man falling out of a tree," was how Walker described the six-feet-six, 195-pound right-hander, who threw sidearm and seemed to show the batter nothing but arms and legs.[17]

The game's most memorable incident was a free-for-all in the eighth inning following the Reds' Babe Young's double off Vic Lombardi. On his way to second, Young collided with shortstop Stan Rojek. After both hit the ground, Young got up, touched second, and then grabbed Rojek. Both men started swinging, while teammates tried to separate them. Meanwhile, fans in the right-field seats began throwing bottles on the field. Umpire Beans Reardon eventually cleared the field, but when play resumed, Young was no longer the runner at second. During the ruckus, Walker had tossed the ball

21. "The place doesn't look the same since you've gone, Dixie"

in from the outfield, where Lombardi picked it up and tagged Young while he was still tussling with Rojek.

When Walker and the Pirates made their first visit to Ebbets Field, on May 21, the Dodgers were in sixth place and had a five-game losing streak, all at home, including the last three to St. Louis. Brooklyn fans welcomed Dixie home with a new car, presented in a pregame ceremony by his old friend, Judge Sam Leibowitz. With Walker, looking strange in his grey Pittsburgh visitor's uniform, standing by his side, Leibowitz expressed the sentiments of a multitude of Brooklynites. "The place doesn't look the same since you've gone, Dixie," Leibowitz said. "You belong among the great immortals of Brooklyn baseballdom."[18] After thanking the fans, Walker drove in the first Pittsburgh run with a sacrifice fly and had a run-scoring single in the ninth to remind them of what was now gone forever. Pittsburgh's 8–4 win extended the Dodgers' losing streak to six games.

The Ebbets Field patrons had begun booing Leo Durocher, who had returned as the Dodgers manager. Within two months, Leo would leave to manage the Giants, with Shotton returning to take over the Brooklyn club. Shotton had been the first pennant-winning manager not to be rehired by his team since Rogers Hornsby of the Cardinals in 1927.

Brooklyn fans, unhappy with the team's poor play, expressed their displeasure by staying away — only 8,803 showed up for this game. A rise in admission prices and the trading of two of the local favorites — Walker and Eddie Stanky — added to their discontent. In March, the Dodgers had traded second baseman Stanky to the Boston Braves to free the position for Jackie Robinson. The Braves went on to win the pennant while the Dodgers slipped to third.

Braves outfielder Tommy Holmes thought the acquisition of Stanky was instrumental in helping them win. He also thought the Dodgers had hurt themselves by getting rid of Walker. "I think Dixie Walker's shift to the Pirates hurt the Dodgers too. If Stanky and Walker stayed with Brooklyn all season it would have been a lot tougher for us to win."[19] But when Shotton was asked if having Walker and Stanky would have made the difference this year, he defended his old pal and boss Branch Rickey. "Stanky and Walker just didn't fit into his plans for the Dodgers of the future," he said.[20]

Unlike the ostentatious charade it has now become, the All-Star Game was still a highlight of the baseball season in 1948. In the days before interleague play and the constant movement of players from team to team, it was a chance for fans to see the star players from the other league. And not only in the city where it was being played; the game was now being televised nationally, making it possible for millions of fans to watch. At a time when the league's separate identities were more clearly defined, both players and fans took greater pride in their league's winning the game. For the players, there was an additional incentive for the game to retain its popularity; proceeds went to their pension fund.

The 1948 game, played at St. Louis and won by the American League, 5–2, was played without controversy, unlike the events leading up to it. Some star players had chosen to bypass the All-Star Game, a move that had angered many of the other players. Members of the Cincinnati Reds had gone so far as to send a letter to Walker, concerning players using the three-day break as a vacation rather than taking part in the game. Following Dixie's trade to Pittsburgh, Hugh Casey had taken his place as Brooklyn's player representative, but Dixie retained his position as the National League's player representative.

The letter did not mention specific names, but based on who had pulled out of the game, it was clear they were targeting Indians pitcher Bob Feller and Cardinals shortstop Marty Marion. Signed by pitcher Bucky Walters, the letter suggested that in the future a fine equivalent to three days' pay be levied against players who skip the game. Walker said that other National League teams endorsed the Reds' plan, as did Tigers pitcher Fred Hutchinson, the American League's player representative.

Reds players had been outspoken in their criticism of the last-minute withdrawal by Marion. They claimed he looked perfectly healthy against them in the last scheduled game before the All-Star break, when he got St. Louis's only hit to spoil Ken Raffensberger's potential no-hitter. Following a meeting of baseball's Executive Council, Commissioner Chandler, while not endorsing the plan, and also without naming names, issued this statement: "I am very much concerned over the failure of club owners and players to take seriously the All-Star Game. We have had some straight talk. I assume that in the future every player who is voted on the All-Star team will show up. We have no plan to punish anybody, but we will take whatever steps are necessary."

After the meeting, Walker said he did not think this was the time to talk about the form of punishment to be administered. "The fellows are not exactly sure what they want," he said, "except they want something done about absenteeism."[21] They wanted something done because the indifference shown to the game by some players could affect future attendance, and therefore the amount of money going to the players' pension fund.

Dixie may have slowed some as he approached his 38th birthday, but he remained a capable and dangerous hitter. "Dixie Walker is giving us a big lift," manager Billy Meyer said on the last day of August. "He knew we never expected a full season out of him, but just wanted him to be ready when needed. He is now, and he is doing a wonderful job."[22]

Led by Dixie, Ralph Kiner's 40 home runs, and the pitching of rookie Bob Chesnes (14–6) and 41-year-old Rip Sewell (13–3), the Pirates improved by 21 games and climbed from last place to a surprising fourth, one game behind the third-place Dodgers. By contrast to Brooklyn's attendance, which decreased 400,000 from 1947, attendance at Forbes Field increased by more than 200,000.

"I wasn't hitting much more than .225 at first," Walker said about his first season in Pittsburgh, "but came back the last half of the season. My final average was .316. I must have hit more than .350 the last half."[23] During the season's final month, Dixie had two four-hit games, the last of his career. But that last half-season had taken its toll. "I knew I was through," he said. He told Meyer not to count on him for 1949, but Meyer and GM Hamey had confidence that he could still do it. "I was just as confident I couldn't," Dixie confessed.[24]

Walker was a new father when he returned for a final season. His fifth child, Sean Casey Shea Walker, was born March 9, 1949, at St. Vincent's Hospital in Birmingham. In returning, Dixie joined future Hall of Famers Joe DiMaggio, Johnny Mize, and Luke Appling as the only ten-year players active in 1949 who had better than a .300 lifetime batting average. He played in just 88 games, and his .282 average marked the first time he failed to better the .300 mark in seven years.

Dixie, however, did lead the National League with 13 pinch hits, including his only home run of the season, the 105th and final four-bagger of his career. Appropriately, it came at Ebbets Field — against Ralph Branca on July 20 — sailing over the

Dixie was the oldest non-pitcher in the National League in 1949 (National Baseball Hall of Fame Library, Cooperstown, New York).

right field fence and landing on Bedford Avenue. Always more of a slashing line-drive hitter than a power hitter, Walker finished his career with 2,064 hits and a .306 batting average.

"Sometimes I wonder how good a ballplayer I could've been if I hadn't got hurt so much," Dixie said. "Pretty good, I guess."[25] Even with those missed years, he was more than "pretty good"; he was among the best players of his era. As for missing the equivalent of three years because of injuries, it was, after all, those injuries that made him unfit for wartime service. Had he not had them, he likely would have missed a similar amount of time in the military.

The second time Walker played a tangential part in American artistic culture was his appearance in the Norman Rockwell painting variously titled "The Three Umpires," "Game Called Because of Rain," or "Bottom of the Sixth Inning." The painting first appeared on the cover of the *Saturday Evening Post* on April 23, 1949. It depicts a discussion at home plate between Brooklyn's Leo Durocher (some believe it to be Clyde Sukeforth) and Pirates manager Billy Meyer, as the three umpires — Larry Goetz, Beans Reardon, and Lou Jorda — check the sky for rain. Rockwell portrays Walker, the right fielder, standing with his hands on his hips in front of the Ebbets Field scoreboard.

That same umpiring crew was working the September 5 Pirates-Cardinals doubleheader at Sportsman's Park. In the tenth inning of the second game, Meyer sent Walker up as a pinch-hitter to face George Munger. Goetz, a National League umpire since 1936 with a reputation of having a short fuse when it came to players or managers protesting his calls, was behind the plate. The Cardinals chose to intentionally walk Dixie, but during the course of that intentional pass, Walker and Goetz got into a shouting match. Goetz accused Dixie of what he called "stretching across the plate" on Munger's pitches, and when Walker loudly protested Goetz ejected him from the game.

"I was not stretching across the plate," Walker insisted the next day. "I saw an outside chance to drive a ball in an opening between second and third and break up the ball game. I even showed Goetz my fresh footprints. He tried to shove me back like he always does with players. Only this time I didn't feel like being shoved. I waited 11 years to tell Goetz off and believe me it was worth the money." The money he referred to was a $100 fine plus a three-day suspension given to him by league president Ford Frick.

Dixie said he resented Goetz's "attitude toward young players," whom he felt Goetz treated as if they had no right to question his decisions. "The fans pay to see legitimate baseball and not a game run the way one umpire wants it run, with the younger players having no right to squawk about anything."[26]

Throughout his final season as an active major-league player, Walker

21. "The place doesn't look the same since you've gone, Dixie"

devoted much of his time to his duties as the National League's player representative. During the All-Star break, he met with Hutchinson to discuss a series of player complaints they planned to submit to the Major League Executive Committee. That committee was now made up of Frick, AL president Will Harridge, St. Louis Browns owner Bill DeWitt, and Pirates owner Frank McKinney.

Walker felt especially strongly about all the bonuses going to young players. "Ballplayers of both leagues feel that signing these youngsters to bonus contracts is forcing older fellows out before their time and is also bringing an inferior brand of baseball before the public." He did not get a satisfactory response on that issue, but McKinney and DeWitt agreed to several other proposals he and Hutchinson made, including the installation of cinder warning tracks in the outfield by the start of the 1950 season.[27]

The news on the financial front, however, was extremely discouraging. Walker and Hutchinson disclosed that the players' pension fund instituted in 1947 was a flop and in danger of collapsing. "It's no use to kid ourselves," Walker said. "The plan has not panned out as well as we hoped it would. We're just not taking in enough money to meet the cost of operation. We went into the hole for $80,000 last year." Walker said the plan needed to take in an additional $200,000 a year for the next eight years to stay in business. He said that the fund had taken in $497,000 and had paid out $572,345.[28]

"We were forced to take more than $80,000 out of our own reserve fund of $272,000 to make up the deficit," Hutchinson said. "Obviously this can't go on. We simply must figure out ways and means to raise money or give up the ghost."[29]

Under the rules of the pension plan then in effect, a five-year man received $50 a month after the age of 50, and a ten-year man received $100 a month. Among the plans being considered to increase revenue were raising the age from 50 to 55 and playing two All-Star games.

Yet a year later Hutchinson was stressing all the positive things that had been accomplished. "The big leaguer's lot today is a thousand times better than it was ten years ago. But don't give me the credit. Most of the groundwork was done by Dixie Walker and Johnny Murphy when they were the player representatives," Hutchinson said. "Look at all the good they did," he continued. "They helped make the retirement pension a success, they saw to it that a player's salary couldn't be cut by more than 25 per cent from one year to another, and they got a better deal for every player in spring training."[30]

Late in the 1949 season, when it was obvious that Walker's playing days were over, there were rumors that he would take a salaried position for the Players Guild. But even at age 39, Dixie Walker was not yet ready to trade in a baseball uniform for a business suit.

22

Managing in the Minor Leagues

Dixie Walker, with a long expressed interest in managing, had spent the last years of his career studying the game with that goal in mind. Following his release by the Pirates, he began almost immediately looking for a team to manage for the 1950 season. Bucky Walters had been let go in Cincinnati, but the Reds filled that position with Luke Sewell, a man with six years of experience leading the St. Louis Browns. With no major league jobs open, Dixie decided to start a step lower and seek out a manager's job in one of the Triple A leagues. He was at the Dodgers-Yankees World Series in New York hoping to find an open spot in the Pacific Coast League, but nothing came of that. After arriving back in Birmingham, he called Jack Dunn, owner of the International League Orioles, asking to be considered for the open manager's job in Baltimore. "Walker is very much in the running," said Dunn, before selecting one-time big-league outfielder Nick Cullop.[1]

Meanwhile, an opportunity much closer to home was developing. Earl Mann, owner of the Atlanta Crackers of the Double A Southern Association, had fired his manager, Cliff Dapper, and was looking for a replacement. Mann wanted Mel Ott, but the former Giants skipper was not interested.[2] When Mann learned that the recently retired Walker was available, he offered him the job. On December 5, 1949, Dixie signed to manage the Crackers in 1950. "Branch Rickey would have dropped dead if Dixie ever returned a signed pact without lengthy quibbling," wrote the *Brooklyn Daily Eagle* when Walker signed his Atlanta contract.[3]

"We are happy to have Dixie back in Dixie," said Mann.[4] Walker was equally pleased at getting his first chance to run a ball club. "This is a great opportunity for me. It is what I have always wanted to do when my playing days were at an end," he said.[5] "I'm gonna see what I can do with this old cerebellum," Dixie said in a mid-winter interview while tapping his head. "Shucks, I've been squinting at fast balls in the twilight and chasing fly balls back to the screen long enough."[6]

Walker had played under a variety of managers in his 18-year big-league career: Joe McCarthy with the Yankees, Mickey Cochrane and Del Baker with the Tigers, Jimmy Dykes with the White Sox, Leo Durocher and Burt Shotton with the Dodgers, and Billy Meyer with the Pirates. While his greatest success had come under Durocher, he said he had no particular managerial model in mind. "I hope I have learned something from each of them that will help me as a manager."[7]

One thing he had learned was the importance of a strong pitching staff. So in late February, Dixie headed to Buchanan, Georgia, where he secured former teammate Whit Wyatt, now 42, to be his pitching coach. "The Boston Braves," said Mann, referring to Atlanta's new major-league affiliation, "are tickled to get Whit into the system."[8]

Two days after landing Wyatt, Walker drove to the Atlanta suburb of Buckhead, where he paid a visit to Hugh Casey. The 36-year-old Casey had pitched for the Pirates in 1949 and briefly for the Yankees, who released him after the season. Casey's big-league career was over; nevertheless, Walker believed his former Brooklyn teammate could still be an effective pitcher, at least at the Double A level, and signed him to pitch for the Crackers.

Not much was expected of the Atlanta club Walker inherited in 1950, but Dixie was not discouraged. He spent most of his time at training camp teaching what he knew best — hitting. He turned his pitchers over to Wyatt, but he was not without his own thoughts on the subject. "More pitchers get sore arms because their legs are not in condition than for any other reason," he said. "A pitcher can never do too much running," Wyatt agreed. "I realized that early on in my career, and I guess that's why I lasted as long as I did."[9]

By midsummer Walker had the Crackers in first place. Harry Walker, back with the Cardinals and at Ebbets Field for a series against Brooklyn, reveled in his brother's success. "Nobody thought Dixie had a chance to win when he took the job of manager," Harry said. "But he's got his kid team right up there fighting for a pennant. I would like to see him make it. I sure would like it."[10]

Aided by his two former teammates, Dixie led the Crackers to a surprising first-place finish. Wyatt cajoled 92 wins out of a rather nondescript pitching staff; Casey, working mostly in relief, led the club with 45 appearances and compiled a 10–4 record. Atlanta won four straight over Memphis in the first round of the Southern Association playoffs, but lost, four games to one, to Nashville in the finals.

A major portion of the credit for the Crackers' success went to Walker, who in addition to managing, served as the third-base coach. Dixie also played in 39 games, mostly as a pinch-hitter, and batted a respectable .273. His most lasting contribution may have been his work in tutoring Eddie Mathews, a scared youngster with only Class D experience. Under Walker's tutelage, the 18-year-old third baseman and future Hall of Famer batted .286 with 32 home runs. Dixie knew as much about hitting as anybody, Mathews later said.

For finishing first with a team given little chance of even having a winning record, Walker won the Southern Association's Manager of the Year award. The difference, according to *Atlanta Constitution* sportswriter Guy Tiller, was Walker's "patient and intelligent handling of each player, and his detailed instructions on how to correct faults and avoid mistakes."[11]

Because of his success in Atlanta, Dixie's name was mentioned as a possible successor to Eddie Dyer in St. Louis. Cardinals owner Fred Saigh had expressed interest in Walker and questioned several baseball people about his qualifications. The responses were positive and led to a meeting between the two, held without fanfare, in St. Louis early in November. A spokesman for Saigh said that Walker was one of 18 candidates, and not necessarily the leading one. Marty Marion, the former Cardinals shortstop, had been the frontrunner all along, and it was Marion whom Saigh hired.[12]

Another scenario, a decidedly more intriguing one, had Walker returning to Brooklyn to replace manager Burt Shotton. In a front-page story in the October 11 edition of *The Sporting News*, editor/publisher J.G. Taylor Spink reported that Branch Rickey probably would move from Brooklyn to the St. Louis Browns. (Rickey did leave, but he went to Pittsburgh.) With Rickey gone, Walter O'Malley would replace Burt Shotton with either Pee Wee Reese or Dixie Walker. Reese appeared to be the top choice, but Pee Wee believed he had several years of playing time left and did not want to burden himself with the managerial duties. Spink speculated that O'Malley would then choose Walker.[13]

A month later, on November 9, Thad Horton, a radio commentator on station WSB in Atlanta, reported that he had an "exclusive announcement." Horton said "sources in New York" had told him Walker was about to be named manager of the Dodgers. "I don't know a thing about it," Walker said. "I've been left out of any such announcement."[14]

Jackie Robinson's reaction to the chance of Dixie getting the job is worth noting. Robinson, on tour with the Negro League's Indianapolis Clowns in late October 1950, was asked his reaction to Walker managing the Dodgers. It was fine with him, Jackie said, adding that he would not mind playing under Walker.

"If there are any arguments against the appointment of Walker," wrote Dan Daniel, "they certainly do not include his possible relationship as an Alabamian to Jackie Robinson, Roy Campanella, Dan Bankhead, and Don Newcombe. The old Dixie-Negro factor no longer carries weight in baseball."[15]

22. Managing in the Minor Leagues

Nevertheless, O'Malley chose Charlie Dressen, Leo Durocher's one-time assistant, to manage the Dodgers in 1951. With all the major league managerial jobs filled, Dixie returned to Atlanta, but strictly in a non-playing capacity. Whatever notions he may have had of again being an active player for the Crackers in 1951 were dispelled after a few batting practice sessions during spring training. "My legs are good for another year or two, but my timing is gone," he said. "I can't meet the ball like I used to. I either get around too late or too fast. I just can't get into the ball anymore. I know it's finished. I've known since the 1948 season with Pittsburgh. I'm strictly a bench manager from now on."[16] For the first time since 1927, Dixie Walker's name did not appear on any team's active players list.

The Southern Association was still segregated in 1951, but on April 8 of that year, the Crackers played an exhibition game against the Dodgers at Atlanta's Ponce De Leon Park. Many in the overflow crowd of 17,522 were blacks who had come to see Jackie Robinson and the Dodgers' other black stars. Walker told his players before the game that they should model their play on the Dodgers. "The Dodgers hustle. They run the bases like rabbits. Don't make any mistakes against 'em or they'll murder you in your sleep." But the Dodgers were mostly listless during the game, including Robinson. They made five errors, and neither of their black pitchers, Don Newcombe or Dan Bankhead, was effective, allowing 15 hits in an 8–6 loss. Kirby Higbe, like Wyatt and Casey, a former Dodgers pitcher and Walker teammate, went all the way for Atlanta.[17]

The 1951 season was a difficult one for Walker, both on and off the field. Eddie Mathews missed the first part of the season serving in the Korean War, and after he returned, the Braves promoted him to their Triple A team in Milwaukee. The Crackers struggled to a sixth-place finish, 17½ games behind the league-leading Little Rock Travelers.

Dixie's friend Hugh Casey was no longer involved with baseball, having failed in his attempt to rejoin the Dodgers for the 1951 season. In addition, Casey's personal life was in crisis. He was now drinking to excess; the Internal Revenue Service was after him for more than $6,700 in unpaid income taxes; and a young Brooklyn girl named Hilda Weissman had filed a paternity suit against him.

On July 3, in an Atlanta hotel, 37-year-old Hugh Casey used a shotgun to kill himself. The funeral was held the following day, with Walker and Wyatt serving as pallbearers. Casey was buried beside his parents in Atlanta's Mount Paran Church of God cemetery.

At the time, Walker was serving a suspension for his actions in a June 29 game against the Mobile Bears. Dixie had disputed umpire Paul Roy's call on a play at the plate after the umpire had first called a Mobile runner out and then ruled him safe. Roy said he changed the call because the Crackers catcher had obstructed the runner by bumping him. Walker was so upset he pulled his players off the field and refused Roy's orders to have them retake their positions. When the Atlanta players remained in their dugout, Roy forfeited the game to Mobile.

Afterwards, Southern Association president Charles Hurth said, "I am suspending Manager Walker indefinitely pending my investigation of the forfeiture."[18] Walker was suspended for 90 days and fined $100. A 90-day suspension would not be over until early in the 1952 season. "There's nothing I can say," Walker told the press. "This leaves me high and dry. I'll tell you though, that I certainly feel it. Why ninety days suspension just never occurred to me."[19]

Walker appealed the fine and suspension, backed by Crackers owner Earl Mann, who blamed Roy for losing control of the situation. At a July 29 meeting attended by Hurth, Roy and George Trautman, the president of all the Minor Leagues, Trautman lifted the remaining 60 games of the suspension and returned the $100.

Walker spent a third and final season in Atlanta in 1952, leading the Crackers to a second-place finish. After the Southern Association season ended, he went to New York to visit Estelle's relatives on Long Island and take in the Dodgers-Yankees World Series. Visiting Ebbets Field for the Dodgers final regular season game, Dixie said he had not forgotten the fans who never forgot him. "The best thing that could happen to the Brooklyn fans would be a victory over the Yanks in the Series," he said.[20]

On September 30, Mann announced Dixie would not be returning in 1953. Mann said the separation, while mutually agreed upon, had come up so suddenly, he had not thought about a replacement. "Dixie thought it would be better to settle it here in New York where he would have a chance to talk to some people," Mann said. Although Mann didn't know Walker's plans, he assumed "the fact that Dixie had initiated the discussion indicated that he might be seeking a position in higher baseball circles."[21]

Mann eventually chose Gene Mauch, who stayed in Atlanta for just a year. In 1954, Mauch was replaced by the man Walker had hired to be his pitching coach, Whit Wyatt. "I guess the best thing that ever happened to me was when Dixie talked me into returning to baseball," said Wyatt, who had been out of the game until Walker brought him back as the Crackers pitching coach in 1950. "I haven't regretted a minute of it."[22]

Meanwhile, Pittsburgh had fired Billy Meyer, and Walker met with Pirates GM Branch Rickey during the '52 World Series to discuss the team's open managerial position. When asked by a reporter if he was interested in managing the lowly Pirates, Walker replied, "Any fellow who's just managed

22. Managing in the Minor Leagues

in the minor leagues and wouldn't take a job in the majors is just plain nuts." About being let go by the Crackers, he said, "It's just one of those things you have to expect in baseball."[23]

After the Pirates hired Fred Haney as their manager for 1953, Walker turned to his second choice. He applied to the Sacramento Solons of the Pacific Coast League. Sacramento had fired their manager, former Yankees second baseman Joe Gordon, the same day Dixie was fired at Atlanta. That job ended up going to Gene Desautels.

Thwarted again in his attempt to return to the big leagues as a manager, Walker made it back as a coach. Two weeks before Christmas, the St. Louis Cardinals hired him to be their first-base coach and to help coach their outfielders. Walker was replacing Terry Moore, who'd had a running feud with Cardinals manager Eddie Stanky since midway through the 1952 season. Owner Fred Saigh said that Stanky made the decision to sign Walker, but that he was in agreement with the choice.

At spring training with the Cardinals in 1953, Walker told the press how happy he was to be back in the big leagues. He mentioned specifically his joy at being in New York City for 22 games. "It's wonderful to be in the big time again, wonderful to know that for 11 games I will be back in Flatbush and for 11 more at the Polo Grounds revisiting the old scenes, meeting old friends, and reviving memories of my nine great seasons with the Dodgers."[24]

However, Dixie was with St. Louis only until July 30, when as part of an organization-wide shakeup, the Cardinals chose him to replace Al Hollingsworth as manager of the Houston Buffs, their affiliate in the Texas League.

Led by future Cardinals Ken Boyer and Don Blasingame, Dixie's Houston club finished second in 1954, one game behind the Shreveport Sports. Houston then defeated Oklahoma City and Fort Worth — both four games to one — to win the Texas League title. It was a very successful season in Houston, a league

After three years of managing in the minor leagues, Dixie was happy to be back in the majors as a Cardinals coach in 1953 (National Baseball Hall of Fame Library, Cooperstown, New York).

championship and an attendance of 310,000, more than twice that of any of the other seven clubs in the league. Dixie also oversaw the integration of the Houston club, as former major leaguers Bob Boyd and Willard Brown joined the Buffs in midseason and were cited by Walker as key contributors to the team's success.

In the Dixie Series, "the South's version of the World Series," Houston faced Walker's former club, the Southern Association's Atlanta Crackers. The Crackers, now managed by Dixie's friend Whit Wyatt, rallied from a three-games-to one-deficit to win the Series. After the game, Walker graciously congratulated his old teammate in the Crackers' clubhouse. "It's bad trying to beat your best friend," Wyatt told Dixie, "but you were trying to beat me."[25]

One unforgettable day for the Houston fans during the 1954 season came on August 3, when the Walker's sixth child, Stephen Vaughn Walker, was born. Dixie's 17-year-old son Fred, who had a job with the club, was working the switchboard. During the game, a call came in to the park to let Dixie know Estelle was just about to give birth. Fred took the call, but when he was unable to reach his father in the clubhouse, he made the following announcement over the public address system. "Will Dixie Walker, Houston Buffs manager, please go to St Joseph's Hospital, your wife is having my brother." With the crowd cheering the good news, and the delightful way in which it was delivered, Dixie stepped out of the dugout, waved, and left the park.[26]

In 1954, seven years after having threatened to strike rather than play against Jackie Robinson, the Cardinals had their first black player — Tom Alston, a left-handed hitting first baseman. Alston had been a disappointment as a rookie, so in 1955, Walker was called back to St. Louis by manager Stanky to work with Alston and the other St. Louis batters. Mike Ryba exchanged places with Dixie, going from coaching in St. Louis to managing in Houston. Walker worked with Alston at training camp in St. Petersburg, telling him "he was striding too quickly and too far." Dixie also tried to improve Alston's mental approach to hitting. "I just straightened him up, told him to quit feeling sorry for himself and take a three-quarter swing instead of trying to kill the ball each time."[27] In his long and productive career as a batting coach, Dixie Walker helped numerous hitters, but Tom Alston was not one of them. Over the next three seasons, Alston appeared in only 25 games as a major leaguer.

In 1953, Dixie's stint as a Cardinals coach had lasted little more than half a season; in 1955, it lasted even less. In May, with the team struggling, the club fired Stanky and brought in Harry Walker, who had been managing the Rochester Red Wings in the International League. Harry was not successful

In the 1954 Dixie Series, Walker managed the Houston Buffalos against his former club, the Atlanta Crackers, managed by his old friend Whit Wyatt (private collection of Ken Fenster).

The 1954 Texas League champions (private collection of Ken Fenster).

either, and in 1956, St. Louis replaced him with Fred Hutchinson. It would be ten years before Harry Walker managed again at the major league level.

Dixie replaced brother Harry at Rochester and stayed with the Red Wings through the 1956 season. He again had applied for the opening in Pittsburgh in 1956, but Rickey, in one of his last acts as Pirates GM, hired another ex–Dodger and Walker teammate — Bobby Bragan. Though Rochester finished fourth in 1955 and second in 1956, they won the International League playoffs in both seasons. In doing so, they twice won playoff series from the Toronto Maple Leafs — in the first round in 1955 and in the finals in 1956.

Walker and Maple Leafs owner Jack Kent Cooke had clashed at the end of the 1956 season over a series of events that can be seen as a classic argument against the playoff system in baseball. Going into the last day of the season, Montreal was in first place, a half-game ahead of Toronto. The Royals were playing a doubleheader against the Red Wings, while the Maple Leafs were playing a doubleheader against Buffalo. Having clinched fourth place and a spot in the playoffs, Walker chose to save his best pitchers for the playoffs, which if his team won, he reasoned, would put money in the pockets of all his players. Dixie was both accused and defended for using "garbage-man" pitchers against Montreal.

"Under the tradition of good sportsmanship and any code of ethics, Rochester was duty-bound to use its best available pitchers and all its front-line players in the final doubleheader," wrote *Binghamton Press* sports editor John W. Fox. Walker had two of his best pitchers available, Duke Markell and Jack Fasholz, but in the opener, he started Jack Kelly, who had not started a game all season and had pitched only 39 innings. Walker thought so little of Kelly he left him off the playoff roster. Montreal scored five runs against Kelly in the first inning and won the game.

League president Frank Shaughnessy was so upset with Walker's pitching selections, he phoned Rochester GM George Sisler, Jr., ordering him to have Walker start Markell or Fasholz in the second game. Walker paid no attention, and Montreal won the second game against seven-game winner Ed Ludwig. Meanwhile Buffalo started their two best pitchers against Toronto, but although Toronto won both games, they were unable to pass the Royals for first place. (The International League did not require teams to make up games that affected the pennant race.) Markell then started against Montreal in the first game of the playoffs and defeated them.

Fox blamed it all on the playoff system. "The incident boils down to the basic weakness of the playoff system in baseball. The pennant should be the all-important goal and every team should be doing its best to beat every other team right down to the last day."[28] The major leagues would face similar problems after they instituted a playoff system, problems that they have yet to solve.

Most of the Toronto complaints came from owner Cooke, whom Fox had called "a sort of combination Bill Veeck and Frank Lane." Walker responded to Cooke's criticism by calling him a cry baby, and saying the Toronto team had no one but themselves to blame. "Instead of trying to manage the Red Wings, Toronto should look in its own closet," Walker said. "The Leafs had a 7½ game lead as late as the end of June and if anybody is looking for a reason why they lost you can start and stop with the simple fact that they blew it to Montreal."

Dodgers GM Buzzie

Manager Walker's use of his Red Wings pitching staff on the last day of the 1956 season spotlighted the weakness of the playoff system in baseball (National Baseball Hall of Fame Library, Cooperstown, New York).

Bavasi, the Royals' parent club, supported Walker: "Walker should resent everything said about him, and the pitcher Kelly should resent things too. Walker's first obligation is to his ball club. Should Dixie use up his best pitchers in a game that doesn't put a dime in the pockets of his players?" Dixie put a further zinger in to Cooke by sending him a telegram the night before the playoffs saying, "Plan on starting Markell tonight. Hope you approve."

Yet despite Cooke's objections to Walker's strategic maneuvers, or maybe because of them, Dixie had impressed the Leafs' owner. In December, Cooke hired him to replace retiring manager Bruno Betzel for the 1957 season.

Dixie Walker always regretted that he never got a chance to manage the Dodgers. Eventually, he realized he never really had been in the running. "The baseball writers in New York kept doing stories about my impending promotion to managership of the Dodgers," Walker told Dan Daniel. "I now can tell you, I never had a chance." Walker said no Dodgers official had ever approached him about the position. The only managerial nibble he ever had, he added, was when Fred Saigh interviewed him in 1950.[29]

His final opportunity had come at the end of the 1953 season. In his three years in Brooklyn, Charlie Dressen had won two pennants — in 1952 and 1953 — and just missed another, in 1951. Dressen thought that merited his receiving a multi-year contract, but the Dodgers stuck by their policy of one-year contracts for managers. In October '53, when Dressen refused a one-year deal, the Dodgers fired him. Once again, the job of managing the Dodgers was open, and once again Dixie Walker's name was in the mix.

Reporters asked Walter O'Malley if Walker was a viable candidate considering the letter he had written in 1947 saying he would not play with Negro players. "If you think that knocks Dixie out of consideration for this job as manager, you've got another think coming," O'Malley said.[30]

Still, Walker did not get the job, which went to Walter Alston, the same man who had taken the St. Paul manager's job that Dixie refused in 1948. Alston had spent two years with the Saints and four more with Montreal, paving the way for the chance to manage in Brooklyn. If Walker had taken the St. Paul offer back in '48, it is possible he might have followed the same career path.

23

Ending His Career in Dodger Blue

Jack Kent Cooke was a great admirer of Branch Rickey. The two men were part of a group that later founded the Continental League, an expansion league that never came to fruition. Cooke brought the first black ballplayers to the Toronto Maple Leafs, three of whom Walker inherited. Dixie led Toronto to a first-place finish in 1957, but the Leafs lost to Miami in the first round of the International League playoffs. Humberto Robinson, a dark-skinned Panamanian, won 18 games for Walker, and Don Johnson won 17 games.

Oddly, the only "racial incident" of the season occurred in mid–July when Johnson, an Oregon-born white pitcher, jumped the club saying, "I will never pitch another game for the Toronto Maple Leafs until they get rid of that rebel S.O.B. who manages them."[1] A few days later Johnson changed his mind and returned to the team.

The Leafs finished second in 1958 but lost in the league finals to Montreal. In 1959, they did a complete turnaround, finishing in last place. It was an all-around unhappy season for Dixie. In mid August, Toronto papers reported that the 49-year-old manager had traded punches with catcher Tim Thompson during a double shutout loss against Miami. It was triggered when Walker fined Thompson $25 for missing a squeeze bunt sign and Thompson responded by cursing at him.[2]

By late August, Walker was openly predicting this would be his last season in Toronto. "When you win," he said, "you get the praise. When you lose, you get the gate."[3] He resigned on August 30, calling the 1959 season "the worst year I've ever had in baseball as a player, coach, or manager."[4] It was the end of Dixie's managerial career. Six months later an era ended when Ebbets Field, one of the game's great landmarks, was torn down to make room for an apartment complex. The Ebbets Field Apartments opened in 1962. Ten years later, it was renamed the Jackie Robinson Apartments.

Dixie was out of uniform — at least temporarily — but not out of baseball.

On November 2, 1959, the Milwaukee Braves signed him to scout players in the Southern states. Walker spent three years in that capacity before again putting on a uniform. In the fall of 1962, he was in Bradenton, Florida, serving as the batting instructor for Braves prospects in the Florida Instructional League, when team president John McHale asked the 52-year-old Walker to instruct the parent club in the art of hitting.

"He did an excellent job as a scout and we would like to keep him in that capacity," McHale said. "But we felt that there was an immediate need for instruction of the young players on our club. We think Dixie will do a real good job for us."[5] Walker signed on for his new coaching job after a meeting with McHale and manager Bobby Bragan. Dixie, who also frequently served as the first-base coach, was happy to be reunited with old friend Whit Wyatt, another of Bragan's coaches.

The Braves had winning seasons in their final three years in Milwaukee, but finished in the middle (sixth, fifth and fifth) of the ten-team National League in each. In 1964, they had the best offense in the league, and much of the credit went to Walker.[6] He was instrumental in the improved hitting of Rico Carty, Lee Maye, and Denis Menke. Carty, a rookie, batted .330, while Maye, a lifetime .269-hitter, batted .304. Menke, with a reputation as a weak hitter during his first two seasons, batted .283 with 20 home runs. Milwaukee's total number of doubles climbed from 204 in 1963 to 274 in 1964. Maye went from 22 doubles in 1963 to 44 in 1964, Menke from 16 to 29. None of this would have happened without the special efforts of the players, Walker insisted. "It's up to the hitter himself," he said. "His attitude is all important. If he wants to improve himself and will try to do it, chances are that something can be worked out."[7]

Walker loved talking about hitting and hitters. "I've seen a lot of great ones," he said, "but the most dangerous of them all with men on base was a man I played with and against, Bill Dickey of the Yankees."[8]

When the Braves moved to Atlanta in 1966, they put Dixie in charge of scouting in the Southeast. Three years later, he was back in uniform as a batting instructor for the Los Angeles Dodgers. Walker had applied for the job in a letter to Walter O'Malley, after Duke Snider left at the end of the 1968 season to take a similar job with the San Diego Padres. "It's just like coming home," he told Dodgers vice president Al Campanis when the Dodgers' chief of scouting informed him of his selection.[9]

So much had changed since he first put on a Brooklyn Dodgers uniform in 1939, but Dixie loved being a Dodger again. In a 1974 interview, he reminisced about his love for Brooklyn and Ebbets Field. "There was a feeling in that ballpark that probably will never be recaptured again. I'll always be fond of my years in Brooklyn, even though I didn't know what I was getting into when I went there. The people loved the Dodgers as if they were a part of them." Speaking of the Los Angeles fans, he said. "They're a different class. They're more subdued, orderly. They seem to have more to relate to in California than just baseball."[10]

Walker got started in his new role by coaching young Dodgers prospects in the Arizona Instructional League. In sizing up his team's chances for the 1969 season, Dodgers manager Walter Alston said Walker's presence had been a big help. Speaking at spring training, Alston said, "Dixie has been able to call a boy aside and work with his hitting. It's difficult to criticize and correct with a six-man audience. Private tutoring is very important."[11]

Early in the season, Walker's lessons earned him high praise from his manager and from the players. According to Alston, "Dixie has a nice, quiet way of suggesting things. Players don't get the idea he's trying to force them to do things."[12] When first baseman Wes Parker was asked why his and some of his teammates' hitting had improved, he attributed it to his new batting coach. "I'll tell you why. Dixie Walker is the reason why and he's the reason a lot of us have changed our attitudes. Ask Andy Kosco or Ron Fairly or any of the guys who worked at Vero Beach and they'll tell you the same thing. Dixie has brought confidence and relaxation to me." Parker added, "It's just the attitude that he's instilled in all of us that's done it."[13] Along with the help he provided at spring training, Walker remained with the club during the season. "Dixie stayed with us most of last year," said

The Milwaukee Braves had the National League's best offense in 1964, with much of the credit going to batting coach Walker (National Baseball Hall of Fame Library, Cooperstown, New York).

Parker. "He's the first hitting coach we ever carried during the season. Dixie not only corrected my swing, he was there to keep it corrected."[14] A mediocre hitter during his first four seasons, Parker raised his average from .239 in 1968 and .278 in 1969 to .319 in 1970, fifth highest in the league. His league-leading 47 doubles were more than twice the 23 he had in 1969.

Center fielder Willie Davis, a nine-year veteran, also profited from Dixie's teachings. "If I'd been swinging in past years the way I'm doing this spring," Davis said, "why I really believe that I could be making $150,000 a year instead of $50,000. You know all Dixie Walker has been doing is saying, 'Line drives. I want to see nothing but line drives.' And when I stop swinging from my heels it comes easy. I can do it."[15] Davis, who had never reached the .300 mark in his eight full seasons in the league, surpassed it in the next three.

Another Dodger who benefited from Walker's instruction was Maury Wills. Wills was batting .222 in 47 games with the Montreal Expos when the Dodgers reacquired him in a June 11, 1969, trade. Wills then batted .297 in 104 games with Los Angeles. "Dixie Walker had a lot to do with my improvement last year. He got me out of the bad batting habits I had picked up."[16] Walker continued to work with Wills. "I'm very pleased with the way I'm hitting and I give a lot of credit to Dixie Walker," said the 38-year-old shortstop in May 1971. "Dixie watches me during batting practice every day and reminds me of the things I should be doing. I don't care how old you are, you can still be reminded. Dixie is a great asset to this club and any player who doesn't listen to him is foolish."[17]

Early in 1970, Walker was part of a group that conducted baseball clinics at military bases in West Germany and England, and for amateur clubs in Holland. Al Campanis led the group that also included Dodgers pitching coach Red Adams, Cardinals first baseman Joe Torre, and Emmett Ashford, major league baseball's first black umpire.[18]

Meanwhile, Walker continued helping improve the Dodgers hitters. Infielder Jim Lefebvre had been the National League's Rookie of the Year in 1965, but injuries and declining batting averages had him contemplating retirement during the 1969 season, though he was just 27. In late August, Walker advised him to begin writing down all the positive things he was doing at the plate. Lefebvre did so and had a solid September, in which he batted .269 and drove in 12 runs, his highest full-month batting average and RBI total of the season. "Dixie said I was doing so many things right," said Lefebvre, "that I should write all the good points down while they were fresh in my mind."[19]

Outfielder Willie Crawford said, "Dixie Walker has opened up my stance, and what I do with my legs now is a lot like what you're supposed to do when swinging a golf club. In fact, the last few days I've gone to a driving range and hit about 100 golf balls so that I can develop a groove."[20]

That Crawford never developed his full potential was a big disappointment to Walker. In his first Dodgers training camp in 1969 Dixie had said of him, "This young man has as much potential as anyone I've ever seen."[21] Among the other Dodgers Dixie worked with were Billy Grabarkewitz, Steve Yeager, Steve Garvey, and Bill Russell.

But Walker went beyond mere hitting tips in trying to help players reach their full potential. When he was at Milwaukee, he had urged Joe Torre, a chubby young catcher, to lose weight. By 1971, Torre, now a Cardinals third baseman, was on his way to a batting championship and a Most Valuable Player Award. Torre credited his success to a diet that reduced his weight from 220 to 200. "It's always been my contention that weight takes a player out of his game a year or two early and that is when he's at his peak salary," Walker said.[22]

Diet and nutrition was a constant theme of his. "I would be inclined to say that fewer players are overweight than when I played. The training today is more intensive and the players get more help on what to eat. They weigh in regularly and they speak of diets more today."[23] Dixie himself stayed in relatively good shape in his post-playing years. On June 6, 1971, at age 60, the man writer Patrick McNulty described as tall and scholarly, a "well-mannered quiet-talking Southern gentleman," hit a sharp single to right in a Dodgers old-timers game.[24] In another old-timers game, a year later, he made a nice running catch off former Yankee Andy Carey.

In December of 1973, the Dodgers traded pitcher Claude Osteen to Houston for slugging outfielder Jim Wynn. Wynn's batting average and run production had fallen sharply in '73, some of the blame for which was due to his disagreements with his manager, Harry Walker. Like older brother Dixie, Harry was also a well-known and respected hitting coach. Harry had tried to get Wynn to cut down on his swing and try to hit the ball to all fields.

Dixie moved quickly to head off any possible controversy involving Wynn, Harry, and himself. Jim Wynn is "some kind of amazing hitter just the way he is," he said, while carefully sidestepping any criticism of Harry. "I was aware that Jimmy and Harry may have had some differences," he said, "but I went to Wynn this spring and told him that I didn't want that to affect our relationship, that I wanted him as my friend, which he has been. Our relationship has been beautiful."[25] Encouraged by Walker to be his natural self at the plate, Wynn raised his batting average by 51 points in 1974, and his 108 runs batted in would be his career high.

Because the Dodgers were a younger team in 1974, Walker suggested to Alston, his contemporary in age, that he take a more open approach in his relations with the players. Dixie made the recommendation after several of the younger players had come to him. "Dixie is the only guy on the staff who can get through to Walt," said one.[26] Taking Walker's advice, the normally tight-lipped Alston made an effort to be more communicative and the Dodgers responded by winning the pennant. Walker even got Alston started on playing golf.

After the 1974 season, Walker stepped down as the Dodgers hitting coach, preferring instead to instruct the club's minor leaguers. In 1975, he worked with the farm teams in Albuquerque, New Mexico, and Bellingham, Washington, but did rejoin the Dodgers for an occasional homestand or road trip. Walker was at Vero Beach in 1976, where his major pupil was newly acquired outfielder Dusty Baker. "Dusty came to me the first day we were in Florida and asked for my help," Walker said. "He's open for suggestion and that makes my job so much easier. I find him a player who's determined to reach his potential."[27] Baker starred for the Dodgers for the next eight seasons and went on to a successful career as a major-league manager.

During spring training at Vero Beach in 1971, Walter O'Malley had presented Walker with a silver bat worth $2,500. The bat was given to Dixie as a symbol of his 1944 batting championship and in recognition of the excellent work he'd done as the Dodgers hitting coach. A silver bat was not awarded to the batting champion in 1944, but it was by 1947, when brother Harry won the batting title. "Walter just thought Harry shouldn't have a bat unless I had one too," Dixie said. "It was all his idea, and I certainly thank him for it."[28] In 1977, O'Malley named Walker, Duke Snider, and Carl Furillo on his all-time Dodgers team.

A vote conducted back in 1954 by the 11 newspapermen then covering the Dodgers also selected Dixie to their all-time Brooklyn team. Voting by position, the writers had Walker in right field, Duke Snider in center, and Zack Wheat in left. The others were pitcher Dazzy Vance, catcher Roy Campanella, first baseman Gil Hodges, second baseman Jackie Robinson, shortstop Pee Wee Reese, and third baseman Arky Vaughn.[29]

On Oct. 24, 1972, Jackie Robinson died at the age of 53. "I'm as sad as I possibly could be about his death," Walker told the press. "Me being a Southern boy and raised in the South, it wasn't as easy for me to accept Jackie when he came up. At that time I was resentful of Jackie, and I make no bones about it. But he and I were shaking hands at the end."[30]

Earlier in the year, during spring training, Walker had spoken to reporter Ira Berkow about Robinson. "My attitude has changed over the years," Dixie told Berkow. "I feel like I've learned. You associate with Negro players, as a manager and a coach, day in and day out, and you get to know them like you do white players." Walker talked about the time Judge Samuel Leibowitz, a friend of both men, tried to get them to pose for a picture shaking hands. Walker refused. "Judge, use common sense," Walker told Leibowitz. "You were down in Alabama a few years ago defending those five [sic] black boys who were accused of raping two white girls. [A reference to the Scottsboro case.] You know what those people are thinkin' down South. You got to picture that to know my predicament." Walker praised Pee Wee Reese for the way he stood up for Robinson. "But at the time I had to do what my own mind dictated." Walker said he ran into Robinson and they were friendly toward each other. "I've grown and Jackie knows it. And he's grown too."[31]

Even after Robinson's death, Walker never missed an opportunity to praise his former teammate. "I'll say one thing for Robinson," he told Berkow in 1981, "he was as outstanding an athlete as I ever saw. He had the instinct to always do the right thing on the field. He was a stem-winder of a ballplayer. But you know we never hit it off well. Over the years, though, Robinson and I would meet at Old-Timer's Day games and we sat and chatted some."[32]

He was also very cognizant of Robinson's place as a civil rights pioneer. "The other night I watched a television program and heard mention of a number of people who were important in the blacks gaining advantages in America," he told Berkow in that 1981 interview. "And the name of Jackie Robinson never came up. It surprised me. I mean, how soon people can forget."[33]

Dixie Walker died on May 17, 1982, at St. Vincent's Hospital in Birmingham. He had been suffering from stomach cancer, and in the weeks before his death, the cancer had spread to his kidneys, gall bladder, and colon. Although Dixie was a Protestant, Monsignor Herman Cazalas conducted a prayer service for him at Our Lady of Sorrows Catholic Church in Homewood, Alabama, and then accompanied the funeral cortege to Elmwood Cemetery in Birmingham, where Dixie was buried. At the same church ten years earlier, on June 13, 1972, Dixie and Estelle went through the Catholic rite of convalidation to have their civil marriage sanctioned.[34]

In addition to his beloved Estelle, who lived for another 20 years, Dixie was survived by his daughters, Mary Ann Estelle and Susan, and his son, Stephen.[35] During their 46 years of marriage, Dixie and Estelle had been blessed with a loving marriage and family. But they also had known tragedy, suffering the heartbreaking loss of three children: four-month old Mary Ann of pneumonia in 1940; 34-year-old Fred Jr. in a scuba diving accident in 1971; and 26-year-old Sean of an accidental gunshot wound in 1975.

On June 3, 1985, Walker, a member of the Alabama Sports Hall of Fame since 1973, was inducted into the Brooklyn Dodgers Hall of Fame. The other inductees, Dolph Camilli, Babe Herman, and Johnny Podres, appeared in person at the ceremony held at the Brooklyn Museum. Walker was represented by son Stephen.[36]

Several other former Dodgers were invited, and that night a group of them, including two of Dixie's children, Susan and Stephen, gathered at the historic Gage and Tollner restaurant in downtown Brooklyn to reminisce and tell stories. Several who had played with Walker related their remembrances of him. Camilli called him an all-around player in the traditional sense. He was fast, a good fielder, a very good contact hitter, and he knew the game.[37] Not for nothing had Dixie Walker been known by his peers as a "ballplayers' ballplayer."

24

Was Dixie Walker a Racist?

Had he played for any of the other 15 major league teams in 1947; or had some other owner chosen to be the first to racially integrate his team — hardly likely given the owners' 15–1 vote in opposition to Jackie Robinson — Dixie Walker would be remembered much differently today. But Walker played for the Brooklyn Dodgers in 1947, and it was his team's president — Branch Rickey — who had opened the door to black players, disgracefully closed for so long.

Walker's initial resistance to Robinson in the spring of 1947 haunted him the rest of his life. He called it the "dumbest thing" he ever did and said on numerous occasions that he wished he had handled it differently. Once the 1947 season began, however, he never did anything to oppose or interfere with Robinson's progress. He not only gave Jackie batting tips, but according to Dodgers executive Buzzie Bavasi, he even advised the game's best baserunner in the fine art of sliding.

There is no evidence of a harsh word ever exchanged between Jackie Robinson and Dixie Walker. Seeing Jackie play in 1947 convinced Dixie that the stereotypes of Negro inferiority he had grown up with were ludicrous. Seeing Jackie play over the next nine years led Dixie to call him as outstanding an athlete as he had ever seen. He told his son Stephen that Robinson had more courage than any man he had ever known. As for skill, he would put him up alongside anybody and wished he could go back and change a few things.

Over the years, Walker's pariah status has diminished, yet for far too many people the only image they have of Dixie Walker is that of a bigoted racist who tried to keep Jackie Robinson out of baseball. "Dixie Walker has paid an unfair price for what later day politically correct baseball historians decry as racism," wrote baseball historian Jack Kavanagh. "If there were amends to be made, Dixie made them." Yet he continued to be condemned for what Kavanagh calls "his reluctance to participate in Branch Rickey's Great

Social Experiment." Kavanagh says that what "Dixie did by initiating his own departure was exactly what much of the borough's white population was also doing."[1]

Dixie, while undeniably wrong in what he did, is a victim of "presentism," and should be judged in the context of the times. Historians define presentism as the practice of viewing the past, and judging the people of the past, in terms of today's standards and orthodoxies. It is the applying of current ideals and moral standards to interpret historical figures and their actions. Presentists are guilty of a lack of regard for context, for the meanings or senses that a given practice had for its historical contemporaries as opposed to how it may read to us now.

"It's when a historian sees events in the past through the prism of present-day standards," lawyer-historian Annette Gordon-Reed told William Safire of the *New York Times*. "For example, Thomas Jefferson is often judged harshly as a sexist even though the notion of complete equality between the sexes was almost unthinkable in his era." Gordon-Reed called it the "why wasn't Jefferson like Alan Alda question."

Some modern-day historians have decried the failure of mid-nineteenth century American literary icons, like Herman Melville, Ralph Waldo Emerson, Henry David Thoreau, and Nathaniel Hawthorne, to take a more active role in the abolitionist movement. In his review of Andrew Delbanco's biography of Melville, literary critic Frederick Crews addressed the problem of revisionist historians oftentimes failing to consider the social context of the times in which events took place. Like many others of his era, Melville was deeply opposed to slavery, but he could not see how it could be abolished without a civil war that would lead to the deaths of hundreds of thousands of Americans. Crews cites Delbanco's annoyance with these historians for "allowing for no middle ground between total condemnation and total vindication of his views."[2] Could not Walker's 1947 request to be traded from the Dodgers be seen as his own version of taking the middle ground?

Baseball historian Norman Macht wrote, "A historian who judges a man in the context of today's time and standards and not the standards and conditions of the time in which the subject lived commits a scholarly sin." Macht was not writing about Dixie Walker; he was writing about what he thought were unfair charges against Commissioner Landis's role in the integration of baseball. "There is a vast, unbridgeable distance between what we like to believe we always were as a society and what we really were," Macht wrote.[3]

Therefore, one has to remember "what we really were" in 1947, a time when the general perception among whites that blacks did not have what it takes to succeed was not limited to baseball. In 2009 Raymond Arsenault wrote a book about another black pioneer, Marian Anderson, specifically about Miss Anderson's groundbreaking concert at the Lincoln Memorial on Easter Sunday, 1939. Arsenault wrote, "After a lifetime of being told they were intellectually and culturally inferior, even many blacks questioned their race's capacity to excel in the 'higher' forms of art, theater, science, literature, sports, entertainment, and music."[4]

That a black woman could sing opera came as a surprise to many whites. "Blacks were born to dance and sing and shout," most whites believed, but classical music was another matter, wrote Arsenault. "Mastery of classical technique required superior intelligence, discipline, and years of training. Most white Americans had never encountered a major black composer, opera singer, or virtuoso violinist. Indeed, one suspects that few whites could even imagine such a thing."[5]

America was an overwhelmingly segregated society in the 1940s. There was hardly a neighborhood in the country that was integrated and very few workplaces where blacks and whites worked as equals. The vast majority of schools were also racially segregated: in the South by law, and in the North by custom and neighborhood design.

Washington, D.C., the nation's capital, was almost completely segregated. Written in the code of ethics of the District of Columbia's real-estate board was the proviso that "No property in a white section should ever be sold, rented, or advertised, or offered to colored people."[6] That code was still in place officially in 1947, and unofficially for many years after.

The schools in Washington remained segregated by law until the Supreme Court decision in *Brown v. Board of Education* outlawed the practice on May 17, 1954, and continued to be mostly segregated even after the ruling. The Washington Redskins, the city's beloved football team, would not have a black player on its roster until 1962.

The American military, fresh off liberating the world from two regimes that preached racial and cultural superiority, remained segregated until February 1948, when President Harry Truman ordered both the armed forces and civil service to integrate their personnel. Fearing he could never get such "radical" legislation through the United States Congress, the president accomplished the desegregation by way of an Executive Order.

On July 27, 1947, Jackie Robinson and Pete Reiser connected for back-to-back home runs in Pittsburgh, helping the Dodgers extend their lead in the National League pennant race to seven games. The next day, the Supreme Court of New York ruled that Stuyvesant Town, a 35-building apartment complex that would contain 8,755 apartments being built by the Metropolitan Life Insurance Company in lower Manhattan, could exclude black families. The court said private developers can "restrict such accommodations on grounds of race, color, creed, or religion." The suit to prevent Stuyvesant

Town from practicing what the *Times* called alleged discrimination was brought by "three Negro war veterans." After reviewing a number of cases, the court said, "It is well settled that the landlord of a private apartment or dwelling house may, without violating any provision of the Federal and State Constitutions, select tenants of its own choice because of race, color, creed, or religion."[7]

Remember, it was not the Supreme Court of Alabama, or Georgia, or Mississippi that made this ruling. It was made by the Supreme Court of New York, the most liberal-minded State in the nation.

As late as December 1955, at about the same time Rosa Parks famously refused to give up her seat and move to the back of a Montgomery, Alabama, bus, Governor Marvin Griffin of Georgia demanded that Georgia Tech not play in the Sugar Bowl against the University of Pittsburgh. His reason: the Panthers team included Bobby Grier, a black running back. "The South stands at Armageddon," Griffin said in a telegram to Georgia's Board of Regents, detailing his request that teams in the state's university system not participate in events in which races were mixed on the field or in the stands. "The battle is joined. We cannot make the slightest concession to the enemy in this dark and lamentable hour of struggle."[8]

As outrageous as this sounds to the modern-day reader, an anachronism we smugly attribute to the benighted backward ways of the American South, this overt racism was not strictly a Southern disease. That same year, home-builder Bill Levitt was building a new development in Bucks County, Pennsylvania, a suburb of Philadelphia. Levitt was one of the nation's leading home builders, having built towns named Levittown in New York and New Jersey. They were huge tracts of relatively cheap houses, which in most cases were an entry into home-ownership for thousands.

When a Bucks County newspaper brought up the exclusion of blacks in his latest town, Levitt replied, "The plain fact is that most whites prefer not to live in mixed communities. This attitude may be wrong morally, and someday it may change. I hope it will. But as matters now stand, it is unfair to charge an individual for creating this attitude or saddle him with the sole responsibility for correcting it. The responsibility is society's. So far society has not been willing to cope with it. Until it does, it is not reasonable to expect that any one builder should or could undertake to absorb the entire risk and burden of conducting such a vast social experiment."[9]

Levitt's claim that "most whites prefer not to live in mixed communities" was true for much of the North, where "public officials claimed that the separation of races was just a fact of life, not mandated by law or controlled by the state. Whites could deny responsibility for racial segregation, for their choices about where to live and where to send their children to school were individualized and ostensibly race-neutral. The logical conclusion of this line of reasoning was that it was the natural order of things that the vast majority of whites lived in all-white communities and that blacks were confined to segregated neighborhoods and mostly minority schools. Like lived with like, birds of a feather flocked together. No one was at fault."[10]

As mentioned, the vote of the owners in 1947 had been 15–1 against the Dodgers bringing Jackie Robinson to Brooklyn. How much had changed over the years? Not as much as we would like to think. At a luncheon in Minneapolis in the early 1970s, Minnesota Twins owner Calvin Griffith gave his reason for relocating his franchise from Washington. "I'll tell you why we came to Minnesota in 1961. It was when I found out you had only 15,000 blacks here. Black people don't go to ball games, but they'll fill up a rassling ring and put up such a chant it'll scare you to death.... We came here because you've got good hard-working white people here."[11]

These are only a few, a very few, examples of the state of race relations in America in 1947. Does the climate of the time, a time in which very few white Americans lived among, worked with, or went to school with black Americans justify Dixie Walker's taking a morally indefensible position? It does not, but I hope I have added some historical perspective to his decision to do so.

Chapter Notes

1 : Born to Play Baseball

1. The four pitchers older than Walker were Rip Sewell (42), Dutch Leonard (40), Harry Gumbert (39), and Schoolboy Rowe (39). The only American League non-pitcher older than Walker was Luke Appling (42).
2. Some baseball sources list Ewart Walker's year of birth as 1887, but both the Social Security Death Index and the 1900 Federal Census list Ewart as having been born in 1888. So too does his World War I draft card, written in his own hand.
3. *The Sporting News*, November 27, 1965.
4. *Washington Post*, October 2, 1909.
5. *New York Times*, September 10, 1911.
6. *Brooklyn Daily Eagle*, September 10, 1911.
7. *Washington Post*, May 31, 1912.
8. *Washington Post*, June 4, 1912.
9. On June 10, 1910, Walker pitched a one-hitter, defeating Ed Walsh and the Chicago White Sox, 1–0.
10. Robert Rice, "The Artful Dodger," *PM*, August 8, 1943.
11. Frank Graham, "The Hottest Guy in Baseball," *New York Sun*, August 21, 1940.
12. Gordon Campbell, *Famous American Athletes of Today* (Ninth Series) (Boston: L.C. Page, 1945), 304.
13. Ibid., 305.
14. Bob Broeg, "Fine Alabama Contribution to Baseball," *St. Louis Post-Dispatch*, June 21, 1949.
15. Irving Vaughan, "Baseball Got Dixie Walker in Steel Mill, Also Got Him Out," *Chicago Daily Tribune*, May 14, 1937.
16. *Binghamton (NY) Press*, July 9, 1940.
17. Ibid.
18. *Brooklyn Daily Eagle*, December 26, 1933.
19. Frank Graham, "The Hottest Guy in Baseball," *New York Sun*, August 21, 1940.

2 : A Minor League Sensation

1. *Brooklyn Daily Eagle*, May 11, 1933.
2. *Brooklyn Daily Eagle*, December 26, 1933.
3. "Southern Clubs Name Reserves," *Atlanta Constitution*, December 1, 1929.
4. Gordon Campbell, *Famous American Athletes of Today* (Ninth Series)(Boston: L.C. Page, 1945), 309.
5. *Brooklyn Daily Eagle*, May 25, 1930.
6. *Hartford Courant*, June 20, 1930
7. Robert Rice, "The Artful Dodger," *PM*, August 8, 1943.
8. In 1946, the International League, American Association, and Pacific Coast League were all designated as Class AAA leagues.
9. Along with Jersey City, there were teams in Newark, NJ; Rochester, NY; Buffalo, NY; Baltimore, MD; Reading, PA; and two in Canada, Montreal and Toronto. Only in mostly segregated Baltimore did civic life resemble that of the South.
10. *Sporting News*, February 5, 1931.
11. *Washington Post*, March 8, 1931.
12. *New York Times*, March 27, 1931. This is the first time the paper called Walker "Dixie" rather than Fred. They would use the

names interchangeably for the rest of the 1931 season.
13. Bill Werber and C. Paul Rogers III, *Memories of a Ballplayer* (Cleveland: SABR, 2001), 132.
14. *Brooklyn Daily Eagle*, February 13, 1944.
15. Irving Vaughan, "Baseball Got Dixie Walker in Steel Mill, Also Got Him Out," *Chicago Daily Tribune*, May 14, 1937.
16. E-mail to the author from Daniel R. Levitt, author of *Ed Barrow*, January 2009.
17. Charlie Good, "League Batting Leader Joins the Toronto Club," *Toronto Daily Star*, August 28, 1931.
18. Gordon Campbell, *Famous American Athletes of Today* (Ninth Series) (Boston: L.C. Page, 1945), 311.
19. Ronald A. Mayer, *The 1937 Newark Bears: A Baseball Legend* (East Hanover, NJ: Vintage Press, 1980), 36.
20. Morton Roth, "Dixie Walker: Farewell to a Boyhood Idol," *Baseball Digest*, 40.

3 : The Guy to Take Babe Ruth's Place

1. *Brooklyn Daily Eagle*, May 11, 1933.
2. Ibid.
3. Ibid.
4. Ibid.
5. *Syracuse Herald Journal*, January 23, 1949.
6. Bill James, *The New Bill James Historical Baseball Abstract* (New York: Free Press, 2001), 808.
7. Bill Wise, "Dixie Does All Right," *Sport Pix*, June 1949, 11.
8. *The Sporting News*, April 13, 1933.
9. Frank Graham, Jr., "Greatest Fight on a Ball Field," *Baseball Digest*, June 1953, 45. The unnamed veteran writer related the story to Graham during a 1953 Cardinals-Phillies game.
10. Bill Werber and C. Paul Rogers III, *Memories of a Ballplayer* (Cleveland: SABR, 2001), 37.
11. Frank Graham, Jr., "Greatest Fight on a Ball Field," *Baseball Digest*, June 1953, 45–46.
12. Alan H. Levy, *Joe McCarthy: Architect of the Yankee Dynasty* (Jefferson, NC: McFarland, 2005), 183.

13. Gary Sarnoff, "War at Griffith Stadium," *The National Pastime* (SABR), 2009, 76.
14. Chicago *Daily Tribune*, April 28, 1933.
15. Frank Graham, Jr., "Greatest Fight on a Ball Field," *Baseball Digest*, June 1953, 45.
16. Gordon Campbell, *Famous American Athletes of Today* (Ninth Series) (Boston: L.C. Page, 1945), 308.
17. *Chicago Daily Tribune*, April 27, 1933.
18. Ray Robinson, *Iron Horse: Lou Gehrig in His Time* (New York: W.W. Norton, 1990), 152–53.
19. *Washington Post*, April 30, 1933.
20. Ibid.
21. *The Sporting News*, May 4, 1933.
22. *Binghamton* (NY) *Press*, July 27, 1933.
23. *Brooklyn Daily Eagle*, May 11, 1933.
24. James P. Dawson, *New York Times*, June 26, 1933.
25. Hank Greenberg hit 58 home runs in 1938. No one came closer to Ruth's record total of 60 in 1927 until Roger Maris surpassed the Babe's mark with 61 in 1961.
26. *New York Times*, June 26, 1933.
27. Ibid.
28. Harold C. Burr, *Brooklyn Daily Eagle*, July 20, 1933.
29. Joe Vila, *The Sporting News*, July 27, 1933.
30. Harold C. Burr, *Brooklyn Daily Eagle*, July 23, 1933.
31. Bob Broeg, "Backward, Turn Backward Oh Time...," *St. Louis Post-Dispatch*, September 23, 1972.
32. *Brooklyn Daily Eagle*, August 25, 1933.
33. Peter C. Bjarkman, *Encyclopedia of Major League Baseball Team Histories: American League* (Westport, CT: Meckler, 1991), 498.
34. *Brooklyn Daily Eagle*, August 31, 1933.

4 : The Lost Years

1. *The Sporting News*, February 15, 1934.
2. Ibid.
3. Dick Young, *New York Daily News*, July 28, 1968. Walker would reach double figures in home runs only one other time in his career. He hit 13 for Brooklyn in 1944, the year he won the National League batting championship.
4. *Chicago Daily Tribune*, February 25, 1934.

5. Harold Parrott, *Brooklyn Daily Eagle*, January 29, 1934.
6. Shirley Povich, "This Morning," *Washington Post*, March 19, 1934.
7. *The Sporting News*, April, 5, 1934.
8. *New York Times*, May 19, 1934.
9. Shirley Povich, *Washington Post*, December 21, 1934.
10. Gehrig had a .363 batting average, 49 home runs, and 165 RBI.
11. Gomez led the league in wins (26), earned run average (2.33), and strikeouts (158).
12. *The Sporting News*, December 20, 1934.
13. *The Sporting News*, November 22, 1934.
14. *The Sporting News*, March 14, 1935.
15. Alan H. Levy, *Joe McCarthy: Architect of the Yankee Dynasty* (Jefferson, NC: McFarland, 2005), 197.
16. *The Sporting News*, March 14, 1935.
17. *Brooklyn Daily Eagle*, March 15, 1935.
18. Dan Daniel, "Dixie Bids for Yank Job," *New York World Telegram*, April 5, 1935.
19. Ibid.
20. *Brooklyn Daily Eagle*, April 4, 1935.
21. *Brooklyn Daily Eagle*, May 24, 1935.

5 : Radical Surgery and a Career Revived

1. Lyle Spatz, *Yankees Coming, Yankees Going* (Jefferson, NC: McFarland, 2000), 66.
2. Ibid., 67.
3. *New York Times*, March 6, 1936.
4. *The Sporting News*, March 19, 1936.
5. *New York World Telegram*, April 24, 1936.
6. *The Sporting News*, May 21, 1936.
7. Gordon Campbell, *Famous American Athletes of Today* (Ninth Series) (Boston: L.C. Page, 1945), 313.
8. Lyle Spatz, *Yankees Coming, Yankees Going* (Jefferson, NC: McFarland, 2000), 69.
9. *The North Castle Historical Society* 24, 1997, 30.
10. E-mail to the author from Mary Ann Walker, April 22, 2010.
11. E-mail to the author from Stephen Walker, October 27, 2009.
12. Edward Burns, *Chicago Daily Tribune*, June 2, 1936.

13. *The Sporting News*, December 23, 1937.
14. Gordon Campbell, *Famous American Athletes of Today* (Ninth Series) (Boston: L.C. Page, 1945), 314.
15. Earl Hilligan, "It's True What They Say About Dixie, Dykes Says," *Burlington (NC) Daily Times-News*, April 17, 1937.
16. Irving Vaughan, "Baseball Got Dixie Walker in Steel Mill, Also Got Him Out," *Chicago Daily Tribune*, May 14, 1937.
17. *The Sporting News*, April, 22, 1937.

6 : The Most Unpopular Man in Detroit

1. *Los Angeles Times*, December 3, 1937.
2. Sam Greene, "Detroit Fans Deride Cochrane for Swapping Walker to Dykes," *The Sporting News*, December 9, 1937.
3. Bump Hadley's beaning of Mickey Cochrane at Yankee Stadium on May 25, 1937, ended Cochrane's playing career.
4. Shirley Povich, "This Morning," *Washington Post*, December 4, 1937.
5. Sam Greene, "Detroit Fans Deride Cochrane for Swapping Walker to Dykes," *The Sporting News*, December 9, 1937.
6. Charles P. Ward, "New Walker Tune Heard in Detroit; It's Swing to Dixie," *The Sporting News*, February 24, 1938.
7. *Brooklyn Daily Eagle*, April 12, 1938.
8. *Chicago Daily Tribune*, April 20, 1938.
9. Art Hill, *I Don't Care If I Never Come Back* (New York: Simon & Schuster, 1980), 130.
10. Although Vern Kennedy won 21 games in 1936 and 14 in 1937, his ERAs were an unimpressive 4.63 and 5.09 in those two seasons.
11. *The Sporting News*, July 21, 1938.
12. *New York Times*, July 23, 1938.
13. John Kieran, "Sports of the Times," *New York Times*, June 10, 1938.
14. Shirley Povich, "This Morning," *Washington Post*, March 19, 1939.
15. Richards Vidmer, "Down in Front, *Washington Post*, March 26, 1939.
16. *Hartford Courant*, March 28, 1939.
17. Detroit traded pitcher Vern Kennedy, pitcher Roxie Lawson, pitcher Bob Harris, pitcher George Gill, outfielder Chet Laabs, and infielder Mark Christman to St. Louis

for pitcher Bobo Newsom, pitcher Jim Walkup, outfielder Beau Bell, and infielder Red Kress.

18. Art Hill, *I Don't Care if I Never Come Back* (New York: Simon & Schuster, 1980), 131.

19. *Binghamton (NY) Press*, March 16, 1958.

7 : "All I knew about Brooklyn was that it was some strange outer world"

1. *Los Angeles Times*, August 16, 1974.

2. Richard Bartell and Norman L. Macht, *Rowdy Richard* (Berkeley, CA: North Atlantic Books, 1987), 311.

3. Richard Applegate, "The Battle of the Hatfields and the McCoys," *Mound City Memories: Baseball in St. Louis* (Cleveland: Society for American Baseball Research, 2007), 89.

4. John Keiran, "The Bronx Cheer for Brannick from Brooklyn," *New York Times*, September 19, 1940.

5. James J. Murphy, *Brooklyn Daily Eagle*, July 30, 1939.

6. Bill Wise, "Dixie Does All Right," *Sport Pix*, June 1949, 8.

7. *Brooklyn Daily Eagle*, February 25, 1944.

8. Roscoe McGowen, "Dixie Walker Drives Two Triples, As Dodgers Set Back Pirates, 5–3," *New York Times*, August 2, 1939.

9. In 1936, the National League team in Boston changed its name from Braves to Bees. In 1941, they changed back to Braves.

10. Roscoe McGowen, *New York Times*, August 8, 1939.

11. Pat McDonough, "Walker Idol of Flatbush," *New York World Telegram*, August 8, 1939.

12. Kirby Higbe with Martin Quigley, *The High Hard One* (New York: Viking, 1967), 69.

13. Gordon Campbell, *Famous American Athletes of Today* (Ninth Series) (Boston: L.C. Page, 1945), 305.

14. Rudy Marzano, *The Brooklyn Dodgers in the 1940s: How Robinson, MacPhail, Reiser and Rickey Changed Baseball* (Jefferson, NC: McFarland, 2005), 67.

15. "The People's Choice: The Cheering of Fans Has Helped Problem-Child Walker More Than Any Amount of Hell from Cochrane," *Esquire*, May 1939.

16. *Brooklyn Daily Eagle*, August 16, 1939.

17. Walker's former team, the Tigers, finished fifth in 1939 but would win the pennant in 1940.

18. *Brooklyn Daily Eagle*, October 2, 1939.

19. Jonathan F. Light, *The Cultural Encyclopedia of Baseball* (Jefferson, NC: McFarland, 1997), 724.

20. *Christian Science Monitor*, December 9, 1939.

21. *New York Times*, February 12, 1940.

22. *New York Times*, February 26, 1940.

23. Ibid.

24. *New York Times*, March 8, 1940.

8 : The People's Choice

1. *The Sporting News*, July 27, 1939.

2. Charles Alexander, *Breaking the Slump: Baseball in the Depression Era* (New York: Columbia University Press, 2002), 244.

3. *Hartford Courant*, "Reese Glad He's Sold to Brooklyn Club Now," July 20, 1939.

4. *New York Times*, May 1, 1940.

5. Ibid.

6. In the Union Association, which existed only in 1884, St. Louis won its first 20 games. That same year, New York of the National League won its first 12.

7. *Brooklyn Daily Eagle*, June 8, 1940.

8. *New York Times*, "Medwick and Davis Join Dodgers for Big Series Opening Against Reds Today," June 14, 1940.

9. *Washington Post*, "Medwick Deal Brings Joy to Flatbush," June 14, 1940.

10. Billy Southworth replaced Ray Blades as manager of the Cardinals on June 7, 1940.

11. Paul Green, "Whitlow Wyatt," *Sports Collectors Digest*, March 28, 1986, 220.

12. Donald Honig, *Baseball When the Grass Was Real* (New York: Coward, McCann & Geoghegan, 1975), 196.

13. John Keiran, "Sports of the Times," *New York Times*, July 6, 1940.

14. David Vincent, Lyle Spatz, and David W. Smith, *The Midsummer Classic, The Complete History of Baseball's All-Star Game* (Lincoln: University of Nebraska Press, 2001), 46.

15. *Brooklyn Daily Eagle*, July 29, 1940.

16. Jack Kavanagh, "A Dodger Boyhood," *Baseball Research Journal 20*, 1991, 127.
17. Lyle Spatz and Steve Steinberg, *1921: The Yankees, the Giants, and the Battle for Baseball Supremacy in New York* (Lincoln: University of Nebraska Press, 2010), 108.
18. Tommy Holmes, *The Sporting News*, September 12, 1940.
19. *Hartford Courant*, September 22, 1940.
20. *Brooklyn Daily Eagle*, September 25, 1940.
21. *Brooklyn Daily Eagle*, September 27, 1940.
22. *The Sporting News*, September 19, 1940.
23. *Brooklyn Daily Eagle*, January 19, 1941.

9 : An Almost Perfect Team

1. *The Sporting News*, October 17, 1940.
2. *Time*, April 21, 1941.
3. *Hartford Courant*, December 19, 1940.
4. *Brooklyn Daily Eagle*, January 29, 1941.
5. *Brooklyn Daily Eagle*, September 15, 1941.
6. *Time*, April 28, 1941.
7. Ike Pearson's pitch to Reiser was high and tight, but it did not appear that Pearson meant to hit him.
8. *Brooklyn Daily Eagle*, April 30, 1941.
9. In July 1945, MacPhail, then running the Yankees, sold Hank Borowy, the team's best pitcher, to the Chicago Cubs for approximately $100,000. Many years later, a plausible explanation surfaced for the Yankees' seemingly inexplicable sale of Borowy to the Cubs. It was, the theory went, MacPhail's repayment to Chicago general manager Jim Gallagher for the 1941 deal that brought Billy Herman to Brooklyn.
10. Jimmy Powers, "The Powerhouse," *New York Daily News*, May 17, 1941.
11. *Brooklyn Daily Eagle*, June 11, 1941.
12. *Brooklyn Daily Eagle*, August 6, 1941.
13. *Brooklyn Daily Eagle*, August 30, 1941.
14. Other Dodgers named to the team were Billy Herman, Cookie Lavagetto, and Joe Medwick.
15. *New York Times*, August 25, 1941.
16. *Time*, September 8, 1941.
17. Rob Neyer and Eddie Epstein, *Baseball Dynasties: The Greatest Teams of All Time* (New York: W.W. Norton, 2000), 172.
18. Donald Honig, *Baseball When the Grass Was Real* (New York: Coward, Mccann & Geoghegan, 1975), 92.
19. Bob Broeg, "The '42 Cardinals," *Sport*, July 1963, 41.
20. Bill Borst, "Showdown in St. Louis," *The National Pastime* 11 (1991), 63–64.
21. *Brooklyn Daily Eagle*, September 12, 1941.
22. Bob Considine, "On the Line," *Washington Post*, September 15, 1941.
23. Bill Wise, "Dixie Does All Right," *Sport Pix*, June 1949, 9.
24. Roscoe McGowen, *New York Times*, September 14, 1941.
25. *Brooklyn Daily Eagle*, December 11, 1952.
26. Thomas Liley, "Whit Wyatt — The Dodgers' 1941 Ace," *The National Pastime* 11 (1991), 47.
27. J.G. Taylor Spink "Always Something Doing with Dixie," *The Sporting News*, December 25, 1941.

10 : A Pennant and a World Series

1. W. C. Heinz, "The Rocky Road of Pistol Pete," in *The Baseball Reader: Favorites from the Fireside Books of Baseball*, edited by Charles Einstein (New York: Lippincott & Crowell, 1980), 162.
2. Ibid., 162–163.
3. Robert W. Creamer, *Baseball in '41* (New York: The Penguin Group, 1991), 207–08.
4. W. C. Heinz, "The Rocky Road of Pistol Pete," 162.
5. *Chicago Defender*, September 20, 1941.
6. *Chicago Defender*, April 16, 1938.
7. John P. Carmichael, *My Greatest Day in Baseball* (New York: A.S. Barnes, 1945), 235.
8. Rudy Marzano, *The Brooklyn Dodgers in the 1940s: How Robinson, MacPhail, Reiser and Rickey Changed Baseball* (Jefferson, NC: McFarland, 2005), 67.
9. *Time*, October 6, 1941.
10. Leo Durocher with Ed Linn, *Nice Guys Finish Last* (New York: Simon & Schuster, 1975), 129.

11. Ron Fimrite, "The Play That Beat the Bums," *Sports Illustrated*, October 20, 1997.
12. Peter Golenbock, *Bums: An Oral History of the Brooklyn Dodgers* (New York: G. P. Putnam's Sons, 1984), 70.
13. *Time*, October 6, 1941.
14. Bill James, *The New Bill James Historical Baseball Abstract* (New York: Free Press, 2001), 207.
15. Ron Fimrite, "The Play That Beat the Bums," *Sports Illustrated*, October 20, 1997.
16. *Brooklyn Daily Eagle*, September 26, 1941.
17. Bill James, *The New Bill James Historical Baseball Abstract* (New York: Free Press, 2001), 207.
18. *Brooklyn Daily Eagle*, October 1, 1941.
19. *Washington Post*, September 20, 1941.
20. *Time*, October 6, 1941.
21. At the same time Dixie Walker was playing against the Yankees in the World Series, Ewart and Flossie's younger son, 24-year-old Harry, was playing for the Columbus (Ohio) Redbirds against the Montreal Royals in the Junior World Series. Columbus was a Cardinals farm team and Montreal was a Dodgers farm team.
22. *Brooklyn Daily Eagle*, October 1, 1941.
23. *Brooklyn Daily Eagle*, September 30, 1941.
24. Ron Fimrite, "The Play That Beat the Bums," *Sports Illustrated*, October 20, 1997.
25. Deacon Phillippe of the 1903 Pirates and Christy Mathewson of the 1911 Giants both lost successive games, but not on consecutive days.
26. John Thorn, *The Relief Pitcher: Baseball's New Hero* (New York: E. P. Dutton, 1979), 79.
27. *Atlanta Constitution*, October 6, 1941.
28. Andrew Paul Mele, *A Brooklyn Dodgers Reader* (Jefferson, NC: McFarland, 2004), 56.
29. The 1930 rule, which was still in effect in 1941, read as follows: An error, but not a passed ball, shall be charged to the catcher if he drops or misses a third strike, allowing the batsman to reach first base. Credit the pitcher with a strikeout. (Information provided by David Vincent, the official scorer for the Washington Nationals.)
30. *Brooklyn Daily Eagle*, October 6, 1941.
31. Norman Macht, "Why did Mickey Miss the Ball?" *The National Pastime* 11 (1991), 45.
32. Leo Durocher, *Nice Guys Finish Last* (New York: Simon & Schuster, 1975), 162.
33. Donald Honig, *Baseball When the Grass Was Real* (New York: Coward, McCann & Geoghegan, 1975), 138.
34. Paul Green, "Whitlow Wyatt," *Sports Collectors Digest*, March 28, 1986, 220.

11 : The 1942 Dodgers Look to Repeat

1. *Brooklyn Daily Eagle*, July 5, 1941.
2. *Brooklyn Daily Eagle*, January 9, 1942.
3. *Brooklyn Daily Eagle*, July 5, 1941.
4. *Washington Post*, January 12, 1942.
5. *Brooklyn Daily Eagle*, November 21, 1941.
6. Ibid.
7. *Hartford Courant*, January 15, 1942.
8. *Brooklyn Daily Eagle*, November 20, 1941.
9. Lyle Spatz, *New York Yankee Openers: An Opening Day History of Baseball's Most Famous Team, 1903–1996* (Jefferson, NC: McFarland, 1997), 178.
10. *New York Times*, February 1, 1942.
11. *Chicago Daily Tribune*, February 19, 1942.
12. *New York Times*, February 22, 1942.
13. *New York Times*, February 26, 1942.
14. *Washington Post*, March 18, 1942.
15. Lew Paper, *Perfect: Don Larsen's Miraculous World Series Game and the Men Who Made It Happen* (New York: New American Library, 2009), 171.
16. *Brooklyn Daily Eagle*, March 17, 1942.
17. *Hartford Courant*, March 19, 1942.
18. Shirley Povich, *Washington Post*, March 18, 1942.
19. Jimmy Powers, *New York Daily News*, April 7, 1942.
20. Lucius (Melancholy) Jones, "Sports Slants," *Atlanta Daily World*, April 6, 1942.
21. E-mail to author from Stephen Walker, April 20, 2010.
22. Joe Williams, *New York World Telegram*, April 11, 1942.

12 : "Men, you are going to lose this pennant"

1. Bob Broeg, "The '42 Cardinals," *Sport,* July 1963, 43.
2. *New York Times,* June 19, 1942.
3. Donald Honig, *Baseball When the Grass Was Real* (New York: Coward, McCann & Geoghegan, 1975), 197–98.
4. Harold C. Burr, "Dixie Walker's More Than Man-of-Week to Brooklyn," *Brooklyn Daily Eagle,* July 7, 1946.
5. Duke Snider with Phil Pepe, *Few and Chosen: Defining Dodger Greatness Across the Ages* (Chicago: Triumph Books, 2006), 57.
6. *Brooklyn Daily Eagle,* July 20, 1942.
7. Donald Honig, *Baseball America* (New York: Macmillan, 1985), 278.
8. Wil A. Linkugel and Edward J. Pappas, *They Tasted Glory: Among the Missing at the Baseball Hall of Fame* (Jefferson, NC: McFarland, 1998), 37–38.
9. Peter Golenbock, *Bums* (New York: G. P. Putnam's Sons, 1984), 78.
10. *New York Times,* August 4, 1942.
11. *Brooklyn Daily Eagle,* August 19, 1942.
12. Stephen D. Boren and Thomas Boren, "The 1942 Pennant Race," *The National Pastime* 15 (1995), 135.
13. *Brooklyn Daily Eagle,* September 2, 1942.
14. *New York World Telegram and Sun,* March 12, 1953.
15. Stephen D. Boren and Thomas Boren, "The 1942 Pennant Race," *The National Pastime* 15 (1995), 134.
16. Bob Broeg, "The '42 Cardinals," *Sport,* July 1963, 40.
17. Stephen D. Boren and Thomas Boren, "The 1942 Pennant Race," *The National Pastime* 15 (1995), 134.
18. Cooper had not lost a start since he began borrowing that teammate's shirt whose number corresponded to the number of the game he wanted to win. For this game, he wore Coaker Triplett's number 20.
19. *Time,* September 21, 1942.
20. Stephen D. Boren and Thomas Boren, "The 1942 Pennant Race," *The National Pastime* 15 (1995), 134.
21. Walter M. Langford, *Legends of Baseball: An Oral History of the Game's Golden Age* (South Bend, IN: Diamond Communications, 1987), 62.
22. *Brooklyn Daily Eagle,* September 28, 1942.
23. Bob Broeg, "Fine Alabama Contribution to Baseball," *St. Louis Post-Dispatch,* June 21, 1949.
24. Bob Broeg, "The '42 Cardinals," *Sport,* July 1963, 43.
25. Richard Applegate, "The Battle of the Hatfields and the McCoys," *Mound City Memories: Baseball in St. Louis* (Cleveland: SABR, 2007), 89.
26. Rob Neyer and Eddie Epstein, *Baseball Dynasties: The Greatest Teams of All Time* (New York: W. W. Norton, 2000), 165, quoting Rick Van Blair in *Dugout to Foxhole: Interviews with Baseball Players Whose Careers Were Affected by World War II* (Jefferson, NC: McFarland, 1995).

13 : The War Begins to Affect Baseball

1. John Drebinger, "Cards Down Yanks with Homer by 4–2; Win World Series," *New York Times,* October 6, 1942.
2. *Brooklyn Daily Eagle,* September 30, 1947.
3. Jack Cuddy, "Dixie Walker Not Sorry That MacPhail Has Left Brooklyn," *Berkshire* (MA) *Evening Eagle,* January 11, 1943.
4. Two of Walker's teammates, Arky Vaughan and Dolph Camilli, also had said that as a way of contributing to the war effort, they would leave baseball and retire to their California farms. (Vaughan did, from 1944 through 1946.)
5. *Brooklyn Daily Eagle,* December 16, 1942.
6. *New York Times,* January 14, 1943.
7. *Brooklyn Daily Eagle,* January 14, 1943.
8. Tommy Holmes, *Brooklyn Daily Eagle,* December 20, 1942.
9. *Brooklyn Daily Eagle,* October 17, 1942.
10. *Brooklyn Daily Eagle,* February 7, 1943.
11. *The Dothan Alabama Eagle,* February 9, 1943.
12. *New York Times,* March 24, 1943.
13. Peter Golenbock, *Bums* (New York: G. P. Putnam's Sons, 1984), 89.
14. Thomas Liley, "Whit Wyatt—The Dodgers' 1941 Ace," *The National Pastime* 11 (1991), 47.

15. Stanley Woodward, "In the Rickey Manner," *Baseball Digest*, July 1950, p. 23.
16. Al Figone, "Larry MacPhail and Dolph Camilli," *The National Pastime* 14 (1994), 108.
17. Donald Honig, *Baseball When the Grass Was Real* (New York: Coward, McCann & Geoghegan, 1975), 198.
18. *Brooklyn Daily Eagle*, August 17, 1943.
19. Paul Scheffels, *Brooklyn Daily Eagle*, July 12, 1943.
20. Robert Rice, "The Artful Dodger," *PM*, August 8, 1943.
21. Ralph C. Moses, "Arky Vaughan," SABR BioProject, www.bioproj.sabr.org.
22. Roscoe McGowen, "Dodgers Revolt Against Durocher," *New York Times*, July 11, 1943.
23. *Brooklyn Daily Eagle*, July 12, 1943.
24. Peter Golenbock, *Bums* (New York: G. P. Putnam's Sons, 1984), 93.
25. Richard Bartell and Norman L. Macht, *Rowdy Richard* (Berkeley, CA: North Atlantic Books, 1987), 311.

14 : The 1944 National League Batting Champion

1. Robert Rice, "The Artful Dodger," *PM*, August 8, 1943.
2. *Brooklyn Daily Eagle*, April 20, 1943.
3. *Brooklyn Daily Eagle*, May 4, 1943.
4. *Brooklyn Daily Eagle*, July 3, 1943.
5. *Brooklyn Daily Eagle*, July 1, 1943.
6. Richard Goldstein, *Spartan Seasons: How Baseball Survived the Second World War* (New York: Macmillan, 1980), 76.
7. William B. Mead, *Even the Browns: The Zany, True Story of Baseball in the Early Forties* (Chicago: Contemporary Books, 1978), 5.
8. *Syracuse Herald Journal*, October 29, 1943.
9. *Brooklyn Daily Eagle*, November 5, 1943.
10. Oscar Fraley, *Binghamton (NY) Press*, May 21, 1948.
11. *Brooklyn Daily Eagle*, December 31, 1943.
12. *Brooklyn Daily Eagle*, March 7, 1944.
13. *Brooklyn Daily Eagle*, March 8, 1944.
14. William B. Mead, *Even the Browns*, 122–23.
15. Rudy Marzano, *The Brooklyn Dodgers in the 1940s* (Jefferson, NC: McFarland, 2005), 97.
16. Tim Panaccio, "How it Was During the War Years," *Baseball Digest*, January 1977, 69.
17. Noel Hynd, *The Giants of the Polo Grounds* (New York: Doubleday, 1988), 331.
18. *Brooklyn Daily Eagle*, September 28, 1944.
19. *The Sporting News*, May 4, 1944.
20. Garry Schumacher, "The Customers Are Finally Right," *New York Journal American*, May 26, 1944.
21. Jimmy Powers, *New York Daily News*, April 7, 1942.
22. Bill Roeder, *New York World Telegram and Sun*, August 13, 1955.
23. *Brooklyn Daily Eagle*, October 3, 1944.
24. Gordon Campbell, *Famous American Athletes of Today* (Ninth Series) (Boston: L. C. Page, 1945), 316.
25. *Brooklyn Daily Eagle*, September 22, 1944.
26. Gordon Campbell, *Famous American Athletes of Today (1945)*, 315.
27. Ibid., 316.
28. Dan Daniel, "Dixie Walker Ascribes Added Power to Change in Bats," *New York World-Telegram*, July 8, 1946.
29. David Jordan, "A Fresh Look at Wartime Baseball," a paper delivered at the 1991 Society for American Baseball Research convention in New York City.

15 : "The most beloved baseball player of recent years"

1. *Brooklyn Daily Eagle*, September 28, 1944.
2. *Brooklyn Daily Eagle*, February 5, 1945.
3. *Brooklyn Daily Eagle*, September 20, 1945.
4. *Brooklyn Daily Eagle*, March 20, 1945.
5. *Brooklyn Daily Eagle*, January 29, 1950.
6. Frank Colman batted .209 in 77 games for the 1945 Pirates.
7. *Time*, April 9, 1945.
8. Walter M. Langford, *Legends of Baseball* (South Bend, IN: Diamond Communications, 1987), 62.

9. Steve Dolan, "Padre Coach Has Near-Miss Career," *Los Angeles Times*, May 12, 1981.
10. Peter Golenbock, *Bums* (New York: G. P. Putnam's Sons, 1984), 90.
11. Bill Roeder, "Walker's Bat Puts New Life in Dodgers," *New York World Telegram*, July 21, 1945.
12. Lew Paper, *Perfect* (New York: New American Library, 2009), 25.
13. *Time*, Sept. 17, 1945.
14. *Brooklyn Daily Eagle*, June 25, 1945.
15. "Dodgers in Train Mishap," *New York Times*, September 16, 1945.
16. Fleetwood Walker played in 42 games for the 1884 Toledo Blue Stockings of the American Association. The American Association of 1884 is recognized as a Major League.
17. Harvey Frommer, *Rickey and Robinson* (New York: Macmillan, 1982), 104.
18. Fay Young, "End of Baseball's Jim Crow Seen with Signing of Jackie Robinson," *Chicago Defender*, November 3, 1945.
19. On January 3, 1946, the Tigers traded Rudy York to the Boston Red Sox for shortstop Eddie Lake.
20. Fay Young, "End of Baseball's Jim Crow Seen with Signing of Jackie Robinson," *Chicago Defender*, November 3, 1945.
21. *Ibid*.
22. Roger Kahn, *Into My Own*, p. 31.
23. Fay Young, "End of Baseball's Jim Crow Seen with Signing of Jackie Robinson," *Chicago Defender*, November 3, 1945.
24. Shirley Povich, "South Protests Entrance of Negro into Majors," *Washington Post*, May 14, 1953.

16 : The War Ends and the Battle with the Cardinals Resumes

1. *Time*, March, 25, 1946.
2. *Brooklyn Daily Eagle*, January 17, 1949.
3. *Time*, March, 25, 1946.
4. Bill Roeder, "Poor Old Dixie Is Out of Job Again, They Say," *New York World Telegram*, March 8, 1946.
5. Bill Roeder, "Dixie Ready to Cavort in Any Field," *New York World Telegram*, March 14, 1946.
6. Roscoe McGowen, *New York Times*, March 18, 1946.
7. *The Dothan* (AL) *Eagle*, March 7, 1946.
8. The Dodgers sold Goody Rosen to the New York Giants on April 27.
9. Wilfrid Sheed, *My Life as a Fan* (New York: Simon & Schuster, 1993), 139.
10. Bill Roeder, "And Who Slapped the Giants Down? Nobody but Dixie," *New York World Telegram*, April 22, 1946.
11. *Brooklyn Daily Eagle*, July 12, 1940.
12. *Brooklyn Daily Eagle*, April 24, 1946.
13. J. Ronald Oakley, *Baseball's Last Golden Age, 1946–1960* (Jefferson, NC: McFarland, 1994), 44.
14. Art Ahrens, "The Old Brawl Game," *The National Pastime* 23 (2003), 5.
15. Bill Roeder, "Walker-Merullo Bout Seen Top Diamond Brawl," *New York World Telegram and Sun,* July 26, 1954.
16. *New York World Telegram*, May 24, 1946.
17. Philip Lowry, *Green Cathedrals: The Ultimate Celebration of Major League and Negro League Ballparks* (New York: Walker & Company, 2006), 40.
18. *Brooklyn Daily Eagle*, June 20, 1946.
19. *New York Times,* June 20, 1946.
20. *New York World Telegram*, December 12, 1945.
21. George Coleman, *Brooklyn Daily Eagle*, June 26, 1946.
22. *Binghamton* (NY) *Press*, June 27, 1946.
23. Harold C. Burr. "Dixie Walker's More Than Man-of-Week to Brooklyn," *Brooklyn Daily Eagle*, July 7, 1946.
24. Dan Parker, "Dixie Walker, the Peepul's Cherce," *New York Daily Mirror*, August 11, 1946.
25. Dan Daniel, "Dodgers Now Look Like Best Bet for World Series," *New York World Telegram*, July 5, 1946.
26. *The Sporting News*, June 5, 1946.
27. *Time*, July 8, 1946.
28. Dan Daniel, "Dixie Walker Ascribes Added Power to Change in Bats," *New York World Telegram*, July 8, 1946.
29. Several Dodgers felt the addition of Chet Ross might have made the difference and allowed them to win the pennant. They showed their feelings toward Tepsic by voting him just one-eighth of a share of the money they received for finishing second.

30. Clifford Blau, "Leg Men," *Baseball Research Journal* 38, no.1 (Summer 2009), 73–74.
31. *Time*, August 26, 1946.
32. *Time*, September 9, 1946.
33. Jimmy Cannon, "Leo Buttons His Lip," *Baseball Digest* (November 1946), 43.
34. *Time*, October 7, 1946.

17 : Playoffs, Pensions, and a Promotion

1. *Time*, October 7, 1946.
2. Rudy Marzano, *The Brooklyn Dodgers in the 1940s* (Jefferson, NC: McFarland, 2005), 126.
3. Peter Golenbock, *Bums* (New York: G. P. Putnam's Sons, 1984), 101.
4. Rob Neyer and Eddie Epstein, *Baseball Dynasties* (New York: W. W. Norton, 2000), 172.
5. Thomas Oliphant, *Praying for Gil Hodges* (New York: St. Martin's Press, 2005), 159.
6. Wilfrid Sheed, *My Life as a Fan* (New York: Simon & Schuster, 1993), 137.
7. Donald Honig, *Baseball When the Grass Was Real* (New York: Coward, McCann & Geoghegan, 1975), 55.
8. Peter Golenbock, *Bums*, 101.
9. Jimmy Cannon, "Leo Buttons His Lip," *Baseball Digest*, November 1946, 43.
10. Charles P. Knorr, *The End of Baseball as We Knew It: The Players Union, 1960–81* (Champaign: University of Illinois, 2002), 16.
11. William Marshall, *Baseball's Pivotal Era, 1945–1951* (Lexington: University Press of Kentucky, 1999), 74.
12. Ibid, 75.
13. *Brooklyn Daily Eagle*, July 9, 1946.
14. Charles P. Knorr, *The End of Baseball as We Knew It: The Players Union, 1960–81* (Champaign: University of Illinois, 2002).
15. Bob Feller and Bill Gilbert, *Now Pitching, Bob Feller* (New York: Harper Perennial, 1990), 204.
16. *New York World Telegram*, August 1, 1946.
17. *New York World Telegram*, August 3, 1946.
18. *New York World Telegram*, September 9, 1946.
19. "Pension Program for Players Voted by Major Leagues," *New York Times*, February 2, 1947.
20. Courtesy of film historian Rob Edelman.
21. *Time*, October 7, 1946.
22. Jocko Maxwell, "Robinson's The Name for '47," *Baseball Digest*, October 1946, p. 58.
23. Peter Golenbock, *Bums*, p. 139.
24. Ibid, 144.
25. Lee Lowenfish, "The Gentlemen's Agreement and the Ferocious Gentleman Who Broke It," *Baseball Research Journal* 38, no. 1 (Summer 2009), 13.
26. Peter Golenbock, *Bums*, p. 145.
27. Red Barber, "Leadoff Man," *The New Republic*, July 4, 1983.
28. "Robinson Set to Appear in Ebbets Field," *New York Amsterdam News*, January 11, 1947.
29. *Los Angeles Sentinel*, January 30, 1947.
30. Roscoe McGowen, "Walker Devises First Base Screen," *New York Times*, February 23, 1947.
31. Lester Bromberg, "Dodger Fans: Dixie's on Job and Will Be Set for Opener," *New York World Telegram*, February 22, 1947.
32. Leo Durocher, "Durocher Says," *Brooklyn Daily Eagle*, March 2, 1947.
33. *New York World Telegram*, April 5, 1947.

18 : "It was the dumbest thing I did in all my life"

1. E-mail to the author from Stephen Walker, October 29, 2009.
2. Roger Kahn, *The Era, 1947–1957: When the Yankees, the Giants, and the Dodgers Ruled the World* (New York: Ticknor & Fields, 1993), 35.
3. Roger Kahn, *The Boys of Summer* (New York: Harper and Row, 1971), 44.
4. Ira Berkow, "Dixie Walker Remembers," *New York Times*, December 10, 1981.
5. Harvey Frommer, *Rickey and Robinson* (New York: Macmillan, 1982), 128
6. Ira Berkow, "Dixie Walker Remembers," *New York Times*, December 10, 1981.
7. Milt Dunnell, "Dixie Lived Down the Racist Image of Robinson Case," *Toronto Star*, May 19, 1982.
8. Jackie Robinson, *Baseball Has Done It* (Philadelphia: Lippincott, 1964), 55.

9. David Falkner, *Great Time Coming: The Life of Jackie Robinson, from Baseball to Birmingham* (New York: Simon & Schuster, 1995), 154.

10. Arthur Mann, "The Truth About the Jackie Robinson Case," *Saturday Evening Post*, May 20, 1950.

11. Both Frank Kalin and Al Gionfriddo had major league experience. Kalin had played three games for the Pirates in 1940 and four games for the White Sox in 1943. Gionfriddo had been with the Pirates since September 1944.

12. William Marshall, *Baseball's Pivotal Era, 1945–1951* (Lexington: University Press of Kentucky, 1999), 458.

13. Duke Snider with Phil Pepe, *Few and Chosen: Defining Dodger Greatness Across the Ages* (Chicago: Triumph Books, 2006), 122.

14. Bob Vanderberg, "Robinson Changed Minds and Won Hearts," *Chicago Tribune*, March 31, 1997.

15. Robert McGee, *The Greatest Ballpark Ever: Ebbets Field and the Story of the Brooklyn Dodgers* (New Brunswick, NJ: Rivergate Books, 2005), 193.

16. Ira Berkow, "Dixie Walker Remembers," *New York Times*, December 10, 1981.

17. Higbe had been Brooklyn's best pitcher in 1946, but on May 3, 1947, less than three weeks into the season, Branch Rickey traded him to the Pirates.

18. Ira Berkow, "The High Hard One," *New York Times*, May 11, 1985.

19. Richard Sandomir, "A Dissident Can Now Embrace the Legacy," *New York Times*, April 5, 1997.

20. Larry Eldridge, "Why Isn't Pee Wee Reese in the Hall of Fame," *Baseball Digest*, July 1978, 81–82.

21. Jules Tygiel, *Baseball's Great Experiment: Jackie Robinson and His Legacy* (New York: Vintage, 1984), 169.

22. Ed Stevens, *The Other Side of the Jackie Robinson Story* (Mustang, OK: Tate, 2009), 43.

23. Ira Berkow, "The High Hard One," *New York Times*, May 11, 1985.

24. J. Ronald Oakley, *Baseball's Last Golden Age* (Jefferson, NC: McFarland, 1994), 50.

25. Scott Simon, *Jackie Robinson and the Integration of Baseball* (Hoboken, NJ: John Wiley & Sons, 2002), 106.

26. Leo Durocher, *Nice Guys Finish Last* (New York: Simon & Schuster, 1975), 166–67.

27. Bob Vanderberg, "Robinson Changed Minds and Won Hearts," *Chicago Tribune*, March 31, 1997.

28. Sam Lacy, *Baltimore Afro-American*, April 12, 1947.

29. Wendell Smith, "The Sports Beat," *Pittsburgh Courier*, April 12, 1947.

30. Irwin Silber, *Press Box Red: The Story of Lester Rodney, the Communist Who Helped Break the Color Line in American Sports* (Philadelphia: Temple University, 2003), 102.

31. *Des Moines Register*, July 25, 1993.

32. Scott Simon, *Jackie Robinson and the Integration of Baseball* (Hoboken, NJ: John Wiley & Sons, 2002), 36.

33. *Brooklyn Daily Eagle*, April 12, 1947.

34. *Brooklyn Daily Eagle*, April 13, 1947.

35. Dan Burley, *New York Amsterdam News*, April 19, 1947.

36. Walter White, "People, Politics, and Places," *Chicago Defender*, April 26, 1947.

37. *Richmond (VA) Afro American*, April 19, 1947.

38. *New York Times*, April 12, 1947.

39. Peter Golenbock, *Bums* (New York: G. P. Putnam's Sons, 1984), 114.

40. Red Barber and Robert Creamer, *Rhubarb in the Catbird Seat* (Garden City, NY: Doubleday, 1968), 84.

41. *New York World Telegram*, April 13, 1947.

19 : Jackie Robinson Joins the Dodgers

1. *New York Herald Tribune*, April 15, 1947.

2. *New York Times*, April 15, 1947.

3. Richard Sandomir, "A Hard-Hitting Profile of Robinson by ESPN," *New York Times*, February 28, 1997.

4. Lester Rodney, *Daily Worker*, April 15, 1947.

5. *New York Times*, April 16, 1947.

6. Herb Goren, *New York Sun*, April 16, 1947.

7. Gus Steiger, *New York Daily Mirror*, April 16, 1947.

8. *Brooklyn Daily Eagle*, April 16, 1947.

9. Arthur Daley, *New York Times*, April 16, 1947.

10. Arch Murray, *New York Post*, April 16, 1947.
11. *Brooklyn Daily Eagle*, April 26, 1947.
12. Peter Golenbock, *Bums* (New York: G. P. Putnam's Sons, 1984), 169.
13. Pee Wee Reese with Tim Cohane, "Reese's Own Story," *Baseball Digest*, May 1954, 36.
14. *Time*, April 14, 1947.
15. J. Ronald Oakley, *Baseball's Last Golden Age, 1946–1960* (Jefferson, NC: McFarland, 1994), 44.
16. Jules Tygiel, *Baseball's Great Experiment* (New York: Vintage Books, 1984), 183.
17. J. Ronald Oakley, *Baseball's Last Golden Age*, 54.
18. Jackie Robinson, *I Never Had It Made* (New York: G. P. Putnam's Sons, 1972), 74.
19. Jackie Robinson, *Baseball Has Done It* (Philadelphia: Lippincott, 1964), 56.
20. Ira Berkow, "Dixie Walker Remembers," *New York Times*, December 10, 1981.
21. *Brooklyn Daily Eagle*, February 27, 1949.
22. Jules Tygiel, *Baseball's Great Experiment* (New York: Vintage Books, 1984), 194.
23. Daniel Okrent and Harris Lewine, editors, *The Ultimate Baseball Book* (Boston: Houghton Mifflin, 1979), 270.
24. Arch Murray, "Frick Admits Breadon Halted Strike by Cardinals Against Jackie Robinson," *New York Post*, May 9, 1947.
25. Don Amore, "'47 Cardinal Says Robinson Boycott Was Planned," *Hartford Courant*, June 29, 2008.
26. Peter Marshall, *Baseball's Pivotal Era, 1945–1951* (Lexington: University Press of Kentucky, 1999), 141.
27. Ira Berkow, "Dixie Walker Remembers," *New York Times*, December 10, 1981.
28. Wendell Smith, "The Sports Beat," *Pittsburgh Courier*, May 24, 1947.
29. Irwin Silber, *Press Box Red* (Philadelphia: Temple University, 2003), 46.
30. Ibid., 103.
31. Data provided by David W. Smith of www.retrosheet.org.
32. This photograph probably was taken prior to the World Series.
33. Jonathan Eig, *Opening Day: The Story of Jackie Robinson's First Season* (New York: Simon & Schuster, 2007), 211.

20 : Dixie and Jackie Bring a Pennant to Brooklyn

1. Saves did not become an official statistic until 1969.
2. Tom Meany, "Hugh Casey," *Sport*, May 1948, 84.
3. *New York World Telegram*, September 13, 1947.
4. Gordon Williams, *Reading* (PA) *Times*, July 1 1947.
5. Ted Reed, *Carl Furillo* (Jefferson, NC: McFarland, 2010).
6. Bill Reedy, *Reading Eagle*, July 11, 1951.
7. Bobby Bragan and Jeff Guinn, *You Can't Hit the Ball with the Bat on Your Shoulder* (Fort Worth: Summit Group, 1992), 125.
8. Sidney Jacobson, *Pete Reiser: The Rough-and-Tumble Career of the Perfect Ballplayer* (Jefferson, NC: McFarland, 2004), 175.
9. Dan Daniel, *New York World Telegram*, December 9, 1947.
10. *Daily Worker*, September 16, 1947.
11. Jonathan Eig, "The Real Jackie Robinson Story," *Wall Street Journal*, March 31, 2007.
12. Harvey Araton, "The Dixie Walker She Knew," *New York Times*, April 9, 2010.
13. Maury Allen with Susan Walker, *Dixie Walker of the Dodgers* (Tuscaloosa: University of Alabama Press, 2010).
14. E-mail to the author from Stephen Walker, April 20, 2010.
15. Bill Roeder, "Cards Best Behaved, Says Jackie," *New York World Telegram*, July 9, 1947.
16. *Chicago Daily Tribune*, May 19, 1947.
17. *Chicago Defender*, May 24, 1947.
18. Red Barber and Robert Creamer, *Rhubarb in the Catbird Seat* (Garden City, NY: Doubleday, 1968), 49.
19. Letter to the author from Marty Adler, founder and president of the Brooklyn Dodgers Hall of Fame.
20. *Time*, August 18, 1947.
21. *Brooklyn Daily Eagle*, August 5, 1947.
22. Roscoe McGowen, "Boss of Bums but Not Bum Boss," August 1947, *Baseball Magazine*, August 1947, 307.
23. *New York World Telegram*, September 13, 1947.
24. Red Barber, "Leadoff Man," *The New Republic*, July 4, 1983.

25. *Brooklyn Daily Eagle*, August 23, 1947.
26. *New York World Telegram*, September 13, 1947.
27. Dan Daniel, *New York World Telegram*, September 20, 1947.
28. *New York Times*, September 27, 1947.
29. Deacon Phillippe of the 1903 Pirates, Jack Coombs of the 1910 Athletics, Red Faber of the 1917 White Sox, and Ray Kremer of the 1925 Pirates all won successive games, but not on consecutive days.
30. Tom Meany, "Hugh Casey," *Sport*, May 1948, 84.
31. Michael, D'Antonio, *Forever Blue: The True Story of Walter O'Malley, Baseball's Most Controversial Owner, And the Dodgers of Brooklyn and Los Angeles* (New York: Riverhead, 2009), 105–06.

21 : "The place doesn't look the same since you've gone, Dixie"

1. *Washington Post*, May 11, 1975.
2. Harold C. Burr, *Brooklyn Daily Eagle*, October 16, 1947.
3. Tommy Holmes, *Brooklyn Daily Eagle*, December 10, 1947.
4. Tommy Holmes, *Brooklyn Daily Eagle*, November 24, 1947.
5. When Walker turned down their offer, the Dodgers chose Walter Alston to manage the St. Paul club.
6. *Brooklyn Daily Eagle*, December 3, 1947.
7. *Utica Observer-Dispatch*, April 13, 1951.
8. *Brooklyn Daily Eagle*, December 11, 1952.
9. Michael Gaven, "What a Load of Rhubarb," *Baseball Digest*, February 1958, 57.
10. Jackie Robinson, "Now I Know Why They Boo Me," *Look*, January 25, 1955.
11. *New York Times*, December 9, 1947.
12. *Los Angeles Times*, August 16, 1974.
13. E-mail to author from Stephen Walker, May 9, 2009.
14. Sam Goldaper, "Dixie Walker, Dodger Star of the 1940's, Dead at 71," *New York Times*, May 18, 1982.
15. *Brooklyn Daily Eagle*, December 12, 1947.
16. *New York Times*, January 18, 1947.
17. Victor Debs, Jr., *Missed It by That Much* (Jefferson, NC: McFarland, 1998), 75.
18. *New York Times*, May 22, 1948.
19. *Brooklyn Daily Eagle*, September 29, 1948.
20. *Brooklyn Daily Eagle*, September 27, 1948.
21. *Nebraska State Journal*, July 23, 1948.
22. *New York World Telegram*, September 1, 1948.
23. *Utica Observer-Dispatch*, April 13, 1951.
24. Ibid.
25. *The Sporting News*, May 31, 1982.
26. *New York Daily Mirror*, September 7, 1949.
27. *Brooklyn Daily Eagle*, July 12, 1949.
28. Players and owners had both put $118,000 into the fund, proceeds from the All-Star game were $111,000, and proceeds from the World Series were $150,000.
29. *New York Times*, July 12, 1949.
30. *Binghamton (NY) Press*, June 8, 1950.

22 : Managing in the Minor Leagues

1. *Associated Press*, October 12, 1949.
2. *New York World Telegram*, December 6, 1949.
3. *Brooklyn Daily Eagle*, January 29, 1950.
4. *Hartford Courant*, December 6, 1949.
5. Ibid.
6. *Brooklyn Daily Eagle*, January 29, 1950.
7. Guy Tiller, "Prospect for Majors: Dixie Walker," *Baseball Digest*, October 1950.
8. *Hartford Courant*, March 1, 1950.
9. *Chicago Daily Tribune*, March 24, 1950.
10. *Brooklyn Daily Eagle*, July 26, 1950.
11. Guy Tiller, "Prospect for Majors: Dixie Walker," *Baseball Digest*, October 1950.
12. *Brooklyn Eagle*, November 29, 1950.
13. *The Sporting News*, October 11, 1950.
14. *Binghamton (NY) Press*, November 10, 1950.
15. *New York World Telegram and Sun*, November 2, 1950.
16. *Utica Observer-Dispatch*, April 13, 1951.

17. *Brooklyn Daily Eagle*, April 9, 1951.
18. *New York Times*, July 1, 1951.
19. *New York Times*, July 7, 1951.
20. *Brooklyn Daily Eagle*, September 29, 1952.
21. *Hartford Courant*, October 1, 1952.
22. *Brooklyn Daily Eagle*, November 20, 1953.
23. *Brooklyn Daily Eagle*, October 3, 1952.
24. *Brooklyn Daily Eagle*, October 15, 1953.
25. *Atlanta Constitution*, September 29, 1954.
26. E-mail to the author from Stephen Walker, October 27, 2009.
27. *Utica* (NY) *Daily Press*, March 9, 1955.
28. John W. Fox, "Dixie Demonstrates Playoff System Evils," *Binghamton* (NY) *Press*, November 9, 1956.
29. Dan Daniel, "Never in Running for Dodger Job, Sighs Dixie," *New York World Telegram and Sun*, March 12, 1953.
30. Ibid.

23 : Ending His Career in Dodger Blue

1. Milt Dunnell, "Dixie Lived Down the Racist Image of Robinson Case," *Toronto Star*, May 19, 1982.
2. *Binghamton* (NY) *Press*, August 13, 1959.
3. *Binghamton* (NY) *Press*, August 27, 1959.
4. Ibid.
5. Bob Wolf, "'Peepul's Cherce' to Coach Braves' Kids in Sock Art," *The Sporting News*, November 24, 1962.
6. The 1964 Milwaukee Braves led the NL in batting average, on-base percentage, slugging percentage, total bases, and runs scored.
7. Bob Wolf, "Dixie Adds Dynamite to Braves' Bats," *The Sporting News*, December 26, 1964.
8. *Los Angeles Times*, September 5, 1974.
9. *Los Angeles Herald-Examiner*, October 5, 1968.
10. *Los Angeles Times*, August 16, 1974.
11. *Los Angeles Times*, February 25, 1969.
12. *Los Angeles Times*, April 23, 1969.
13. *Los Angeles Times*, April 21, 1969.
14. *New York Times*, January 23, 1970.

15. John Wiebusch, "The New Willie Davis," *Baseball Digest*, May 1969, 15.
16. *Los Angeles Times*, February 5, 1970.
17. *Los Angeles Times*, May 13, 1971.
18. *Los Angeles Times*, February 12, 1970.
19. *Los Angeles Times*, March 17, 1970.
20. *Los Angeles Times*, May 22, 1970.
21. *Los Angeles Times*, March 28, 1969.
22. *Los Angeles Times*, August 8, 1971.
23. *Los Angeles Times*, March 30, 1972.
24. *Los Angeles Times*, May 9, 1971.
25. *Los Angeles Times*, April 18, 1974.
26. *Los Angeles Times*, October 3, 1974.
27. *Los Angeles Times*, April 11, 1976.
28. *Los Angeles Times*, March 10, 1971.
29. *Brooklyn Daily Eagle*, August 27, 1954.
30. *Los Angeles Times*, October 25, 1972.
31. Ira Berkow, "Dixie Walker: You Associate with Blacks Till You Know Them," *Burlington* (NC) *Times-News*, March 29, 1972.
32. Ira Berkow, "Dixie Walker Remembers," *New York Times*, December 10, 1981.
33. Ibid.
34. Convalidation is a ceremony in which a previous civil marriage, in which at least one partner is Catholic, is later sanctioned in the Catholic Church.
35. As the wife of a former major leaguer, Estelle Walker was receiving a pension of $38,000 a year at the time of her death.
36. *New York Times*, June 3, 1985.
37. Letter to author from Marty Adler, founder and president of the Brooklyn Dodgers Hall of Fame.

24 : Was Dixie Walker a Racist?

1. Jack Kavanagh, "Dixie Walker," *Baseball Research Journal* 22 (1993), 83.
2. Frederick Crews, "Melville the Great," *New York Review of Books*, December 19, 2005.
3. Norman L. Macht, "Does Baseball Deserve This Black Eye," *Baseball Research Journal* 38, no. 1 (Summer 2009), 5.
4. Raymond Arsenault, *The Sound of Freedom: Marian Anderson, the Lincoln Memorial, and the Concert That Awakened America* (New York: Bloomsbury Press, 2009), 67.
5. Ibid., 75.

6. Norman L. Macht, "Does Baseball Deserve This Black Eye," p. 6.
7. *New York Times,* July 29, 1947.
8. *New York Times,* January 1, 2006.
9. David Kushner, *Levittown: Two Families, One Tycoon, and the Fight for Civil Rights in America's Legendary Suburb* (New York: Walker and Company, 2009), 75–76.

10. Thomas J. Sugrue, *Sweet Land of Liberty: The Forgotten Struggle for Civil Rights in the North* (New York: Random House, 2008), 184.
11. Ira Berkow, "Ice Water in the Veins," *New York Times,* April 10, 1987.

Bibliography

Ahrens, Art. "The Old Brawl Game." *The National Pastime,* Society for American Baseball Research 23 (2003): 3–6.

Alexander, Charles C. *Breaking the Slump: Baseball in the Depression Era.* New York: Columbia University Press, 2002.

_____. *Our Game: An American Baseball History.* New York: Henry Holt, 1991.

Allen, Maury, with Susan Walker. *Dixie Walker of the Dodgers: The People's Choice.* Tuscaloosa: University of Alabama Press, 2010.

Amore, Don. "'47 Cardinal Says Robinson Boycott Was Planned." *Hartford Courant,* June 29, 2008.

Anderson, Dave. "Honoring Robinson's Achievement and Carrying on His Legacy." *New York Times,* April 16, 2007.

Applegate, Richard. "The Battle of the Hatfields and the McCoys," *Mound City Memories: Baseball in St. Louis.* Cleveland: Society for American Baseball Research, 2007.

Araton, Harvey. "The Dixie Walker She Knew." *New York Times,* April 9, 2010.

Arsenault, Raymond. *The Sound of Freedom: Marian Anderson, the Lincoln Memorial, and the Concert That Awakened America.* New York: Bloomsbury Press, 2009.

Bailey, Judson. "New Players Put Brooklyn There—MacPhail." *Atlanta Constitution,* August 22, 1941.

Barber, Red. "Leadoff Man." *The New Republic,* July 4, 1983.

_____. *1947—When All Hell Broke Loose in Baseball.* Garden City, NY: Doubleday, 1982.

Barber, Red, and Robert Creamer. *Rhubarb in the Catbird Seat.* Garden City, NY: Doubleday, 1968.

Bartell, Richard, and Norman L. Macht. *Rowdy Richard.* Berkeley, CA: North Atlantic Books. 1987.

Beale, Morris Allison. *The Washington Senators.* Washington, D.C.: Columbia, 1947.

Berkow, Ira. "Dixie Walker Remembers." *New York Times,* December 10, 1981.

_____. "Dixie Walker: You Associate with Blacks Till You Know Them." *Burlington (NC) Times-News,* March 29, 1972.

_____. "Ice Water in the Veins." *New York Times,* April 10, 1987.

_____. "The High Hard One." *New York Times,* May 11, 1985.

Bjarkman, Peter C., editor. *Encyclopedia of Major League Baseball Team Histories: American League.* Westport, CT: Meckler, 1991.

_____. *Encyclopedia of Major League Baseball Team Histories: National League.* Westport, CT: Meckler, 1991.

Blau, Clifford. "Leg Men." *Baseball Research Journal,* Society for American Baseball Research 38, no. 1 (Summer 2009): 70–81.

Bloodgood, Clifford. "The Abnormal Season of '46." *Baseball Magazine,* December 1946.

Boren, Stephen D., and Thomas Boren. "The 1942 Pennant Race." *The National Pastime,* Society for American Baseball Research 15 (1995): 133–135.

Borst, Bill. "Showdown in St. Louis." *The National Pastime,* Society for American Baseball Research 11 (1991): 63–64.

Boston, Talmage. *1939, Baseball's Pivotal*

Year. Fort Worth: The Summit Group, 1994.
Bragan, Bobby, and Jeff Guinn. *You Can't Hit the Ball with the Bat on Your Shoulder: The Baseball Life and Times of Bobby Bragan*. Fort Worth: The Summit Group, 1992.
Branch, Taylor. *At Canaan's Edge: America in the King Years, 1965–68*. New York: Simon & Schuster, 2006.
Broeg, Bob. "Backward, Turn Backward Oh Time ..." *St. Louis Post-Dispatch*, September 23, 1972.
____. "Fine Alabama Contribution to Baseball." *St. Louis Post-Dispatch*, June 21, 1949.
____. "The '42 Cardinals." *Sport*, July 1963, 40.
Broeg, Bob, and William J. Miller, Jr. *Baseball from a Different Angle*. South Bend, IN: Diamond Communications, 1988.
Bromberg, Lester. "Dodger Fans: Dixie's on Job And Will Be Set for Opener." *New York World Telegram*, February 22, 1947.
Burr, Harold C. "Dixie Walker's More Than Man-of-Week to Brooklyn." *Brooklyn Eagle*, July 7, 1946.
Campbell, Gordon. *Famous American Athletes of Today* (Ninth Series). Boston: L. C. Page, 1945.
Cannon, Jimmy. "Leo Buttons His Lip." *Baseball Digest*, November 1946.
Cantor, George. *World Series Fact Book*. Detroit: Visible Ink Press, 1996.
Carmichael, John P., editor. *My Greatest Day in Baseball*. New York: A.S. Barnes, 1945.
Charlton, James. *The Baseball Chronology*. New York: Macmillan, 1991.
Creamer, Robert W. *Baseball in '41*. New York: Penguin, 1991.
Crepeau, Richard. "Landis, Baseball, and Racism." *Baseball Research Journal*, Society for American Baseball Research 38, no. 1 (Summer 2009): 31–32.
Crews, Frederick C. "Melville the Great." *New York Review of Books*, December 1, 2005.
Cuddy, Jack. "Dixie Walker Not Sorry That MacPhail Has Left Brooklyn." *Berkshire (MA) Evening Eagle*, January 11, 1943.
Daley, Arthur. "Overheard at the Polo Grounds." *New York Times*, September 8, 1947.
Danforth, Ed. "Lefties Finally Foil Dixie Walker." *Baseball Digest*, August 1951, 75.

Daniel, Dan. "Dixie Bids for Yank Job." *New York World Telegram*, April 5, 1935.
____. "Dixie Walker Ascribes Added Power to Change in Bats." *New York World Telegram*, July 8, 1946.
____. "Dodgers Now Look Like Best Bet for World Series." *New York World Telegram*, July 5, 1946.
____. "Never in Running for Dodger Job, Sighs Dixie." *New York World Telegram and Sun*, March 12, 1953.
D'Antonio, Michael. *Forever Blue: The True Story of Walter O'Malley, Baseball's Most Controversial Owner, And the Dodgers of Brooklyn and Los Angeles*. New York: Riverhead Books, 2009.
Debs, Victor, Jr. *Missed It by That Much*. Jefferson, NC: McFarland, 1998.
Delbanco, Andrew. *Melville: His World and His Work*. New York: Knopf, 2005.
Dewey, Donald, and Nicholas Acocella. *The Ball Clubs*. New York: Harper Collins, 1996.
____. *The Biographical History of Baseball*. New York: Carroll & Graf, 1995.
Dolan, Steve. "Padre Coach Has Near-Miss Career." *Los Angeles Times*, May 12, 1981.
Dorinson, Joseph, and Joram Warmund, editors. *Jackie Robinson: Race, Sports, and the American Dream*. Armonk, NY: M. E. Sharpe, 1998.
Dunnell, Milt. "Dixie Lived Down the Racist Image of Robinson Case." *Toronto Star*, May 19, 1982.
Durocher, Leo, with Ed Linn. *Nice Guys Finish Last*. New York: Simon & Schuster, 1975.
Eig, Jonathan. *Opening Day: The Story of Jackie Robinson's First Season*. New York: Simon & Schuster, 2007.
Eldridge, Larry. "Why Isn't Pee Wee Reese in the Hall of Fame?" *Baseball Digest*, July 1978.
Falkner, David. *Great Time Coming: The Life of Jackie Robinson, from Baseball to Birmingham*. New York: Simon & Schuster, 1995.
Feller, Bob, and Bill Gilbert. *Now Pitching, Bob Feller*. New York: Harper Perennial, 1990.
Fenster, Kenneth R. "The 1954 Dixie Series." *Baseball in the Peach State*, Society for American Baseball Research, 2010, 82–92.
Figone, Al. "Larry MacPhail and Dolph

Camilli." *The National Pastime,* Society for American Baseball Research 14 (1994): 106–109.
Fimrite, Ron. "The Play That Beat the Bums." *Sports Illustrated,* October 20, 1997.
Freese, Mel R. *The St. Louis Cardinals in the 1940s.* Jefferson, NC: McFarland, 2007.
Frommer, Harvey. *New York City Baseball: The Last Golden Age: 1947–1957.* New York: Macmillan, 1980.
_____. *Rickey and Robinson.* New York: Macmillan, 1982.
Gallagher, Mark. *The Yankee Encyclopedia.* Champaign, IL: Sagamore, 1997.
Garner Dwight. "'Voice of the Century' Broke Racial Barriers." *New York Times,* April 2, 2009.
Gaven, Michael. "What a Load of Rhubarb." *Baseball Digest,* February 1958.
Gies, Joseph, and Robert H. Shoemaker. *Stars of the Series, A Complete History of the World Series.* New York: Thomas Y. Crowell, 1965.
Gillette, Gary, and Pete Palmer, editors. *The ESPN Baseball Encyclopedia, Fifth Edition.* New York: Sterling, 2008.
Goldaper, Sam. "Dixie Walker, Dodger Star of the 1940's, Dead at 71." *New York Times,* May 18, 1982.
Goldblatt, Andrew. *The Giants and the Dodgers: Four Cities, Two Teams, One Rivalry.* Jefferson, NC: McFarland, 2003.
Goldstein, Richard. *Spartan Seasons: How Baseball Survived the Second World War.* New York: Macmillan, 1980.
Golenbock, Peter. *Bums: An Oral History of the Brooklyn Dodgers.* New York: G. P. Putnam's Sons, 1984.
Good, Charlie. "League Batting Leader Joins the Toronto Club." *Toronto Daily Star,* August 28, 1931
Gough, David. "A Tribute to Burt Shotton." *The National Pastime,* Society for American Baseball Research 14 (1994): 99–101.
Graham, Frank. "The Hottest Guy in Baseball." *New York Sun,* August 21, 1940.
Graham, Frank, Jr. "Greatest Fight on a Ballfield." *Baseball Digest,* June 1953.
Green, Paul. "Whitlow Wyatt." *Sports Collectors Digest,* March 28, 1986, 172–220.
Greene, Sam. "Detroit Fans Deride Cochrane For Swapping Walker to Dykes." *The Sporting News,* December 9, 1937.

Heinz, W. C. "The Rocky Road of Pistol Pete." In *The Baseball Reader: Favorites from the Fireside Books of Baseball,* edited by Charles Einstein. New York: Lippincott & Crowell, 1980, 162–176.
Higbe, Kirby, with Martin Quigley. *The High Hard One.* New York: Viking Press, 1967.
Hill, Art. *I Don't Care if I Never Come Back: A Baseball Fan and His Game.* New York: Simon & Schuster, 1980.
Hilligan, Earl. "It's True What They Say About Dixie, Dykes Says." *Burlington* (NC) *Daily Times-News,* April 17, 1937.
Honig, Donald. *Baseball America.* New York: Macmillan, 1985.
_____. *Baseball When the Grass Was Real.* New York: Coward, McCann & Geoghegan, 1975.
_____. *The Brooklyn Dodgers: An Illustrated Tribute:* New York: St. Martin's Press, 1981.
Hynd, Noel. *The Giants of the Polo Grounds.* New York: Doubleday, 1988.
Jacobson, Sidney. *Pete Reiser: The Rough-and Tumble Career of the Perfect Ballplayer.* Jefferson, NC: McFarland, 2004.
James, Bill. *The New Bill James Historical Baseball Abstract.* New York: Free Press, 2001.
Jordan, David M. *A Tiger in His Time.* South Bend, IN: Diamond Communications, 1990.
Kahn, Roger. *The Boys of Summer.* New York: Harper and Row, 1971.
_____. *The Era, 1947–1957: When the Yankees, the Giants, and the Dodgers Ruled the World.* New York: Ticknor & Fields, 1993.
_____. *Into My Own: The Remarkable People and Events That Shapes a Life.* New York: St. Martin's Press, 2007.
Kavanagh, Jack. "Dixie Walker." *Baseball Research Journal,* Society for American Baseball Research 22 (1993): 80–83.
_____. "A Dodger Boyhood." *Baseball Research Journal,* Society for American Baseball Research 20 (1991): 119–132.
Keiran, John. "The Bronx Cheer for Brannick from Brooklyn." *New York Times,* September, 19, 1940.
Kirksey, George. "MacPhail's Spending Due to Net Dodger Flag." *Atlanta Constitution,* December 22, 1940.
Knorr, Charles P. *The End of Baseball as We Knew It: The Players Union, 1960–*

81. Champaign: University of Illinois, 2002.

Kushner, David. *Levittown: Two Families, One Tycoon, and the Fight for Civil Rights in America's Legendary Suburb.* New York: Walker, 2009.

Langford, Walter M. *Legends of Baseball: An Oral History of the Game's Golden Age.* South Bend, IN: Diamond Communications, 1987.

Levitt, Daniel R. *Ed Barrow: The Bulldog Who Built the Yankees' First Dynasty.* Lincoln: University of Nebraska Press, 2008.

Levy, Alan H. *Joe McCarthy: Architect of the Yankee Dynasty.* Jefferson, NC: McFarland, 2005.

Light, Jonathan F. *The Cultural Encyclopedia of Baseball.* Jefferson, NC: McFarland, 1997.

Liley, Thomas. "Whit Wyatt — The Dodgers' 1941 Ace." *The National Pastime,* Society for American Baseball Research 11 (1991): 46–47.

Linkugel, Wil A., and Edward J. Pappas. *They Tasted Glory: Among the Missing at the Baseball Hall of Fame.* Jefferson, NC: McFarland, 1998.

Lowenfish, Lee. *Branch Rickey: Baseball's Ferocious Gentleman.* Lincoln: University of Nebraska Press, 2007.

_____. "The Gentlemen's Agreement and the Ferocious Gentleman Who Broke It." *Baseball Research Journal,* Society for American Baseball Research 38, no. 1 (Summer 2009): 12–13.

_____. *The Imperfect Diamond: A History of Baseball's Labor Wars.* New York: De Capo Press, 1991.

Lowry, Philip J. *Green Cathedrals: The Ultimate Celebration of Major League and Negro League Ballparks.* New York: Walker, 2006.

Macht, Norman L. "Does Baseball Deserve This Black Eye." *Baseball Research Journal,* Society for American Baseball Research 38, no. 1 (Summer 2009): 5–9.

_____. "Why did Mickey Miss the Ball?" *The National Pastime,* Society for American Baseball Research 11 (1991): 44–45.

MacPhail, Lee. "Year to Remember Especially in Brooklyn." *The National Pastime,* Society for American Baseball Research 11 (1991): 41–43.

Mann, Arthur. "The Truth About the Jackie Robinson Case." *Saturday Evening Post,* May 20, 1950.

Marshall, William. *Baseball's Pivotal Era, 1945–1951.* Lexington: University Press of Kentucky, 1999.

Marzano, Rudy. *The Brooklyn Dodgers in the 1940s: How Robinson, MacPhail, Reiser and Rickey Changed Baseball.* Jefferson, NC: McFarland, 2005.

Maxwell, Jocko, "Robinson's the Name for '47." *Baseball Digest,* October 1946, 58.

Mayer, Ronald A. *The 1937 Newark Bears: A Baseball Legend.* East Hanover, NJ: Vintage Press, 1980.

McDonough, Pat. "Walker Idol of Flatbush." *New York World Telegram,* August 8, 1939.

McGee, Robert. *The Greatest Ballpark Ever: Ebbets Field and the Story of the Brooklyn Dodgers.* New Brunswick, NJ: Rivergate Books, 2005.

McGowen, Roscoe. "Boss of Bums but Not Bum Boss." *Baseball Magazine,* August 1947.

_____. "Dodgers Revolt Against Durocher, Then Play and Win Game, 23–6." *New York Times,* July 11, 1943.

McNeil, William F. *The Dodger Encyclopedia.* Champaign, IL: Sports Publishing, 1997.

Mead, William B. *Even the Browns: The Zany, True Story of Baseball in the Early Forties.* Chicago: Contemporary Books, 1978.

Meany, Tom. "Dixie Deal Strictly Business." *Baseball Digest,* March 1948, 55–56.

_____. "Hugh Casey." *Sport,* May 1948.

Mele, Andrew Paul. *A Brooklyn Dodgers Reader.* Jefferson, NC: McFarland, 2004.

Miller, Patrick B., and David K. Wiggins, editors. *Sport and the Color Line: Black Athletes and Race Relations in Twentieth-Century America.* New York: Routledge, 2004.

Morris, Peter. *A Game of Inches: The Game Behind the Scenes.* Chicago: Ivan R. Dee, 2006.

Murray, Arch. "Frick Admits Breadon Halted Strike by Cardinals Against Jackie Robinson." *New York Post,* May 9, 1947.

Nack, William. "The Breakthrough." *Sports Illustrated,* May 5, 1997.

Neft, David S., Richard M. Cohen, and Michael L. Neft. *The Sports Encyclopedia: Baseball, 25th Edition.* New York: St. Martin's Press, 2005.

Neyer, Rob, and Eddie Epstein. *Baseball Dy-*

nasties: The Greatest Teams of All Time. New York: W. W. Norton, 2000.

Oakley, J. Ronald. *Baseball's Last Golden Age, 1946–1960: The National Pastime in a Time of Glory and Change.* Jefferson, NC: McFarland, 1994.

Okkonen, Marc. *Baseball Uniforms of the 20th Century.* New York: Sterling Publishing, 1991.

Okrent, Daniel, and Harris Lewine, editors. *The Ultimate Baseball Book.* Boston: Houghton Mifflin, 1979.

Oliphant, Thomas. *Praying for Gil Hodges.* New York: St. Martin's Press, 2005.

Panaccio, Tim. "How it Was During the War Years." *Baseball Digest*, January 1977.

Paper, Lew. *Perfect: Don Larsen's Miraculous World Series Game and the Men Who Made It Happen.* New York: New American Library, 2009.

Parker, Dan. "Dixie Walker, the Peepul's Cherce." *New York Daily Mirror*, August 11, 1946.

Paxton, Harry T. "It's Raining Dollars in Pittsburgh." *Saturday Evening Post*, May 8, 1948.

Pietrusza, David, Matthew Silverman, and Michael Gershman, editors. *Baseball, The Biographical Encyclopedia.* Kingston, NY: Total/Sports Illustrated, 2000.

Porter, David L., editor. *Biographical Dictionary of American Sports: Baseball, Revised and Expanded Edition.* Westport, CT: Greenwood Press, 2000.

Povich, Shirley. "South Protests Entrance of Negro into Majors." *Washington Post*, May 14, 1953.

Powell, Larry. "Jackie Robinson and Dixie Walker: Myths of the Southern Baseball Player." *Southern Cultures* (Summer 2002): 56–70.

Reed, Ted. *Carl Furillo: Brooklyn Dodgers All-Star.* Jefferson, NC: McFarland, 2010.

Reese, Pee Wee, with Tim Cohane. "Reese's Own Story." *Baseball Digest*, May 1954.

Rice, Damon. *Seasons Past.* New York: Praeger, 1976.

Rice, Robert. "The Artful Dodger." *PM*, August 8, 1943.

Robinson, Jackie. *Baseball Has Done It.* Philadelphia: Lippincott, 1964.

_____. "Now I Know Why They Boo Me." *Look*, January 25, 1955, 23–28.

Robinson, Jackie, as told to Alfred Duckett. *I Never Had It Made.* New York: G. P. Putnam's Sons, 1972.

Robinson, Ray. *Iron Horse: Lou Gehrig in His Time.* New York: W. W. Norton, 1990.

Roeder, Bill. "And Who Slapped the Giants Down? Nobody but Dixie." *New York World Telegram*, April 22, 1946.

_____. "Dixie Ready to Cavort in Any Field." *New York World Telegram*, March 14, 1946.

_____. "Poor Old Dixie Is Out of Job Again, They Say." *New York World Telegram*, March 8, 1946.

_____. "Walker-Merullo Bout Seen Top Diamond Brawl." *New York World Telegram and Sun*, July 26, 1954.

Roth, Morton. "Dixie Walker: Farewell to a Boyhood Idol." *Baseball Digest*, February 1983.

Sandomir, Richard. "A Dissident Can Now Embrace the Legacy." *New York Times*, April 5, 1997.

_____. "A Hard-Hitting Profile of Robinson by ESPN." *New York Times*, February 28, 1997.

_____. "In Print, Cheerleading and Indifference." *New York Times*, April 13, 1997.

Sarnoff, Gary. "War at Griffith Stadium." *The National Pastime,* Society for American Baseball Research (2009): 73–76.

Schumacher, Garry. "The Customers Are Finally Right." *New York Journal American*, May 26, 1944.

Shatzkin, Mike. *The Ballplayers.* New York: William Morrow, 1990.

Sheed, Wilfrid. *My Life as a Fan.* New York: Simon & Schuster, 1993.

Silber, Irwin. *Press Box Red: The Story of Lester Rodney, the Communist Who Helped Break the Color Line in American Sports.* Philadelphia: Temple University. 2003.

Simon, Scott. *Jackie Robinson and the Integration of Baseball.* Hoboken, NJ: John Wiley & Sons, 2002.

Skipper, John C. *Charlie Gehringer: A Biography of the Hall of Fame Tigers Second Baseman.* Jefferson NC: McFarland, 2008.

Smith, Wendell. "The Sports Beat." *Pittsburgh Courier*, April 12, 1947.

Snider, Duke, with Phil Pepe. *Few and Chosen: Defining Dodger Greatness Across the Eras.* Chicago: Triumph Books, 2006.

Solomon, Burt. *The Baseball Timeline.* New York: Avon Books. 1997.

Spatz, Lyle. *New York Yankee Openers: An*

Opening Day History of Baseball's Most Famous Team, 1903–1996. Jefferson, NC: McFarland, 1997.

_____. *Yankees Coming, Yankees Going.* Jefferson, NC: McFarland, 2000.

Spatz, Lyle, and Steve Steinberg. *1921: The Yankees, the Giants, and the Battle for Baseball Supremacy in New York.* Lincoln: University of Nebraska Press, 2010.

Spink, J.G. Taylor. "Always Something Doing with Dixie." *The Sporting News*, December 25, 1941.

Stevens, Ed. *The Other Side of the Jackie Robinson Story.* Mustang, OK: Tate Publishing, 2009.

Sugrue, Thomas J. *Sweet Land of Liberty: The Forgotten Struggle for Civil Rights in the North.* New York: Random House, 2008.

Thorn, John. *The Relief Pitcher: Baseball's New Hero.* New York: E. P. Dutton, 1979.

Thorn, John, Phil Birnbaum, Bill Deane, et al., editors. *Total Baseball, Eighth Edition.* Wilmington, DE: Sports Media Publishing, 2004.

Tiemann, Robert L. *Dodger Classics.* St. Louis: Baseball Histories, Inc. 1983.

Tiller, Guy. "Prospect for Majors: Dixie Walker." *Baseball Digest*, October 1950.

Tygiel, Jules. *Baseball's Great Experiment: Jackie Robinson and His Legacy.* New York: Vintage Books, 1984.

Van Blair, Rick. *Dugout to Foxhole: Interviews with Baseball Players Whose Careers Were Affected by World War II.* Jefferson, NC: McFarland, 1995.

Vanderberg, Bob. "Robinson Changed Minds and Won Hearts." *Chicago Tribune*, March 31, 1997.

Vaughan, Irving, "Baseball Got Dixie Walker in Steel Mill, Also Got Him Out." *Chicago Daily Tribune*, May 14, 1937.

Vincent, David, Lyle Spatz, and David W. Smith. *The Midsummer Classic, The Complete History of Baseball's All-Star Game.* Lincoln: University of Nebraska Press, 2001.

Vecsey, George. "Dixie Walker's Home Run." *New York Times*, May 20, 1982.

Ward, Charles P. "New Walker Tune Heard In Detroit; It's Swing to Dixie." *The Sporting News*, February 24, 1938.

Werber, Bill, and C. Paul Rogers III. *Memories of a Ballplayer.* Cleveland: Society for American Baseball Research, 2001.

White, Walter. "People, Politics, And Places." *Chicago Defender*, April 26, 1947.

Wiebusch, John. "The New Willie Davis." *Baseball Digest*, May 1969.

Wise, Bill. "Dixie Does All Right." *Sport Pix*, June 1949.

Wolf, Bob. "Dixie Adds Dynamite to Braves' Bats." *The Sporting News*, December 26, 1964.

_____. "'Peepul's Cherce' to Coach Braves' Kids in Sock Art." *The Sporting News*, November 24, 1962.

Woodward, Stanley. "In the Rickey Manner." *Baseball Digest*, July 1950, 23.

Yardley, Jonathan. "Jonathan Yardley on 'Levittown.'" *Washington Post*, February 15, 2009.

Young, Fay. "End of Baseball's Jim Crow Seen with Signing of Jackie Robinson." *Chicago Defender*, November 3, 1945.

Index

Numbers in **_bold italics_** indicate pages with photographs.

Abrams, Al 200
Adams, Ace 132
Adams, Red 222
Ahrens, Art 148
Alabama Sports Hall of Fame 225
Albany (Georgia) Nuts 13
Alda, Alan 228
Ali, Muhammad 104
Allen, Johnny 33–34, 38–50, 90, 105, 118
Allen, Maury 191
Allen, Mel 124
Allen, Nick 15
Almada, Mel 55, 65, 68
Alston, Tom 214
Alston, Walter 218, 221, 223–24, 245n
American Baseball Guild 160
American Legion 99
Anderson, Ferrell 154
Anderson, Marian 228–29
Andrews, Nate 130
Appling, Luke 74, 205, 233n
Army Emergency Relief Fund 109
Arsenault, Raymond 228–29
Ashford, Emmett 222
Atlanta Crackers 104, 136, 208, 214, **_215_**
Atlantic Basin Iron Works 100
Averill, Earl 54

Baker, Del 52–53, 209
Baker, Dusty 2, 224
Ball, Lucille 150
Baltimore Orioles 9, 19, 208
Bankhead, Dan 210–11
Barber, Lylah 163
Barber, Red 4, 58, 62, 64, 93, 124, 153, **_154_**, 162–63, 174–75, 179, 191, 193
Barlick, Al 88
Barney, Rex 118
Barr, George 140
Barrett, Red 156
Barrow, Ed 15–18, 29–31, 34, 36, 38
Barrymore, Ethel 86

Bartell, Dick 59, 90
Barton, Bruce 78
Baseball War Bond League 124
Basgall, Monty 7
Basinski, Eddie 138
Battan, Eddie 155
Bavasi, Buzzie 217–18, 227
Beazley, Johnny 110, 113
Beggs, Joe 81
Behrman, Hank 149, 154
Bell, Beau 53, 236n
Bell, Fern 61
Benson, Rev. Benney S.C. 155
Benswanger, Bill 142
Berkow, Ira 166, 224–25
Berra, Yogi **_184_**
Berres, Ray 61
Betzel, Bruno 218
Bevens, Bill 185
Bill Slocum Memorial Award 134
Billingsley, Sherman 41
Birmingham Barons 12–14
Bishop, Max 33
Bithorn, Hi 108
Blackwell, Ewell 197, 202
Blades, Ray 125, 176, 236n
Blasingame, Don 213
Bluege, Ossie 22
Boggess, Dusty 148
Bokina, Joe 40
Bonham, Ernie 97, 162
Bonham, Ruth 162
Boone, Ike 18
Bordagaray, Frenchy 108, 118, 129, 138
Borough Hall 93, 155, 194
Borowy, Hank 126, 237n
Bottomley, Jim 43
Boudreau, Lou 133
Bowman, Bob 72, 75
Boyd, Bob 214
Boyer, Ken 213
Boys High School 116

256 INDEX

Bradley, Alva 38
Bragan, Bobby 121, 168–69, 171, 188, 216, 220
Branca, Ralph 118, 157, 159, 180, 182, 186, 189, 192, 197, 205
Brannick, Eddie 60
Breadon, Sam 86, 112, 114, 160, 182
Brecheen, Harry 127, 152, 155, 157, 189
Bridges, Tommy 52
Briggs, Walter 49, 52
Broeg, Bob 28
Bromberg, Lester 164
Brooklyn Bushwicks 78
Brooklyn Club 124
Brooklyn Dodgers Hall of Fame 119, 193, 225
Brooklyn Football Dodgers 100
Brooklyn Museum 225
Brooklyn Navy Yard 124
Brooklyn Paramount Theater 95, 123
Brooklyn Rotary Club 101, 115
Brooklyn Technical High School 105
Brooklyn Trust Company 58, 82
Brooklyn Week for the Blind 123
Brouthers, Dan 131
Brown, Jimmy 107
Brown, Jumbo 26
Brown, Tommy 129, 136
Brown, Willard 214
Buffalo Symphony 138
Buker, Cy 138
Bulova Clock Company 149
Burley, Dan 173
Burns, Edward 43
Burr, Harold C. 20, 27, 107, 151, 194, 199
Bush, Donie 19, 67
Byrd, Sammy 13, 17–22, 25, 34
Byrnes, James F. 135

Cagney, James 106
Cagney, Jeanne 106
Caledonian Hospital 81
Camilli, Dolph 4, 58, 61, 63–67, 69, 82, 88, 93–95, 97, 100, 102, 105–107, 109, 114, 118–119, 201, 225–26, 239*n*
Campanella, Roy 210, 224
Campanis, Al 220, 222
Cannon, Jimmy 154, 159
Carey, Andy 223
Carleton, Tex 68–69
Carmichael, John P. 55
Carty, Rico 220
Casey, Hugh 4, 61, 68–70, 72, 75, **75**, 81–84, 88, 90, 92, 94–95, **96**, 97–98, 117–118, 146, 154, 168, **175**, 186–87, **195**, **196**, 195–97, 204, 209, 211
Cashmore, John 70, 100, 177
Cavarretta, Phil 133, 139, 148–49, 178
Cazala, Monsignor Herman 225
Chandler, Albert "Happy" 141–42, 160, 162–63, 174, 204

Chandler, Spud 95–96, 194
Chapman, Ben 2, 12–13, 16–17, 19–26, 28–30, 33–34, 36, 40–41, 46, 128–29, 136, 141, 181–82
Chennault, Gen. Claire 135
Chesnes, Bob 202, 204
Chester, Hilda 162
Chicago Bears 100
Chipman, Bob 139, 185
Christman, Mark 235*n*
Clay, Dain 154
Cobb, Ty 132, 189
Cochrane, Mickey 33, 45, 47–52, 63, 209, 235*n*
Coleman, George 150
Collins, Eddie 35
Collins, Rip 15
Colman, Frank 136, 240*n*
Columbia Broadcasting System 150
Columbus (Ohio) Red Birds 51, 238*n*
Combs, Earle 16, 19–20, 25–31, 33–36
Comiskey, Louis J. 40
Commodore Hotel 30, 82–83
Conlan, Jocko 90
Conn, Billy 150
Connelly, Tom 74
Considine, Bob 88
Continental League 219
Cooke, Bob 91
Cooke, Dusty 17, 21
Cooke, Jack Kent 216, 219
Coombs, Jack 245*n*
Cooper, Mort 71, 82–83, 86–89, 106–8, 110, 111, 113, 117, 120, **120**, 127, 147, 156, 239*n*
Cooper, Walker 86, 106, 117, 119–20, **120**, 127, 147, 152, 156
Corriden, John "Red" 132, 176
Coscarart, Joe 40
Coscarart, Pete 65, 67, 73, 84, 100
Cox, Billy 200–1
Crabtree, Estel 88
Cramer, Doc 46
Crawford, Willie 222–23
Creamer, Robert 85
Crespi, Frank 88, 107
Crews, Frederick 228
Cronin, Joe 22–26, 33, 35, 67
Crosby, Bing 202
Crosetti, Frank 21, 38, 52
Crosley, Powell 142
Crouch, Bill 79
Crowder, Alvin 22
Cuddy, Jack 115
Cullenbine, Roy 53, 64–65, 68, 70
Cullop, Nick 208

Daley, Arthur 179
Daniel, Dan 35, 40, 60, 151–52, 189, 194, 210, 218
Danning, Harry 79–80, 99

Index

Dantonio, John "Fats" 138
D'Antonio, Michael 197
Dapper, Cliff 208
Daubert, Jake 131
Davis, Curt 71, 73, 81–82, 87–88, *96*, 96–97, 105–6, 110, 118, 121, 127–28, 136, 138
Davis, Spud 142
Davis, Willie 222
Dawson, James P. 26
Day, Lorraine 174
Delbanco, Andrew 228
Demaree, Frank 84–85
Derringer, Paul 15, 84, 90, 101
Desautels, Gene 213
DeShong, Jimmie 39
Desmond, Connie 162, 179
Detroit Yacht Club 49
DeWitt, Bill 207
Dickey, Bill 22, 25, 29, 32–34, 40, 220
Dickson, Murry 7, 152, 157
Dietrich, Bill 45, 69
Digby, George 143
DiMaggio, Joe 2, 34, *39*, 39–41, 52, 85, 95, 97–98, 105, 117 131, 139, 194–95, 205
Dixie Series 214
Dixie Walker Liquor Store 99
Dobbs, Johnny 13
Dodger Sym-phony 155, 162
Doerr, Bobby 133
Donald, Atley 97, 196
Doyle, Carl 71
Drebinger, John 114
Dressen, Charlie 72, *96*, *137*, 141, 157, 159, 165, 176, 188, 211, 218
Dunn, Jack 9, 208
Dunn, Tom 140
Durocher, Leo 4, 53, *59*, 59–61, 63–64, 67–69, 71–75, 79, 81, 84, 87–89, *91*, 91–94, 96–98, 101–103, 105, 107–8, 110–13, 118, *121*, 121–22, 125–27, 129, 132, 138, 140–41, 145–48, 151, 153–55, 157, 159, 162, 164, 170–71, *175*, 174–77, *180*, 180, 188, 193, 203, 206, 209, 211
Dusak, Erv 152
Dyer, Eddie 147, 152–53, 157, 183, 191, 210
Dykes, Jimmy 43–48, 51–52, 209

Earnshaw, George 17
Edwards, Bruce 154, 171, 181, 187, 189, 197
Effrat, Louis 177
Eig, Jonathan 185, 190
Eisenstat, Harry 54
Elliott, Bob 140, 197, 202
Elmira Pioneers 76
Emerson, Ralph Waldo 228
Engleberg, Memphis 174
Epworth League 151
Erickson, Paul 108, 148
Etten, Nick 112
Evans, Red 60

Faber, Red 245*n*
Fairly, Ron 221
Falkner, David 167
Fasholz, Jack 216–217
Feller, Bob 50, 69, 102, 161, 204
Ferrell, Wes 36
Ferriss, Dave 141
Finney, Lou 73
Fitz Gerald, Ed 202
Fitzsimmons, Freddie 68, 74, 77, 80, 88, 96–97, 99, 102, 105, 116, 118, 136
Flatbush Court 114
Flatbush Theater 77
Fletcher, Art 36
Fletcher, Elbie 158
Floridian Hotel 167
Floyd Bennett Field 70
Fonseca, Lew 25, 31
Ford, Russ 9
Fox, John W. 216–17
Fox, Pete 53
Fraley, Oscar 125
Frederick Loeser & Company 127
French, Larry 86–87, 108, 112, 117–18, 122
Frey, Lonny 84
Frick, Ford 57, 76, 85, 88, 90, 138, 140–41, 160, 182
Frisch, Frankie 111, 126, 140
Furillo, Carl 145, 155, 168, 181, 187–89, *188*, 193, 196, 200, 234

Galan, Augie 87, 102, 107, 119, *128* 136–37, 140–41, 145, 148, 155–56, 160
Galbraeth, John 202
Gallagher, Jim 82, 237*n*
Gallagher, Joe 70, 75
Garagiola, Joe 156–57, 189–91
Garms, Debs 76
Garvey, Steve 223
Gaven, Mike 200
Gehrig, Lou 25, 27–29, 33, 53, 95, 130, 134, 235*n*
Gehringer, Charlie 50–52
Geisel, Harry 23–24
General Eisenhower Medal 132
Gilbert, Charlie 68–70, 82
Gill, George 235*n*
Gionfriddo, Al 167–68, 178, *192*, 192, 195, 243*n*
Gladstone, William Ewart 8
Gleeson, Jimmy 74
Glenn, Joe 38
Goetz, Larry 97, 206
Gomez, Lefty 24, 28, 33, 95, 235*n*
Good, Charlie 18
Gooding, Gladys 177
Goodman, Ival 69
Gordon, Joe 49, 95, 124, 194, 213
Gordon-Reed, Annette 228
Goren, Herb 179

258　INDEX

Goslin, Goose 22, 25
Grabarkewitz, Billy 223
Graham, Frank, Jr. 23–24
Grand Central Station 93–94
Gray, Dolly 8
Greater New York Fund 100
Green, Paul 98
Greenberg, Hank 26, 50, 52, 74, 102, 124, 169, 202, 234n
Greene, Sam 48–49
Greensboro (North Carolina) Patriots 13
Greenville (South Carolina) Spinners 14–15
Gregg, Hal 118, 128, 138–39, 149, 154, 181, 200
Grier, Bobby 230
Griffin, Marvin 230
Griffith, Calvin 231
Griffith, Clark 8–9, 14, 23–25, 163
Grimes, Burleigh 58–59
Grimm, Charlie 137
Groom, Bob 8
Gulfport (Mississippi) Tarpons 13–14
Gumbert, Harry 69, 92, 154, 233n
Gutteridge, Don 74

Haas, Bert 71, 154
Haas, Bruno 17
Hack, Stan 75
Hadley, Bump 39, 48, 235n
Hafey, Chick 132
Hague, Frank 15
Hale, Odell 38
Hamey, Roy 167–68, 201, 205
Hamlin, Luke 63, 69, 71, 79, 81, 100
Haney, Fred 213
Harder, Mel 38, 50
Harridge, Will 22–24, 28, 160, 207
Harris, Bob 235n
Harris, Bucky 48, 176, 194
Hart, Bill 127
Hartnett, Gabby 75, 82
Hatten, Joe 146, 148, 152, 155, 157, 172, 186, **195**
Hawthorne, Nathaniel 228
Hayworth, Ray 33
Head, Ed 76, 147, 168
Hecht, Ben 150
Heintzelman, Ken 149
Heinz, W.C. 91
Hemsley, Rollie 28
Henrich, Tommy 75, 97, 194
Herman, Babe 58, *137*, 225
Herman, Billy 4, 70, 82–83, 87–90, 94, 98, 102, 108, 111, 118, 125, 127, 165, 202, 237n, 237n
Hermanski, Gene 145–47, 171, *175*, *184*, 188, 200
Herring, Art 154
Higbe, Kirby 4, 62, 79–82, *82*, 84–86, 92, 94, *96*, 97, 102–3, 105, 108, 117–18, 127, 146, 156–57, 168–70, 186, 189, 211, 243n

Higgins, Pinky 48, 52
Hill, Art 51, 54
Hill, Jesse 35, 39
Hoag, Myril 17–19, 21, 35–36, 40, 50
Hobbs, Roy 149
Hodges, Gil 118, 200, 224
Hollingsworth, Al 213
Holmes, Tommy (player) 133, 139, 203
Holmes, Tommy (sportswriter) 76, 103, 116, 179, 199–200
Holy Name Society 99, 115, 151
Hopp, Johnny 82, 101, 127, 133, 151–52, 202
Hopper, Clay 162–63
Hornsby, Rogers 36, 136, 142, 203
Horton, Thad 210
Hotel Astor 134
Hotel Bossert 74, 101, 115
Hotel Nacional 166–67
Houston Buffs 86
Hubbell, Carl 76, 84, 90, 104, 124
Hudson, Johnny 82
Huggins, Miller 16, 29
Hurth, Charles 212
Hutchinson, Fred 52, 204, 207, 216
Hyland, Dr. Robert F. 34, 108

Immerman, Connie 174
Indianapolis Clowns 210

Jackson, Reggie 167
Jacobs, Mike 52
Jacobson, Baby Doll 87
Jamaica High School 123
James, Bill 21, 94
James Madison High School 105
Javery, Al 110
Jefferson, Thomas 228
Jersey City Skeeters 14–15, 18
Johns Hopkins Hospital 36
Johnson, Art 86
Johnson, Don 219
Johnson, Roy 22, 35, 38–40
Johnson, Thomas P. 202
Johnson, Walter 8, *9*, 22
Joint Major League Committee 160
Jones, Jersey 52
Jones, Lucius 104
Jones, Sam 17
Jorda, Lou 206
Jordan, David 133
Jorgens, Arndt 33
Jorgensen, Spider 187
Junior World Series 19, 238n
Jurges, Billy 78, 109

Kahn, Roger 166
Kalin, Frank 167–68, 243n
Karst, Gene 59
Kavanagh, Jack 74, 227
Keeler, Willie 139

Index

Kehn, Chet 105
Keller, Charlie 95, 97, 194
Kelly, Jack 216–18
Kelly, Mike "King" 151
Kennedy, Vern 43, 47–49, 51–53, 139, 235*n*, 235*n*
Kieran, John 52, 73
Kimball, Newt 68
Kiner, Ralph 168, 202, 204
King, Clyde 138
Kipke, Harry 49
Kluttz, Clyde 152
Knaupp, Cotton 14
Knights of Pythias 99
Knott, Jack 43
Kosco, Andy 221
Koy, Ernie 63, 65, 67–68, 71
Kreevich, Mike 43, 46
Kremer, Ray 245*n*
Kress, Red 236*n*
Kreuscher, Dr. Philip 44, 50
Krist, Howie 90
Kuhel, Joe 22
Kurowski, Whitey 107, 151, 153, 157

Laabs, Chet 53, 235*n*
Lacy, Sam 171
Ladies Aid Society 125
Lafayette High School 180
LaGuardia Field 69
Lake, Eddie 241*n*
Landis, Kenesaw 64, 101, 124, 141, 228
Lane, Eddie 74
Lane, Frank 217
Lanier, Max 72, 82, 84, 86, 107–8, 110, 112, 117, 119, 127
Lanigan, Ernie 15
Lardner, John 80
Lary, Lyn 30
Laurice, Shorty 155
Lavagetto, Cookie 4, 61, 63, 65, 67, 72–73, 76, 82, 93–94, 97, 101–2, 138, *146*, 146, 189, 194–95, *196*, 237*n*
Laval, Pierre 104
Lawson, Roxie 235*n*
Lazzerri, Tony 25, 38, 49
Lebourveau, Bevo 17
Lee, Bill 61
Lee, Thornton 45–46
Lefebvre, Jim 222
Leiber, Hank 73
Leibowitz, Samuel 100, 181, 203, 224–25
Leonard, Emil "Dutch" 233*n*
Leslie, Sam 20
Levitt, Bill 230–31
Levitt, Daniel 18
Lewis, Buddy 135
Libke, Al 140
Lieb, Fred 41
Little Rock Travelers 211

Litwhiler, Danny 126
Livingston, Mickey 79
Lohrman, Bill 118
Lombardi, Ernie 69
Lombardi, Vic 7, 138, 152, 156–57, 168, 186, 192, 200, 202–3
Lopez, Al 64, 67
Louis, Joe 52, 92, 104, 150, 173
Louisville Colonels 67
Lowrey, Peanuts 148
Luckman, Sid 100
Ludwig, Al 217
Lukon, Eddie 154
Luna Park 130
Lyons, Ted 46

Macht, Norman 228
Mack, Connie 114, 142
Macon, Max 70, 109
MacPhail, Larry 4, 54–55, 57–60, 63–66, 68–72, 79–85, 88, **89**, 90, 92–94, 100–4, 108, 110–12, 114–15, 120, 134, 142–43, 153, 160, 163–64, 174, 176, 237*n*
Magerkurth, George 109
Maglie, Sal 140
Major League Executive Committee 207
Malamud, Bernard 149
Mamaux, Al 19
Mancuso, Gus 79, 88–89
Mann, Arthur 167
Mann, Earl 208–9, 212
Mantle, Mickey 91–92, 131
Manush, Heinie 22, 34, 38
Marion, Marty 82, 107, 117, 120, 132–33, 141, 151–52, 160, 162, 183, 191, 204, 210
Maris, Roger 234*n*
Markell, Duke 216–18
Marshall, Willard 105
Martin, Pepper 127
Marzano, Rudy 63
Masi, Phil 85
Mathews, Eddie 209–11
Mathewson, Christy 150, 238*n*
Mauch, Gene 200, 212
Maye, Lee 220
Mays, Carl 17
Mays, Willie 86, 91–92
McCarthy, Joe 15–17, 20–21, 23, 25–29, 31–32, 34–36, 38–41, 65, 95, 130, 175–177
McCormick, Frank 77, 80, 84
McCoskey, Barney 53, 74
McCullough, Clyde 148
McDonough, Pat 62
McGowan, Bill 46
McGowen, Roscoe 61, 89, 102, 145, 164, 179
McGraw, John 74
McHale, John 220
McKechnie, Bill 35, 64, 90–91, 130, 134
McKinney, Frank 202, 207
McNulty, Patrick 213

McQuinn, Bob 64
McQuinn, George 35
Meany, Tom 175, 186
Medwick, Joe 4, 71–73, 75, 80–82, 90, 94, 97104, 107–8, 133, 191, 237n
Melton, Rube 84, 110, 128
Melville, Herman 228
Memphis Chicks 61
Menke, Denis 220
Merullo, Lennie 2, 139, 148–49, **149**
Meyer, Billy 7, 202, 204–6, 209, 212
Miksis, Eddie 187
Milan, Clyde 14
Minneapolis Millers 19
Mize, Johnny 77, 82, 85–86, 94, 100–1, 104, 117, 151–52, 168, 178, 197, 205
Mobile Bears 154, 211–12
Montauk Club 115
Montreal Royals 70, 82, 141–42, 145, 153, 162–64, 171–72, 174, 216–17, 219, 238n
Moore, Gene 63–64, 67–68, 70
Moore, Terry 73, 82, 85–86, 89–90, 101, 157, 160, 183, 213
Mooty, Jake 71, 75
Morgan, Chet 51
Morgan, Eddie 58
Moriarty, George 23–24, 32
Munger, George 206
Mungo, Van Lingle 59
Murphy, James J. 60
Murphy, Johnny 19, **39**, 95, 97, 160–62, 195, 207
Murphy, Robert 160
Murray, Arch 179
Murtaugh, Danny 7
Musial, Stan 86, 101–2, 117–120, 126–27, 130–31, **131**, 133, 136, 149, 151–52, 156, 159–60, 183
Music Corporation of America (MCA) 42
Myer, Buddy 22–25
Myers, Hy 196

Nahem, Sam 71
National Association for the Advancement of Colored People 173
National Fathers Day Committee 132
Navy Relief Fund 109
Nee, Johnny 14, 34
Nevins Bowling Center 116
New York Football Giants 100
New York Jets 42
Newark Bears 15, 19, 36–37, 49
Newcombe, Don 184, 210–11
Newsom, Bobo 53, 110, 118, **121**, 121–22, 236n
Nicholson, Bill 108, 132–33, 165
Norworth, Jack 72
Nova, Lou 92

Ocean Shipscaling Company 100
O'Doul, Lefty 131
O'Dwyer, William 100
Oliphant, Tom 157

Olmo, Luis 118, 137–41
Olson, Paul 108
O'Malley, Walter 197, 210–11, 218, 220, 224
Orengo, Joe 118
Osteen, Claude 223
Ostermueller, Fritz 147, 181
Ott, Mel 76, 79, 105, 133, 150, 208
Owen, Marv 47, 51
Owen, Mickey 75, 79–80, 82, 85, 87–88, 94, 97–98, 108, 114, 118–19, 127, 136, 138, 154

Padgett, Don 100–2, 154
Pafko, Andy 139
Page, Joe 194–95
Painter, Earle "Doc" 36, 40
Parker, Dan 151
Parker, Wes 221–22
Parks, Art 59, 63
Parks, Rosa 230
Parrott, Harold 31, 98–100, 170
Passeau, Claude 75, 85, 148
Peacock, Johnny 136, 138
Pearson, Ike 81, 237n
Pearson, Monte 38
Peck Memorial Hospital 153
Pennock, Herb 30
Perini, Lou 163
Phelps, Babe 64, 67, 70, 73, 79, 100
Phillippe, Deacon 238n, 245n
Pierre, Bill 13
Piet, Tony 47
Pinelli, Babe **184**
Pintar, John 79
Podres, Johnny 225
Poffenberger, Boots 50
Pollet, Howie 86–87, 152, 156–57, 159
Posedel, Bill 68, 73
Povich, Shirley 31, 33, 48, 51–52
Powell, Jake 41
Powers, Jimmy 77, 83, 104, 130
Pressnell, Tot 73
Pyle, Ewald 141

Quinn, Bob 64

Rabbitt, Joe 18
Racine, Hector 142
Rackley, Marv 145
Radcliff, Rip 43, 46, 74
Raffensberger, Ken 204
Raven, Julius A. 41–42
Reardon, Beans 189, 202, 206
Red Cross 116, 127
Reed, Ted 187
Reese, Dottie Walton 103
Reese, Pee Wee 4, 67–71, 73–76, 81–82, 87–88, 94, 96–97, 100, 102–3, 106–7, 109, 112, 117, 138, 146, 148–49, 153–55, 162, 169–71, **175**, 180, 187, 189, 194, **195**, **196**, 196–97, 200, 210, 224–25

Index

Reichler, Joe 150
Reiser, Pete 4, 53, 76, 80–85, 87–88, 90–92, *91*, 94–95, 97, 101–2, 104–6, 108, 117, 131, 145–46, 152–55, 159, 162, 168, 170–71, *175*, 178–81, 188–89, 191, 193–94, *196*, 196, 229, 237n
Rennie, Rud 93
Rensa, Tony 50
Reynolds, Allie *184*, 194, 196
Reynolds, Carl 22, 38
Reynolds, Quentin 134
Rice, Grantland 12, 86
Rickey, Branch 4, 57, 59, 71, 86, 101, 114–15, 117–19, 121–22, 125–27, 129, 135–36, 141–45, *142*, 151, 153, 157, 159, 162–63, 165–79, 181, 186, 189, 193, 199–201, 203, 208, 210, 212, 216, 219, 227, 243n
Rickey, Branch, Jr. 138, 143, 152, 200
Riddle, Elmer 117, 142
Rikard, Culley 188
Ripley, Robert 140
Ripple, Jimmy 68
Rizzo, Johnny 102, 107–8
Rizzuto, Phil 95
Robinson, Humberto 219
Robinson, Jackie 1, 4–5, 129, 141–42, *142*, 145, 153, 162–63, 166–74, 177–86, 189–91, 193–94, 196–97, 200–1, 203, 210, 224–25, 227, 229, 231
Robinson, Wilbert 74
Rochester Red Wings 15, 86, 214
Rockwell, Norman 206
Rodney, Lester 172, 178, 184
Roe, Preacher 136, 200–1
Roeder, Bill 130–31, 140
Rojek, Stan 149, 187, 202–3
Rolfe, Red 19, 36, 97
Rooney, Agnes 41–42
Roosevelt, Franklin Delano 101, 104
Root, Charlie 60
Rosen, Goody 63, 137–39, 141, 145, 241n
Rosenthal, Harold 193
Ross, Chet 153, 241n
Roth, Morton 19
Rowe, Schoolboy 52, 233n
Rowell, Carvel "Bama" 76, 85, 149
Roy, Paul 211–12
Ruchser, Lou 164
Ruffing, Red 28, 51, 95–96
Ruppert, Jacob 15–16, 19, 28, 31, 58
Russell, Bill 223
Russell, Rip 61
Russo, Marius 95–97
Ruth, Babe 1, 16, *16*, 18–21, 25–29, 31, 33–35, 40–41, 52, 151, 196, 234n
Ryba, Mike 214

Sabin, Gen. Dominick 146
Sacramento Solons 213
Safire, William 228

Saigh, Fred 210, 213, 218
Sain, Johnny 7, 10, 178
St. George Hotel 72
St. Joseph's Hospital 214
St. Paul Saints 118, 199, 201, 218
St. Vincents's Hospital 205, 225
Salveson, Jack 45
Sanders, Ray 127
Sandlock, Mike 138, 154
San Francisco Seals 39
Sayles, Bill 118
Scheffels, Paul 120
Schepner, Joe 14
Schmeling, Max 52, 92
Schmidt, Freddy 183
Schmitz, Johnny 148
Schoendienst, Red 151
Schultz, Howie 118, 122, 137–38, 157, 162, 178
Schumacher, Hal 76
Scott, Everett 27–28
Scott, Jack 17
Seats, Tom 138
Seattle Symphony 138
Selkirk, George 19, 35–36, 40–41
Sewell, Joe 17, 29
Sewell, Luke 25, 134–35, 208
Sewell, Rip 7, 83, 117, 204, 233n
Shaughnessy, Frank 217
Shawkey, Bob 15, 18, 36
Shea, Catherine 42
Shea, Frank 194–96
Shea, Patrick 42
Sheed, Wilfred 146, 158
Shotton, Burt 125, 179–80, *180*, 186–87, 193, 203, 209–10
Shoun, Clyde 118
Shreveport Sports 213
Shuba, George 200
Simon, Scott 173
Sington, Fred 63
Sisler, George, Jr. 217
Slaughter, Enos 82–83, 86, 89, 101–2, 108, 117, 124, 149, 157, 159, 191
Smith, Red 149
Smith, Wendell 171, 183
Snider, Duke 118, 165, 168, 200, 220, 234
Soden, David F. 77
South Nassau Communities Hospital 70
Southworth, Billy 15, 72, 82, 88, 100–2, 106, 111, 113, 127, 147, 156, 236n
Spink, J.G. Taylor 89, 210
Stainback, Tuck 64
Stalin, Josef 172
Standard Oil Company (Esso) 124
Stanky, Eddie 2, 4, 137, 140–41, 148, *149*, 152–53, 155, 157, 162, 168, 171–72, 175, 178, 180–81, 187, 191, *195*, 197, 203, 213–14
Steiger, Gus 179
Stengel, Casey 17–18, 40, 60, 62, 74, 111, 113
Stevens, Ed 137–38, 170–71, 178, 202

Stewart, Bill 61
Stirnweiss, George 145
Stoneham, Horace 58, 75, 109, 142, 163
Stratton, Monty 43, 45–46
Strincevich, Nick 168
Strull, Stan **184**
Sugar Bowl 230
Sukeforth, Clyde 138, 177–179, 206
Sundra, Steve 38
Supreme Court of Alabama 230
Supreme Court of Georgia 230
Supreme Court of Mississippi 230
Supreme Court of New York 230
Suzuki, Ichiro 159

Tamulis, Vito 71, 74, 79
Taylor, Harry 186
Taylor, Zack 33
Tebbetts, Birdie 47, 50
Tepsic, Joe 153, 241*n*
Terry, Bill 20, 76, 79–80, 84
Thompson, Tim 219
Thomson, Bobby 97
Thoreau, Henry David 228
Tiller, Guy 210
Tinker, Joe 15
Tobin, Jim 92, 138
Toledo Mud Hens 17–18, 62
Toporcer, George 18
Toronto Maple Leafs 18, 55, 216–17
Torre, Joe 222–23
Trautman, George 212
Tresh, Mike 47
Triplett, Coaker 239*n*
Trout, Paul "Dizzy" 52, 54
Truman, Harry 229

United Orphans 151
United States Supreme Court 229

Van Atta, Russ 22, 33–34
Van Blair, Rick 113
Vance, Dazzy 224
Vanderbilt, Alfred Gwynne 86
Vander Meer, Johnny 58, 81, 84, 154
Vaughan, Arky 4, 61, 100, 102, 106, 118, **121**, 121–22, 124–27, 171, 193, 224, 239*n*
Vaughan, Irving 45
Vaughn, Annie 19
Vaughn, Susie 10
Vaughn, William 10
Veeck, Bill 217
Vicksburg (Mississippi) Hillbillies 14
Vidmer, Richards 53
Vila, Joe 27
Voiselle, Bill 132
Vosmik, Joe 65, 68, 70

Wagner, Allen 199
Wagner, Honus 132

Walberg, Rube 46
Waldorf-Astoria Hotel 124, 162
Walker, Alfred 8, 10
Walker, Earnest 8, 10
Walker, Estelle 41–42, 45, 65, 70, 77, 83, 99, 103–4, 117, 121, 151, **190**, 225, 246*n*
Walker, Ewart "Dixie" 8–13, **9**, 95, 233*n*, 238*n*
Walker, Fleetwood 141, 241*n*
Walker, Flossie 10–12, 42, 95–96, 238*n*
Walker, Fred "Dixie": All-Star Game 73–74, 120, 132, 138, 151, 192, 203–4; brawls 22, 25, 107, 139–41, 148; civic endeavors 72, 99–101, 105, 115–16, 123–25, 151, 180; as coach with Braves 220, 246*n*; as coach with Cardinals 213–14; as coach with Dodgers 220–224; creation of first base screen 164; games against Athletics 17, 36, 43, 54; games against Braves 7, 62, 68, 73, 77, 85, 92–93, 106, 130, 140–41, 149, 178, 193; games against Browns 26–28, 36, 43, 45, 53, 69; games against Cardinals 71–72, 74, 87–89, 107, 111, 119, 152, 206; games against Cubs 60–61, 70, 105, 139–40, 148; games against Dodgers 203, 205–6; games against Giants 68–69, 76, 84, 104–5, 109, 132, 139–40, 146, 193–94; games against Indians 43, 50–51, 53; games against Phillies 83, 105, 110, 119–20, 131, 138, 181; games against Pirates 61, 83, 114, 121–22, 147, 149, 181, 188; games against Red Sox 26, 36, 45–46, 51; games against Reds 61–62, 64, 69, 71, 81, 84, 90, 124, 139–40, 150, 152, 154, 194, 202–3; games against Senators 17, 21–27, 40, 51; games against Tigers 25–27, 32; games against White Sox 26–28, 50–51; games against Yankees 45, 51–54; injuries 31–34, 36, 43–44, 54, 60, 107, 112, 126–27; International League Hall of Fame 197; as manager of Atlanta Crackers 208–9, 211–12; as manager of Houston Buffs 213–214; as manager of Rochester Red Wings 216–18; as manager of Toronto Maple Leafs 218–19; marriage 41–42, 225; Most Valuable Player award 113, 132, 139, 159, 164, 197; in movie 162; Player of the Year award 134; player representative 160–62, 204, 207, 245*n*; relationship with Branch Rickey 115, 135–36, 144, 151, 166–68, 171, 199–201; relationship with Brooklyn fans 62–63, 74, 77, 81, 94, 99, 103, 105, 109, 115, 123–-26, 131, 134, 150–51, 164; relationship with Leo Durocher 60, 81, 84, 101, 103, 121–22, 125–26, 145–51, 159, 164–65, 170, 175; relationship with Jackie Robinson 1, 4–5, 117, 142, 162–64, 166–68, 171–74, 178, 181–85, 189, 191, 197, 200, 210–11, 224–225, 227; relationship with Larry MacPhail 64–65, 80–81, 84, 88, 101–104, 110–11, 114–15, 120, 153, 164–65; salary negotiations 30–31, 38, 65, 78, 80,

102, 135–36, 144, 201, 208; sale to Dodgers 55, 57, 60; sale to White Sox 40–41; spring training with Dodgers 65, 68, 80–81, 102–4, 117, 127, 132, 135–36, 144, 166–67; spring training with Pirates 202; spring training with Tigers 49, 53; spring training with White Sox 44–45; spring training with Yankees 16–17, 19–21, 31, 34–35, 39–40; as team leader 191–92; trade rumors 36, 38, 40, 64, 79, 84, 101, 165, 167–68, 199; trade to Pirates 199–201; trade to Tigers 47–49, 51, 53; USO tours 126, 134–35; working for Sperry Gyroscope Corporation 115–17, 123, 126; World Series 95–97, 194–96
Walker, Fred, Jr. 45, 99, *190*, 214, 225
Walker, Gerald "Gee" 47–51
Walker, Harry 2, *3*, 10, 12, 113–14, 117, 120, *120*, 127, 157, 192–93, 201, 209, 214, 216, 223–24, 238*n*
Walker, Jimmy 124
Walker, Mary 8
Walker, Mary Ann 65, 70, 225
Walker, Mary Ann Estelle 42, 83, 99, *190*, 191, 225
Walker, Robert 8
Walker, Sean *190*, 205, 225
Walker, Stephen 42, 104, 166, *190*, 191, 201, 214, 225–27
Walker, Susan 117, 190, *190*, 225–226
Walkup, Jim 236*n*
Walsh, Ed 8–10, 233*n*
Walters, Bucky 64, 69, 71, 204, 208
Waner, Lloyd 129
Waner, Paul 80–81, 85, 101, 103, 106118, 127, 129, 134–35, 145
War Bond All-Stars 124
War Charities Day 124
War Mobilization Board 135
Waring, Fred 109
Warneke, Lon 82, 90, 111, 139
Wasdell, Jimmy 70, 83, 100
Weaver, Monte 22, 25, 40
Webber, Les 119

Weintraub, Phil 129
Weissman, Hilda 211
Welch, Johnny 26
Wendler, Harold "Doc" 181
Werber, Bill 17–18, 23, 143
Werblin Sonny 42
West, Max 64, 93
West, Sam 36
West Point 36, 117
Westlake, Wally 7, 168, 202
Wheat, Zack 131, 224
White, Ernie 82, 84, 86–88, 108
White, Walter 173
Whitehill, Earl 2, 22–27
Whitman, Dick 145
Wilks, Ted 127
Williams, Dewey 178
Williams, Gordon 187
Williams, Joe 105
Williams, Ted 85, 117, 131, 152, 165
Wills, Maury 2, 222
Wilson, Jimmie 82, 108, 111, 113
Witek, Mickey 146
Woodward, Stanley 182
Wright, Taft 74
Wrigley, Philip K. 82, 160
Wyatt, Whit 4, 64, 68–69, 72–74, 76, *82*, 81–89, 93–94, *96*, 96–98, 102, 105–6, 108, 111–12, 118–19, 136, 147, 189, 209, 211–12, 214, *215*, 220
Wynn, Jim 2, 223
Wyse, Hank 178

Yawkey, Tom 160
Yeager, Steve 223
York, Rudy 52, 142, 241*n*
Young, Babe 202–3
Young, Dick 30, 177, 193
Young, Fay 142
Young, Michael 159

Zeller, Jack 142

www.ingramcontent.com/pod-product-compliance
Lightning Source LLC
Chambersburg PA
CBHW021342230426
43666CB00006B/378